Princeton Studies on the Near East

FROM MADINA TO METROPOLIS

METROPOLIS

Heritage and Change in the Near Eastern City

edited by L. Carl Brown

The Darwin Press
Princeton, New Jersey

Library of Congress Cataloging in Publication Data

From Madina to Metropolis.

Based on papers presented at a conference
entitled "Urban Planning and Urban Prospects
in the Near East and North Africa" held at
Princeton University in April 1970.
    Includes bibliographies.
    1. Cities and towns—Near East—Addresses,
essays, lectures. I. Brown, Leon Carl, 1928- ed.
HT147.N4F76   301.36'3'0956   76-161054
ISBN 0-87850-006-5

Printed in the United States of America

CONTENTS

ILLUSTRATIONS

HALF-TONE PLATES

The abbreviation **Pl.** followed by a number, and then a second number in parentheses, found in the outside margin of the text page, refers to an illustration keyed to the text at that point. The first number is that of the illustration (Plate); the second is that of the page on which the Plate is located, e.g., **Pl. 1 (16).** The references to other illustrations that refer in a general way to the topic discussed in the text appear in italics, e.g., *Pls. 52-53 (146-147).* References to figures in the margin of the text, e.g., **Fig. 18 (306),** follow the above explanation.

7

MAPS, GRAPHS AND DRAWINGS IN THE TEXT

ACKNOWLEDGMENTS

Warmest thanks are due to several members of the staff, students and friends of the Princeton University Program in Near Eastern Studies who assisted generously in making possible the original conference and the graphic exhibit on "The Near Eastern City" that was held in the University Art Museum at the same time. This was an example of a community effort in the best sense, and among the "community leaders" were Dorothy J. Dalby and Christine Lieggi Brennan; also Anne Stokes Brown, Edward H. Breisacher, Martin Chasin, Robert McChesney, Brinkley Messick, Leila Poullada, Marion Stark, Robert Van Vranken, Jr., and Lewis Ware.

Elizabeth S. Ettinghausen must be singled out for a special word of acknowledgment and gratitude. She organized the graphic exhibit and left as a legacy of her work a graphic collection on the Near Eastern City that will continue to be of use to staff and students for years to come. The overwhelming majority of photographs and figures appearing in this book were brought together thanks to her efforts.

The Program in Near Eastern Studies, finally, wishes to acknowledge with deepest thanks the permission to reproduce photographs and figures granted by the following contributors:

Aramco
Carol Baldwin
Sir Archibald Creswell
Direction de l'Urbanisme et de
    l'Habitat, Rabat
William Dix, Jr.
†Bayard Dodge
Egyptian Tourist Office
Elizabeth S. Ettinghausen
Exxon
Government of Iran
Government of Pakistan
Government of Turkey
Kuwait Municipality
Library of Congress
Middle East Technical University
Ministry of Economics, Yemen
    Arab Republic
Ministry of Guidance and
    Information, Kuwait

Ministry of Public Works, Yemen
    Arab Republic
Abbott L. Moffatt
National Geographic Society
Office National Marocain du
    Tourisme, Rabat
Pan American World Airways
Pantomap Israel Ltd.
Richard Parker
Frederic C. Shorter
Wim Swaan
Kathe Tanous
Atila Torunoğlu
William Trousdale
Lewis Ware
Donald N. Wilber
John Witmer
H. Conway Zeigler

THE CONTRIBUTORS

Janet Abu-Lughod is Professor of Sociology at Northwestern University.

L. Carl Brown is Professor of Near Eastern history and Director of the Program in Near Eastern Studies at Princeton University.

Jean Dethier, formerly Chief of Information Service (1968-1970), Department of Housing and Urban Planning, Morocco, is now working in Paris as architect and urban planner.

Paul English is Professor of Geography at the University of Texas.

Cevat Erder is Chairman, Department of Restoration, Faculty of Architecture, Middle East Technical University, Ankara.

Richard Ettinghausen is Hagop Kevorkian Professor of Islamic Art, Institute of Fine Arts, New York University and consultative chairman of the Department of Islamic Art, Metropolitan Museum of Art, New York.

Hassan Fathy, formerly Professor of Architecture, Faculty of Fine Arts, Cairo University, is now a practicing architect and urban planner in Cairo.

Samir Khalaf is Associate Professor of Sociology, American University of Beirut.

Per Kongstad is Research Director, The Institute of Development Research, Copenhagen.

Karol Jozef Krótki is Professor of Sociology, University of Alberta, Edmonton, Canada. He was Census Controller in charge of the population census office in Sudan from 1949 to 1958.

Ira Lapidus is Professor of History, University of California, Berkeley.

The late **Saba George Shiber,** a native Palestinian and naturalized American citizen, taught at various universities and was consultant to several municipalities in both the United States and the Arab world before his untimely death in 1968.

Ilhan Tekeli is a staff member of the Regional Planning Department, Middle East Technical University, Ankara.

FROM MADINA TO METROPOLIS

Introduction

by L. Carl Brown

THIS is a study of modern Near Eastern cities, and these are eventful times for the study of cities. Urban affairs demand the attention of the man in the street as never before. And, with an ever increasing proportion of the world's population clustered in cities, never was that old cliché for everyman—the man in the street—more apt.

The urban concerns of politicians and people are also matched by those of academicians, professionals, and opinion molders. As universities turn their attention to creating new chairs and special programs in urban studies, schools of architecture, public administration faculties, and social science departments eye each other warily and stake out their claim in this field of growing interest—and concern.

Students of modernization note the apparent iron law yoking together urban growth and economic development while elsewhere urban planners, public officials, and assorted amateur prophets wonder whether megalopolis can survive.

In the confusing welter of new thought about cities one can often discern strands of dichotomous old themes, some as venerable as civilization itself. There is the city as virtue or the city as vice, the city as parasite or the city as generator, the city as a complex that makes possible the arts and a high cultural tradition or the city that dehumanizes.

The present interest in cities may lead at times to polarized views and exaggerated notions, but few would dare argue that the concern, itself, has been artificially over-stimulated. There is a growing awareness that, for better or worse, the fate of our cities provides a key to the fate of our civilizations, East and West. Before a common urbanism, the world's races, religions, and political ideologies seem to lose a bit of their distinctiveness. The diversity distinguishing rural regions throughout the world is still to be perceived. No one could confuse the Dalmatian Coast with the Great Plains, the thatched huts of Ivory Coast villages with the stone and red tile construction of Mount Lebanon, the intensive agricultural use of limited land in Japan with extensive dry farming in Russia or the United States.

Not so the urban scene, which reveals increasing uniformities. There is traffic congestion in Beirut and Tunis as well as Rome and Boston. The immigration of   Pl. 1 (16)

15

1. Traffic congestion on a side street in Beirut, Lebanon. (Photo: Pan American World Airways.)

2. Istanbul, Turkey, the Hilton Hotel. Beautiful, rational, and utilitarian, but thoroughly "international" in conception and effect. (Photo: Pan American World Airways.)

3. Aerial view of downtown Casablanca, Morocco. A sleepy port city of 25,000 persons in 1907, Casablanca now numbers over 1,400,000. (Photo: Pan American World Airways.)

Pl. 70-71
(210)
Pl. 83 (267)

Pl. 38 (110)
Pl. 3 (17)
*Pl. 52-53
(146-147)*
yesterday's rural poor now form black ghettos in Detroit, Akron, and Newark, bidonvilles in North Africa and *gecekondu* in Turkey. The old city boundaries merge imperceptively into suburbs which are themselves major urban agglomerations in Cairo as well as London and Paris. The mushroom city knows no East or West. Casablanca in this regard may be set alongside Houston. In Aleppo and Alexandria, just as in Glasgow and Marseilles, substantial and architecturally interesting quarters are now so antiquated that the bleak prospects are either destruction and urban renewal or restoration at a forbiddingly high unit cost.

Technology and economic imperatives seem to conspire in assuring that the world's cities will look increasingly similar. An economic use of limited space dictates high-rise buildings, and this requirement, in turn, is satisfied best—in both economics and engineering—by similar building materials: steel, glass, and reinforced concrete. And that most of the architects and engineers trained to construct such "modern" buildings have been educated in a limited number of places in Europe and the Western world only increases the homogenizing potential.

Pl. 2 (16)
The world's cities are now strung together by jetports with monotonously similar terminal buildings from whence today's Marco Polo or Ibn Battuta is whisked away to Hiltonesque hotels of steel, glass, and international cuisine. Such hotels are usually tucked into the midst of newer structures and spatial organizations bearing the marks of "international modern." Indeed, the untrained tourist eye can often gauge the extent to which a city has entered into the mainstream of international social, political, and economic life by appraising the extent and pervasiveness of its "modern sector."

There is, accordingly, a growing sentiment to regard cities from other parts of the world not as far away places with strange sounding names but as recognizable varieties of a familiar species—the modern urban agglomeration. A number of historians and social scientists are now providing working hypotheses to buttress, with added sophistication and refinement, just such categories of thought.

Instead of looking for characteristics to distinguish the cities of different cultures, these scholars believe it is more useful to classify according to "pre-modern" and "modern"—or, to adapt the terminology used in one of the seminal books on this subject—"preindustrial" and "industrial."[1]

The growing tendency to emphasize how technology, population pressures, and economic imperatives serve as a powerful solvent partially dissolving cultural and earlier ecological differences in the process of creating a distinctive generic type—the modern city—is properly to be applauded as a bold intellectual leap that will permit an increase in man's knowledge of the urban phenomenon.

It may be especially important in Western man's study of non-Western cities, for in spite of progress made in cross-cultural scholarship in the past few decades, there remains a tendency to view the non-West either as a residual category or as an exotic organism resisting comparison. A perspective that can

---

[1] Gideon Sjoberg, *The Preindustrial City: Past and Present* (Glencoe, Ill.: Free Press, 1960; paperback edition, 1965).

advance such categories as "oriental despotism" and "oriental mode of production" can equally well embrace the notion of an "oriental city" existing beyond history and analysis. Emphasis on the common fate of modern cities may provoke reconsiderations of earlier lazy assumptions. We may, as a result, begin to find that the Near Eastern city (and other "oriental" cities) had a vibrant history not all that dissimilar from the Western experience. We could uncover more clearly the rise and fall of cities linked not just to the fate of dynasties but to economic, technological, and demographic change. We could discern Near Eastern equivalents to the many useful sub-categories put forward in the unfolding of Western urban historiography—examples would include the role of socio-economic classes from bourgeoisie to lumpenproletariat, the dynamics of rural-urban ties and antipathies, "church-state" and government-society relation-ships in the urban context, and the extent to which a city's spatial organization and architectural style is determined by the constant interaction of operative ideals and class structure (i.e., what in any time, place, and cultural context makes a suitable "monument" and who are the possible patrons?).[2]

As a result of this new stimulus, we will be better prepared to resist the temptation, already observable in certain quarters, to substitute underdeveloped world, Third World, or some other equally residual egregious euphemism for the earlier "mysterious East." The contributions to this volume are to be squarely placed within an intellectual framework that presupposes a world-wide significance to the subject under discussion. This work is committed to the proposition that a study of Near Eastern cities is not only important in its own right, but can also provide insights and guidance for anyone interested in cities in other parts of the world as well.

Even so, this very laudable effort to think and act in terms of universal values and a sense of common humanity can, if due care is not exercised, be pushed, ironically, to a dehumanizing approach in which all individuality is swallowed up in a contrived paradigmatic model. Or, alternatively, all other urban cultures may, however inadvertently, be forced upon the Procrustean bed of the urban pattern best known to the examiner (an especially insidious problem since the very process of modernization is ineluctably tied up with Westernization).

Cities are, in one sense, becoming increasingly alike or at least faced with similar problems and prospects. Yet, anyone who has had the opportunity to experience, say, Fez, Istanbul, or Isfahan would argue that such cities possess a cultural core, however elusive to describe, that is and will ever be distinctive. And even if experts and laymen might dispute what generic label to apply—whether Islamic, Near Eastern, Western Asian, or some hyphenated sub-category such as Arabo-Islamic or Turko-Islamic—there could be a consensus that these cities are

---

[2] Indeed, for the Near Eastern and Islamic city such scholarly work, bringing the region into the mainstream of urban studies, is already underway. Many of the contributors to this volume have made their mark in this endeavor. In Near Eastern and Islamic studies, one of the pioneers in insisting on the common "medievalness" of pre-modern Europe and the Islamic Near East has been Claude Cahen, whose influence has been even more profound since he had impeccable credentials as an "Orientalist" and could present his arguments to that rather rarified body of cognoscenti on their own terms. See, especially, his *Mouvements populaires et autonomisme urbaine* (Leiden, 1959).

4. This aerial view of Fez, Morocco, to both sides of the Oued bou Khareb (river), conveys well both the hodgepodge pattern of street communication and the orderly, square internal arrangement—showing each house built around a courtyard. (Photo: Office National Marocain du Tourisme, Rabat.)

properly distinguishable from New York, Paris, Calcutta, Nairobi, or Shanghai. Let us, without attempting too carefully to justify the name, call this phenomenon "the Near Eastern city."

A distinguished American Arabist and student of modern North Africa tells the story of one of his early visits to Fez. A native of the city offered his services as guide; but the American, feeling he knew the city well enough and seeking to avoid the inherently superficial role of a "guided" Western tourist, declined. "All right, but you'll get lost," the Moroccan smugly retorted. The scholar set out, relishing his quiet absorption at his own pace, into this venerable Islamic city while carefully keeping mental note of his orientation as he went down one after another of Fez's labyrinthine streets. Nevertheless, caution was not enough; and some 45 minutes after his stroll had begun, he realized he was lost. Just as he began to look furtively for someone to give him directions, the spurned guide materialized and chortled, "See, I told you!"

Pl. 4 (20)

Of course, the Near Eastern city—even Fez—eventually yields its topographical secrets to the Westerner. Equally, it might be argued that the city of broad boulevards and grid patterns is more a phenomenon of the modern West than of Western civilization as such (leaving aside, for present purposes, the argument about Roman city planning and how much of that legacy survived the Roman Empire). Paris, after all, had an entirely different physiognomy before Napoleon's rue de Rivoli and Baron Haussmann's *grands boulevards*. Nor is it always the narrow, winding streets and the absence of straight lines and right angles in spatial organization that most characterize the Near Eastern city. Indeed, the map of the old city of Herat reveals two intersecting main arteries that veritably reproduce the oldest known symbol for the city—the cross enclosed in a circle.[3] Further, certain of the cities that may be appropriately included in the Near Eastern cultural area have relatively wide streets and a reasonably "open" use of space. A good example is Marrakech plus other cities located closer to Black Africa and blending in more African forms of city organization.

Fig. 2 (76)

No, the Near Eastern city is not readily categorized according to a pre-determined check-list, but it nevertheless possesses its own elusive essence. A more poetic writer would dare to assert that it has its own soul. Perhaps in a certain sense the Near Eastern city is like Near Eastern music: it can be readily analyzed and described, but to all but the most perceptive ears, considerable time, a slowly nurtured familiarity, and a subtle shifting of psychological gears on the part of the listener are needed before this music can be understood and appreciated on its own terms.

A jaded American whose career had given him the opportunity of living in several Near Eastern cities once begged off from joining a party intent on visiting the bazaar area in a North African city with the weary observation that "if you've seen one suq you've seen them all." In a superficial sense he was right. He would, indeed, have been able to describe the paradigmatic Near Eastern bazaar. His statement is as true—and as inadequate—as the assertion "if you've

---

[3] See Robert S. Lopez, "The Crossroads within the Wall," in *The Historian and the City*, eds. Oscar Handlin and John Burchard (Cambridge, Mass.: Massachusetts Institute of Technology Press, 1963; paperback edition, 1966).

seen one Midwestern city, you've seen them all." Are we, then, content to rest at this level of passing familiarity?

Herein lies another challenge that is faced in this book. The goal of depicting Near Eastern cities within the context of world urban studies should not be pursued in a way stifling to the individuality of this culture. At the same time, emphasis on the "Near Eastern-ness" of things treated in this book should not be exaggerated to the point where these cities are filed away beyond reach on that shelf reserved for incomparable exotica.

The most appropriate answer would appear to be in making a virtue of the dialectic process and the dynamic tension realized in pitting the unique against the category, the thing-in-itself against the thing-in-comparison-with-others, and the cultural principle of classification against the structural-functional. The contributors to this volume have been selected, in part, with these aims in mind. They come from a variety of professional specializations. The views of the architect, urban planner, public official, sociologist, geographer, Islamicist, demographer, and art historian are expressed in the chapters which follow. All of them have something important to say about Near Eastern cities, but they are not, because of their professional specializations, accustomed to expressing their ideas in such a deliberately multi-disciplinary forum. The urban historian concerned with socio-economic institutions may be poorly informed of the training and ideas of the present-day architect or, for that matter, the architect of any earlier age. The public official concerned with economic development may not be attuned to understand the aspirations and fears of art historians working on the preservation of historical sites and their integration into the existing city. Practitioners of many of the specializations brought together in this book could be expected to have only passing acquaintance with the "central-place theory."[4] And so on.

The contributors to this book first came together and presented their papers in a conference entitled "Urban Planning and Urban Prospects in the Near East and North Africa" held at Princeton University in April 1970. They had been alerted to expect a variegated audience representing many specializations and a combination of "doers" and "thinkers" plus a saving remnant of laymen. They were urged to draft their papers with this audience in mind. Following the discussion at the conference, they returned to their homes to rewrite their chapters in the form they now appear in this book. As a result of this multi-disciplinary—and also, let it be noted, multi-national—approach, each contributor has been obliged to express his argument with due concern for universally accepted categories of thought and to eschew the jargon and "in-group" assumptions of his own profession.

The result, we hope, is more than a work of *vulgarisation* (although even such an aim is not to be renounced, for the mayor, the architect, the irate

---

4 The author recalls an informal meeting in which a social scientist explained the central-place theory to an art historian. The latter responded that he felt like Molière's M. Jourdain upon learning that he had been speaking prose all his life. He had thought in categories similar to the central-place theory without knowing of the theory's existence. This post-eighteenth-century problem of increasing specialization of knowledge is more acute than many realize. It is equally a problem, and this is even more often ignored, in the area of so-called non-Western studies.

taxpayer, and the student of Everytown would be the richer for learning a bit about the Near- Eastern city). It is, rather, a bringing together in collaboration and confrontation of the major themes concerning the Near Eastern city; and for that matter, the city in general—the historical legacy, the confrontation of "old" and "new," the challenge of preserving and integrating the old forms and styles without turning parts of the city into an anachronistic museum, the vagaries of urban planning on a national scale, the intimidating interaction of geography, economics and culture, and so on.

Geographically, the Near Eastern city is here defined to include the urban experience that lies in the regions of Arabic, Turkish, and Persian language and culture.[5] In cultural terms, this embraces the area that has sometimes been called the Islamic heartland, and in certain ways the subject of this book is almost equally to be described as the Islamic city. Almost, but not quite; for the Islamic world extends well beyond Arabic, Turkish, and Persian lands to include the millions of Muslims in the Indian subcontinent, Indonesia, Central Asia, and Black Africa. These areas beyond the concern of this book boast their own rich architectural and urban forms.

Even so, there is an unavoidable arbitrariness in our classification. Persian motifs are clearly present in Pakistani cities. The Muslim cities of what is now Soviet Central Asia are not generically separable from the Turko-Persian-Islamic cultural areas to the South and West. In architecture and urban patterns it is a sliding scale, not a sharp break, from Muslim Northern Africa to Muslim Black Africa.

The geographical and cultural boundaries chosen are, therefore, not completely satisfactory, but on balance they are probably more useful than any conceivable alternative. An attempt to cover cities in the entire Islamic world would be so broad as to obscure any cultural distinctiveness, somewhat comparable to coverage of the "Western" city, from Santiago to Moscow. On the other hand, confining the Near Eastern city to the Arabic, Turkish, and Persian areas does, as already noted, concentrate on the Islamic heartland. It also focuses attention on that portion of Western Asia where a form of urbanism and civilization began and where Islamic urban forms took shape in confrontation with the Byzantine and Sassanian heritage. And, in geographical terms, these boundaries enclose an area wherein "the desert and the sown," not to mention the particularism of mountain life vis-à-vis the urban-dominated lowlands, are major determinants. This is surely a sharp ecological separation from the Muslim, but tropical, climes of Bengal, Indonesia, and much of Muslim Black Africa.

An even more precise way to label the subject of this book might be the somewhat cumbersome expression "the Islamic Near Eastern city." On the one hand, it is a bit presumptuous at times to speak categorically about things Islamic when the book is deliberately designed to cover only a minority of the

[5] Near East is admittedly an arbitrary geographical designation for a part of the world that has been especially afflicted with imprecise geographical labels. Why not Middle East, since clearly Afghanistan is not properly included in the Near East? Yet, can Morocco, which is west of most of France, be placed in the Middle East? Compound terms such as "Near and Middle East and North Africa" would be too cumbersome. We have, therefore, chosen to retain the older "Near East" since it, at least, connotes proximity to Europe geographically and culturally.

world's Muslims.[6] On the other hand, a central organizing theme—in many ways *the* central organizing theme—of this book is the way in which Islam and Islamic culture molded patterns of urban life in the area from Morocco to Afghanistan. Instead of an imposed uniformity in terminology, our authors have been left free to refer at times to Islamic or Muslim cities, at other times to Near Eastern cities, and on even other occasions to traditional or modern cities. These variations can help to clarify by revealing each author's own judgment of where the emphasis should lie in the point under discussion. Nor, it is hoped, will any confusion arise if the reader keeps in mind the geographical, cultural, and religious definitions and limitations mentioned before.

There remains, however, one problem concerning the usage "Muslim" or "Islamic" which should, in fairness to the reader, be noted even though no effort will be made to resolve the problem in this book. A few prosaic points in what might be called cross-cultural conceptualization can explain what is at issue. Suppose a reader were handed a book on Christian architecture. He would expect, of course, a study largely devoted to churches and monasteries. He would not expect the book to deal with all forms of buildings, public and private, religious and secular. If he were given a book on the Christian city he would probably be a trifle confused and not know what it might contain. Is it Saint Augustine's *civitas dei* (i.e., not an individual urban agglomeration at all but the whole body of believers, or Christendom)? Does it refer to the New Jerusalem, the metaphorical expression of Christian paradise described in Revelation? In any case, the book would not readily be assumed to deal with the social and spatial organization of cities.

Not so for Islam. By an unfortunate convention, we have all become accustomed to speak of Islamic cities[7] just as we refer glibly to Islamic society. Now, it may well be that Muslims continue to be organized in ways more directly linked to religious values and institutions than Christians, or for that matter, Hindus, Buddhists, and other large religious groups. Nevertheless, to label everything "Islamic" is to assume a poverty of cultural response which does an injustice to these peoples and their rich heritage. There is nothing in Islam as such that predisposes narrow, winding streets (or wide boulevards and a grid pattern). No Islamic norm prefigures the traditional bazaar pattern of occupational and professional segregation wherein all the blacksmiths are to be found in one section, all the tailors in another, and so on. Nor has Islam been the major determinant in the pattern of female sequestration.

---

6 Only approximately one-third of the over half billion Muslims in the world live in the area being considered (i.e., the Arab world, Turkey, Iran, and Afghanistan). The Indian subcontinent alone (India, Bangladesh, and Pakistan) contains almost as many Muslims. Indonesia, with a population of over 115 million, is overwhelmingly Muslim. Islam is the most rapidly expanding religion in Black Africa. There are also several million Muslims living under Soviet rule in Central Asia.

7 An example of the terminological confusion in reverse: Father Louis Gardet, one of the most perceptive Catholic scholars of Islam, has written a stimulating book on basic Islamic religious and humanistic values, or what might be called the Muslim concept of the *civitas dei*. And it is clearly to convey this latter notion, plus perhaps to underscore a sense of the common Semitic religious roots of Islam and Christianity, that he entitled his work *La Cité Musulmane* (Paris, 1954). The book, apparently because of this title, found its way into a bibliography entitled "A Selection of Works relating to the History of Cities," contained in Handlin and Burchard, *The Historian and the City*. Would such a book have been listed in such a bibliography if it had been entitled *La Cité Chrétienne*?

Of course, the traditional Muslim self-image posited a certain integrity and completeness distinguishing the Islamic community (the *umma*) in all aspects from any non-Muslim society. To this extent, the traditional Muslim feeling of self-sufficiency and **distinctiveness** vis-à-vis the non-Muslim may be compared with the Chinese. This, too, helps to explain the Western scholar's tendency to use the adjective "Islamic" with such abandon, but the approach remains, nevertheless, faulted by its implicit a priorism. It is much better to keep clearly in mind that Islam, as a system of religious values and law, has acted upon and interacted with every institution and social group in those parts of the world where it has gained a body of adherents, but that the resulting civilizations, as with all civilizations, have been made up of many parts. The "Muslim-ness" of any component part is a subject well worthy of study, but it is not a matter to be taken for granted.[8]

This book on the Near Eastern city does not seek encyclopaedic comprehensiveness. It attempts to offer adequate examples from the different regions and cultural areas being considered, but even more important than any notion of "geographical balance" is the presentation of major themes. For example, the problem of preserving historical sites, discussed in Chapter Nine, is based essentially on the author's (Cevat Erder's) experience in Turkey; but he is talking of fundamental themes and approaches that would be equally present in Iran or the Arab world. Similarly, Mr. English's study of Herat not only seeks to explain the social and spatial organization of that traditional city. It also tries to place this empirical data within the framework of the several hypotheses that attempt to present a model of the traditional city in the Islamic world.

The select bibliographies to be found at the end of most chapters are also intended to support and emphasize the thematic organization of the book. Each bibliography represents the author's own view of which books and articles could be usefully consulted by anyone wishing to pursue in greater detail, or from other perspectives, the subject treated in his chapter. For this reason, the same works are often cited in more than one bibliography.

This is not a study in Near Eastern urban history. The major focus is clearly the contemporary Near Eastern city. Nevertheless, a concern to understand today's Near Eastern city in its cultural context and to discern the pattern of transition has imposed a historical framework upon most of the chapters, whether it be a general over-view of the traditional city, as set out by Mr. Lapidus, or a demonstration of the types of changes that have occurred in one section of Beirut during the past several decades, as shown in the chapter by Messrs. Khalaf and Kongstad. The Near Eastern city is, at present, besieged by so many forces of change that only an acute historical sense of process and flux is likely to be adequate for the necessary description and analysis.

A group endeavor, such as this book, is often stimulated by a desire to do something a bit different or to overcome what are thought to be weaknesses or

---

[8] The late Marshall G. S. Hodgson sensed this confusion of many things under one label and pointed the way toward a solution by suggesting that "Islamic" be reserved for things purely religious and "Islamicate" for components of higher civilization created by the blending of Islam as religion with the cultural milieu where it struck root. Islamicate could then be equivalent to "Western" in designating an entire civilization. We could then speak unambiguously about Islamic law and Islamicate cities, or even more precisely Islamic architecture and Islamicate architecture.

imbalances in previous work. And this desire, which usually begins in inchoate musings and vague feelings of "why don't they . . .," can sometimes crystallize into the guiding principle that informs the entire effort. The "something different" in this case is, as already noted, the confrontation of themes and ideas about the Near Eastern city by specialists whose professional disciplines do not usually take note of each other—architects and historians, art historians and sociologists, and so on. The authors contributing to this book were especially eager to get around the barrier artificially created to divide what might be labelled the problem-solving approach from the aesthetic approach. They reject any notion of a separation between the practical and the pleasing. The book accordingly emphasizes such culturally-oriented ideas of architecture as spatial organization, life-style and, in a broader sense, the Near Eastern aesthetic factor; but these themes are interwoven with the more familiar "problems" of cities in this part of the world such as the population explosion, the rural-to-urban migration and the bidonvilles, urban adjustments to the post-colonial period and the over-all socio-political dimensions of urban planning.

Nor does the synthesis sought in this book lead to a set of precise recommendations, and most of the individual chapters are equally modest on the matter of what is to be done. To certain readers more accustomed to a diagnosis culminating in prescription, the way chosen may seem overly restrained if not, indeed, Pollyannaish. Let the reader be assured on one point: the choice made represents not an unconscious flight from reality but a deliberate intellectual option. It is based on the conviction that we owe it to ourselves and to our subject to view such inquiries not just as problems to be solved but as varieties of human hope and achievement to be understood and appreciated on their own terms. Perhaps we can even agree that the really effective solutions to problems are inextricably linked to the very human endeavors out of which they arose.

Since this book is intended to be also of use to readers with little background in Islamic or Near Eastern studies,[9] it may be helpful here to offer a few basic observations about Near Eastern cities in order to:

1. Put the Western reader on guard against likely misconceptions growing out of the tendency to hazy generalizations about the "non-Western world."

2. And also (the obverse of the above) suggest areas where an unconscious application of Western conceptualizations about the city to the Near Eastern city may be misleading.

3. Describe briefly two of the issues that have divided the handful of scholars who have concerned themselves with the Near Eastern city.

The following pages are intended to be evocative—if not provocative—rather than comprehensive. Accordingly, the risk of distorting a complex and subtle

---

[9] As well as students of Islam or the Near East lacking background knowledge in urban studies; but this latter group is better served by a wide variety of accessible sources, from general surveys and textbooks to detailed monographs. To mention only a few: the classified and annotated bibliography appended to Handlin and Burchard, *The Historian and the City*; Gideon Sjoberg, *The Preindustrial City: Past and Present*; Max Weber, *The City* (Glencoe, Ill: Free Press, 1959, paperback; it includes the useful introduction "The Theory of the City" by Don Martindale); Gerald Breese, *Urbanization in Newly Developing Countries* (Englewood Cliffs: Prentice-Hall, 1966), and Gerald Breese, ed., *The City in Newly Developing Countries: Readings on Urbanism and Urbanization* (Prentice-Hall, 1969).

reality through oversimplification is assumed. Many of the points adumbrated here will be treated in a different context, and with greater care in the chapters to follow. If this section helps prepare the reader to appreciate more fully some of the major issues that will recur throughout the book, then it will have served its purpose.

* * * * * * *

The Near East has been a region of cities since the dawn of history, the example, par excellence, of urban civilization. And with the rise of Islamic civilization, beginning in the seventh century, this urban tradition was in no way diluted. It was, instead, strengthened while being modified and given an Islamic stamp. In the ninth century the Abbasid capital of Baghdad possibly reached a peak of one and one-half million inhabitants, and Basra supported a population perhaps half that size. During the same period at the western-most reaches of the Islamic world, the Umayyad capital of Cordova must have numbered several hundred thousand.[10]

Indeed, during the Middle Ages the contrast in city life between the Muslim Near East and Europe was striking. "For the greater part of the Middle Ages and over most of its area, the West formed a society primarily agrarian, feudal and monastic, at a time when the strength of Islam lay in its great cities, wealthy courts and long lines of communications."[11]

Individual cities in the Islamic Near East endured the expected fortunes and adversities meted out in history. The once majestic Baghdad began to decline starting in the tenth century and suffered a devastating defeat and capture at the hands of the Mongols in 1258. The Arab world's largest city, Cairo, was by contrast only beginning its history, having been founded by the Fatimids in 969 near the site of the older Fustat. In Tunisia the earlier Kairouan was yielding primacy to Tunis. Many present-day capitals such as Beirut, Ankara, and Teheran were, until modern times, very modest settlements.

As in other parts of the world, some cities rose to new heights while others declined to near oblivion, but throughout these vicissitudes the deeply-etched urban pattern characterizing the Islamic Near East remained. In the early sixteenth century, Istanbul, with a population of perhaps 400,000, was the largest city in Europe.[12]

This urban character of Islamic Near Eastern civilization has been emphasized by the last generation or so of scholars if only to overcome the earlier layman's misconception about Islam being the "child of the desert." After all, Muhammad

[10] For a discussion of the population estimates of Baghdad and Basra, see the articles by that name in the *Encyclopaedia of Islam*, 2nd ed. On Cordova, see E. Levi-Provençal, *Histoire de l'Espagne Musulmane*, vol. 3 (Paris, 1953). These estimates are to be taken with caution, for historians estimating pre-modern city populations must work with extremely elusive data. In addition, there is, alas, still very little consensus or standardization concerning the exploitation of the data which is at hand. Levi-Provençal, for example, simply records the lowest estimate for Cordova in its prime as 100,000 and the highest, one million. Beyond asserting that the former is clearly too low and the latter too high, Levi-Provençal refuses to speculate. However gross the margin of error, these estimates do suffice to indicate that the early Islamic civilization boasted great cities and a deep-rooted urban tradition.

[11] R. W. Southern, *Western Views of Islam in the Middle Ages* (Cambridge, Mass.: Harvard University Press, 1962), p. 7.

[12] See p. 246. And, of course, Istanbul is a "European" city, being on the European side of the Bosporus.

was not a bedouin. He was born and grew up in the sophisticated trading city of
Mecca. When he and his small band of followers experienced political difficulties
in Mecca, they emigrated (the *hijra* of 622 which marks the beginning of the
Muslim epoch) not to the countryside, not to a bedouin encampment, but to
another city, Yathrib (renamed Medina). In the same way, after the death of
Muhammad, the great traditions of religious sciences, philosophy, law, and
mysticism were hammered out in the highly urban environments of Damascus,
Baghdad, and other cities. As these facts about the urban roots of Islamic
religion and culture become better known, many scholars are inclined to go so
far as to assert that Islam as religion and culture is inconceivable stripped from
its matrix of city life.

These observations about the venerableness of urban life in the Near East,
trite to the specialists, may not seem too jarring to the layman either. The
Westerner, as part of his *own* cultural heritage, can evoke images of Babylon and
Nineveh, Alexandria, the Constantinople that became Istanbul, the urban
achievements of Muslim Spain, and the cosmopolitan urbanity that characterized
Harun al-Rashid's Baghdad in the *Thousand and One Nights.* This is all very well,
but there remains among many of us a subconscious tendency to associate
urban-ness with modernity, or even more precisely Westernization. Nothing could
be more misleading. The Near East has approached modernity from a different
path, but one studded with urban landmarks all along the way. It is not easy to
determine just what impact this urban heritage has had upon modern Near
Eastern cities. How is this Near Eastern urban heritage to be compared with the
quite different past of European feudalism with political power dispersed in the
countryside, or the Americas growing out of colonization, or parts of Black
Africa characterized by relatively low population density, cohesive village, and
tribal groups but limited urbanization? These are questions not easily answered,
but it is surely wise to begin with an accurate assessment of the past.

Modernization, or more precisely, Westernization, therefore, reached the Near
East as a cultural area already endowed with a venerable, well-established
urbanism. The result, especially when it took the more openly intrusive form of
Western colonialism, was a juxtaposition of urban styles which often had clearly
delineated physical boundaries. Tunis provides an especially striking example.
The old city—the madina—is now surrounded with a ring road that follows
precisely the line of earlier city walls (only scattered sections of the wall and a few
of the babs, or gates, now survive). Within this circle lies a spatial and
structural organization attuned to the life-style of medieval and early modern
Tunis, to the Tunis of the Hafsids and the early Husaynids. Beyond is a radically
different city organization. Admittedly, some of the areas outside the circle
enclosing the old madina still reveal signs of the old forms and patterns. Such
zones might better be labelled transitional or hybridized, since they reveal
interesting combinations of Western and indigenous, but these are neither so
extensive nor so important as the thoroughly westernized zones. These
transitional zones are, in any case, satellites of the new city, responding to
imperatives and attractions lying outside of the old madina.

As with many such cities in this part of the world, Tunis has moved its
center of gravity under the Western impact. The economic, professional, and

cultural center of Tunis now lies between the old madina and the port. Indeed, the principal street of the modern city, the wide, tree-lined Avenue Habib Bourguiba (formerly Jules Ferry) appears on maps of modern Tunis much like a battering ram pressing against the vulnerable old city. This modern part of Tunis holds the world of vehicular traffic, high-rise buildings, a grid pattern of streets and angular buildings—everywhere straight lines and sharp edges, the realm of the geometric, the planned, the practical, and the accessible. What a contrast to the narrow, meandering, kaleidoscopic old madina!

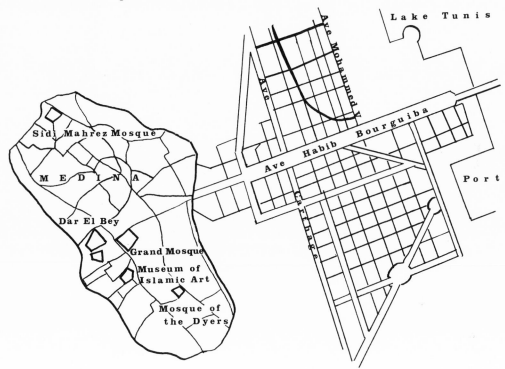

Fig. 1. Tunis showing juxtaposition of old and new city, and Bourguiba Avenue as battering ram against old city.

The old madina has lost its venerable claim to being the educational center. The new University of Tunis is developing on the city's edge, and the celebrated Zitouna School devoted to higher Islamic studies (often called Zitouna Mosque-University in earlier Western sources) is now a *faculté* in the new University of Tunis. Perhaps the educational exodus from the old madina may be said to have begun as early as 1875, even before the French Protectorate, when a westernizing Tunisian minister established Sadiqi College as an institution specifically intended to train needed government officials by means of a combined Western/indigenous curriculum. A few primary and secondary schools linger within the confines of the old madina, sometimes housed in venerable madrasas, but the prestigious institutions and the pacesetters are to be found in the modern sectors.

The old madina remains, therefore, somewhat like the inner city in American urban experience—abandoned by the great and powerful, their former places taken over by the poor who are also often newcomers to the city. And, as a result of this change, the considerable architectural integrity of these former core-areas and the urban culture these structures and spaces embodied go largely ignored.[13]

The contrast between old madina and new modern city is not always as visually sharp and topographically delineated as in Tunis. In Algeria, for example, the infinitely more intensive French colonization all but eliminated the physical evidence of old madinas. Elsewhere, as in Beirut, the old city (which was quite small in the much more modest urban agglomeration that was Lebanon's capital a few generations ago) has been, for all practical purposes, swallowed up and digested by the restless new city. Sometimes, the old-new dialectic is worked out by a distinct new city challenging the old as with Khartoum and Omdurman or Port Sudan as the British-inspired new port on the Red Sea replacing the earlier Suwakin.

Pls. 54-55
(151)

More similar to Tunis are Jerusalem and Aleppo among major cities plus a great variety of provincial towns throughout the Near East, for they tend to reveal more strikingly the physical confrontation between old and new.[14]

Whatever the specific physical form taken, the conflict and contrast between two urban styles is always present. It is, in part, as suggested before, somewhat like the Western problem of the inner city—abandoned splendor now semi-derelict in its presumed obsolescence. Yet, unlike the problem of the decaying inner city, the "old madina-new city" phenomenon is caught up in a situation of cross-cultural borrowing with all its attendant psychological strains. In such cases, man's view of the problem is even more likely to transcend aesthetic and utilitarian considerations. Old and new are then likely to become symbols for ultimate values—the old madina as refuge and locus of traditional religious piety, the old-time religion in the old-time city. Or the old city becomes a stifling museum of antiquities and the very symbol of "our backwardness." Complementary polarities can also exist in the conceptualization of the new city.

Much of the social commentary and creative writing on the Near East has addressed itself to this confrontation of old and new. Some of this writing is itself now venerable (a few of the earliest examples going back over a century), and in some quarters the theme itself is deemed *passé*. Nevertheless, the dialectic process itself, of indigenous old versus intrusive new, continues apace; and many of the more sensitive individuals involved still conceptualize their present

[13]   And, as M. Dethier's chapter demonstrates, the classic case of a colonial government's deliberate effort to separate old and new cities is to be found in Lyautey's Morocco.

[14]   The problem is not readily solved. Let a once imposing urban area stand derelict for awhile, and it will be regarded with distaste. Yet, an overly deliberate restoration, creating a sort of museum, fosters the tendency to view the past as a plaything. And where a portion of the madina is turned into a kind of Near Eastern "Dodge City" or "Carcassonne" catering to tourism, the results can be abominable. Anyone with respect for the old culture can only shudder at the sight of groups of foreign tourists sporting tawdry reproductions of Near Eastern traditional clothing being offered thoroughly misleading guided tours through "attractions" and *manifestations folkloriques*. In this age of mass tourism the "living museum" approach, however well intended, is probably best avoided. A genuine economic integration into the living city provides a better opportunity to preserve the historical legacy, but such efforts demand a bit of intuitive brilliance—and luck. In some cases, the appeal to social snobism may be a useful stimulus. The restoration of Georgetown over the past few decades into the most prestigious and expensive of Washington's residential areas has guaranteed the preservation of a charming eighteenth-century colonial architectural style. If only the old madina could again become the "in" place to live. . .? This could be a realistic and just approach were it coupled with effective housing plans to accommodate those lower class and declassé peoples now living in squalor in these potentially restorable portions of the old madina.

Two mid-nineteenth-century views of city walls and gates.
5. Sousse in Tunisia as seen from the sea. Note the second line of walls surrounding the qasba located on high ground within the city. (Source: Charles de Chassiron, *Aperçu pittoresque de la Regence de Tunis.*) 6.(below) The Damascus Gate, Jerusalem. (Source: David Roberts.)

situation in such terms. No study of the modern Near Eastern city will be adequate that does not keep clearly in mind this confrontation of two highly-developed urban traditions as well as the value-laden atmosphere in which the struggle has taken place.

This insistence on the highly-developed Near Eastern urban tradition that existed before the impact of the West suggests a related point worth noting: the pre-modern Near Eastern city was a reasonably well-organized urban ag-glomeration. Its several parts held together and they, further, blended together into an over-all entity that "made sense." This should be axiomatic. Historians, anthropologists, and the structural-functionalists among social scientists have long been in implicit accord that social organisms surviving over long periods of time must lay claim to some inherent logical and ecological adaptability. Nevertheless, the anachronistic tendency to regard as slightly absurd what is outdated runs deep in modern man's psyche. Let us then reaffirm that there must have been something solid and "workable" about the Islamic Near Eastern city, for otherwise it would not have survived for so long. Two of the chapters in this book deal directly with the traditional cities and several other chapters touch upon one or another aspect of the pre-modern urban heritage. Here it will suffice to offer a few general points designed mainly to answer the utilitarian modernist's implicit question, "how could they have been so foolish. . . ?"

Pls. 5-6 (31)
Pl. 8 (36)
Pls. 41-42 (115)

The traditional city walls, including in many cases internal walls dividing quarter from quarter, were, of course, to provide security. The security sought was not, in the first instance or in most cases, against an invading army. The walls were, rather, a form of what we moderns would call police protection. When the gates were closed, as at night, the city would turn its back on both brigand and bumpkin and could therefore guard against those whose profession was to disturb the peace as well as those whose lack of roots in the city might exacerbate the possibility of tension or disorder.

Pl. 40 (114)
Pl. 69 (198)

The same logic held for gates and walls dividing the city's different quarters. The ultimate rationale may be grasped in terms of a security arrangement that relied less on personnel (police, watchmen, inspectors, etc.) than on a spatial organization controlling mobility. The walls and the quarters served to divide the city into manageable component parts, and in each part there was at least the potential for a kind of intimacy and primary-group relationships that Western theorists are inclined to connect more with village culture. It therefore followed that the *shaykh* of a city quarter (or whatever title he might bear according to the city and period being considered) could control his home area with virtually no formal staff in the same way that the archetypal English squire held sway over the English countryside.

Pl. 7 (33)

This form of security and spatial organization is easily over-romanticized. The idea that control was maintained through the checks and balances of social pressures mediated, where individual human intervention was required, by urban Muslim equivalents of Squire Western is overly idyllic. Such a control system was, as with any human organization, purchased at a price which included in this case an emphasis on ascriptive roles and loyalties, the potential for unchecked

7. Part of the street called Straight in Damascus, Syria, *ca.* 1900. This photograph conveys a less romantic aspect of the traditional city. The inadequately paved streets were a problem in the rainy season. Also, many of the outside walls are in disrepair. This is, to some extent, a natural result of the "introverted" organization of space in which families and small groups tend to turn their back on, and accordingly be less concerned with, the outside. (Photo: Library of Congress.)

petty despotisms, and a generally diffuse pattern of political and economic organization with a concomitant low level of resource mobilization. Indeed, it can well be argued that the security organization suggested above was bound to fall apart under the impact of the industrial revolution with its requisites for infinitely greater human mobility and human adaptability to new skills and roles. Nevertheless, the logic of the traditional city security organization must be understood. Only then can the observer analyze and appreciate the confrontation of old patterns and new socio-economic requirements that characterize each Near Eastern city today.[15]

What then of those narrow, labyrinthine streets? Were not these inefficient? Again, a closer examination reveals a rather tidy adaptability. First, consistent with the above point concerning spatial arrangement as a form of police protection, the pattern of street arrangement was confusing and cumbersome only to the modern mind seeking to move men and things readily through all parts of the city. One might well reflect how completely the grid pattern of broad thoroughfares presupposes high levels of mobility and exchange. The traditional Near Eastern city was designed not to generalize and ease mobility and exchange but to control and compartmentalize it. On the level of the individual city dweller, this meant that there were only certain parts of the city that he needed to know or cared to know, his own residential and market area plus a few central points of exchange and communication.

Pls. 13-16
(61-62)
Pls. 20-21
(67)
Pls. 23-24
(71)
Pl. 29 (91)

The narrow, winding streets were, accordingly, a sort of built-in system of traffic control, inhibiting the movement of men, animals, and commodities through areas where it was preferable that they be barred or at least limited. It all added up to an informal, but nevertheless, effective zoning plan. Certain areas were deliberately given narrow streets and relatively less accessible locations. Others, responding to the needs of bulky or heavy exchange, were situated where this could be achieved with a minimum of confusion, usually close to or just beyond the city's outer walls. Still other city activities were located in conformity to their industrial needs. Tanners and dyers, for example, needed water as well as space open to the sun's natural drying powers.

Pls. 59-60
(169)

As a result of this "city-plan," the student in the *madrasa,* the pious at prayer in the mosque, or the shopper in the cloth bazaar could go about his

---

15 It might well be argued that the traditional security organization of the Muslim city sketched here differed more in degree than in kind from Western cities, even in modern times. In the United States, the increased awareness of communal sub-sectors in major cities (Black especially, but also Italian, Irish, Polish, Puerto Rican, Jewish, Catholic, WASP, etc.) and the arguments of the revisionist historians that the melting pot notion was a myth have provoked a revaluation of the received wisdom. Probably, earlier generations of American urban scholars did exaggerate the anonymous, contractual, and rationalized (in the Weberian sense) nature of the city as opposed to the ascriptive, face-to-face, and traditional nature of rural life. It is even more evident that comparable forms of security control emphasizing spatial organization rather than numbers of police personnel characterized pre-modern Western cities. The major point, it seems, to keep clearly in mind is that here one is necessarily dealing at the level of "ideal types," to be used as heuristic working hypotheses for better organizing our knowledge and not as rigid categories of thought to be imposed upon empirical study. All of this underlines in yet another way the importance of studying Near Eastern cities in a comparative context, but at the same time the special mix developed in the traditional Near Eastern city must not be too readily lost sight of in our passion for general comparisons.

affairs undisturbed by a constant stream of porters and heavily-laden donkeys. The blacksmith, on the other hand, could be found on the edge of the city, more available to the men and animals requiring his service; and at the same time, the din of his hammer was far enough away not to disturb customers in the *suqs* of the booksellers or perfumers.

The caravansaries tended to be located in a single quarter at the city's edge, for there was no need to disturb the tranquility of the inner city by introducing "wholesale" commodities there. Also, the foreign merchants were better kept in their own quarter in a peripheral area of the city. The same dual reasoning dictated having what we might now call "farmers' markets" just outside the city walls.

Pls. 8-9 (36)
Pl. 25 (72)

Of course, there were individual variations in city spatial organizations. To use the classification adopted by some urban historians, certain Near Eastern cities were "spontaneous," others were "created." That is, some had grown slowly over time, adapting in the process to new circumstances and changing dynasties. Others had been deliberately created by a political sovereign: Baghdad, Cairo, Isfahan, Meknes, and Khartoum are major examples, ranging in date of creation from the eighth century to the early nineteenth. This latter group might boast a more open communication system coupled with a more ostentatious assertion of the political presence, or at least some part of the city may continue to bear witness to a strong ruler's desire to immortalize his reign in stone and luxurious use of space. Nevertheless, as has been demonstrated, the distinction between spontaneous and created Near Eastern cities tended to become eroded with time.[16] Eventually, the city's own inner mechanisms wore down the fitful whims of rulers. Indeed, this was even more easily done because in the traditional Near Eastern urban culture the "state" intervened only lightly and spasmodically in the city's daily life. There remained an urban life that was traditional in the sense of being slow to change, traditional in the sense of placing heavy emphasis on ascriptive values, traditional in that it largely dispensed with central control or centralized efforts at resource mobilization. Traditional, but for all of that, far from illogical, incomprehensible, or absurd![17]

---

[16] E. Pauty, "Villes spontanées et villes créées en Islam," *Annales de l'Institut d'études orientales*, no. 9 (1951).

[17] And for that matter, far from foreign to pre-modern European styles of urban organization. For example, scholars of Muslim North Africa have made much of the manner in which the political sovereign, or the state, seems to form a city apart. Or, at least, the "state" seems to be in, but not of, the city. Brunschvig, writing of Central North Africa, in the period from the thirteenth century to the sixteenth century, notes that "in certain great cities the citadel of Qasba was likely to form a government distinct from that of the city." R. Brunschvig, *La Berberie orientale sous les Hafsides des origines à la fin du XVe siècle*, 2 vols. (Paris, 1940, 1947), 2:112. And Le Tourneau cites as "veritable separated cities" the sectors housing "government" such as the Qasba of Marrakech, the Qasba of Tunis, Fez Jdid (vis-à-vis Fez), and the Qasba of Algiers. Roger Le Tourneau, *Les Villes Musulmanes de l'Afrique du Nord* (Algiers, 1957), pp. 12-13. It is, of course, as if the "state" were warily guarding the city. Yet, how different was this from the medieval European city in which castles were built to defend against inhabitants of the town as well as against outsiders? The Tower of London dominated that city on the East, Barnard's Castle on the West. And King Phillip Augustus built the Louvre on the edge of the merchant settlement in Paris; the fourteenth century brought the Bastille built at the opposite end of Paris; and the two small fortresses—Chatelets—held the bridgeheads leading from the Ile de la Cité to the left and right banks of the Seine (all within the city of Paris). See Sidney Painter, *Medieval Society* (Ithaca: Cornell University Press, 1951), p. 86.

In the traditional city, the "farmers' market" and the livestock market were appropriately placed just outside the city walls, thus avoiding noise and congestion within the city proper. 8. (above) The site for the open air market in Fez, Morocco. (Photo: Pan American World Airways.)

9. The animal market at the edge of the city in Marrakech, Morocco. (Photo: Abbott L. Moffatt.)

Now, a word about that most elusive subject—the city as an ideal in Islamic culture. It might be well to begin with a reminder that Western culture approaches the city-as-ideal with considerable ambiguity. "See Rome and die," but for all that as William Cowper insisted, "God made the country and man made the town." Cities with their concentrations of resources and intelligences are, of course, prized in the West; but there remains that haunting notion—much older than the nineteenth-century Romantic movement—that the pastoral simplicity of rural life is closer to the divine plan. Cities are hierarchy and status. The countryside is self-reliance and stolid independence. Commenting on a deserted village, Oliver Goldsmith could epitomize this theme:

> *Princes and lords may flourish, or may fade;*
> *A breath can make them, as a breath has made;*
> *But a bold peasantry, their country's pride,*
> *When once destroyed, can never be supplied.*

These themes of rural simplicity and virtue as opposed to urban complexity and vice are, perhaps, especially marked—even if often in an implicit or dormant fashion—in American urban studies.

How, then, does Near Eastern Islamic culture stand on this matter? Interestingly enough for an area with such an overwhelming majority of peasants, there is virtually no idealization of a "bold peasantry." In Arabic culture, there is an idealization of bedouin life—somewhat comparable to the frontiersman motif in American history and literature. The classical period of Arabic poetry brought the creation of the ode, vaunting bedouin virtues, and the period and genre are highly prized to this day. Yet, in fact, even by the time of the Abbasid Caliphate, such poetry had become conventionalized as a means of expressing individual virtuosity rather than a living tradition. The urbane, half-Persian Abu Nuwas (died *ca.* 803) could even go so far as to satirize the absurdity of city aesthetes pretending to care about bedouin life:

> *The lovelorn wretch stopped at a (deserted) camping-ground to question it,*
> *And I stopped to inquire after the local tavern.*
> *May Allah not dry the eyes of him that wept over stones,*
> *And may He not ease the pain of him that yearns to a tent-peg.*
> *They said, 'Dids't thou commemorate the dwelling places of the tribes of Asad?'*
> *Plague on thee! Tell me, who are the Banu Asad?* [18]

A disdain for the peasant, a certain stereotyped but increasingly artificial exploitation of bedouin themes in literature, and an implicit assumption that the good life was to be worked out in an urban environment—such seems to typify the Near Eastern traditional response to the city as ideal. The location of imposing religious or secular buildings may well offer another clue to the priority of values in the Islamic Near East. The relative absence in the countryside of castles (the major exceptions being a number built by the Crusaders or during the Crusader period in the Levant), country houses, or

---

[18] Reynold A. Nicholson, *Translations of Eastern Arabic Poetry and Prose* (Cambridge University Press, 1922), p. 33.

imposing architectural edifices equivalent to parish churches contrasts with the luxuriant architectural styles in traditional Near Eastern cities patronized by princes and private citizens. Of course, Western architecture extending out into the countryside was a natural response to feudalism, with resulting power (and patronage) to be found beyond the cities in the countryside, whereas the Islamic Near East provided nothing comparable to feudalism. True, but this is merely to use the approach of socio-economic history, rather than that of the more nebulous intellectual history, to arrive at the same place.

One careful attempt to delineate Islamic ideal-types in the medieval period goes as follows: "Islam prefers the sedentary to the nomad, the city dweller to the villager. It accepts the artisan but respects the merchant. The sword ranks lower than the pen. Religious knowledge is more desirable than wealth ... Power is fascinating and awesome but transient, the king and the officials a disturbing body in the peace-loving but war-ridden, industrious and exploited community."[19]

The idealization evokes images not of a squirearchy, not a warrior nobility, not of a restless, individualistic frontiersman, but of an urban bourgeoisie.

Etymology offers a bit more evidence of an urban prejudice. The two Arabic expressions for civilization (*hadara* and *madaniya*) both derive from roots meaning settlement or cities (comparable to the Western: civilization-*civitas*). Variant forms of these two words are also used to convey the notion of refinement, sophistication, or education. Other words in Arabic, Turkish, or Persian might be marshalled to show the etymological—and, so we would argue, socio-psychological as well—links between the idea of concentration of human population and prosperity.

Pejorative terms also underscore the urban bias. Until quite modern times the word "Turk" was used in Turkish to indicate a rustic with all the connotations of the boorish lout. "Arab" was used with equal disdain to label those nomads and transhumants living outside of sedentary life, and it tended to be synonymous with crude, uneducated, and uncivilized. Modern nationalism has, of course, completely reversed the usage, and, in addition, the torrent of populist thought that has covered the Near East in the last few decades has acted to challenge the old urban prejudice against non-urban life.[20] It remains, nevertheless, useful in any contemporary analysis of Near Eastern cities to keep clearly in mind the high valuation on urban-ness and urbanity that has always characterized these cultures, as well as the relative lack of a primitivist ideal expressed in terms of a return to nature or at least away from the city.

This is an appropriate place to introduce one of the themes now subject to a revisionist challenge by a growing body of scholars working in Near Eastern

---

[19] Gustave von Grunebaum, "The Profile of Muslim Civilization," in *Islam: Essays in the Nature and Growth of a Cultural Tradition*, ed. Von Grunebaum (London, 1955), p. 25.

[20] For example, it is no longer deemed proper for a resident of Tunis to refer to those of rural background as *afaqi* or *barrani*, with the connotation of "hick" or "rube." Both the socio-geographical mobility achieved in the past decades and the ideological imperative, sparked by the nationalist movement, to think in terms of a common Tunisian-ness have brought about the change. Indeed, there is a trend toward a complete reversal of prejudice. Those of the old *baldiya* class (the traditional urban bourgeoisie) who are reluctant to adapt to the new ways and new ideology find themselves disapproved. To some extent, the word *baldi* is now a term of reproach.

urban studies—the notion of a sharp separation between urban and non-urban life in the Near East. The revisionists, among whose number are contributors to this volume, would argue instead that to view the matter in terms of a rural-urban continuum would better capture the complex reality. The older view was energetically expressed by Gibb and Bowen: "The contrast which exists between the rural community and the city in every society was rarely more striking than in the medieval Islamic world. Here it was not merely a contrast between isolation and congregation, between the dispersed economy of the village and the concentration economy of the town, between oppressed poverty and relative freedom and wealth, between producer and consumer. It was a contrast of civilizations."[21]

An appropriate summation of the revisionist argument has been given elsewhere by a contributor to this volume. "We can no longer think of Muslim cities as unique, bounded or self-contained entities . . . . None of the characteristic social bodies of Muslim society—the quarter, the fraternity, the religious community and the state—were specifically urban forms of organization."[22]

The revisionist challenge is eminently welcome. It provokes a renewed concentration on the total society—to give a trite example, an equal emphasis on the push in the countryside with the pull of the city in order to analyze rural-to-urban migration. Further, the idea of a rural-urban continuum also emphasizes, in a subtle fashion, the notion of a dynamic historical process by concentrating attention on changing rural-urban patterns throughout time. It would be unfair to those formulators of the older interpretation to infer that they denied such rural-urban links and historical changes in the pattern of those links. They were quite aware of this process. Nevertheless, the tendency to conceptualize in terms of two separate worlds—urban and rural—created as well an inclination to think of categories that could properly be studied in isolation, Pls. 10-11 (42) one from the other.

Those emphasizing the rural-urban continuum in Near Eastern studies have already demonstrated certain distortions and exaggerations in the earlier formulation. As a result, the Near Eastern urban-rural dichotomy can no longer be accepted as dogma. This is clear progress, for good scholarship can do without dogmas. It would, therefore, be ironical if the continuum notion came now to be accepted uncritically as new dogma. There are, after all, differences between city and countryside throughout the world, and perhaps especially in the Near East. Possibly we have not yet found ways to classify and analyze these differences, but we must not let the continuum theory divert our attention from further work along these lines. That there are different dialects *within* the city does not, for example, make any less important the existence of distinguishing urban-rural dialects. Although it may well be more a sliding scale than earlier scholars appreciated, at some point along that scale irrefutable quantitative and qualitative differences emerge to distinguish rural from urban; and this whole matter demands further clarification.

[21] H. A. R. Gibb and Harold Bowen, *Islamic Society and the West*, vol. 1, pt. 1 (Oxford University Press, 1950), p. 276. Or, note for North Africa the following: ". . . city and countryside formed two completely separate worlds." Le Tourneau, *Les Villes Musulmanes de l'Afrique du Nord*, p. 21.

[22] Ira M. Lapidus, "Muslim Cities and Islamic Societies," in *Middle Eastern Cities*, ed. Lapidus (University of California Press, 1969), p. 73.

At the same time, the city, as ideal in Muslim society, remains to complicate the problem. Clearly, a culture's self-image must not be used as the basis of explanation and analysis in the teeth of contrary empirical evidence, but the reverse is equally compelling. The self-image and the event, the thought and the deed, must both be weighed in any comprehensive appreciation of a society.

A second matter of concern to scholars working in Near East urban studies—or more precisely, one that promises to provoke a useful scholarly debate in the near future—is that of political control and the concomitant sense of political loyalty existing in the Near Eastern city, traditional or modern. The older view, which still prevails, but no longer without challenge, was succinctly stated by Von Grunebaum in his bold effort (already cited) to assert ideal types: "No Muslim was ever rebuked for damaging the civic spirit. No Muslim government ever tried to develop the civic spirit."[23] This interpretation ties in with the idea of government (or the state) as being something in but not of the city. It also overlaps with the generally held view that Islamic political institutions usually manifested a certain formlessness, a certain lack of preciseness by comparison with that which the West inherited from its Greco-Roman past.

How this cluster of ideas revolving around the alleged lack of a civic spirit in Islamic cities came into being is not difficult to see. It gew out of the intellectual baggage Western scholars brought with them as they turned to study this sister civilization. Accustomed to think in terms of the agora and the forum, of Athenian democracy, the binding force of Roman law, the city-states of the Renaissance in Italy, and the role of European burghers in advancing modern capitalism as well as modern democratic institutions by their jealous defense of their urban rights against kings and nobility, they looked in vain for comparable institutions and parallel historical developments in the Islamic Near East. Finding little or no comparison, this school of thought lapsed into negative forms of description. The Near Eastern urban political culture was defined by what it was not.

The above charge is too harsh and is certainly unfair to earlier pioneers in this field without whose insights and contributions the possibility of more sophisticated analysis would be unthinkable. Even so, there is a weakness in this approach to Near Eastern urban politics, and the time has come for it to be challenged. One fundamental fault is that this whole line of enquiry compares the ideal of one culture (Greco-Roman-Renaissance in the West) with the reality or alleged reality (the traditional Near Eastern city) of another. And it follows that we must begin by comparing the comparable. There was slavery in ancient Athens and in the Baghdad of Harun al-Rashid. A lumpenproletariat ready to riot in times of scarcity or breakdown of public order existed in medieval Cairo as well as in medieval London and Paris. Both Istanbul and Venice in the sixteenth century were partially molded by certain governmental policies toward trade. These things

---

[23] Von Grunebaum, "Profile of Muslim Civilization," in *Islam*, p. 26. Admittedly, the author was trying to sketch ideal-types. He fully realized, as he noted in another part of the same book, that "actual (Muslim) government resembles rather closely medieval government elsewhere" ("Government in Islam," p. 136). Nevertheless, the idea that medieval Islam lacked the notion of citizenship or the equivalent of a civic spirit is what seems to have stuck with most scholars of medieval Islam.

may be studied and compared with benefit, and equally one may usefully compare the self-image and ideal structure of different urban cultures.

In narrowly political terms, the traditional Near Eastern city found in its midst a very small number of persons who were linked with the state. The state, as such, tended to confine its activities in the city to the minimum. Accordingly, the city, or more precisely its several component parts representing an appreciably larger spectrum of religious and ethnic diversity than in Europe, was largely left to govern itself. To approach such a political culture with the unconscious assumption of a neat hierarchy of authority culminating in a political sovereign is to invite misunderstanding.

Having said this, however, it remains to note that the classification and analysis of urban political institutions in the Islamic Near East remains somewhat elusive. We still know rather more about the ideal government than how politics and government actually worked. Several authors in this book touch on the subject, which is only natural, for some of them have been in the vanguard of those suggesting new interpretations and new methodologies. Mr. Lapidus, for example, emphasizes the mediating and integrating role of the Islamic law schools. He also suggests the importance of the venerable Western Asian tradition of strong, bureaucratically organized state-systems. Mr. Tekeli in his contribution on the Ottoman Empire offers an overview of one dynasty's political impact on cities under its rule. Mr. English properly warns against pitfalls of any overly-rigid monocausal theory of interpretation. Other suggestions and approaches are to be found throughout this book.

As the reader comes across this theme in the chapters to follow he may well wish to keep in mind the following challenge: the Islamic Near Eastern city seems relatively fluid and formless by Western standards. Yet, this type of city survived for centuries, forming the matrix for a high cultural tradition. Something clearly held these cities together. If not a civic spirit, then what was it?

* * * * * * *

The first two chapters in Part I, entitled "The Traditional Near Eastern City," provide a historical benchmark against which urban change in modern times can be measured. Mr. Lapidus undertakes the difficult task of suggesting certain basic characteristics that link together traditional Near Eastern cities in the Muslim period. He emphasizes the intermediary role of the law schools in holding together the various parts of the traditional Muslim city.

Mr. English then explores one traditional Muslim city—Herat, in Afghanistan—comparing and contrasting it with the general theories and models proposed for traditional cities. As a geographer, Mr. English is especially attuned to the city's spatial organization, and he sees the quarters as providing a "common organizing principle of pre-industrial Muslim urban life." He notes in Herat a relative absence of guild organizations and spatial groupings by occupation and suggests that perhaps certain models of pre-industrial cities have exaggerated the concept of social segregation.

Each of these chapters reflects a careful effort to provide useful generalizations about the traditional Near Eastern city, for without these

10. Medina, Saudi Arabia, *ca.* 1787. (From: Mourradja d'Ohsson, *Histoire de l'Empire Ottomane.*)

11. Plan of Algiers, *ca.* 1818. (From: Pananti, *Narrative of Residence in Algiers.*) Both convey the exaggerated European image of the Near Eastern city—much congestion within a surrounding wall and a comparatively deserted countryside.

"building blocks" it is impossible to assemble our data into any kind of meaningful intellectual edifice. At the same time, each author is concerned not to distort a complex reality with glib categorizations. The sense of the dynamic interplay between the abstract and the concrete is, accordingly, never obscured.

Part II, "Urban Development and Change—Some Individual Examples," offers a series of "case studies" on specific cities. Mrs. Abu-Lughod's chapter traces the ebb and flow of Cairo's long past, putting to rest the notion of a traditional Near Eastern city that has slumbered throughout the centuries beyond the context of history. She then emphasizes the contrast of the old and new city as created, and then aggravated, during the period of British hegemony. She sees the period since 1952 as marking a partially successful effort at re-integration of the greater city. Another theme worthy of note is the city's resiliency in the face of mushrooming growth, accelerated rural-to-urban immigration, and the backwash of Egypt's many domestic and international vicissitudes. It is, after all, heartening to be reminded, while absorbed in the study of myriad urban problems, that the cluster of peoples and institutions making up a great city such as Cairo combine to provide great reserves of perseverence, adaptability, and durability. These assets need only to be used, or at least not over-abused, by the human planners.

Messrs. Khalaf and Kongstad are concerned with one section of a major city, in this case the Hamra district of Beirut. After an introductory background sketching the rapid growth of Beirut in general and demonstrating how this city, with 40% of Lebanon's total population, is an exaggerated example of primary city dominance, the authors move on to a precise examination of the Hamra section. Hamra, they urge, is not so much a "typical" example of the type of change virtually inundating Beirut as it is an especially striking example. Their careful documentation of land use, rents, man-space ratios, and other such quantitative criteria adds up to a gripping story. Beirut is the example, par excellence, of the mushrooming, modern laissez-faire city, and the data compiled by Khalaf and Kongstad demonstrates the strengths and weaknesses of this approach.

The authors trace three distinct "phases" of architectural style in the Hamra section—all within a time considerably shorter than the Biblical three score and ten—from farmhouse to neo-traditional villa to high-rise apartment. All three are now found juxtaposed in the increasingly confined space, offering a graphic illustration of the city's prospects . . . and growing pains.

Karol Krótki, a statistician and demographer who directed Sudan's first population census in the 1950s, combines his professional expertise and his intimate knowledge of Sudan in presenting a mélange of statistical and impressionistic observations about Omdurman. This city, made famous by the Sudanese Mahdi in the 1880s has been, as Mr. Krótki suggests, more nearly a "desert port" than a river port and has served as an urban center for nomads and transhumants coming from the vast expanses of Sudan that lie beyond the Nile Valley. It is now a city that has lost the political, economic, and cultural initiative to the capital, Khartoum, that lies across the river. What could more clearly underline this transition than Mr. Krótki's terse observation that coups succeed in Khartoum but fail in Omdurman? Nevertheless, Omdurman is an important urban agglomeration (or, in another sense, a major element in what is increasingly called "Greater Khartoum"), and in terms of population it is by no means a dying city. Mr. Krótki's treatment, therefore, of a city that has been to some extent "passed by" but by no means "counted out" represents yet another important theme in our study of the urban phenomenon in the modern Near East. In many ways, Omdurman exemplifies the obverse of the mushroom city, and as such it is a vital piece in the total picture.

And the prize mushroom city of them all—whose fabulous rate of growth outstrips even the latter-day Phoenician genius of Beirut—is Kuwait, the city that oil built. During those brief years of its rise from minor oasis and port to modern capital of a small, underpopulated country suddenly offered the Midas-touch in the form of oil revenues, Kuwait was fortunate to have as its biographer, planner, goad, and gadfly an architect and urban-planner named Saba George Shiber. Mr. Shiber would obviously have been among those invited to participate in this volume, but unfortunately, he died in July 1968, at the age of 44, just when he was reaching the maturity of his intellectual and planning powers. With the permission of his family, we have selected extracts from several of his works (updating where appropriate) to compose the chapter on Kuwait appearing in this book. The resulting chapter, we believe, stands now as a tribute to the man and his work as well as to the city he loved and knew so intimately.

Mr. Shiber's description of the old city is almost lyrical. Clearly, his ideal of the new city involved an integration and adaptation of what was best from the old. He was also keenly aware of the need to work within a national developmental plan.

In a sense, Mr. Shiber also showed a touch of what might be called the Pygmalion syndrome. A dynamic man caught up in the challenge of a virtually new city abuilding, he was by no means a dispassionate technician. His writings reveal the intensity of his commitment. One can only marvel at his seemingly limitless reservoir of enthusiasm and ideas and his desire to get on with the job. Yet, he also reveals considerable impatience with, and perhaps a misunderstanding of, the political process in which urban planning is ineluctably encased. Mr. Shiber's *cri de coeur* may, therefore, also be read from another perspective that transcends urban planning in Kuwait: the harnessing of his kind of planning zeal to the existing political, social, and economic institutions and interests is, and will always be, a major concern in the most effective use of human resources and opportunities.

Cities, of course, do not exist in isolation. They are better conceived as the nerve centers of regions which, in turn, coalesce to form sovereign political units—or, in modern parlance, "nation-states." Part III, "Country Planning," is concerned with cities as part of this larger whole. M. Jean Dethier traces in considerable detail the changing pattern of national urban planning in Morocco from the time the French Protectorate was established in 1912 to the present. The author calls attention to the different styles and approaches of the successive chronological periods, differences both in inspiration and application. In M. Dethier's account, the reader can contrast the creative genius of a Marshal Lyautey with the different tendencies of lesser lights who followed in his wake. And, more pertinent to architects and urban planners, one can follow the unfolding of the modern Moroccan urban scene through the influence of major architectural figures linked at points in their career with Morocco, such as Henri Prost and Michel Ecochard. Yet, behind these fluctuations of policy and plans, one detects certain constants: (1) French Morocco as a settler colony marching to the urban needs and aspirations of the European settler class; (2) an approach to urban planning that has a static, urban bias and thereby attempts to ward off, block from view, or in other ways wish out of existence the problem of bidonvilles; (3) a resistance to over-all national planning; and (4) finally (and most ironically) an inability—even in times of genuine response to popular needs—to best utilize native skills and styles. M. Dethier's account is hard-hitting, but for all that not lacking in empathy and understanding. He keeps in balance both the necessity and the limitations of central planning. As he so persuasively demonstrates with this study of Morocco during 44 years of colonial rule and now almost a generation of independence, centralized professional competence must be wedded to the resources, aspirations, and life-style of those to be served.

Mr. Tekeli treats a longer chronological period and a radically different pattern of "decolonization" in his study of transition in spatial organization and urban planning from the Ottoman Empire to the Turkish Republic. In the process he demonstrates in terms of spatial organization and resource allocation both the extensiveness and the impressively rational system undergirding this vast empire that embraced Anatolia, the Balkans, the Fertile Crescent, and Northern Africa to the borders of Morocco. This is an interpretation readily to be accepted by the handful of Ottomanists and scholars of Near Eastern history, but it is worth emphasizing in a book of this kind. The layman is still all too likely to be mislead by hazy half-truths about the "sick man of Europe" or the "unspeakable Turk." Mr. Tekeli goes on to catalogue the disruptions wrought in Anatolia by the European hydra that sapped the strength of a declining empire from the late eighteenth century until the final Ottoman collapse following the First World War. This background makes understandable and meaningful the changes ushered in by Atatürk's Turkish Republic, symbolized by the move of the capital from Istanbul to Ankara. It was not just the recapturing of a people's destiny from the hectoring semi-control of outsiders, although this was clearly involved. It was also the formidable move from an extensive, multi-national empire to a cohesive nation-state.

Part IV deals with "The Cultural Heritage and Aesthetic Factors." These chapters are much more than a traditional obeisance to the fine arts, cloistered away from the hurly-burly of everyday urban life in museums and "national monuments." Except for the post-eighteenth-century prejudice against long titles, this section might more accurately be labelled: "The cultural heritage and aesthetic factors and their application in the orderly and practical planning of tomorrow's cities, with due consideration of how ignorance or misapplication of these same factors will cause unnecessary waste and discomfort."

Mr. Erder, in discussing the care of historical monuments and sites in Turkey, makes it clear that Ottoman rulers were generally inclined to preserve old edifices and impose few structural changes. Ironically, the present age of supposedly greater cosmopolitanism has brought with it the greatest threat to the cultural heritage preserved in stone, wood, and mortar. The economics of tourism catapults historical monuments and sites out of a phase of benign neglect to one of oppressive attention—often for the wrong reasons. The resulting misplaced motels and improper restorations can be not only aesthetically unattractive; they can, over time, radically depreciate a country's touristic appeal—which these days can be measured in hard cash. Here, then, is a pressing need for coordination of the many authorities involved—urban planners, administrators, tourist officials plus a small, but let us hope increasing, number of scholars in art and architectural history capable of appraising and reconstructing the past. Mr. Erder also emphasizes the need for a clearer notion of the historical monument—not a relic in the midst of modernity but a structure of contemporary validity, integrated artistically and functionally into its surrounding environment.

Mr. Ettinghausen begins his chapter by calling attention to the unfortunate and artificial disciplinary compartmentalization that hampers communication between art historians and contemporary architects and urban planners. He then goes on to show the continued validity, in both functional and aesthetic terms, of many of the more fundamental canons of "traditional" urban planning. His argument is in no way based on romantic nostalgia of things past nor contrived neo-traditionalism. Rather, he clearly sees that in architecture and urban planning as in any other creative enterprise (as literature, music, or for that matter, science and technology) what is to survive must be comprehensible, pleasing, and—that important, if much-abused word—authentic in its own cultural context.

Hassan Fathy is concerned with this same important theme. He expresses alarm that all too many architects working in the modern Arab city (for this is the focus of his own experience, but his comments apply with equal force in other parts of the Near East—and beyond!) have an imitative, distorted idea of modern architecture which amounts to a poor, hybridized borrowing from other cultures of elements poorly adapted to the Near East. He proceeds to document both the positive and negative aspects of his argument.

One can hardly more fittingly close this introduction than with the final sentence in Mr. Fathy's chapter: "When the full power of human imagination is backed by the weight of a living tradition, the resulting work of art is much greater than any that an artist can achieve when he has no tradition to work in or when he willfully abandons his tradition."

12. Ministry of Finance, Riyadh, Saudi Arabia. An attractive building, reasonably effective in screening sun and heat while emphasizing an extroverted, outward-looking mien; but there is little that is traditional Arab or Islamic in its style. (Photo: Aramco.)

Part I
THE TRADITIONAL
NEAR EASTERN CITY

1

Traditional Muslim Cities: Structure and Change
by Ira P. Lapidus

CITIES and civilizations—the words, the concepts, the experiences are implicit in each other. The study of traditional Muslim cities touches on all aspects of Islamic civilization, and to understand traditional Muslim cities we must appraise the historical context in which they have developed, the nature of the society they embodied, and their cultural significance. At the same time, we will see how historical and social experiences and religious and aesthetic ideals influenced their physical and architectural form.

The world of Islam, of course, is not one world but many, and each harbors its own type of traditional city. Each city has unique qualities and its own *gestalt*. However, few Muslim cities of the period before the eighteenth century are well known to us. Only Fez, Cairo, Damascus, Aleppo, Baghdad, Samarra, and Nishapur and a few smaller places have been the subject of detailed studies. Still, to speak of traditional Muslim cities as a type and to analyze the essential qualities of such cities may be justified because the scholar who engages himself in history seeks to understand the "facts" in hand as an introduction to a larger world of meanings. Any worthy enterprise of the mind extrapolates, searching forward with the light of ideas for new areas of understanding, all the while referring each new hypothesis or intuition back to what is known. In this sense history, though essentially an intellectual craft, has something in common with the work of planners and officials. Both move from an ever insufficient supply of information toward the larger whole, which must be understood if the true significance of the facts can be comprehended or a practical work be accomplished.

In this spirit I offer an overall view of traditional Muslim cities. I shall not describe any one city, but I shall focus on aspects of city life which seem essential in the Muslim experience. Though I do not describe any single city in its unique quality, and leave aside the special features which make cities beloved to the people who are born and who live in them, I try to point out those elements of political, social, economic, and geographical organization which,

51

abstracted from the particular circumstances, enable us to comprehend features which are essential to all Muslim cities. Though my thoughts are based upon a knowledge of Muslim cities in the region from the Nile to the Jaxartes, excluding such important Islamic lands as North Africa and Indonesia, from the seventh to the sixteenth centuries, the experiences of this region and period seem to me an enduring legacy for our own times. But the reader rather than the author may best judge the meaning of the past for the present.

The pre-Islamic past was the foundation of Muslim city experience. Millenia-old experiences in the organization of urban societies and the cultural and religious appreciation of cities underlay the Muslim experience. From the past came a highly differentiated society, stratified by classes, divided into subcommunities, and dominated by a hierarchical form of social organization with developed imperial governments at the apex. From the past came also the complex techniques of industries and crafts, norms for commerce, and market institutions. Cultural traditions assigned a great importance to religion in the organization of urban society, and valued city living as an essential element in a fully developed human life. This tradition was, of course, a living tradition in the thousands of cities, towns, and villages founded in ancient times but continuing into the Islamic era.

The Arab conquests did not introduce urbanity, but for quite specific reasons they lent a special impetus to the construction and expansion of cities and towns. Cities had to be built to canton bedouin peoples migrating from Arabia in order to prevent them from dispersing, seizing, and dividing the conquered lands into individual or tribal properties; and to segregate them from the conquered peoples so that they could be organized into armies for future campaigns and could be tutored in Islam. Basra, Kufa, Fustat, and Kairouan were among the bedouin camp cities created by the Arabs.

The Arab conquests also entailed the formation of new empires which had their own reasons for city, suburb, and fortress construction. The Umayyad and Abbasid caliphs and governors, as rulers before and since, built new capitals to segregate loyal forces from other elements of the populations, to provide secure headquarters, and to symbolize the dominance of a particular regime or ruler and his capacity to bring order and civilization to his domains. Such new capitals varied in importance from Baghdad, the administrative center which evolved into a world city, to small suburbs and fortresses built throughout the Arab empires.

The overall effect of city, suburb, and fortress construction was to stimulate urbanization and economic prosperity, notably in Iran and Iraq. However, the dedication of the Arabs and their rulers to city building had limits. Early efforts at city building were restricted to settling migrants and garrisons and assuring the power of rulers and governors, but nowhere, to my knowledge, did these endeavors entail a general regional urbanization. In fact, newly-founded Arab cities or other favored settlements often drained previously established towns of their livelihood and population. In some provinces, as in Mesopotamia, the net effect of the conquests was a regression of urban life. Thus for both settlement and administrative and political reasons the Arabs, as other conquerors before and since, generated a wave of city building notable in intensity but too limited in scale to be equated with Muslim-era Near Eastern urbanization.

Arab town building, then, must be seen in the context of pre-Arab urbanization. But what was its significance for Islam? Students of Islam sometimes suppose that in this early period, and indeed ever since, it was essential to live in a city to be a Muslim. Indeed, Arab-founded cities were the main centers of Islam, and the migration of pagan Arabs to the newly-founded cities entailed a hijra—movement from a bedouin or village life to city life and a transition from pagan to Muslim beliefs. Still, to equate cities and Islam in any exclusive way is misleading. Many Arab-Muslim migrants, especially in Iran, settled in villages, and many, as in Mesopotamia, continued to live as bedouins. In addition, as time passed, many Arab-Muslim city dwellers seeped away from the caliphal-dominated cantonments to take up civilian pursuits in villages surrounding the garrison towns. Moreover, Islam made converts in towns and villages outside of the original Arab settlements. Thus, Islam was not entirely identified with city dwellings as such or with dwelling in particular cities. Cities had a notable but not an all-absorbing importance for early Islam.

In the main, what the Arab conquests meant for the Near Eastern urban situation was the emergence of a double city tradition. The towns and cities established in ancient times, harboring the bulk of the Near Eastern population, confronted Arab-founded or Arab-settled places. From the first, however, each type of city influenced the development of the other. Populations mixed. Islam became the religion and Arabic the language and literature of formerly non-Arab, non-Muslim towns, while the pre-Islamic kind of urban society, economy, and culture were transmitted to the Arab places. We may infer that this merging of cities and their traditions went on for many centuries, though in differing ways and in different degrees in different places. We know too little about these processes to trace the historical development of cities in general, but a few aspects of early Muslim city evolution may be mentioned. To simplify our presentation, let us assume the persistent presence of pre-Islamic urban society and trace the evolution within Arab- or imperial-founded and settled cities and towns.

In the early Arab cities, the clan or tribal elements of organization were characteristic. Early Arab society was devoted to war and relatively little differentiated by occupation or stratified by class; nor was there a sharp distinction between tribal, religious, and political elites. Governors and generals, often selected from the Quraysh or other elite clans, were the caliph's delegates for both administration and prayer, just as the caliph himself embodied the primal institutional unity of Islam.

The early Arab cities did not long retain their primitive form. Broadly speaking, though the process is still obscure because we cannot separate the internal evolution of the Arab towns from the influences of pre-Islamic towns and peoples, a more diversified community came into being. At Basra, for example, Arab-Muslims attracted a large non-Arab population and themselves became involved in the great variety of occupations characteristic of urban places. Class distinctions became more pronounced as opportunities in commerce, land speculation, trade, government, and religious teaching led individuals and families into new lives. The clan remained the crucial unit of society, although in many spheres of life it became less important as new distinctions of class, status, and power and new commercial, political, and religious ties between the residents of the town came into being.

Another of the early cities, Baghdad, is known to us in some detail. The capital of the Abbasid Empire, Baghdad was the largest city in the Near East, one of the largest cities in the world, and a city with a heterogeneous and cosmopolitan population. The people of Baghdad included Arab and non-Arab migrants from Basra and other Iraqi towns, a local Nestorian community, merchants from all over Iran, administrators from eastern Iran, Khurasanian-Arab, Central Asian, and Turkish soldiers, workers from Syria and Egypt, and others. Baghdad was a microcosm of Near Eastern peoples. In this metropolis of the early Islamic world parochial affiliations competed with cosmopolitan identifications. On the one hand, peoples with the same religious, ethnic, or clan background resided together. Arab clans, migrants from the same village or town, merchants from the same region, and regiments of soldiers from different localities inhabited their own part of the city. Christians, Jews, and, among the Muslims, groups of Sunnis and Shiites lived in their own quarters. This is not to say that all of Baghdad's populace was organized into tight parochial communities but that such groups were an important component in the organization of the population.

On the other hand, Baghdad was a city of peoples with universal identifications. Merchants who traded with their home cities or other far off places, administrators and soldiers with imperial careers, and itinerant scholars made Baghdad a city of cosmopolitans. Diverse peoples learned to speak Arabic as a common tongue and were joined together as converts to Islam. Baghdad was the capital of the Islamic Empire, the chief center of Islamic religious learning, and an important place for conversion and absorption within the Islamic community. Divided and parochial, Baghdad's peoples were, however, united on the basis of Islam and empire.

As the capital of the Islamic world, Baghdad was also a foyer for the development of specifically Muslim communal institutions. In the early centuries of Islam, Muslims had no church, in the sense of an organized hierarchy, to maintain doctrines and worship and to provide believers with a congregational or parish life. Though Muslims worshipped in mosques, they were not organized into congregations, nor were they directed by an authoritative religious hierarchy. In the first few centuries of Islam, the caliph and the caliph alone represented the community of Muslims. Prayer leaders, *qadis,* and governors were simply his understudies. In principle, Muslims were individual believers grouped in a worldwide brotherhood whose unity as a people and whose destiny to rule was symbolized by the caliph.

In fact, there were many intermediate communities. Informal groups of scholars who studied the Quran, *hadith*, law or theology, ascetics or mystics and their faithful devotees, preachers and their loyal audiences, Shiite *Imams* and their clienteles were of great importance in the daily life of Muslims, but they had no official status. Nonetheless, in time, some of these informal groups, such as the schools of lawyers, became the cadres for an organized Muslim social life. Groups of scholars who gathered to discuss religion and law came to take a part in the administration of legal affairs and provided the personnel for an emerging Islamic legal system. The schools provided judges and court officials, notaries, administrators for community trusts and properties, and advisers to the caliphs and the government administration. In addition, in ninth-century Baghdad, the Hanbali law school also amassed a popular following, faithful to the teachings of the school, loyal to their religious chiefs, even opposed to the caliphs for having corrupted the succession to the prophet for political ends, and eager to impose their special views on the Muslim community as a whole. By the late ninth century, in Baghdad, Hanbali Muslims, loyal to particular teachings and to the scholars and preachers who upheld these teachings, had banded together to administer communal affairs, to live their religious and social lives in common, and to press their views in opposition to other versions of Islam. Only further research can say whether this "sectarian" development was unique to the Hanbalis, but in any case, we see the Hanbali movement as an early experiment for organizing Muslims into communities and for resolving the tension between parochial subcommunities and the sense of universal Muslim brotherhood.

Baghdad, to my knowledge, was the first Arab-Islamic city to present the formal aspects—diverse and differentiated populations, parochial communities, organized Muslim religious bodies, and a strong state apparatus—of later Muslim urban communities. But what relationship there was between Baghdad in the late ninth century and later Muslim cities we do not know. We know only that in the tenth and eleventh centuries the Near East went through a revolutionary upheaval. The Abbasid Empire disintegrated. New regimes independent of the Caliphate came to power in various parts of the old empire. Turkish nomads invaded the eastern and European Christians the western regions. In these upheavals, the old official, landowning, and merchant elites in many provinces were swept away. The conversion of Near Eastern peoples to Islam was substantially completed. Islamic culture diffused throughout the region, and Islam at last became the predominant religion of the masses as well as the religion of the governing elites. Muslim preachers and religious leaders emerged, bolstered by control of public offices and by connections with landowning, commercial, and official interests, as a new urban notability. We know little about the phases of this evolution. At best we have a scanty knowledge of the places involved, and we face difficult methodological problems in exploring this subject. But setting the difficulties aside, we may draw the conclusion that by the middle of the eleventh century one concomitant of these immense changes was the merger of the two streams of urban traditions. Four centuries after the Arab conquests, we finally enter fully into the Muslim era of Near Eastern urban development. From the eleventh down to the fifteenth century, to the rise of the Ottoman and Safavid empires, Arab cities and cities with pre-Islamic origins need no longer be distinguished. The cities best known to us—Nishapur, Bukhara, Baghdad, Damascus, Aleppo, and Cairo—now show formal similarities in social organization derived both from the Muslim and the pre-Islamic past. These common features are aspects of social organization which seem to be found in all Muslim cities, though these similar qualities do not exhaust the character of individual places.

The parochial element in Muslim cities remained pronounced. Almost any town or city would be composed of some grouping of families, neighborhood quarters, Muslim sects or fraternities, Christian or Jewish minorities, ethnic strangers, settlers from other villages or towns, manufacturing or trading groups, or a combination of the foregoing parochial bodies. Medieval Muslim cities echoed both the Arab clan heritage of small, tightly-knit communities and the ancient Near Eastern tradition of incorporating diverse peoples into town populations. Indeed, this diversity was the very essence of urbanity.

Equally prominent in this period were organized Muslim religious communities. Though less intimate, less binding, and more diffuse, schools of law had an important role to play in the organization of urban community life.

The schools were groups of scholars devoted to the study of the Shari'a—Islamic law. In the early centuries of Islam various groups sponsored several versions of the Shari'a which differed in matters of detail and to some degree in the jurisprudential principles upon which they were based. Nonetheless, the different school versions were essentially similar. By the eleventh century, only four of the early schools had effectively survived—the Hanafi, Maliki, Shafi'i, and Hanbali—each recognizing the others as equally orthodox. The four schools persist to the present day, representing four definitive versions of the Islamic holy law. By the eleventh century, the Shafi'i, Hanafi, and Maliki schools, as well as the Hanbali school, had also developed into administrative and community bodies. By this period, most townspeople seem to have been affiliated with one or another of the schools. In the most common cases town populations were affiliated with one or two of the schools, perhaps with minority membership in a third or even a fourth.

The schools performed many functions for their members. They formed study groups of scholars, teachers, students, and interested laymen who kept alive the school traditions in the study of the Quran, hadith, law, and theology. The schools maintained formal institutions of learning, madrasas, which were endowed to pay salaries to the teachers and stipends to the students. The madrasas also functioned as mosques and meeting houses for the schools and their followers.

From the law schools came the notaries, *muftis,* and judges who witnessed contracts, gave legal advice, and adjudicated disputes. The schools applied their teachings to maintain the religious norms for family and commercial life. Leading members of the schools were also consulted by their lay followers on many other social and communal matters, and the *ulama,* or school scholars, represented their constituencies to the political authorities and dealt with the state on their behalf in matters of public order and security, taxation, and the maintenance of streets, roads, and other public facilities. Thus, in each town the several law schools formed the cadre of everyday community life. The schools represented the values and norms of the community and preserved the religious and scholarly traditions through which these ideals were kept alive. They provided for education and especially higher education, legal and commercial administration, political representation, and general counsel to the populace.

The law schools also mediated between their members and other town communities. Within a given town, the schools were generally, but not necessarily, more encompassing bodies than neighborhood quarters or other parochial communities. To a degree they served to integrate various town populations, but they did not form local governments. No single school normally embraced the whole of a town population; no school had jurisdiction over territory or a military or administrative bureaucracy. Only in times of great emergency might the leaders of the schools come together to represent the whole of the populations of their towns.

Furthermore, the law schools mediated between town populations and the outside world. Town-centered schools often had adherents in villages surrounding the towns. Villagers who normally marketed in the central town of their district, or came for holidays, Friday prayer, loans, protection, or whatever, were often affiliated with the schools. The schools reached from town into hinterlands, forming communities of the people living in a given region. However, just as the presence of several schools was a divisive element in town populations, the rural adherents of different schools might also be hostile to each other. Muslim community affiliations were governed by personal and communal loyalties rather than by loyalties determined by proximity in space.

At another level, the law schools bound townsmen to the worldwide community of Muslims. The scholars of a school in any given locality were but a cell in a vast network of affiliations which often spread across the Islamic world. Loyalty to a common literary tradition, the movement of students to favored centers of learning, and the migration of scholars knit the individual law school cells on a world basis. Through the schools, local loyalties were translated into cosmopolitan religious identities. The law schools, as organized local communities, were intermediaries bridging the gap between extremely parochial loyalties and the sentiment of universal Muslim brotherhood.

This kind of religious community was of central importance in the post-Abbasid Near Eastern town. Clearly it derived from the early informal organization of Muslim scholars, amplified in Baghdad, and matured over centuries. Devoted to an Islamic life, the law schools made medieval Near Eastern urban communities "Muslim" communities. Yet from another point of view, this "Muslim" city organization may also be regarded as deriving from an older and pre-Islamic Near Eastern urban tradition. In ancient times, city temples played a crucial role in the organization of a coherent urban community. In Christian times the church was decisive in local society. In each epoch, the prevailing religions represented a different set of values and understandings, a different type of organization, and a different form of society; but in all ages, ancient, Christian, and Muslim, community life seems to have been inextricably bound up with religion. From religious teachings come the ideals and the norms of social action; from religious organizations, the structuring of social life.

Though the precise historical relationships have yet to be explored, the cities of the Muslim era belong at once to an Arab-Islamic and an ancient Near Eastern tradition.

In these divided Near Eastern cities of the eleventh to the fifteenth centuries, with their parochial communities and sectarian religious associations, the large states and empires which dominated the Near East were another important organizing force. Various Seljuq, Seljuqid, and Mamluk regimes, based on slave-military elites and quasi-bureaucratic administrative machines, provided the physical protection, albeit a poor one, against invasion from without and civil war from within. The regimes controlled the bulk of the resources generated by the urban economy by heavily taxing the populations, but at the same time they helped maintain local economies, kept open the flow of goods between cities and between towns and their rural hinterlands, and invested in religious and communal institutions and in general urban maintenance. We may well question whether the services were worth the price, but the Muslim residents of Near Eastern cities, too divided within to govern themselves, had little choice. Military regimes dominated the towns, both as patrons and as exploiters.

The central importance of the state in urban affairs was also a legacy of the Islamic Empire and an echo of ancient patterns. The slave military regimes of the post-empire period had their origins in the Abbasid effort to maximize the military force of the state and to centralize administration to the highest possible degree. But behind the Abbasid experiences lay a tradition of powerful empires dominating society, and an ethos glorifying the state and the ruler, indeed elevating the ruler to a quasi-divine status. The Islamic political order had unique qualities, but qualities which appeared as an extension of older traditions.

The three types of urban bodies—parochial groups, religious schools, and state military regimes—were the decisive actors in the Muslim towns. In different places the character of each type, or its relative importance, no doubt varied; in different places different relationships were established between the elements. However, there are two advantages to stressing the common structural components rather than the individuality of each city. The structural approach helps to compare specific situations and to keep in view the fact that the social organization of Near Eastern cities had common features as the result of a long historical process. Through the formation of a Muslim urban subculture in the wake of the Arab conquests and the eventual merger of ancient and Arab-Muslim traditions, a Near Eastern city type, bearing the imprint of Islamic culture while descending from the ancient pre-Islamic Near Eastern world, had come into being.

In the context of this analysis, Muslim cities may be understood from several points of view. From one point of view, we see an organization which, abstractly considered, could belong to cities in any region or culture. The analysis by states, intermediate communities, and parochial bodies may be applied virtually without cultural connotations. We can describe urban organization in purely structural terms without reference to specific cultural qualities.

From another point of view, the organizational features of Muslim Near Eastern cities can be seen in the context of pre-Islamic and ancient Near Eastern traditions. The types of communities one finds in the Islamic period are echoes of past forms of organization. The relative strength of empire and the local importance of religious bodies, for example, reflect a more ancient pattern of social organization.

Yet at the same time these cities were not just Near Eastern, but they were clearly Muslim in quality. The family one found in these cities was molded by the teachings and laws of Islam as well as by the Arabian heritage. The schools of law preserved Muslim scriptures and applied them in social life. They represented a variant form of religious organization different from the temple communities or churches of the past, different precisely because of the Islamic teaching and the Islamic historical heritage they embodied.

These cities may also be uniquely Muslim in the sense that cities have a distinctive importance in Islamic culture. European students of Islam have pointed out that Muslim authors emphasize the sacred character of some cities. Mecca, Medina, and Jerusalem were particularly sacred. Other cities were holy by virtue of biblical events, by virtue of the presence of shrines and graves of scholars and saints, and by the presence of religious schools and mosques. Indeed, mosques made the city a city for they were the characteristic symbol of the presence of a Muslim community. Furthermore, it is said that in Islam collective worship, serious religious learning, and the sophisticated fulfillment of daily religious obligations all require an urban environment. Ever since the conquest it has been a part of Islamic lore to consider migration to the cities from the desert or from villages a hijra—an entry into Islam. The religious virtuosity and virtue of the city dweller as opposed to the countryman or bedouin is commonly emphasized. Cities, then, seem to have a sacred importance, a practical religious significance, and an emotional value to urban Muslims far in excess of what our analysis of the history and social organization of classical and medieval cities would suggest. How are we to reconcile these cultural appreciations with the actualities of organization?

First, we may say that the discrepancy is more apparent than real. The traditional Muslim view was more subtle than we have sometimes allowed. In the Muslim view, a city was a superior place for religious life but not an exclusive center for the living of a Muslim life. We have already spoken about the early conquests and the attachment of the Arab-Muslim migrants to cities. In the early centuries, Islam was closely associated with cities for the very good reason that Arab-Muslims had, by and large, settled in a few cities, and these were, until the eventual conversion of Near Eastern peoples, the most important places for Islam. Towns with large Muslim populations had Friday mosques which were supervised by the caliph, as the head of the community. As conversions occurred and Islam spread, the relatively few cities and mosques which had constituted the early establishment of Islam were joined by numerous towns and villages. Mosques came to be located in many new cities and in villages as well. Islam seems to be associated with cities because of historical circumstance rather than religious principles.

Similarly, one must be cautious in attributing the sacred quality of shrines and mosques to the cities themselves. Only Mecca, Medina, and Jerusalem were sacred in their entirety. In other places, the shrine was sacred, the city blessed to have it. Also, shrines were not confined to cities: they were found in villages and even on the open road.

One index of the traditional Islamic understanding of cities is the legal theory of worship and especially of congregational worship. Some law schools required forty persons to be present for a valid Friday worship at which the *khutba* was pronounced. Other schools relaxed this requirement, some acknowledging that two persons make a sufficient community for a Friday mosque. In any case, neither forty persons nor two make a place a city as opposed to a village or other settlement. In fact, the legal requirements for worship stress persons rather than locality as essential to Islam. For an Islamic community one does not need a city but a small number of Muslims. The community of Muslims, as we have seen, was composed of persons who adhered to the faith or to particular schools and not of persons who belonged to any particular territory or space.

Still, there was a strong Near Eastern feeling for the superior virtue of townsmen and town living as opposed to peasants and rural living. In part, this was compounded of prejudices natural to townsmen and of the undoubted cultural superiority of towns. Variations in the cultural or religious quality of places is only natural. Whether there is anything specifically Islamic about this or whether an Islamic religious principle is involved may be doubted until more evidence can be presented.

In Islam, we may conclude, it is not cities or physical settlements which are essential but rather communities of persons. A Muslim community may be a bedouin group, a village, a sect, law school, or Sufi brotherhood. Such communities must have a physical setting, but they do not have to embrace all persons living within a town (or other settlement), and they may include persons living outside of a town. In the Muslim world cities were manifestly the crucial centers of worship, learning, and administration, as cities everywhere are the important centers of culture and government. Cities were always the center of a richer and more ample Muslim life, but this is not to say that they had some intrinsic virtue for Islam. Islam seems no more or less a civilization of cities than any other civilization.

Thus far we have considered some historical, social, and cultural aspects of traditional Muslim cities. Before concluding, let us broach one last question and ask how historical circumstances, social organization, and cultural preferences have influenced the physical and aesthetic qualities of Muslim cities. This will be an important theme in other contributions to this volume, and since it is more adequately treated in the context of contemporary investigation, I shall make only a few remarks about the medieval past.

Scholars have devised various approaches to the description of the physical characteristics of traditional Near Eastern cities. Some focus upon the patterns of streets and houses, stressing the apparent shapelessness of the city interior, the preference for narrow lanes and cul-de-sacs as opposed to traffic arteries, the lack of public spaces, and so on. Others see in this apparent jumble a quite definite interior form. The relationships between markets, mosques, schools, and

Examples of narrow streets in residential areas of traditional cities, emphasizing a concern for privacy and security. 13. Arched alley between houses in Rabat. (Photo: Wim Swaan.)

14. A narrow street in Algiers, early twentieth century, showing cantilevered upper stories. (Photo: Library of Congress.)

15. A Tunis Street. Note in both foreground and background how streets lead through houses (the houses are primary, streets secondary), enhancing the cloistered intimacy of the street. (Photo: William Dix, Jr.)

16. A narrow side street with old houses and enclosure walls in Birgi (Izmir District), Turkey. (Photo: Middle East Technical University.)

other public facilities, the placement of quarters, and the location of trades all show a precise pattern. The Near Eastern city may look formless, it is argued, but in fact it has a quite definite and logically patterned organization. Other students of city form have concentrated on the great monuments and the history of artistic and architectural styles.

One suggestion which I make toward understanding the physical form of traditional cities involves the relationships between social organization and spatial patterns. Many cities can be divided between the parts which were suqs (markets) and *haras* (residential quarters). This is not to say that no one resided in the markets or that no marketing was carried out in the quarters. Rather, some districts were primarily residential and others primarily commercial and the center of public life. In the residential quarters, the preserve of women, children, and families, the emphasis on privacy and security was most pronounced. Here were the gates which could be locked at night, the cul-de-sacs which opened into a house or compound of houses, the high, windowless, blank walls, a complete lack of public spaces, and so on. Here suspicion attached most keenly to strangers.

Pls. 13-16
(61-62)
Pl. 7 (33)
Pl. 59 (169)

In the market areas of the city, not only commercial, but religious and political life were concentrated. The suqs had shops, workrooms, storerooms, and also mosques, and madrasas or higher schools. From within or near the markets, the qadis, the notaries, and the *muhtasibs,* as well as other public officials operated, and in some cities the main markets were adjacent to the citadel or fortress of the town. The markets presented the same jumbled appearance as the residential quarters, but here the apparent jumble had a different logic. In the markets, shops and mosques and schools and offices were mixed together because of the undifferentiated life style of Muslim townsmen. Prayer, learning, and public consultations and adjudication were not highly specialized activities segregated in special centers. They were part of the everyday life of the working population and bourgeoisie. The scholar who worked part time as a merchant or craftsman wanted to be near his teacher. The artisan who prayed regularly had his mosque at hand. The merchant who served as a notary found the qadi or the muhtasib in the immediate vicinity. Thus the physical facilities were juxtaposed to permit easy movement from one to another. Mixing integrated the town. In the obvious economic sense, the markets also brought together the residents of the town and of the surrounding countrysides. In a social sense, the suqs also permitted the integration of the various levels—commercial, religious, and political—of urban activity. The mixing of facilities in the suqs signified the fluid bringing together of the various elements of urban society.

Pls. 17-21
(64-67)

Muslim towns had internal divisions, but they were themselves parts of larger entities. Many towns were parts of double or composite bodies—bodies formed by adjacent communities grown together, or a core unit and its surrounding suburbs and villages. Suburbs and villages whose inhabitants shared in the daily life of particular towns radiated for miles around and might even be ringed by outer walls to protect them as well as the dense core of the township from attack. Thus, Muslim towns appeared not only as densely settled places divided

17. Mid-nineteenth-century lithograph of the Coppersmith's Bazaar in Cairo. Note how the shops are clustered right up to the walls of the mosque (far left). The open loggias above other shops in the center background housed Quranic schools. In all, a typical bazaar mixture of "shops and mosques and schools and offices." (Source: David Roberts.)

18. Another Roberts lithograph—the silk merchants' bazaar of the "el Ghooreeyeh" of Cairo—illustrates a similar combination. (Source: David Roberts.)

19. Marrakech, Morocco. Moroccan countryman leading his donkey through the straw bazaar of Marrakech. (Photo: Pan American World Airways.)

20. Tunis, Tunisia. The perfumers' suq: the blank wall on the left is part of the Zitouna Mosque. The perfumers have only to step across the narrow street for prayers. Around the corner is the bookdealers' suq, customarily located close to the principal mosque. (Photo: Lewis Ware.)

21. Kabul, Afghanistan. Country people shopping in the city bazaar. (Photo: William Trousdale.)

into residential and commercial districts, but as complex settlements made up of a number of towns, suburbs, and villages, interrelated by social and commercial contacts and sometimes united by the construction of encompassing walls. Just as the schools of law reached into the countryside outside of town cores proper and just as political administration reached from the fortress to the town and the surrounding districts, physical organization may be understood in terms of relationships between towns and countrysides rather than in terms of the isolation of the town from surrounding settlements. In various ways the physical structure reflected both the parochial and the integrating aspects of Muslim urban society.

This brief introduction to some of the historical, social, religious, and physical aspects of traditional Muslim cities brings to the fore the problem of the relationship between Muslim and Near Eastern civilization. In many respects Muslim cities were created by larger historical developments—migrations of peoples, the formation and collapse of empires, the diffusion of political and religious institutions, economic growth and regression, and the transmission of religious values and aesthetic preferences—which transcended any individual city experience and gave form to cityscape, city society, and city culture. Muslim cities, then, were the product of Islamic civilization, a microcosm of the whole, a reflection of the larger forces by which the history of Islam has been made. On the other hand, cities generated the forces which made for civilization. Political institutions, religious values, and forms of social organization were the creation of city peoples. The relationships between Muslim cities and Muslim history and civilization were dialectical. The unique properties of each city played against the participation of each city in a common Near Eastern Muslim civilization. Historically, we cannot understand any city in isolation from the experience of the region as a whole. Socially, we cannot see its institutions apart from the Muslim world formation of social organizations. Culturally, the religious values of Islam were universal ideals embodied in particular places. Physically, cities interacted with the surrounding environment in ways which merged the city into a larger complex of settlements. In this chapter I have tried to introduce the aspects of traditional Muslim cities held in common as part of a more encompassing historical, social, and cultural experience. By yet another dialectic, the dialectic of discussion, other contributions will balance this emphasis by focusing on the unique condition of particular cities.

BIBLIOGRAPHY

Various theories about the nature of Muslim cities are set forth in R. Brunschvig, "Urbanisme médiéval et droit Musulman," *Revue des Études Islamiques* (1947), pp. 127-55; G. E. von Grunebaum, "The Sacred Character of Islamic Cities," *Mélanges Taha Husain* (Cairo, 1962), pp. 25-37 and "The Structure of the Muslim Town," *Islam: Essays on the Nature and Growth of a Cultural Tradition*, 2nd ed. (London, 1961), pp. 141-58; G. Marçais, "Considerations sur les villes Musulmanes et notamment sur le rôle du Mohtasib," *La Ville* 6 (Brussels: Société Jean Bodin, 1955): 248-62; and "La conception des villes dans l'Islam," *Revue d'Alger*, no. 2 (1956), pp. 517-33; W. Marçais, "L'Islamisme et la vie urbaine," *Comptes Rendus, Académie des Inscriptions et Belles Lettres* (1928), pp. 86-100; E. Pauty, "Villes spontanées et villes créées en Islam," *Annales de l'Institut d'Études Orientales*, no. 9 (1951), pp. 52-75; Xavier de Planhol, *Le Monde*

Islamique (Paris, 1957); I. M Lapidus, "Muslim Cities and Islamic Societies," in *Middle Eastern Cities*, ed. Lapidus (Berkeley, 1969), pp. 47-79. These essays seek to define the "essential" characteristics of Muslim city organization.

More empirically oriented studies of various cities include studies of Aleppo and Damascus by J. Sauvaget, *Alep* (Paris, 1941) and "Esquisses d'une histoire de la ville de Damas," *Révue des Études Islamiques*, no. 8 (1934), pp. 421-80; C. Cahen, *Mouvements Populaires et Autonomisme Urbain* (Leiden, 1959); I. M. Lapidus, *Muslim Cities in the Later Middle Ages* (Cambridge, 1967). Classical Baghdad has been studied by G. Le Strange, *Baghdad during the Abbasid Caliphate* (Oxford, 1924); G. Salmon, *L'Introduction topographique à l'histoire de Baghdad* (Paris, 1904); M. Streck, *Die alte Landschaft Babylonien nach den arabischen Geographen* (Leiden, 1900); J. Lassner, *The Topography of Baghdad in the Middle Ages* (Detroit, 1970). For Samarra, see E. Herzfeld, *Geschichte der Stadt Samarra* (Hamburg, 1938). For Cairo, see M. Clerget, *Le Caire*, 2 vols. (Paris, 1934) and E. W. Lane, *Modern Egyptians* (London, 1908). For Nishapur, see C. E. Bosworth, *The Ghaznavids* (Edinburgh, 1963) and R. Bulliet, *Nishapur*, Ph.D. dissertation; Harvard University, 1968. Important studies of Fez have been made by R. Le Tourneau, *Fès avant le protectorat* (Casablanca, 1949) and *Fez in the Age of the Marinids* (Norman, Oklahoma, 1961). For Istanbul, see R. Mantran, *Istanbul dans la seconde moitié du XVIIe siècle* (Paris, 1962). Some recent collective works include A. Hourani and S. M. Stern, *The Islamic City* (Oxford, 1970); I. M. Lapidus, *Middle Eastern Cities* (Berkeley, 1969). See also J. and D. Sourdel, *La Civilisation de l'Islam classique* (Paris, 1968), pp. 397-466 and E. Reitemeyer, *Die Stadtgründungen der Araber im Islam* (Munich, 1912).

For general works on ancient cities see R. M. Adams, *The Evolution of Urban Society* (Chicago, 1968) and *Land Behind Baghdad* (Chicago, 1966); A. H. M. Jones, *The Greek City from Alexander to Justinian* (Oxford, 1940); N. V. Pigulevskaya, *Les villes de l'État Iranien* (Paris, 1963).

For theoretical or comparative approaches to the study of medieval cities see G. Sjoberg, *The Preindustrial City* (Glencoe, Illinois, 1960); L. Mumford, *The City in History* (New York, 1961); Max Weber, *The City* (Glencoe, Illinois, 1958).

22. Alexandria, Egypt. Urban rooftop view of the city, *ca.* 1800. (From: *Description de l'Egypte.*)

Different types of "public space" in the traditional city.

23. The covered clothing suq in Tunis, near the heart of the old madina. It is heavily trafficked but peaceful. (Photo: Lewis Ware.)

24. A traditional "industrial" sector. This is the street of the dyers in Marrakech, Morocco. (Photo: Abbott L. Moffatt.)

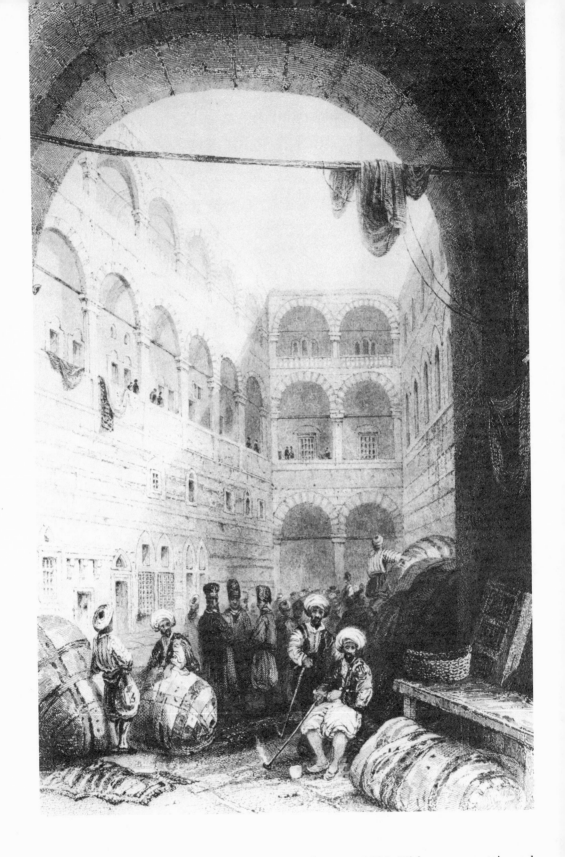

25. An important caravanserai in Istanbul, Turkey, *ca.* 1830. With rooms upstairs and storage below, the caravanserai served as a combined hotel and warehouse. (From: J. Pardoe, *The Beauties of the Bosphorous.*)

2

The Traditional City of Herat, Afghanistan
by Paul English

THE conceptual frameworks and techniques of urban geographers and planners have been designed to cope with the complexities and conditions current in modern Western industrial cities. Cross-cultural comparisons of urban conditions have been few, but this circumstance will undoubtedly change as urbanists expand their horizons and even their theories to encompass urban forms and processes in the Old World. As this occurs, the literature and thought devoted to the preindustrial city and the Muslim town by men like Sjoberg, Von Grunebaum, and others will be of importance.

In his book, *The Preindustrial City: Past and Present,* Gideon Sjoberg proposed the notion that all cities prior to the rise of the scientific and industrial revolutions shared important "structural characteristics" and demonstrated a startling degree of communality despite their distinctive cultural content and style.[1] Sjoberg attempted to establish that urban nuclei in the civilized societies of the Orient, the Islamic East, medieval Europe, Africa, and America were similarly structured whatever their cultural context and that they differed from modern industrial centers in form, function, and spirit. Briefly stated, the "preindustrial city" was small (rarely containing populations of more than 100,000) and political or cultural rather than commercial in orientation. These cities functioned primarily as seats of the dominant ideology and culture of the region, and a few were bases for trade or manufacturing. Central space, therefore, was allotted to governmental and religious institutions, though overall there was a minimum of specialization in land use, and sites frequently served multiple purposes. Social patterning in the preindustrial city stressed the positive value of central location, presumably because of relative safety and ease of communication. Wealthy and powerful people lived near the center; those segregated on account of religion, race, occupation, or poverty lived on the

---

[1] Gideon Sjoberg, *The Preindustrial City: Past and Present* (Glencoe, Ill.: Free Press, 1960); idem, "Cities in Developing and in Industrial Societies: A Cross-Cultural Analysis," in *The Study of Urbanization,* ed. Philip M. Hauser and Leo F. Schnore (New York: John Wiley, 1965), pp. 213-263.

urban fringe. Within this concentric pattern of residential desirability, certain sections of the city were set aside as quarters for religious minorities, kinship communities, or even occupational groups. Status was attained at birth and social mobility was weak. Society was divided into a wealthy literate elite, a mass of commoners, and small outcaste groups. The elite usually controlled the political and religious institutions of the city. By and large, economic activity was poorly developed, and the key unit was the community-bound guild.

At a more specific level of generalization, Von Grunebaum and others have proposed a model of Muslim cities based on a comparison of the spatial organization and institutional structure of Muslim towns with cities of the Greco-Roman or modern industrial worlds.[2] For the Muslim town the key definitions were the centrality of the mosque, the formlessness of the quarters, the concentration of crafts in the bazaar, the lack of civic self-expression, ethnic division of labor, and segregation by race, religion, and occupation. In both of these models, differences between traditional and modern cities rather than shared similarities form the thrust of the argument. In each case, a single key explanatory variable (for Sjoberg, technology; for Von Grunebaum, cultural tradition) is used to explain the complex of forces of urban life in traditional societies and to illuminate a distinctive urban experience.

Yet, it is clear that in all cities the urban system has been determined by the needs, capabilities, and ethos of its society. The allocation of central space to certain institutions, the positioning of shops, the selection of household location, and the criteria for status are universal problems faced and resolved in one way or another by every urban society. It is unreasonable to expect any society to adhere rigidly to a single principle of organization, particularly if it is dysfunctional or based on a single criterion. Thus, Western industrial cities are products of a rational, economic, materialistic society, but it is not axiomatic that choices of household or even business location should be purely economic decisions or, on the other hand, that in the traditional sacred centers of Islam economic factors were ignored. In describing Herat's urban environment, then, it is assumed that city-dwellers there as elsewhere faced complicated decisions and resolved them in terms of a complex of social, cultural, and economic needs and perceptions. In Herat, at least, these motivations created a more flexible and varied urban structure than that proposed in the models, an urban environment which shares principles of organization with other preindustrial and modern cities. To support these premises, this chapter first describes briefly the origin

---

[2] General discussions of the Muslim town can be found in: Claude Cahen, "Mouvements populaires et autonomisme urbain dans l'Asie musulmane du moyen âge," *Arabica* 5 (1958): 225-250; 6 (1959): 25-26, 223-265; idem, "Zur Geschichte der Städtischen Gesellschaften im Islamischen Orient des Mittelalters," *Speculum* 9 (1958): 59-76; G. E. von Grunebaum, "The Structure of the Muslim Town," in *Islam and the Growth of a Cultural Tradition*, 2nd ed., ed. Von Grunebaum (London: Routledge and Kegan Paul, 1961), pp. 141-158; Ira M. Lapidus, *Muslim Cities in the Later Middle Ages* (Cambridge: Harvard University Press, 1967); idem, ed. *Middle Eastern Cities: A Symposium of Ancient, Islamic, and Contemporary Middle Eastern Urbanism* (Berkeley: University of California Press, 1969); M. Lombard, "L'Évolution urbaine pendant le haut moyen âge," in *Annales: économies-sociétés-civilisations* 12 (1957): 7-28; G. Marçais, "La conception des villes dans l'Islam," *Revue d'Alger* 2 (1945): 517-33; Edmond Pauty, "Villes spontanées et villes créées en Islam," in *Annales de l'Institut d'études orientales* 9 (1951): 52-75; Xavier de Planhol, *The World of Islam* (Ithaca: Cornell University Press, 1959), pp. 1-41; J. Weulersse, "La primauté des cités dans l'économie syrienne," in *Comptes rendus du congrès international de géographie* 2 (Leiden, 1938): 233-239.

and development of Herat and the functional structure of the old city, and then analyzes the three major elements in that structure: the organization of space, the quarters system, and the bazaars.

THE ORIGIN AND DEVELOPMENT OF HERAT

The history of Herat is essentially that of Central Asia.[3] Located in the fertile Hari Rud Valley, Herat (Haraiva) existed in Avestan times and took its present form at the time of the Greek conquest of Western Asia. It was one of the seventy Alexandrias founded by the young conqueror, Alexander, and was called "Alexandria in Aria." Herat was conquered by the Arabs in the seventh century, and during the Abbasid period it became one of the great trading centers on the Silk Road connecting East and West. The city was pillaged by the Mongols in the thirteenth century and by Tamerlane a century later, but at the end of the fifteenth century Herat became a major center of culture during the reign of the Timurid prince, Husayn Baiqara (1469-1506).[4] In the Timurid period, many of the magnificent structures of the city—the Musalla quarter north of the walls, the religious college of Gowhar Shah, and the winter residence of the governors inside the city, Chahar Bagh—were built.[5]

The physical plan of the city was dictated by the Milesian mentality of its Greek conquerors and remains intact today. The old city of Herat, as distinct from its modern suburbs, occupies a near perfect one-mile square which is oriented north-south, east-west. This square is superimposed on a lateral northeast-southwest pattern of surrounding fields and villages which slope with the land and the distributaries of the Hari Rud. Inside the walls of the old city two major avenues intersect at the approximate center of the square, dividing it into four superblocks which define the four recognized quarters of the city. The bazaars of Herat line these major avenues: the Malek Bazaar to the north; the Khush Bazaar to the east; the Qandahar Bazaar to the south; the Iraq Bazaar to the west. Their point of convergence, appropriately called the Chahar Suq or "Four Bazaars," is the economic crossroads of this star-shaped central business district.

Until this century, the old city of Herat was surrounded by a huge embankment 250 feet wide at the base and 90 feet high topped by the still higher walls of the city.[6] The gates of the city were located where the major

---

[3] The best précis of Herat's history is Richard N. Frye's "Herat," in *Encyclopaedia of Islam*, 2nd ed.

[4] The Timurid period is discussed in: A. K. Borovkov, ed., *Alisher Navoi* (Moscow: Academy of Sciences, U.S.S.R., 1946), pp. 175-202; Donald N. Wilber, *Afghanistan* (New Haven: Human Relations Area Files Press, 1962), pp. 102-107; P. I. Zestovsky, "Esquisses d'architecture Afghane," *Afghanistan* 4 (1949): 1-25.

[5] The monuments of the city are described in A. Khalili, *Athar-i Harat*, 3 vols. (Herat: privately published, 1930-31); F. Seljuqi, *Khiaban* (Herat: privately published, 1954).

[6] A number of nineteenth-century European travelers recorded their impressions of the city. See: Arthur Conolly, *Journey to the North of India*, 2 vols. (London: Richard Bentley, 1834); Joseph P. Ferrier, *Caravan Journeys* (London: John Murray, 1857); Thomas H. Holdich, *The Indian Borderland: 1880-1900* (London: Methuen, 1901); Nicolas De Khanikoff, "Mémoire sur la partie méridionale de l'Asie centrale," in *Reçueil de voyages et de mémoires publiés par la société de géographie* 7 (1861): 239-451; Charles Masson, *Journeys in Balochistan, Afghanistan, and the Panjab*, 3 vols. (London: Richard Bentley, 1842); Arminius Vambéry, *Travels in Central Asia* (London: John Murray, 1864); Charles E. Yate, "Notes on the City of Herat," *Journal of the Asiatic Society of Bengal* 56 (1887): 84-106; idem, *Northern Afghanistan* (Edinburgh: William Blackwood and Sons, 1888).

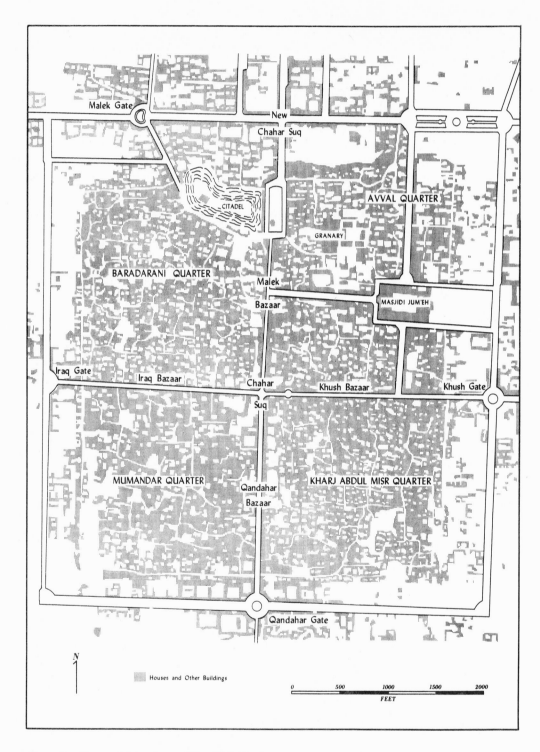

Fig. 2. Herat, Afghanistan (The Old City).

avenues intercepted the walls. The Khush Gate faced westward, the Qandahar Gate to the south, and the Iraq Gate to the east. In the north of the city this pattern was disrupted by the monumental structures of a preindustrial Muslim society, the citadel, the Friday-prayer mosque (Masjidi Jum'eh), and the granary. The citadel had its own entry port in the northwest called the Malek Gate, and a second gate provided access to the mosque quarter. Availability of water probably explains the location of these major structures in the northern part of the old city, through the fact that the Masjidi Jum'eh is oriented east-west rather than towards Mecca suggests that this sacred space was already occupied in pre- and early Islamic times, possibly by a Buddhist monastery. Outside the north wall of the city lay a magnificent walled suburb of fine houses and walled gardens (the Musalla Quarter).

THE FUNCTIONAL STRUCTURE OF THE OLD CITY

The physical form of the old city of Herat embodies the conscious and inadvertent decisions of its past generations; decisions made by the total society, by influential groups, and even by individual Heratis. These judgments concerning the organization of urban life were forged in a complex social environment, no simpler than our modern world. They took account of the physical setting of the city, the technology and resources available, the distribution of power and wealth within the community, and the functional needs of day-to-day life. The Heratis were influenced by the ideals and aspirations embodied in the Islamic cultural tradition, although these were often compromised for other purposes. The city created by these men, therefore, incorporated the substance of what the Heratis valued most, rather than their value system per se. Its urban form can be viewed as a physical realization of their judgments, the same kind of judgments based on the same priorities that have made cities what they are in all societies. In discussing the organization of space, the quarter system, and the bazaars of the old city of Herat, then, we are observing the verdict of its inhabitants on what an urban environment ought to provide. It is because of the complexity of that verdict, the conflicting and divergent motivations that contributed to the physical structure of Herat, that the city does not conform to the existing models of preindustrial Islamic cities.

The Organization of Space

In organizing space, the people of Herat perceived and valued the special qualities of their city, and first among these properties was security. The architecture and plan of Herat were in the first place designed to provide citizens with enclosure, protection, and privacy. Great earthworks and high walls were constructed around the old city at great physical cost. The walls both isolated and insulated the city; all contacts with the outer world were carefully filtered through the five gates, and the gates themselves became the meeting points of urbanites and rural people. Inside the walls, the higher fortifications of the citadel towered over the city, a symbol of the power of its ruler, a haven in times of crisis, and a warning to hostile invaders. After a century in ruins, it is still unclimbable without equipment; it took a determined enemy, indeed, to

Pl. 5 (31)
Pl. 88 (292)

scale the citadel under fire. Excepting the citadel, the only other monumental structures in the old city of Herat are the mosque and the granary. All three of these provided security and comfort to Heratis.

This theme of enclosure and security is also evident in the organization of the four residential sections of old Herat: Avval, Kharj Abdul Misr, Baradarani, and Mumandar. The organic, irregular plan of these quarters of the old city is universal in the Muslim world. The streets and lanes are narrow and twisting, often subterranean, with many sharp turns and frequent cul-de-sacs. The street as a means of circulation is exceptional; there is no traffic network because there is virtually no traffic. Since neither wheeled vehicles, water pipes, nor sewage drains were used here, the alleyways tend to follow slight contours of the land along which water is channeled. These lanes are heavily shaded, for the walls of household compounds are heavily studded and barred, and windows ten feet above the ground have iron grills. Even the small openings at the base of the walls which allow sewage to flow into the alleys are baffled to prevent entry. There are no street signs and no numbers, and one cannot find a specific residence without a guide. This is not accidental. The emphasis in this city has been on security and privacy. The memory of earlier periods of violence is still vivid, and women are so jealously hidden that they wear a net of woven hair across their eyes in addition to the body-covering *chadur,* a fact that has made them vulnerable targets for wheeled vehicles on the major avenues.

This contrast between the geometry of Herat's general plan and the irregularity of its quarters highlights a second theme in urban structure and society which is widespread throughout the Muslim world. Public life and private life are quite separate in Herat, and as a result public and private space are clearly differentiated. As in other Muslim towns, community institutions are weak and occupy virtually no space. There are no communes in Herat, no guild halls, no playgrounds, and few professional organizations. The Sufi brotherhoods are weak except among Shiites and even the Iranian "house-of-strength" (*zurkhaneh*) is absent. A man's actions as a merchant or artisan, as a Muslim or an Afghan, are public actions which take place in a public space, such as in the four bazaars of the city, the few parks located along them (notably Pay'eh Hisar at the base of the citadel), the courtyard of the Masjidi Jum'eh, and the public gardens outside the old city. Here the men of the city practice their trades, barter for goods, worship together, drink tea, and converse. Though most contacts in Herat, even business dealings, are well-established ones based on family relationships, there is a rigid allocation of space for public purposes, divorcing the place of business from the place of residence. There are no shops or other facilities in the residential quarters excepting mosques, shrines, and associated baths. This is the domain of private space and private life. Here, in the inner space of the household compound, a man's roles as father, husband, and member of an extended family are played out. Only the twisting alleyways of the residential quarters, the pathways of the journey to work, are not defined as either public or private.

This public-private polarization in the organization of space and society in Herat can be seen in the use of these three areas. The government, representing

Two contrasting aspects of San'a, Yemen. 26. (above) This view of the old city reveals an intensive use of space with buildings close together, narrow streets and no open spaces. 27. (below) This view of the newer main street (Ali Abdul Mognie Street) reveals an extensive use of open space, including even a public garden. Note the open balconies of the buildings lining the far side of the main street, a style of residential building (and occasionally commercial building) introduced from Central Europe by German and Austrian architects. (Photos: Ministry of Economy and Ministry of Public Works, respectively, Yemen Arab Republic.)

the total society, cares for the public space within the city. Men are hired each day to clean the water channels in the bazaar, and to dampen the roadways each morning and afternoon to keep the dust down. Gardeners tend the flowerbeds at the mosque and in the parks, and policemen patrol the shaded streets to prevent anyone from removing the trees in winter, when wood is expensive. The private space in household compounds is cared for equally well, depending, as in every society, on the temperament and economic position of the owner. The mud dwellings are swept and watered daily, and if enough water is available, flowers and fruit trees are planted in the courtyards. But the alleys of the old city are cared for by no one. They were created by the space remaining after structures were raised, and their condition provides evidence of the weakness of social integration in the quarters. They are garbage-laden, sewage-choked, constricted spaces which, lacking drains, stink at all times of day, particularly since the disposal of filth is a persistent problem in the old city of Herat. Lacking neighborhood organizations, individual removal of waste makes little sense and as a result the surface water supply is constantly polluted.

A third theme in the structure of the old city of Herat is the rational way in which space is organized. In this city there is a functional allocation of land in the commercial districts, the quarters, and even the household compounds which is well adapted to the climate, economy, and social practices of the city. Urban planners have rarely discussed this aspect of Muslim cities, and they were rarely consulted in the construction because most structures in Herat excepting the monumental ones were erected by the men who lived and worked in them. These men built within a more general Near Eastern cultural tradition which clearly designated the correct form a house or shop should take.[7] In Herat, at least, this tradition incorporated a wisdom distilled from the corrected errors of the past.

The Hellenistic quadrilateral which governs the general design of the old city of Herat is an efficient system of organizing urban space.[8] The four major avenues of the city provide access for wheeled vehicles and marching men to the caravanserais of the center, and in these major arteries are located the bazaars of the city. More expensive and permanent goods like copper pots, jewelry, and cloth are sold at the center of the city, near the Chahar Suq, the point of minimum travel for most people in the old city. There are 5,500 shops located within easy walking distance of 80,000 people, and the organization of commercial space is such that any bazaar is within ten minute's walk of any home.

Pls. 13-16
(61-62)
The lanes of the residential quarters of the old city, despite their unsanitary condition, represent a second economic and rational use of space. Fundamentally, they are footpaths for walking from one center of life to another,

---

[7] See the discussion of the "unselfconscious" design process in Christopher Alexander, *Notes on the Synthesis of Form* (Cambridge, Mass.: Harvard University Press, 1966), pp. 46-54.

[8] A summary statement is presented in Dan Stanislawski, "The Origin and Spread of the Grid-Pattern Town," *Geographical Review* 36 (1946): 105-120.

from the home to the bazaar. Though narrow and twisting, they are not equally narrow, and some of the wider ones (as wide as ten feet) cross entire quarters to provide easy routes of travel for transients. In them one rarely finds congestion, and by this measure, these streets are adequate for their purposes and anything wider and more elaborate would be wasteful of land.[9] The application of a grid-pattern in these quarters would reduce the amount of space available for housing, and as a result, it would raise rents and increase the cost of land in the city by allocating an unnecessary amount of land to roads and streets. Since there is no access problem in Herat, such a plan would be uneconomic. In addition, the twisting, well-shaded alleys are far better adapted to the climate of Herat than the broad boulevards of the new city, which resemble wind tunnels when the "wind of 120 days" blows in the summer months. In short, the conditioned view of Western observers that straight, wide grid-patterned streets are more efficient and satisfying than those of traditional Muslim residential quarters is not relevant to Herat, given its society and technology.

The houses of the residential quarters in the old city of Herat also reflect a concern with functional use of space and adaptation to local conditions, despite—or perhaps because of—their forms, which are virtually the same as they were a thousand years ago. (Detached, free-standing houses set in low-walled gardens are becoming the model dwellings of the suburbs of Herat, but being exposed to the elements, wasteful of land on either side, and hard to heat in winter, they are rarely seen in the old city.) Most houses in the old city are rather small (thirty feet square is probably average), one- or two-storied structures built of sun-dried brick faced with mud. The house is attached to thick compound walls at a corner and these form two of its sides. Functional differentiation of space within the house decreases with income; most are divided into two rooms, one of which is set aside as the *harim* or women's quarter. These dwellings ameliorate the diurnal temperature fluctuations of Herat's desert climate, maximize the amount of courtyard space available for other purposes, and are less expensive to construct than free-standing houses. For these reasons they are used in the old city of Herat and throughout the Near East.

Pls. 62 (171), 64 (174), 75 (223)

But there are certain aspects of Herat's urban environment that have remained persistent problems in the life of her people. First among these is water, which is carried to the city in a sizable distributary of the Hari Rud, the Juie Angil. This stream enters the city from the northeast, at the Avval or "First Quarter," so-called because it receives water first. Locally, all other quarters are identified by their place in the water rotation system, thus Kharj Abdul Misr is the "Second Quarter," Baradarani the "Third," and Mumandar the "Fourth." In the first quarter (Avval), clean water flows in channeled streams down the alleys, through the Masjidi Jum'eh, to the covered reservoir at the Chahar Suq. By

---

[9] Mumford stresses this theme in discussing medieval cities: Lewis Mumford, *The City in History* (New York: Harcourt, Brace and World, 1961), pp. 281-305.

contrast, the last quarter, Mumandar, receives very little water during the summer and for that reason is the worst residential section of the old city. Water is here stored in unlined surface reservoirs and distributed throughout the quarter. The water stands and is polluted; after a few days, the light-green scum of algae on its surface becomes thick enough to support small birds. The people of this quarter dislike this situation and the more perceptive among them recognize it as a source cf the plagues which periodically sweep the city. But no planned approach to the problem has yet been organized, partly because the quarters are not meaningful social units in the old city of Herat.

The Quarters System

In most preindustrial Muslim cities, the population is segregated into residential quarters which are social as well as geographic entities, coherent communities within the urban whole. In these quarters, people are bound together by ties of religion, occupation, family, or common origin. During the Ottoman period, this arrangement was formalized into the *millet* system, which officially recognized the existence of a large number of separate and distinct social communities.[10] In Antioch, for example, there were forty-five identifiable quarters. In most cities Jews, Armenians, Greeks, Europeans, and the various Muslim sects were identified with a distinct section of the city. Each quarter formed a nearly independent community walled off from the others, a city within a city, with its own mosque, bath, and market, its own customs, laws, and milieu. These autonomous cells had their own civic and religious leaders, administrative organization, and even watchmen. The quarter was a common organizing principle of preindustrial Muslim urban life, and its absence as a meaningful unit of social organization in Herat merits discussion.

   Each of the four quarters (*hesai*) of the old city of Herat is administered by an important civic official called *mamur-i mahal*, who represents the government in the quarter and is responsible for collecting the head tax and the house tax. The mamur-i mahal selects draftees for the army, records all purchases and sales of property, and keeps records of births, marriages, and deaths in the quarter. If one decides to raze a house, add a room, replace a wall, or open a shop, permission of the mamur-i mahal is needed. He reports all disorders or crimes in the quarter to the mayor's office; informally he settles many minor disputes

roof
heights:
Pl. 28 (87)
Pls. 22 (70),
57 (167) 63
(174)

concerning the blocking of a lane, water rotation, or the height of roofs (important for privacy since people sleep on them in summer). His jurisdiction extends to the bazaars on the margins of the quarter. The mamur-i mahal is not elected by the people, nor does he have a fixed term of office. He receives a small salary from the government, supplemented by fees for services rendered the people of the quarter. Recently, a particularly difficult official was replaced because of discontent among the merchants under his rule; but this is rare. Of

---

[10]   The *millet* system is discussed in H. A. R. Gibb and Harold Bowen, *Islamic Society and the West*, vol. 2 (London: Oxford University Press, 1950), pp. 207-261; Albert H. Hourani, *Minorities in the Arab World* (London: Oxford University Press, 1947).

the four men now in office, three are Sunni and one is a Shiite (the major religious schism in the town); and all are landlords.

The four major divisions of the old city are clearly too large and populous to form meaningful social units within the city. What is apparently absent in Herat are the smaller, more coherent ethnic, religious, or occupational groupings that are frequently described for other traditional Muslim cities. The Shiites are the most important religious minority in the city, forming about one-quarter of the population. They are generally rather prosperous tinsmiths, jewelers, shoemakers, and shopkeepers in the bazaar and live predominantly in the Avval Quarter south of the Masjidi Jum'eh and in the northern half of Kharj Abdul Misr. All six mosques which are exclusively Shiite are found in this sector, locally called Dudulan after a double arch which once existed there. But this area is not a Shiite quarter in a social sense. Shiite households are widely distributed throughout the central part of the old city and some have already moved to the newly-built suburbs. Their houses are intermingled with those of the Sunni majority and are located in that sector of the city where, given their economic status and the slope of land values with water distribution, one would expect to find them. Further, the Shiites insist that they are fundamentally Muslims (and, therefore, like everyone else), and though they are called "Persians" by the less educated Sunnis, there is little evidence of social segregation. The Jews (six families total) and Turkomans of the city are so few in number that it is impossible to discuss them as social groups. Nor can one talk of occupational quarters or districts in the old city of Herat; there are no spontaneous groupings of tradesmen in the residential quarters. Individual streets are often named after particular crafts so that Herat has its Street of the Gunsmith, the Cloth Seller, the String Maker, the Potter, and even the Egg Seller. Where the origin of the name can be traced, however, it refers to a particularly successful individual who died or lives nearby. In no case does it represent a concentration of artisans' households in a special district, and if such a pattern ever existed in the city, it has been forgotten.

In the old city of Herat, then, there are apparently no rigid regional principles of household location other than the common factors of economics, nearness of family or friends, availability of space, access to place of work, and personal preference—the same factors found in many other societies. The inflexibility of the Turkish millet system and the models of preindustrial Muslim cities are not replicated in Herat. Neighborhood activity focuses mostly around the small mosques and shrines dotted throughout the quarters, providing one of the few collective experiences in which the people of Herat, wealthy and poor, can unite. In the crowded quarters, the small mosque is a place where the men of surrounding lanes worship together. Local residents have built and maintained 68 mosques and 36 shrines. No quarter is so poor that it is without a mosque or a shrine containing the bones and relics of a saint. These shrines are frequented by women (they never enter mosques) who are childless or have sick children. Given the sanitary conditions of the city, they are visited often. Men help each other to build houses, lend and borrow tools to defray expenses, and watch one another's home when neighbors visit relatives in surrounding villages. Generally, however, the patterns of community cooperation are weak and the foci for common efforts are few.

The question remains, why are socially coherent, separate quarters not found in the old city of Herat, which embodies so many other characteristics of the preindustrial Muslim town? While historical sources may suggest that distinct aggregations of people in specific districts of the city existed in nineteenth-century Herat, there is virtually no field evidence to support this possibility and informants are agreed that occupational or religious quarters never, to their knowledge, existed in the city. It is more likely that the principle of social segregation has been overstressed in models of preindustrial cities, and that the pattern of household selection for the majority of the population was not based on a single variable. A price in convenience and access must be paid in order to implement a segregated system, and this price was certainly paid by those who could not choose otherwise, by non-Muslim minorities and certain Muslim sects in times of religious fervor, and by artisans engaged in particularly noxious trades at all times. Yet, unless Muslims were, as some have suggested, "building a city of God" rather than a city for men, it seems clear that in this case cross-cultural similarities in urban behavior have been disregarded in favor of differences.

The Bazaars

The concept of cross-cultural similarities is also demonstrated in the bazaars of the old city of Herat, the major centers of personal transactions, commerce, and communication. Now rigidly aligned along the major avenues, small remnants of the older bazaars indicate that earlier markets in Herat had a more irregular, amorphous though still linear form. To a certain extent this evanescent informality remains. Each morning, peasants from neighboring villages set up temporary stalls in the open spaces of the bazaar and sell melons, tomatoes, and fruit to the urbanites. On Sunday and Wednesday, periodic bazaars are held at the Qandahar and Iraq gates and more valuable merchandise—woven silk, hides, wheat, and animals—are brought to market from villages the length of Hari Rud Valley. Through these functions the bazaar has become the most vital and distinctive element of Herat.

The bazaars of Herat have 5,542 shops and an aggregate length of approximately six miles. The city has one shop for every fifteen citizens, indicating its importance as a regional marketing center for the million or so people who live in the valley of the Hari Rud. This population provides the goods to trade as well as the customers to purchase them. Thus, most shops in the Herat bazaars are small retail outlets for the basic staples of life in western Afghanistan. One of every three (1,600 in all) sells either candy, cloth, spices, fruit, or a cup of tea. The traditional artisan skills are represented by shoemakers, tailors, carpenters, iron smiths, and coppersmiths. But the market is changing. Already the dyers have been virtually replaced by precolored yarns and thread, the weavers by factory woven cloth, and the potters by tin pans and

TABLE 1. SHOPS IN THE BAZAARS OF HERAT

Traditional Shopkeepers			*Modern Shopkeepers*		
Candy Seller	515		Sundry	220	
Cloth Seller	421		Auto Parts	137	
Spice Seller	355		Used Cloth		
Fruit Seller	309		(Western)	85	
Teahouses	239		Shoe Seller		
Grain Seller	132		(Western)	78	
Wool Seller	110		Pots & Pans Seller	59	
Wood Seller	102		Kerosene Seller	48	
Butchers	89		Motor Oil Seller	38	
Jewelers	88		Pharmacy	37	
Bakers	86		Teapot Seller	34	
Cooking Oil	63		Mirror Seller	31	
Salt Seller	50		*Total*	767	(13.8%)
Karakul Seller	34				
Animal Fodder	25				
Total	2,618	(47.2%)			

Traditional Artisans & Craftsmen			*Modern Artisans & Craftsmen*		
Cobbler	233		Auto Repair	116	
Tailor	170		Bicycle Repair	94	
Carpenter	164		Tin Trunk Maker	56	
Ironsmith	125		Shoes from Tires	51	
Coppersmith	116		Watch Repair	28	
Barber	94		*Total*	345	(6.2%)
Silk-Rayon Weaver	90				
Donkey Bag Maker	58		*Empty*	331	(6.0%)
Tinsmith	46				
Carriage *(Gadi)* Repair	26		*Miscellaneous* (less than		
Dyer	25		25 shops)	309	(5.6%)
Leather Worker	25				
Total	1,172	(21.2%)			

Total Shops   5,542   *(100%)*

plastic containers. To use an old distinction, the society and its marketplace is beginning to change from one of status to one of contract.

Despite these incipient changes, the bazaars of Herat do exhibit the same general structure found in other preindustrial Muslim cities. Central location is highly valued and the best shops therefore are found around the Chahar Suq and, given the particular historical development of Herat, in the Malek Bazaar adjacent to the Masjidi Jum'eh. This section of the bazaar, which was covered with a domed roof until 1930, is occupied by dealers in high-value permanent merchandise. The bazaars of the cloth merchants, with their beautiful halls (*timcheh*), the coppersmiths, the jewelers, the carpet merchants, the booksellers, and the leatherworkers are all concentrated here. Consistent with the general Near Eastern pattern, each trade is highly localized, with retailers and producers occupying adjacent stalls. The degree of concentration varies from trade to trade,

Pls. 17-18 (64-65),20 (67),23-24 (71)

but 55% of the coppersmiths, 76% of the jewelers, and 83% of the cloth sellers in the city are found near the Chahar Suq in the Khush, Malek, and Qandahar bazaars respectively. Moving outwards from this clearly compartmentalized core, the structures of the various bazaars assume different characters. In all of them, candy shops, teahouses, barber shops, butcheries, bicycle repair shops, shoe repair shops, and fruit stalls are found. Such concentration as does exist is related to clientele. Thus, the auto repair shops of the city are located in the caravanserais of the New Bazaar where the major highway from Iran enters the city, while caravanserais for animals are found at the other three gates. The lower section of the Qandahar and Iraq bazaars, which are particularly oriented to villagers, are occupied by grain sellers and merchants, plowshare makers, gunsmiths and bullet sellers, salt, kerosene, and cooking oil dealers.

Except in the clearly defined central core of the bazaar, where the shops of wealthy merchants are located, the shops and shopkeepers of the bazaar are perpetually changing as some men grow wealthy and move closer to the center of the bazaar, and others less fortunate move outward to the margins. Rents are low on all shops in Herat, ranging from ten dollars per month at the center to less than one on the outskirts, but a great deal of money—key money—is needed to gain the right to rent a shop and may amount to as much as several thousand dollars. Clever and resourceful shopkeepers save their money in order to pay the higher amount of key money required for the better, centrally located shops. A man with financial problems moves his shop to a more peripheral location and pays his debts with the difference in key money for the two locations. Except in the center, then, the shops of Herat change from time to time. One shop in the Khush Bazaar, for example, was occupied by a carpenter, a fruit seller, and a tinsmith at different times during a single summer. The laws that govern the distribution of these shops dealing in inexpensive, low-order goods and services appear to be those that influence retail trade elsewhere. The barbers, bakers, candy sellers, teapot repairers, spice sellers, and fruit sellers are evenly distributed throughout the bazaars.

These distributional differences among crafts and trades are not caused by differences in the integrity of their guilds, for guilds are loosely articulated, weak organizations in the city of Herat. Every craft in Herat has a guild (*sinf*) and a guild leader (*vakili sinfi*) appointed by the government. The primary function of these men is to act as liaison between the artisans and the government. They do not collect taxes or receive a formal salary. Among dyers, the vakili sinfi does not regulate the quality of the product, the length of tenure or salaries of apprentices, or the marketing of products. Dyers with complaints come to him for assistance, but he has no formal power. Most crafts are still hereditary. Some 70% of the practicing jewelers of Herat, for example, followed their father working in his shop from childhood. The remaining 30% apprenticed with an uncle, cousin, or some other relative, or alternatively married into a jeweler's family, or followed some other equally informal path in learning the trade. But there is no central organization to these procedures, no special social activities,

28. Herat, Afghanistan. General view from the Great Mosque showing wide shopping street cut through in the 1950s. (Photo: William Trousdale.)

no shrine or particular feast day associated with guild activity.[11]   A man follows naturally in his father's path in a preindustrial society, but the highly structured guilds of medieval Europe which are claimed to have existed in some preindustrial Islamic cities are not found in Herat.[12]   The bazaars of Herat, then, appear to be organized on the basis of economics rather than religion, status, or guild societies. The finest shops selling expensive, durable merchandise pay the highest rents (through key money) and occupy the most favored location in terms of accessibility. Other shops are distributed with reference to particular clienteles or are evenly distributed along the bazaars of the city to serve neighboring customers. On the outer fringes of the bazaar, artisans from nearby villages work in the city during the week and cater to people from their local region who visit the city. In short, the principles of shop location in the city are rational in terms of both land values and service functions.

THE CHANGING CITY

Such is the structure of the old city of Herat, a structure which has survived for 2,000 years because it formed a satisfactory, functional urban milieu for its citizens. In the last century, major modifications in Herat's urban structure occurred when the values, technology, and urban perception of the West penetrated this region. The process began in the 1880s when British engineers demolished the magnificent northern suburb of Musalla to provide a field of fire for their cannons, the better to kill Russians who then inconsiderately failed to appear. It continued with the razing of the old fortifications of the city, which became obsolete by advances in weaponry, and the straightening of the old bazaars to provide access to wheeled vehicles. Grid-pattern suburbs consistent with Western planning principles now exist north, east, and south of the city (the city casts a water shadow to the west), and powerful and influential citizens are leaving the crowded quarters of the old city to live in the villas of these new suburbs. Broad avenues simulating the Baroque vistas of Europe now lead to the Masjidi Jum'eh, though these wide streets are so hot, dusty, and unpleasant that the city fathers had to import unsuspecting cloth merchants from Qandahar to occupy shops along them.

Pl. 28 (87)

This expansion of Herat into a New City (*Shahreh Nou*), as distinct from the traditional Old City (*Shahreh Khuneh*), and the attendant changes in social structure, patterns of living, and economics, are processes which have been carefully observed in many cities of the Near East—in Cairo, Baghdad,

Pls. 26-27
(79)

[11]   As compared, for example, with descriptions in Bernard Lewis, "The Islamic Guilds," *Economic History Review* 8 (1937): 20-37; Louis Massignon, "Les corps de métier et la cité islamique," *Revue internationale de sociologie* 28 (1920): 473-489.

[12]   The earlier idea that medieval Islam had a flourishing guild system comparable to what prevailed in medieval Europe has now been convincingly challenged. See, especially, S. M. Stern, "The Constitution of the Islamic City," and Claude Cahen, "Y a-t-il eu des corporations professionelles dans le monde musulman classique?" both in A. H. Hourani, ed., *The Islamic City*. Quite possibly, the weak guild structure that exists now in Herat reflects not so much a decline from earlier vitality but a continuation of a venerable pattern.

Teheran, Kirman, Tripoli, Aleppo, and Damascus, among others.[13] They are at once the symptoms and agents of change from a traditional to a modern way of life. The process is very recent in Herat because the city has been virtually isolated since the British in the last century abandoned the "great game" in Central Asia, the Afghans gained firm control over the province of Herat, and the great trade routes of past centuries were fragmented by international boundaries. As a result, Herat today is one of the most traditional large cities in Asia, reflecting more accurately than others the spirit and tenor of preindustrial urban life precisely because it has been less accessible to the forces of modernization.

Yet, despite its relative isolation, Herat's functional structure, organization of space, and residential quarters differ from those ascribed to other preindustrial Islamic cities. Even as the questions are raised, the opportunities to answer them satisfactorily diminish. To what degree is the form of the city the form of its society? Are cities, all cities, simply expressions of the cultures which build them, or are there constraints of distance, time, energy, and economics which will create parameters which societies must respect, thereby creating underlying similarities in urban solutions over broad value systems, institutions, social imperatives, and histories outside the Western tradition? In the Near East, at least, few cities provide sufficient historical documentation to support detailed analysis, and the rapid restructuring of these limit possibilities for future field work. But if conditions in the old city of Herat are representative of preindustrial Muslim urban life, the distinctions between old and new, traditional and modern, have been too finely drawn.

---

[13] Major studies include: Morroe Berger, ed., *The New Metropolis in the Arab World* (New Delhi: Allied Publishers, 1963); J. Berque, "Medinas, villes neuves et bidonvilles," *Cahiers de Tunisie* 6 (1958):5-42;John I. Clarke, *The Iranian City of Shiraz* (Durham: Department of Geography, University of Durham, 1963); Paul W. English, "Culture Change and the Structure of a Persian City," in *Traditionalism and Modernism in the Muslim Middle East,* ed., Carl Leiden (Austin: University of Texas Press, 1968); John Gulick, "Baghdad: Portrait of a City in Physical and Cultural Change," *Journal of the American Institute of Planners* 33 (1967): 246-255; idem, *Tripoli: A Modern Arab City* (Cambridge, Mass.: Harvard University Press, 1967); H. Hahn, "Die Stadt Kabul und ihr Umland," in *Bonner Geographische Abhandlungen,* vol. 34 (1964); Roger Le Tourneau, *Fès avant le protectorat* (Casablanca: Institut des hautes études marocaines, 1949); Xavier de Planhol, "Abadan: morphologie et fonction du tissu urbain," *Revue géographique de l'Est* 4 (1964): 338-385; Jean Sauvaget, *Alep des origines au milieu du XIXe siècle* (Paris: Bibliothèque archéologique et historique de l'institut français d'archéologie de Beyrouth, 1941); K. Scharlau, "Moderne Umgestaltungen im Grundriss iranischer Städte," *Erdkunde* 15 (1961): 180-191; Jacques Weulersse, "Antioche, essai de géographie urbaine," *Bulletin d'études orientales* 4 (1934): 27-79; Eugen Wirth, "Strukturwandlungen und Entwicklungstendenzen der Orientalischen Stadt," *Erdkunde* 22 (1968): 101-128.

A SELECTED BIBLIOGRAPHY

I. *Urban Theory.*

Hauser, P. M. and Schnore, L. F., eds. *The Study of Urbanization.* New York: John Wiley, 1965. A superb reader on the nature of urbanization in the modern world. The articles by Lampard and Sjoberg delineate the historic dimensions of the problems and are especially interesting.

Martindale, Don. "Prefatory Remarks: The Theory of the City." In Max Weber, *The City*, trans. and ed. by D. Martindale and G. Neuwirth. New York: Collier Books, 1962. A succinct summary of approaches to the city introduces Weber's classic volume.

Reissman, Leonard. *The Urban Process: Cities in Industrial Societies.* New York, 1964. See chapter on "ecologists." Although not devoted to preindustrial cities, Reissman's comprehension of the conceptual framework utilized by urbanists is of value.

Sjoberg, Gideon. *The Preindustrial City: Past and Present.* Glencoe, Ill.: Free Press, 1960. A basic theoretical exposition of the similarities of cities throughout the world prior to the Industrial Revolution. For Sjoberg, "technology" is as explanatory as "Islam" is to Von Grunebaum.

Wirth, Louis. "Urbanism as a Way of Life." *American Journal of Sociology* 44 (1938): 1-24. A classic article which redirected the attention of urbanists for a generation.

II. *The Muslim Town.*

Cohen, Claude. "Zur Geschichte der Städtischen Gesellschaft im Islamischen Orient des Mittelalters." *Speculum* 9 (1958): 59-76. A description of the major components of medieval Islamic cities.

Clark, J. I. *The Iranian City of Shiraz.* Durham, 1963. A geographical description of a specific city, characteristic of much recent literature.

Grunebaum, G. E. von, ed. "The Structure of the Muslim Town." In *Islam and the Growth of a Cultural Tradition,* 2nd ed. London: Routledge and Kegan Paul, 1961, pp. 141-158. The classic article which identifies the uniqueness of Muslim towns as compared with those of other culture regions.

Hourani, A. H., and Stern, S. M., eds. *The Islamic City.* Philadelphia: University of Pennsylvania Press, 1970. Another valuable recent symposium devoted to specific aspects of the Muslim town.

Lapidus, Ira. *Muslim Cities in the Later Middle Ages.* Cambridge, Mass.: Harvard University Press, 1967. A masterful scholarly treatise on the Mamluk cities of Aleppo and Damascus. See also the symposium he edited, *Middle Eastern Cities.* Berkeley, 1969.

Le Tourneau, R., *Fès avant le protectorat.* Casablanca, 1949. Perhaps the best and most comprehensive analysis of a city in the Muslim world.

Marçais, G. "La conception des villes dans l'Islam." *Revue d'Alger* 2 (1945): 517-533. An exposition of Islamic attitudes towards the city.

Pauty, Edmond. "Villes spontaneés et villes créées en Islam." *Annales de l'Institut d'études orientales* 9 (1951): 52-75. Pauty differentiates between planned and spontaneous cities in the Muslim world.

29. Tripoli, Libya. Although a narrow street by modern vehicular traffic standards, this is better seen as exemplifying a wide, "public" traditional street—adequate to permit passage of laden donkeys or donkey-driven carts. (An Exxon photograph.)

30. Taif, Saudi Arabia. Changing times. Traditional wooden latticework (mashrabiya) on projecting bays alongside buildings with new open balconies. (Photo: Aramco.)

31. Baghdad, Iraq, *ca.* 1900. A pleasing traditional equivalent of the modern "riverside drive"—wooden and brick row-houses (only foundation walls and part of near wall are brick) each with one or more projecting bays or alcoves overlooking the Tigris. The round boat in the right foreground, made of reeds and sealed with pitch, is typical of this area. (Photo: Library of Congress.)

Part II
URBAN DEVELOPMENT
AND CHANGE—SOME
INDIVIDUAL EXAMPLES

3

Cairo: Perspective and Prospectus
by Janet Abu-Lughod

In 1969 Cairo celebrated her thousandth anniversary on the same site with the same name and, cotemporaneously, marked her hundredth year as a modern metropolis. Given this impressive longevity and current population in excess of six million, her claim to be one of the most important urban communities ever known to man can scarcely be challenged. As symbolic and cultural capital for more that 100,000,000 citizens of the Arab world and as an important religious center for some 500,000,000 adherents to Islam, Cairo serves a hinterland matched by few. And as prototype for the developing cities of the emergent world of Asia and Africa, Cairo demands attention and study, for her growth and her problems are those which will occur elsewhere. On objective grounds, then, Cairo warrants our concern; on subjective grounds, she also rewards our interest, since among all the fascinating cities which man in his diversity has produced, she remains one which continues to captivate and intrigue. What unique factors governed her past and what problems face her at this juncture?

Memphis, located near where Cairo stands today, was a thriving city more than three thousand years before Christ. The Giza pyramids, which mark the extreme southwest limit of the Cairo metropolitan area, and the obelisk of ancient Heliopolis, which lies near the northeast edge of the city, recall a pharaonic heritage dating back more than five thousand years. Between these points stretches a gigantic mélange of historic accretions— the contemporary city of Cairo. Most of the city, however, has nothing to do with the pre-Islamic period, for while the ancient Egyptians and the conquering Greeks and Romans left a trace or two, Cairo's true history did not begin until the Arab invasion of Egypt in A.D. 640 and the founding in that year of an army encampment just outside the preexisting Christian town of Babylon-in-Egypt.

With time, this settlement, called Fustat, grew to be an important commercial emporium for the expanding Islamic Empire and became a center of

This chapter is based on Janet Abu-Lughod's book, *Cairo: 1001 Years of the City Victorious* (Princeton: Princeton University Press, 1971).

culture and religious innovation. Always the capital of the Egyptian province, Fustat occasionally commanded an even wider area and often played a critical if peripheral role in the power struggles that accompanied the rise and spread of Islamic hegemony during the first few centuries following Muhammad's message. As an Islamic city, then, Cairo is more than 1,300 years old, but the town of Fustat now lies buried within the southern part of the city, and only that portion of the metropolis added after A.D. 969 bears the same name and has been incorporated into the contemporary city. Our perspective, therefore, really begins about one thousand years ago.

In 969, a rectangular, walled, military-palace city was staked out on the plains just northeast of Fustat by Jawhar, a conquering general whose army hailed from that part of North Africa known today as Tunisia. He conquered in the name of a dissident branch of Islam (the Shiites), and the Fatimid dynasty, which his ruler consolidated, governed Egypt and a wide empire for the next two hundred years. Al-Qahirah (meaning "The Victorious," and distorted in European tongues to Cayro, Le Caire, and Cairo) became the name of this royal city when Muizz li-Din Allah, the Fatimid caliph, took up residence there in 973; during the ensuing five hundred years of medieval splendor, the city proved to be worthy of her name.

Under Fatimid rule an enlarged Fustat and her palace suburb of Al-Qahirah flowered. The wealth of an extensive empire flowed through her port. Craftsmen fashioned textiles, delicate lusterware, and elaborate sewage systems, and embellished mosques that still stand. Scholars and lawgivers similarly fashioned the details of state and religion. This continuity was abruptly shattered in 1168 when the rippling waves of the European Crusades finally reached Egypt. Saladin was part of the Sunni (Orthodox Islam) army that defeated a European vanguard perilously close to occupying Cairo. The defenders put the unfortified city of Fustat to the torch, and its large population sought refuge behind Al-Qahirah's walls. There, most remained afterward, converting what had been a carefully planned, low-density suburb for the ruling elite and its army into a teeming metropolis. Although Fustat recovered and was rebuilt in part, Al-Qahirah became *the city,* while Fustat was reduced to *its* suburb.

During the next 350 years, Cairo waxed and finally waned as the most important city of the Islamic world. And at that time, given the low estate of Europe's urban centers, to be the most important city of the Islamic world was to be the most important city of Europe and Africa as well as of Asia Minor. Growth was vigorous under Saladin and his successors (the Ayyubid period) and even more marked under the early rule of the manumitted Mamluks, slaves-turned-sultans, who held power from about A.D. 1250 onward. Cairo reached her largest dimensions and peak population by the middle of the fourteenth century,[1] and while she never managed to equal ancient Rome, which some historians believe contained a million inhabitants, she certainly reached a population of half a million and was an object of awe and wonder to the few travelers from underdeveloped Europe who came to see her. An extensive empire

---

[1] The Black Death, which in 1353 reduced Europe to terror, also took its toll in Cairo.

and a thriving spice trade fed the aesthetic tastes and supported the intellectual activities of this "Mother of Cities" (*mater-polis*, or metropolis) or even "Mother of the World," as she was called. Still standing today as constant reminders of this period of greatness are the incredibly beautiful mosques and mausoleums which the Mamluks left dotting the medieval and funereal quarters of the older, eastern portion of the contemporary city.

By the fifteenth century, however, her moment of glory had begun to pass. At the beginning of that century, Tamerlane attacked the eastern flank of the Mamluk Empire, sacking Damascus and inflicting serious losses upon the Mamluks who failed in the defense of their provinces. The century ended with Vasco da Gama's successful circumnavigation of Africa, which altered world trade routes and took the spice trade out of the hands of those who had needed Egypt for transit. The Ottoman Turks invaded a weakened Egypt and occupied its capital in 1516, reducing Cairo from her former role as center of a vast tributary empire to that of a provincial capital subservient and financially responsible to Istanbul. By this time, however, not just Cairo but the whole eastern Mediterranean world as well was stranded in backwater. Western Europe was the new locus for emergent nations, and her small naval powers were busy reshaping the known world and competing for its wealth. In this reshaped world, the eastern Mediterranean receded, its internal struggles eddying only locally.

When European competitions enlarged to touch Egypt once again, the positions of the protagonists had been significantly altered. Napoleon, seeking to outflank British seapower, sailed his forces to Egypt in 1798 and set up headquarters in Cairo for three brief years. The relative sizes of the French and Egyptian capitals reflect the intervening shift. Paris, which had been but a mud village when Cairo was an elegant "queen of broad provinces," had grown to a cultured capital with more than half a million inhabitants; Cairo, unkempt, cluttered with crumbling structures, weak and divided, had declined to a quarter of a million souls producing shoddy goods for local consumption and seeking to stay out of the way of the unpredictable rival Mamluks, who fought among themselves and with the titular overlords, the Turks.

While dates dividing "epochs" are always arbitrary, the year 1800 is often given, not unreasonably, as initiating the re-entry of Egypt into the "modern" world. Certainly, it serves as a convenient point in time from which to trace Cairo's transformation from a preindustrial, relatively unimportant town of straggling outline to the gigantic modern metropolis which today includes twice as many people as had inhabited all of Egypt at the time of the French Expedition in 1800. While the true impact of Europe was not felt in the city until late in the nineteenth century (and we therefore date the emergence of "modern" Cairo at about 1869), the intervening period was preparatory and consolidating, at least with respect to city-building.

Picture, if you will, the Cairo which Muhammad Ali (who, like Saladin, had come to Egypt as a member of the army which repelled a European invasion) inherited in 1806 when he was elevated to the Pashalik of Egypt, thus founding the dynasty which ruled Egypt until the deposition of his descendant, King Farouk, in the bloodless revolution of 1952. Most of Cairo's population was

Enduring Cairo.
32. (left) A David Roberts print of the "Mosque el-Mooristan" in mid-nineteenth-century Cairo. (Source: David Roberts.)

33. (right) A recent photo of the same site. (Photo: Hassan Fathy.)

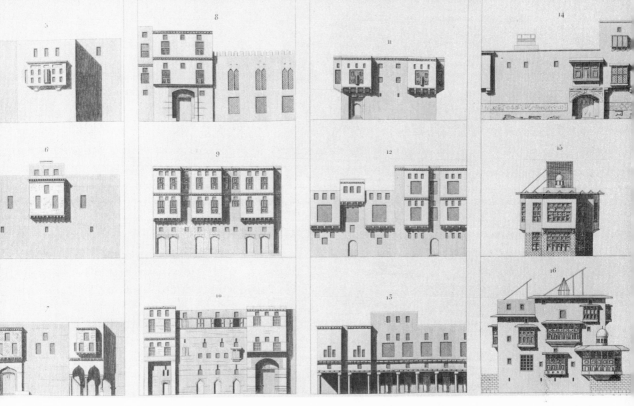

34. Examples of traditional Egyptian housing styles, *ca.* 1800. Nos. 5-7 from Alexandria, 8-10 Rosetta, 11-13 Damietta and 14-16 Cairo. (From: *Description de l'Egypte.*)

35. Lithograph depicting traditional upper-class housing styles along the canal in Cairo during the early years of the nineteenth century. (From: M. J. Marcel, *Egypte depuis la conquête des Arabes,* Paris, 1877.)

concentrated in the walled nucleus of Al-Qahirah, only slightly expanded from its Fatimid dimensions. A sizeable number, however, inhabited the area sprawled outside the walls, chiefly to the south and west, for suburban developments had withered on the north and were blocked by desert on the east. Most densely developed of the extra-mural areas was the region between the southern wall and the high perch of Saladin's Citadel; there were also spotty developments to the west: at the old land-locked port of Al-Maqs (now Cairo's train station); along the borders of the still periodically-flooded Azbakiyah (now the modern central business district); and in the "disorderly" quarter of Al-Luq (near the American University in Cairo). In all, about 250,000 persons lived in this core. Most were unskilled or semi-skilled peasants, laborers, and artisans; a small proportion was engaged in commerce; and a very tiny proportion of ethnically-distinct Turks, Circassians, and Albanians constituted the governing elite. Another 10,000-15,000 persons lived in the geographically distinct port town of Bulaq, while a few thousand others, chiefly Christians and Jews, lived in the tiny nucleus that had survived from Fustat (by then called Misr al-Qadimah, or "the old center").

Over the centuries, the narrow streets of the city had suffered from encroachment and were often completely choked by structures. The residential and even commercial-industrial quarters were subdivided into numerous cells, each with a single access that was barricaded and guarded. Dirt roads (no longer sprinkled and cleaned as they had been in the Middle Ages when urban Europeans were still sloshing through their own garbage-strewn pathways) were dusty and offal-laden, crowded with men, donkeys, and camels. Shopkeepers, perched on their high stone benches in front of tiny inventory cubicles,

Pls. 17-18 (64-65)
Pls. 32-33 (98)
Pl. 108 (327)

preferred ceremonial pipes to high-ranking customers, performed their prayers, and cajoled passersby with running advertisements. Workmen pounded metal pots and vessels, worked leather into saddles and sandals, and wove cloth and rugs on hand-shuttle looms. Venders hawked breads, grilled meats, and cool drinks. Vegetable stalls and open markets displayed redundant items in season only. All but slave women were veiled, and once a week a special flag hanging

Pls. 34-35 (99)
Pls. 102-103 (321)
Pl. 105 (323)

before the public baths signaled "ladies' day." The houses of the wealthy boasted delicately turned and intricately detailed wooden lattice windows, and turned inward on fountained courtyards from which diverged the separate male and female quarters; the poor often squatted in deserted ruins. The few European residents of the city huddled in isolation within the Muski quarter, pacing the Rosetti Gardens in the evening and dreaming of a home continent not easily reached, since there were no regular ships between Egypt and Europe. Cairo was, then, a not atypical example of a preindustrial city, but its transformation had already begun.

When Muhammad Ali had a European carriage delivered, it was the first such vehicle most Cairenes had ever seen.[2] When some wealthy Turks built houses along the newly-opened Shubra Road and installed rectangular glass windows in them, people came to stare. When Muhammad Ali began to construct his "enormous" factories—a foundry, a bleaching plant, some textile mills, and a

----

2 Napoleon had one earlier and briefly.

printing press—near the new ship-building installation at Bulaq port, the novelty drew gawkers. Municipal housekeeping was revived; streets were once again swept and sprinkled; refuse was carted to the outskirts to be sifted and burned; dun-colored structures were shored up and white-washed; a police force supplemented the private guards; and pedestrians were required to carry lanterns at night. By the end of his reign in 1848, links with Europe were well established. Steamships plied regularly between Bulaq and European ports; Muhammad Ali was reading a private Turkish translation of Machiavelli's *The Prince;* and Egyptian scholars recently returned from Europe were busy describing its technology and translating histories of the various countries and the writings of Montesquieu.[3] Ten years before his death, Muhammad Ali had even begun to negotiate with an English engineer for a railroad which would have been, had the plans gone through, one of the first in the world. These changes all laid the foundation for a new form of city building, but the city was not yet ready for expansion. The levelling of refuse heaps on the outskirts, the draining and filling of marshy depressions, and the landscaping of peripheral palaces prepared the way for an urban growth which could not take place until population increase and economic prosperity demanded it.

That period arrived by the 1860s. By then, Muhammad Ali's grandson, Ismail, had inherited the throne. He came in on the crest of a boom which in itself testified to Egypt's new relationship with the world. During the American Civil War, the supply of cotton from the American south to the textile mills of Lancaster was virtually cut off, and the British turned to Egypt, where long staple cotton had been introduced as an important crop by Muhammad Ali. By then, a railroad was in operation to supplement the ships, and the Suez Canal was under construction. The price of Egyptian cotton soared, creating fortunes for a few, stimulating population increase, and yielding capital which Ismail needed to finance his industrialization program and to support his lavish court. When the boom collapsed, these activities were not curtailed; the spiralling deficits were simply filled through usurious loans which Ismail contracted with the less-than-scrupulous financial houses of Europe.

Cairo's decisive turning point came between 1867 and 1869, before the delayed impact of Ismail's fiscal irresponsibility struck. In the former year Paris hosted an *Exposition Universelle* to introduce the "Haussmannized" city to the world. Egypt was invited to participate, and she won medals and acclaim for elaborate displays. Ismail personally opened the exhibits and toured the redeveloped city with Baron Haussmann as his guide. Shamed—or jealous—he returned to Cairo resolved to renovate his own capital and play host to European royalty in a gigantic celebration which would commemorate the opening of the Suez Canal and would display a new, "modern" Cairo. Importing a French landscape architect who had helped plan the *Exposition Universelle* and harnessing considerable Egyptian talent as well, he began to "set the stage." Two years of furiously-paced activity followed. By 1869, not only had a French-style

---

[3] Their headquarters was the Palace of Muhammad Bay al-Alfi which Napoleon had used for his command office and which Abbas I later give to Samuel Shepheard for his first hotel.

town been built along the Canal but an attempt had been made to "convert" Cairo into a similar image. The newer central business district at Azbakiyah was enlarged by additional structures (including an opera house for which he commissioned the writing of *Aida*) and embellished with a French-landscaped park on the filled lake; the parts of the older city that could not be hidden were ambitiously cleaned and painted; and a vast new quarter, Ismailiyah, was laid out west and southwest of the existing city, complete with straight paved streets and *ronds points* following the latest Parisian fashion. Hastily landscaped thorough-fares connected Cairo with the pyramids. Gas lights illuminated a few selected spots, and a water system was partially installed. Behind this papier-mâché mask

Pl. 38 (110)

lay the real Cairo basically unchanged. At this point, modernization remained merely symbolic and superficial. The next few decades saw the fleshing out of this skeleton, but in a manner not quite anticipated by Ismail.

Only ten years after the optimistic opening of the Suez Canal which was to bring prosperity, progress, and national power, the European creditors had foreclosed on Egypt (now a tempting target); Britain had purchased at bankruptcy price all the Egyptian shares in the Canal; Ismail had been deposed and sent into exile; and an abortive constitutionalist movement was ready to be crushed. The autonomy Egypt had so recently "purchased" from Istanbul was lost to the British Foreign Office, operating under nominal Turkish fore-bearance. From 1882 until 1936 (and even beyond), Great Britain was *the* power in Egypt. Under her protective umbrella, Europeans built a self-contained, exclusivist city on the land planned and subdivided by Ismail. Once this zone had been filled in, expansion continued still farther to the west. In the first decades of the twentieth century, the luxurious Nile front came into being when that land was finally made flood-free by a low dam at Aswan; still later, the city expanded onto the island in the middle of the Nile (the Gezira) and, with the completion of bridges, onto the western shore of the river as well. Even before this, however, Cairo had become a dual city, and her physical mitosis clearly reflected the deeper bifurcation—social, cultural, and political—within Egyptian society.

On one side of this "great divide" was the mass of Egyptians who still lived and worked in the traditional city that covered all the terrain that was in urban use before Ismail. The rhythm of their life still revolved around Islam, around their neighborhood cells, around their small-scale crafts and highly personalized commerce; technologically, the driving force was still animate energy, and few of the "newfangled" improvements of paved passable streets, electric lights, water conduits, and telephones touched upon their quarters or, indeed, upon their lives.

On the other side of the social divide, and on the other side of the city, was the "elite," a peculiar amalgam of British civil servants and army officers, Italian, Belgian, French, and Greek entrepreneurs as well as descendants of the Cir-cassian-Turkish-Albanian ruling class with French-culture pretensions. There were Egyptian Copts benefiting from preferential British employment, Syrian and Lebanese Christian exiles, a motley assortment of Maltese, Cypriots, and even erstwhile Egyptians clever enough to claim foreign nationality and thus gain the protection and special privileges accorded to non-Egyptians under the Capitulations. These groups coalesced in the western quarters of the city, supporting a host of self-contained institutions and facilities (the Turf Club, the Gezira Sporting Club and racetrack, the opera, special cotillions and balls) and demanding even more elegant urban amenities from a government to which they paid no taxes. *Their* city had horse-drawn victorias clattering down wide, tree-lined streets; *their* citizens held elegant teas and dinner parties in ornately embellished Parisian apartments or classic villas furnished in the style of Louis XV; *they* were served not only by municipal electric and water systems but by an enormous army of menials drawn from "the natives."

The peak of this bifurcation was reached by 1917, when foreigners constituted more than 10% of the city's population. In that year, the exclusive quarter of Azbakiyah-Ismailiya contained more than 56,000 residents, of whom only 14,000 were Egyptian Muslims—and many of these were resident servants! Cairo was to spend the next fifty years erasing this fissure in her physical and social constitution which had become so marked by World War I. The gap was still clearly evident in the 1940s and only recently have the final traces of it been disappearing.

To evaluate the radical transformation which Cairo achieved within the most recent fifty years, we must reconstruct Cairo as she appeared at the end of World War I. At the time of the census of 1917, the city, generously bounded to include an area of about 160 square kilometers on both sides of the Nile, registered a population of close to 800,000 inhabitants. In addition to the oldest quarters, which by then housed only half of the total population, there were the newer quarters to the west (European in style) which accounted for slightly more than one-fourth of the total, and in addition a newly developing urban quarter on the north where one out of five Cairenes resided. Both population growth and physical expansion had quickened their pace since the turn of the century, the former the result of a demographic revolution within Egypt, the latter the result of a revolution in transport technology which had introduced mass transit and then automobiles to the city. The war stimulated even more changes, and these were consolidated during the prosperous 1920s.

Formerly a debtor nation, Egypt emerged after World War I as a creditor, with England owing her large sums. War dislocations and the requirements of the British army had protected and encouraged local entrepreneurial efforts, and a nascent industrialization was underway. Labor had flocked to the city; their increased demand for housing and the capital accumulated from war-stimulated industries and service ventures combined to generate locally-financed urban expansion on a large scale. While political progress fell far short of nationalist demands, by 1924 the British Protectorate status had been converted to constitutional monarchy, although Britain continued to exercise her will through the Egyptian royal family. While true autonomy remained elusive, symbolic political and economic autonomy had been gained.

The heyday of foreign control, while not over, was ending. New developments within the city reflected this reorientation. Of all quarters, middle- and working-class zones for Egyptian residents expanded most rapidly. These districts worked their way into the interstices between the "medieval" city and the fancier "western" city, sprawled to the north and northeast along transportation routes, jumped the river to proliferate on the western shore, and spread southward toward Misr al-Qadimah. As the emerging Egyptian semi-elite of businessmen, bankers, lawyers, and other professionals began to move up in the social structure and out in the urban structure, their places were more than filled by a growing stream of rural migrants. These rural folk, both those newly arrived and those newly incorporated into the city by boundary enlargements, added an element of peasantry to the city.[4] The original preindustrial traditional core, only slightly transformed since 1800, persisted. To this had been added the foreign and as yet undissolved "lump" of European urbanism, exemplified by the colonial appendage-city. At the edge of these historic accretions was being added a vast, rapidly-growing, jerry-built city for Egyptians who were neither peasants, medieval residuals, nor locals "disguised" as Europeans. These zones contained elements of each of these "cultures" but were beginning to demonstrate a new strain of coalescence in Egyptian society.

During the next few decades these trends continued. The British political presence, officially removed by the Treaty of 1936 but reestablished as a military force in the strategically-essential Canal Zone, was increasingly viewed as a total affront. The colonial appendage became more and more of an anomaly, as Egyptians increasingly proved themselves capable of running a modern state. All the symbols of wealth, power, and oppression were concentrated in the "western" city. And it was clear that this wealth and power were not being used to lighten the load of peasants and urban workers; rather, the latter were being exploited to support a standard of living which drew its inspiration from Europe. The class structure, which still evidenced enormous gaps between the very rich and the very poor, was gradually beginning to develop in the middle ranks. These changes in the economic structure, however, were not paralleled by commensurate changes in the distribution of power.

In 1952, Cairo remained fundamentally bifurcated near the center of the city, despite the fact that to the north and extreme west vast working- and middle-class "cities" had grown up. At the central business district the social and physical boundary between "East" and "West" was still sharply drawn along a north-south axis that ran from the Bab al-Hadid train station southward behind the Azbakiyah Gardens and on down to the vicinity of the Abdin Palace. This line corresponded roughly to the boundary between the historic city of Al-Qahirah (and its peripheral outcroppings) and the modern city built in the nineteenth and twentieth centuries. The pressures building up at this symbolic wall exploded spontaneously and symbolically, ushering in a new era in the histories of Egypt and Cairo.

The explosion, known as "Black Friday," occurred early in 1952. In response to news that the British had killed almost 90 Egyptian policemen in the Canal Zone, which they still occupied, Cairo's outraged masses stormed the

---

[4] Throughout the twentieth century, at least one-third of Cairo's population has been born outside the city, primarily in the rural provinces of Egypt.

invisible barrier between the "two cities," venting incendiary hostility upon the symbols of the oppressor. In the riot that swept the western "downtown," Shepheard's Hotel, the British Turf Club, the foreign "cinema palaces," and the elegant shops owned by foreigners were all set on fire. The Egyptian revolution had begun, although it was not until July that it achieved political expression and form by an overdue military coup, and it was not until 1956 that the hated British were finally expelled from the Canal.

The city has undergone substantial change since that critical moment in Egyptian history. If we assume that cities reflect their circumstances, this could not have been otherwise. Land reforms instituted after 1952 truncated the old Turco-Egyptian elite whose urban consumption style had been unwillingly subsidized by the labor of destitute rural serfs; the Western European elite was finally destroyed in 1956 at the time of the Suez invasion, when many left the country; middle-class southern Europeans—Greeks and, to a lesser extent, Italians—were displaced more gradually through "nationality laws" governing business management. The royal and foreign apex of the social structure was thus cut off. On the other hand, programs of land reform, industrial development, expanded educational facilities, and income redistribution caused a significant leavening from below. If Cairo is no longer so elegant in certain quarters as she was twenty years ago, she is not nearly so destitute and pathetic in others. The knitting together of Egypt's torn social structure has been perhaps the greatest and most lasting achievement of the Revolution of 1952. What is emerging today in Cairo, and what is likely to constitute her most essential quality in the future, is a more culturally unified, and a more economically homogeneous city in which the symbols of class and cultural extremes have been truncated. While historic inheritances have left massive traces on the physical appearance of many quarters, and while differences in speech, dress, and culture   Pl. 40 (114) are still quite obvious to an observer viewing her for the first time, these are but dim and blurred residuals from the sharp cleavages and contrasts which constituted her essence only a decade or two ago. Thus, the final perspective from which to view Cairo's prospects for tomorrow is mid-century.

The critical turning point came between the national census of 1947 and that of 1960, and data from these years best prepare us for an understanding of the contemporary city. By the former year, Egypt's population had increased to almost twenty million (as compared to three million in 1800), of which Cairo's population accounted for two million. The city's inhabitants were distributed throughout the metropolitan region in a manner that reflected the declining importance, demographically and economically, of the older traditional form of urbanism and the expanding significance of indigenous and modern urbanization. Only a third of the population lived, tightly packed, in the oldest quarters of the city—the medieval core and the two slum quarters that had developed around the old ports of Bulaq and Misr al-Qadimah (Fustat). The western city, despite vigorous growth and expanding dimensions, contained only one-fourth of the city's population, and it was no longer as exclusive as it had been. Almost 40% of the population lived in the newer northern quarters which were making deeper and deeper inroads on the rich agricultural land of the Egyptian Delta.

By 1960, the date of the first post-revolution census, Egypt's population had increased to over twenty-six million, and Cairo's had grown even more rapidly to approach three and a half million.[5] By then, the oldest quarters were bulging at the seams and a sizeable overflow had invaded the desert cemetery cities to the east and south. Even so, the oldest quarters contained less than a fourth of the city's inhabitants. The "western" city, by then equally saturated and absorbing numbers only through the replacement of open areas and the few remaining villas with tall apartment houses, contained another quarter of the population. In marked contrast to the declining relative status of the medieval and nineteenth-century cities was the continued growth of the twentieth-century city on the north, which, by 1960, could claim with a fair degree of accuracy to have become the *real* Cairo, even though her undistinguished architecture and nondescript streets still kept her virtually invisible and off the beaten track for most outsiders. Half of Cairo's population lived in this sprawling accretion. And here, more than anywhere else, was the crucible in which the Cairo of tomorrow was being forged.

Since 1960, population growth has continued to constitute the basic parameter of urban change and the critical root cause of Cairo's problems, which have increasingly become less exotic and more familiar to those of us who take metropolitan America as an unconscious model of urbanism. As yet, Cairo's population remains uncounted, awaiting the next census. Estimates vary widely. A simple exponential projection from 1960 would yield a 1970 population for Egypt as a whole in the vicinity of thirty-three to thirty-five million, and a population of Cairo in excess of five million. Most Cairo planners gave an even higher estimate, when interviewed in the summer of 1969, the unanticipated spurt attributable to evacuations from the Canal Zone forced by the Israeli invasion of 1967. Newspaper accounts place the size of that evacuation at half a million persons, most of whom have been resettled in Cairo; private estimates agree that the number is even larger. The Higher Planning Committee of Greater Cairo is working with six and a half million as the estimated population of the metropolitan region which exceeds the official boundaries of the Cairo Governorate. This is probably an accurate figure.

Thus, Cairo's population almost doubled in the decade 1960-70. The sources of growth were threefold. First, there was continued rapid growth through natural increase; the difference between birth and death rates in the city suggests an estimated *annual natural increase* rate of 3% per year. Furthermore, large-scale migration from the rural hinterlands has continued, contributing annually almost as many new Cairenes as were added through natural increase. Suddenly supplementing these steadier sources of population growth was a massive dose of urban-to-urban "migration," as refugees from the highly developed Canal cities of Port Said, Ismailiya, and Suez were relocated in Cairo. The result has been as dramatic as if another ten million persons had been added to New York in a decade. What city, no matter how well prepared, would be

---

[5] Boundaries of the city were changed in the interim. This is our estimate of the population within the older 1947 city limits.

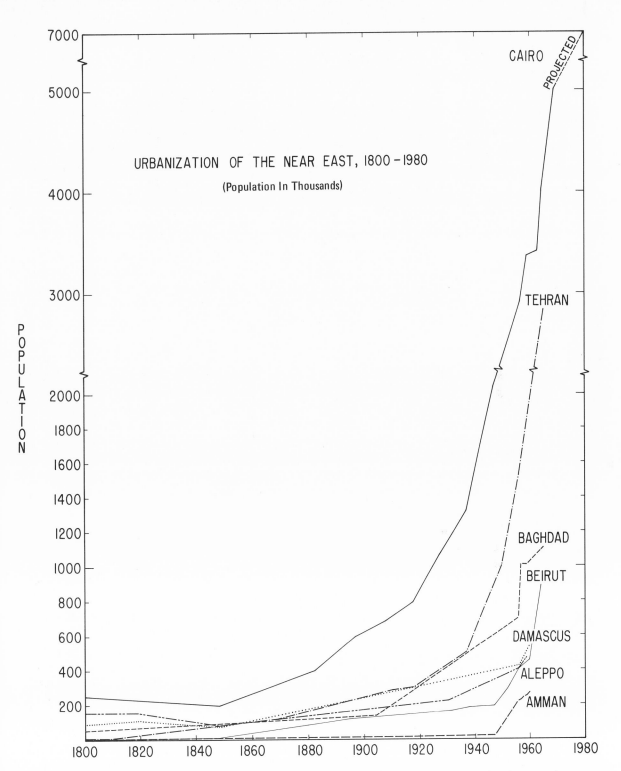

Fig. 3. Urbanization of the Near East, 1800-1980. Urban population has increased at a dramatic rate since 1900, and so has the proportion of total population living in cities. For instance, Amman contained 2.1% of the total population in Jordan in 1915; in 1957, the percentage rose to 9.7%. About 13% of Egypt's population lives in Cairo. The population density of the "Old City" throughout the Near East has reached a high level: 610 people per hectare in Damascus; 750/hectare in Aleppo. The ideal is considered about 300/hectare. (The European average is 150-200/hectare.) (Compiled by Edward H. Breisacher based on information extracted from *The New Metropolis in the Arab World* [Morroe Berger, ed., 1961] and *Middle Eastern Cities* [Ira P. Lapidus, ed., 1969], as well as from this book.)

able to cope adequately with the consequences? It should not surprise us, then, that Cairo has serious problems; what continues to surprise me is how well the city survives and develops under conditions which would have long since defeated a less resilient society. Civility and order persist, despite density conditions that drive Norway rats and New Yorkers alike into destructive, anti-social behavior.

Population pressures have overloaded most urban facilities and have overtaxed Cairo's housing supply. After World War II, Cairo, like many other cities caught by war-time backlogs, suffered from a deficit of housing, from a circulation system inadequate to accommodate increasing numbers of cars and trucks, and from a growing demand for water, sewers, electricity and telephones generated by an expanding population and their heightened expectations. The social revolution intensified these needs by giving ideological legitimacy to demands that came from all quarters of the city, no longer just from the "fortunate few."

Substantial progress was made in the 1950s and early 1960s to solve many of the worst problems and to distribute urban amenities more evenly—until the war of June 1967 when all projects were halted temporarily. Essential highways, such as the Corniche, Ramses, and Port Said streets, and most recently the Salah Salim by-pass route, were built or improved to relieve vehicular congestion. A vigorous program of public housing was initiated, following the lead of Workers' City in Imbabah and expanding to over ten thousand new units in projects scattered throughout the city. A modest beginning was made in publicly-supported, middle-income housing, and whole "new town" develop-ments were begun on the western shore (Madinat Awqaf and Madinat al-Muhandisin) and on the eastern, desert-mountain edge (Muqattam City, some-what of a disappointment, and Nasr City,[6] an impressive achievement thus far). Industrial developments and associated housing estates were judiciously located beyond the built-up city to take some of the load off the central zones. Plans were reactivated for an old and recurring dream, the installation of a subway system to supplement the severely overcrowded surface system of electric trams, metros, and buses.

Pl. 37 (109)

Some of these projects progressed more slowly than anticipated, since they required foreign exchange and hard currencies. Some, no matter how quickly they were executed, still could not keep pace with the rapidly increasing needs of people and cars. We must remember that Egypt had more problems than those which plagued Cairo, and that even many of Cairo's best-laid plans foundered on external, not internal, difficulties. The hard currencies for which the sewerage system went begging (until it finally burst and was replaced in an emergency "war") were needed for arms and defense. Peasants, who had for centuries been shortchanged by the urban-based power elite, commanded a legitimate share of the national resources. Capital investments in industrial plants wisely took precedence over consumer needs such as housing. Desperate if relatively unsuccessful efforts were directed toward slowing down the rate of migration to the capital and toward checking the rate of population increase.

---

[6] This new town will eventually contain 500,000 residents.

36. View of Cairo from the Nile showing the Arab League Building on the left and the Nile Hilton hotel on the right. (Photo: Bayard Dodge.)

37. Cairo. New Boulevard and bridge over the Nile. Gezira Island can be seen in the background. (Photo: Carol Baldwin.)

38. Panorama of Cairo. Most buildings in the foreground represent the Westernized architectural style that predominated from the time of Khedive Ismail (1863-79) until well into
the twentieth century. In the background, especially along the Nile, are to be seen more
recent forms of Westernized architecture. The cylindrical tower in the center background is
post-1952. The relative absence of indigenous architectural forms in this picture strikingly
demonstrates the extent of Westernization. (Photo: Egyptian Tourist Office.)

By 1967, while one certainly could not say that Cairo had even begun to solve her incredibly challenging problems, she was not doing too badly. Because of the undeniable redistribution of income, it was difficult to reconcile that relatively prosperous-looking city with tales of financial insolvency. Here was no Delhi or Calcutta. Most people were adequately fed and well-dressed. Most of them had made the transition from the older style garments—the black gown and head veil of the women and the flowing Gallabiyah "nightshirt" of the men—to European style clothing. New Czech rolling stock had been added to the archaic public transit system. Tourism, a "natural" resource, was doing well, stimulated by lowered air fares, new or renovated hotels administered by the Ministry of Tourism, and a trained staff manning information offices and travel agencies. Decrepit taxis and cars, which had given Cairo a reputation for being an auto graveyard, had been increasingly replaced and supplemented by locally-assembled Fiats. Whereas the Suez War in 1956 had suddenly restricted imports and left the shops of Cairo devoid of all luxuries and a good many "almost necessities," like canned foods, paper products, and even pencils and matches, this was an experience not likely to recur. Since that time, Egyptian industry had filled the vacuum and all but highly complex producers' goods were being manufactured locally. These industries had given employment to many within the city and had provided training and experience for their workers as well as inexpensive products for their growing number of local customers. Thus, modernization was beginning to touch more and more Cairenes; it was only the newly-arrived peasant and the aged hard-core traditionalist who remained insulated. There was, in short, no reason to believe that, although Cairo was temporarily caught in the updraft of development and consequently experiencing crises due to rapid change and growth, she would not eventually pull out with a measure of control and mastery. Certainly, her modernization was broader-based than ever before and was guided by an increasingly trained and experienced elite.

The June War of 1967 suddenly clouded this optimistic prospectus and, at least during the few years that have elapsed, crystal gazing has become impossible. There are moments in any city's history when the future can be foretold from a judicious understanding of the present; there are other periods when discontinuities and extra-urban events loom so unpredictably that prayers supplant predictions. Today, Cairo's future hangs more upon externalities than upon simple trend projections. The present fragile state of neither peace nor outright war has bred among Egyptians that strangely subdued psychology of people at the edge of the volcano. Planning and urban improvements go on, but the conviction had waned that these efforts will solve the more basic problem that besets Egypt. Cairo has, however, remarkable staying power. Throughout the peaks and troughs of a thousand years, Cairo survived as the city victorious. Many times, when invaders were at the gates or even within, those who loved the city must have feared and despaired. History, however, has proved the pessimists short-sighted. Even now the city beats with a vital pulse of recovery, urban improvements are strikingly visible (Maydan Tahrir has just been totally replanned), and the rising decibel level in the streets indicates that the irrepressible Egyptian exuberance cannot remain subdued for too long without breaking through.

Pl. 36 (109)
38 (110)

BIBLIOGRAPHIC NOTES

The literature dealing with Cairo prior to the nineteenth century is significantly richer than that covering the modernization of the city. Few books cover both the old and new cities, and even fewer are oriented toward contemporary problems. The following bibliographic notes reflect more the availability of sources than the writer's evaluation of their significance in the larger picture.

Among the literally hundreds of general social histories of Cairo, the most comprehensive and scholarly are Marcel Clerget, *Le Caire: Étude de géographie urbaine et d'histoire économique* (Cairo: E. & R. Schindler, 1934) in two volumes, which traces city development from inception to 1927, and Janet Abu-Lughod, *Cairo: 1001 Years of the City Victorious* (Princeton: Princeton University Press, 1971), which analyzes the dynamics and structure of Cairo up to 1967 and focuses upon the emergence of modern problems. Briefer, somewhat less scholarly, general studies are to be found in Desmond Stewart, *Cairo: 5500 Years* (New York: Thomas Y. Crowell, 1968) and James Aldridge, *Cairo: Biography of a City* (Boston: Little, Brown and Company, 1969). General histories, focusing primarily on early developments (pre-nineteenth century), are also available in Arabic, notably Shihatah Ibrahim, *Al-Qahirah* (Cairo: Dar al-Hilal, no date but probably 1959), and 'Abd al-Rahman Zaki, *Al-Qahirah...969-1825* (Cairo: Dar al-Tiba'ah al-Hadithah, 1966), for which a sequel for the modern period is promised. The most comprehensive study in Arabic thus far is Fuad Faraj's three-volume work, *Al-Qahirah* (Cairo: Dar al-Ma'arif, 1946). An attractive book consisting chiefly of illustrations and photographs of the city was issued by the Egyptian Ministry of Culture in honor of the thousandth anniversary of the city. Available in English, French, or German editions, it is entitled *Cairo: Life Story of 1000 Years.*

Primary sources are indispensable and available but they must be culled to extract the history of Cairo from the general history of Egypt. Among the most basic are: Taqi al-Din Ahmad al-Maqrizi, *Al-Mawa'iz wa al-I'tibar fi Dhikr al-Khitat wa al-Athar,* in two volumes (Cairo: Bulaq Press, 1853), which covers the city's growth up to about A.D. 1420; and Abu al-Mahasin ibn Taghri Birdi's *History of Egypt,* which has been translated into English by William Popper and printed serially between 1954 and 1960 in the University of California Publications in Semitic Philology; it covers the period between A.D. 1382 and 1469. These have traditionally served as major sources on pre-Ottoman Cairo. Numerous fragmented accounts must be used for the Ottoman period.

By the late eighteenth century, the sources become fuller again. Perhaps the three most important sources for anyone wishing to reconstruct the city just before it entered the modern transformative period are: selected essays (especially that by Jomard) in *Description de l'Égypte,* a multi-volumed work produced by the scholars attached to Napoleon's expedition to Egypt; the voluminous work by 'Abd al-Rahman al-Jabarti, translated into French under the title, *Merveilles Biographiques et Historiques,* which covers the pre- and post-French period; and the observations (beginning around 1826) of Edward William Lane, incorporated into his *An Account of the Manners and Customs of the Modern Egyptians* (first issued in two volumes by Charles Knight and Company, London, 1836, but most commonly available in third-edition form, as published by Dent, London, 1860, and subsequently reissued) and even more explicitly in the volume his nephew, Stanley Lane-Poole, edited from his notes, *Cairo Fifty Years Ago* (London: John Murray, 1896).

For the nineteenth century, the basic primary source on the city is Ali Mubarak, *Al-Khitat al-Tawfiqiyah al-Jadidah* (Cairo: Bulaq Press, 1888) in twenty volumes, which includes, in addition to encyclopedic information on Egypt, large sections on developments in Cairo. The multi-volumed archival documents assembled by Amin Sami, in his *Taqwim al-Nil* (Cairo: Dar al-Kutub al-Misriya, 1936), are also indispensable for the nineteenth century. In Western languages, the best source for the era of Ismail, when the modern city of Cairo was begun, is Georges Douin's *Histoire du règne du Khèdive Ismail* (Rome, 1933 and 1934) in two volumes.

By the twentieth century, the research becomes more complex. The encyclopedic efforts of earlier historians were not duplicated by contemporary scholars. As the city became more complex, specialized studies superseded overall accounts of the city. The only comprehensive study, albeit one of spotty quality, was that prepared between 1953 and 1956 for the *Master Plan of Cairo*. This was printed but never released to the public. The student must look, instead, to the specific studies that have been published in the periodic literature or issued as specialized monographs. While it is well beyond the scope of this note to cite them, a few examples can be given: on traffic and transportation, the monograph by Mustafa Niyazi, *Al-Qahirah: Dirasat Takhtitiyah fi al-Murur wa al-Naql wa al-Muwasalat* (Cairo: Anglo-Egyptian Library, 1958-1959); on local government, Harold Alderfer, et al., *Local Government in the United Arab Republic* (UAR: Institute of Public Administration, 1963, and revised in 1964); as well as an increasing number of official publications by various ministries. The only comprehensive attempt to discuss the twentieth-century transformation of the city appears in Abu-Lughod, *Cairo: 1001 Years of the City Victorious*, cited earlier.

39. Residential quarters for foreign students, primarily of the Al-Azhar University, in Abbassiya district of Cairo. Severely utilitarian, uniform, and Neo-Western except for a passing nod to Near Eastern architectural style in mosque (center picture). (Photo: Bayard Dodge.)

40. Cairo. Gate and bazaar street near Khan Khalili; men in traditional and Western attire, traditional craftsmen and modern jewelry store. (Photo: Carol Baldwin.)

41. Cairo. Bab al-Futuh, built in 1092, a gate of the old city walls. (Photo: Richard Parker.)

42. Fez, Morocco. Bab Shorfa, entrance gate of the Madina. (Photo: Office National Marocain du Tourisme.)

4

Urbanization and Urbanism in Beirut: Some Preliminary Results

by Samir Khalaf and Per Kongstad

THE growing literature on urbanization and comparative ecology is finally beginning to free scholars from exclusive reliance on Western models and experience for understanding the dimensions of urbanization in the Third World. Encouraged by the promising conceptual and methodological advances recently made by Janet Abu-Lughod and Brian Berry in social area analysis and factorial studies of Cairo and Calcutta,[1] the authors are undertaking a broad, multi-dimensional study of urbanization in Beirut, surveying the changing urban patterns and ecological processes that continue to unfold in Beirut, and studying the impact of such transformations on the quality of urban life. More specifically, the study seeks to explore the ways various socio-economic groups and communities have reacted to swift urbanization, and particularly to what extent "urbanization" as a physical phenomenon has been accompanied by "urbanism" as a way of life.[2] This chapter sets forth some of the preliminary results of this study.

A Few General Observations

Beirut is a most challenging and inviting place for the urban scholar and city planner because it is one of the oldest cities on the Eastern Mediterranean shore and has a rich and eventful history and because it has always displayed some curious and paradoxical features which have shaped its rise and fall as an urban

Part of a broader study of urbanization in Beirut undertaken by the authors. Research is sponsored by the Middle East area program, AUB, with funds granted by the Advanced Research Project Agency and the Danish International Developing Agency.

[1] Janet L. Abu-Lughod, "Testing the Theory of Social Area Analysis: The Ecology of Cairo, Egypt," *American Sociological Review* 34 (April 1969): 198-211; Brian J. L. Berry and P. H. Rees, "The Factorial Ecology of Calcutta," *The American Journal of Sociology* 74 (March 1969): 445-491.

[2] The study has three dimensions: 1) *Historical*: travelers' accounts, archives, and oral history are being used in an effort to survey the rise and fall of Beirut as a primate city. 2) *Ecological*: through an exhaustive land-use survey and door-to-door mapping, densities, land-use patterns, and ecological processes are being surveyed. Grid-net techniques are employed to analyze data cell by cell. 3) *Sociological*: through a household survey, the socio-demographic characteristics of the residential units and the impact of urbanization are analyzed.

center. As an imposing Roman colony it manifested a rational planning which is tragically absent today. The city was completely wiped out by a score of earthquakes and fires, threatened by plagues and famines, and ransacked and destroyed by successive waves of unfriendly invaders. Yet it has survived all. Despite its compelling site and favorable geographic location, it remained for centuries, surprisingly, a small and insignificant agglomeration. As recently as the late eighteenth century, the population of Beirut was estimated at 6,000 and in 1848 at not more than 15,000. After 1860, however, a rural exodus began which has never ceased.

As in Egypt, migration from rural areas has been mainly responsible for Lebanon's soaring rates of urbanization. Since almost two-thirds of this internal migration has been directed towards Beirut, the capital has trebled its residential population between 1952 and 1964, totalling an estimated 893,000 in 1964. In more striking terms, Beirut now comprises nearly 72% of Lebanon's urban population and 41% of the inhabitants of the country. In addition, the city has to accommodate an estimated 120,000 daily commuters from neighboring suburbs.[3] In this sense, urbanization in Beirut is associated with primacy or

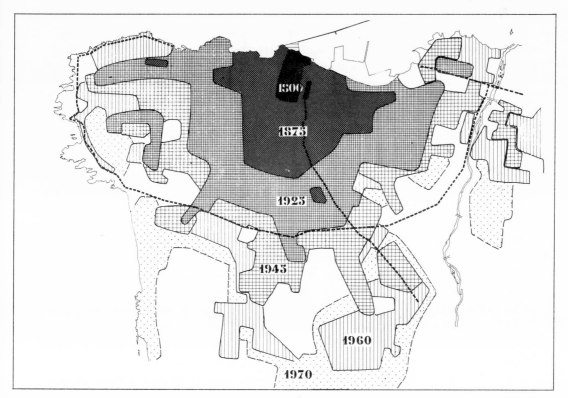

Fig. 4. Beirut's development in stages. (Executive Board of Major Projects for the city of Beirut.)

[3] Isis Raghleb (Southall), "Patterns of Urban Growth in the Middle East," in *The City in Newly Developing Countries*, ed. Gerald Breese (Englewood Cliffs: Prentice-Hall, 1969), p. 110.

metropolitan dominance: the primate city of Beirut now having five times the population of the second largest city (Tripoli), and the second four times that of the third (Zahle). The degree of urbanization is higher than would be expected from the level of industrialization, and Lebanon is among the few countries—along with Egypt, Greece, and Korea—that may be considered "over-urbanized." [4]

As a result, Beirut exhibits nearly all the disquieting symptoms of an exploding metropolis. The scale and scope of urbanization has outstripped the city's resources to cope effectively with the mounting demand for urban space. All the successive efforts of master planning and zoning—the Danger Plan of 1932, the Ecochard Plan of 1944, the Egli Report of 1950, and the general Master Plan of 1954—have failed to curb its haphazard and unguided growth.[5] It is estimated that the area of Beirut is now three times what it was in 1900 and about 100 times what it was in 1800[6] (see Fig. 4). Because of the survival of personal and communal loyalties and interests, planning schemes and zoning ordinances are still unrealized blueprints. Beirut today remains a curious and rare anomaly: perhaps one of the few modern and bourgeoning cities in the world without any exclusively residential zones.

Beirut is also equally forbidding for the scholar who is eager to render its growth and structure more intelligible. Its patterns of growth and ecological processes defy all available concepts and models. Unlike Western cities, Beirut in general presents more types and varieties of urban settlement: more varieties of internal adaptation, of spatial patterning, and of architectural structure. Street plans and block arrangements are not consistent or uniform.

Until 1860, Beirut was a walled medieval town displaying many of the features of the preindustrial city portrayed by Sjoberg.[7] Like most fortified cities, it was organized simply with six main gates enclosing one quarter of a square mile surrounded by gardens. Reminiscent of its seafaring, Phoenician origins, the core of the city was built around the historic port and mole. As in most European preindustrial towns, people in Beirut lived and worked in the same urban quarter. Except for a few social needs met by the suq and public bath, the neighborhood was almost a self-sufficient "cell" with which the individual identified. There was a strong sense of neighborliness, and patterns of behavior were largely regulated through kinship and religious ties. Physical and social space, in other words, were almost identical. Ethnic and religious affiliation created relatively homogeneous and compact quarters or haras. Though traditionally the coastal towns of Lebanon were predominantly Muslim, Beirut eventually became a largely Christian city after 1860.

Residential quarters or "cells" developed in sectors radiating from the urban center and a segregated pattern of residential location based on religion or sect began to emerge. Except for the suq, there was little evidence of areal

[4] N. S. Sovani, "The Analysis of 'Over-Urbanization,' " *Economic Development and Cultural Change* 12 (June 1964): 113-122.

[5] For further details see, Executive Board of Major Projects, *Comprehensive Plan Studies for the City of Beirut* (Beirut: J.S. Saikali, 1968), pp. 5-13.

[6] Ibid., p. 43.

[7] Gideon Sjoberg, *The Preindustrial City: Past and Present* (Glencoe, Ill.: Free Press, 1960).

specialization. Gross density was high—around 300 per hectare—as in most cities at the threshold of urban expansion.

With rapid urbanization this pattern could not naturally sustain itself, and Beirut has been undergoing some swift transformations since the turn of the twentieth century. In this sense, the genesis of true urbanization in Beirut is of recent vintage. Gross densities have remained high with an average of 200 per hectare for Beirut proper and 90 per hectare for the entire metropolitan area, mainly as a consequence of the constant pressure for living space. The supply of developed urban land is very limited compared with the mounting demand; and since the market mechanism is the only factor regulating land use, land values have skyrocketed during the last fifteen years to a level of $200-$400 per square meter for vacant plots in some parts of Beirut. Rents in new housing have gone up correspondingly to a level beyond the reach of most newcomers. Consequently, they have to settle in already crowded houses in the central city now left by the middle class and upper-income groups who prefer modern high-rise apartments at the urban fringe or suburban residence in detached houses.

As zoning regulations are virtually ignored by landowners, additional floors are built on existing houses in densely exploited areas, and courtyards are filled in by new constructions. These constructions also limit the possibilities of street enlargement because high-rise apartments are erected directly at the street limit. The results are painfully obvious: congested traffic and virtually no breathing space in the form of parks, gardens, or playgrounds.

Finally, in the absence of low-cost housing programs—public or private—the overflow of new migrants cannot be accommodated in the central city, and consequently they have to resign themselves to a marginal existence in one of the shantytowns on the urban fringe.

There is nothing unusual about such developments. They are commonly found in most rapidly urbanizing societies of the Third World. What is remarkable about urbanization in Beirut is that the process has not been disruptive or dysfunctional in its consequences. True, urbanization everywhere is nearly always accompanied by dissociative processes and by imbalances, but somehow the mosaic and pluralistic structure of Beirut has managed to cushion some of the discontinuities and tensions inherent in rapid urbanization. Five general observations are worth noting here:

1. Given the multitude of forces which have conditioned the rise and fall of Beirut and the diversity of functions it has continued to play, it is extremely difficult to place Beirut in any one category.[8] In some instances, one may marshal evidence to support the view that the rise and fall of Beirut as an urban center has been associated with its rise and fall as a seat of power. In this sense, it comes close to what Pirenne calls the "Liège type"—i.e., a town of administrative functions. In its historical growth, Beirut also displays some "Flemish" features—a city with primarily commercial and financial functions. As a city of seafaring traders, Beirut has always been the home base of merchants

---

[8] For a historical and theoretical perspective on the changing role of the city see, Gerald Breese, ed., *The City in Newly Developing Countries*, pp. 217-330.

engaging in international trade. But Beirut has also been an intellectual and cultural center. Beginning with its famous law school under the Romans, Beirut's initial and ultimate development is intimately associated with its growth as a center of learning. In brief, Beirut, like the capitals of many European countries, is a multifunctional city.

2. Generally, urbanization in Beirut has been associated with economic growth, industrial diversification, technological change, and social mobility. As a "primate city," to borrow Bert Hoselitz's term, Beirut has been more "generative" than "parasitic."[9] In other words, the growth of Beirut has been more of a stimulus rather than a curb on economic activity. In fact, the increasing scale of urbanization in Beirut has been an integral part of the process of modernization in the entire region.

3. Throughout its history, Beirut has been an effective organ for the fusion of different ethnic, confessional, and socio-economic groups. With increasing urbanization, it has absorbed and assimilated successive waves of migrants and political refugees without any apparent degree of mass violence or urban strife. Except for the civil crisis of 1958, urban life has been marked by little of the mob and street riots or other symptoms of mass protest which accompanied urbanization in other growing cities.

4. In much the same vein, the increasing scale of urbanization·has not been accompanied by increasing rates of social disorganization. Surprisingly, the incidence of criminality and juvenile delinquency in Beirut has not increased over the past ten years in proportion to both the urban and rural populations.[10]

5. Finally, and perhaps most striking, urbanization in Beirut has not meant the erosion of kinship ties, communal loyalties, and confessional affinities and the emergence of impersonality, anonymity, and transitory social relations. As in other dimensions of social life in Lebanon, the network of urban social relations and the character of voluntary associations in the country's capital still sustain a large residue of traditional attachments despite increasing secularism and urbanization. In many respects, Beirut is more of a "mosaic" of distinct urban communities than a "melting pot" of amorphous urban masses. Apart from the multiple agglomerations of village migrants and refugees in specific settlements, one can easily identify three broad communities or urban sub-cultures within Beirut: Achrafieh, Basta, and Ras-Beirut (see Fig. 5).

Achrafieh is a homogeneous Christian (mainly Maronite and Greek Ortho-dox) residential quarter with definite Francophile leanings in both style of life and cultural orientation. The area is predominantly middle and upper class with exclusive residential mansions of the traditional urban aristocracy. Basta is almost entirely Sunni Muslim and of visibly lower socio-economic status. In style of life, the inhabitants are tradition-oriented. Despite their striking differences, both areas have remained relatively homogeneous residential quarters. Since

---

[9] Bert F. Hoselitz, "Generative and Parasitic Cities," *Economic Development and Cultural Change*, no. 3 (April 1955), pp. 278-94.

[10] See Amal Nassar, "Crime in Lebanon" (Master's thesis, Sociology Department, American University of Beirut, 1969); Najla Najjar, "Juvenile Delinquency in a Changing Society" (Master's thesis, Sociology Department, American University of Beirut, 1970).

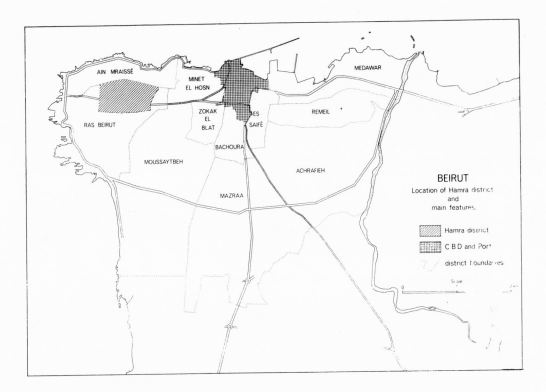

Fig. 5.   Beirut: Location of Hamra district and main features.

Basta is not an administrative unit, it is not shown on Fig. 5. However, Basta is the traditional Sunni Muslim community flanked by Bachoura, the eastern part of Moussaytbeh, and the central part of Mazraa (see Fig. 5). Ras-Beirut (Hamra in particular) is a fast-growing, fashionable and cosmopolitan district with almost no unifying character. Though predominantly middle class and Anglo-Saxon in life style, the area has a heterogeneous ethnic and religious composition. Unlike the two other communities, it has a mixed land-use pattern and because of the invasion of commercial and cultural activities, it is beginning to lose its residential quality and is attracting an increasing proportion of transient and marginal groups.

While the broad metropolitan study of Beirut which will provide us with the necessary comparative data is far from complete, this chapter presents in a more preliminary and descriptive fashion some of the pertinent results of the Hamra survey. As will become readily apparent, Hamra is certainly not a typical urban area in Beirut; perhaps no such comparable metamorphosis exists in other Arab cities. But as a predominantly middle-class area which has gone through a full cycle of swift urbanization in the short span of twenty years, it offers a vivid and interesting case study.

This chapter explores three dimensions of urbanization in Hamra. First, the ecological transformation of Hamra is described through processes of invasion and succession, increasing density, and land-use patterns. Second, the socio-economic profile of the inhabitants is drawn. Finally, an attempt is made to assess

43. Bliss Street, around 1900, with its cactus hedges, flat-roofed farm houses and garden fields.

44. A view of Hamra from the College Tower of the American University of Beirut, around 1900, when the area was still untouched by the encroaching residential invasion.

45. The intersection of **Abdul Aziz** and **Bliss** streets around 1900. Farm houses and suburban villas of the type seen here were the predominant form of housing until the mid-1940s. Curiously, around 70 such farm houses can still be spotted today in the area.

46. A typical example of a modern apartment house which evolved between 1945 and 1955 to cope with the growing demand for urban space. This continues to be the most common form of housing and accounts for nearly 28% of all building types in the area. The ground floor has now been typically converted to a sidewalk cafe.

the extent to which rapid urbanization in Hamra has been accompanied by a significant shift from primary to secondary-group social relations.

THE ECOLOGICAL TRANSFORMATION OF HAMRA

Ecological processes are perhaps the most crucial factors in shaping the physical features and structure of an urban area. The competition for space, the constant influx of diverse population elements, the clustering of people and urban functions, and the resulting areal differentiation are usually instrumental in determining the scale and intensity of urbanization. Hamra is certainly no exception. Throughout its short but intensive history, the process of urbanization in Hamra has been marked by some underlying ecological processes which together have shaped the urban character of the area.

What might be slightly unusual is that its urban growth has been regulated more through the free play of market forces than through deliberate planning or urban zoning. In fact, Hamra grew despite the general conception of the approved Master Plan of 1954 to divert the urban development along the southern axis of metropolitan Beirut.[11] Because of the absence of traditional patterns of land holding, the transfer of land was rendered possible through cadastral legislation. Parcels were individualized as early as 1928, a tendency which must have encouraged land transactions and speculation in real estate as a viable economic venture.

The initial emergence of Hamra might well be considered as a historical accident, more a result of fortuitous circumstances than deliberate urban planning. What could have happened, one might ask, had not Daniel Bliss first laid eyes on this deserted stretch of sand dunes and wild cactus and persuaded the American Board of Commissioners for Foreign Missions to transform the "city's garbage dump" into the site of what has become the most distinguished American academic institution in the Near East? One cannot possibly begin to gauge the consequences of such a likelihood without too much conjecture. One thing is certain though: the scale of urbanization, the physical features, and the quality of urban life in the area would not be what they are today. No other single factor has been as persistent and instrumental in shaping the urban growth of Hamra than the compelling presence of the American University of Beirut (AUB). The growth patterns, the overriding street structure, the ensuing ecological processes as a result of competition for space and location, and the general socio-economic character of the population have all been, in one respect or another, a by-product of this historic accident.

Invasion and Succession

The founding of AUB in 1866 can be clearly singled out as the first instance of institutional invasion of a garden-farming area. The vivid descriptions of Daniel

---

[11] See Executive Board of Major Projects, *Comprehensive Plan Studies for the City of Beirut*, pp. 5-11; George Riashi, "Beirut" in *The New Metropolis in the Arab World*, ed. Morroe Berger (New Delhi: Allied Publishers, 1963), p. 106.

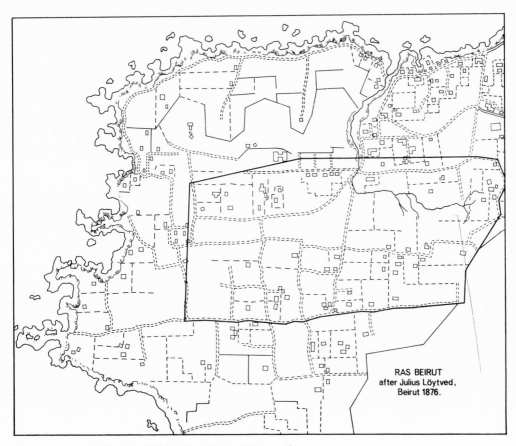

Fig. 6. Ras Beirut in 1876 (after Julius Löytved).

Fig. 7. Beirut, Hamra district, 1967.

Pls. 43-45
(122-123)

Bliss and others attest to this. By the 1870s, as shown on the Löytved map of 1876 (Fig. 6), only a handful of buildings were visible. Apart from a score of twenty-five to thirty scattered farm houses, a few residential villas south of AUB can already be discerned on the map.

By 1919, the two main arteries—Jeanne d'Arc and Abdul Aziz streets—radiating from the university were beginning to attract new constructions, and were laid out as regular streets. (For location of streets see Fig. 7.) The only visible and significant development, however, was in areas adjoining the AUB hospital.

This process of residential invasion was intensified further in the area between Jeanne d'Arc and Abdul Aziz. While the plot ratio (i.e., built-on area divided by parcel area) was 0.04 in 1919, it more than doubled to 0.1 by 1930. The magnitude of this invasion can be expressed in more pointed terms: While only 13% of the area was urbanized in 1919 (i.e., having plot ratios higher than 0.1), the urbanized component increased to 45% in 1930. Although the foot path marking what was to become the main street had been transformed to a regular road, Hamra Street remained virtually untouched by this residential invasion.

This pattern seems to have persisted during the entire inter-war period: further condensation in areas already urbanized, while areas flanking Hamra Street remained relatively undeveloped. By 1945, 64% of the area could be considered urban.

It was not until the late 1940s that Hamra Street and its outlying southward areas began to attract new population groups. The waves of Palestinian migrants shortly after 1948 must have no doubt been responsible for a sizeable portion of this influx. Two striking features stand out here: First, areas previously urbanized tended to stabilize in terms of plot ratios while a marked growth in the central parts of Hamra began to be visible. This is seen further by the declining proportion of empty land along both sides of Hamra Street. In 1945, 58% of such land was undeveloped. By 1955 the proportion decreased to 31%.

Pl. 46 (123)

Second, land parcellation preceding urban construction reached its peak in 1955. As shown earlier, the number of parcels increased from 275 in 1930 to 671 in 1955. This is definitely a by-product of increasing speculation in real estate and the accompanying rise in land value. All this has meant an increasing scale of urbanization. Compared to 64% in 1945, by 1955, 87% of the area could be considered urban.

Though generated by different groups, the influx had remained predominantly residential in character. By the mid-1950s, a third wave brought commercial establishments to Hamra. Initially, it took the form of construction on empty land; but as the competition for scarce space was intensified, residential buildings began to be converted for commercial use. Finally, it was during this period that we first encounter some symptoms of urban succession. This is clearly seen in the increasing number of specialized buildings constructed for non-residential activities. In 1967 there were already fourteen office buildings of which eleven were located in the central district of Hamra.

Urban succession may also be seen in the proportion of non-residential to residential floor space. In 27% of the grid-cell area, non-residential floor space is already dominating, and in 10% of the area there is a complete succession.

Conversion of buildings from residential to non-residential use is also another index of ecological succession. By 1967, 10% of all buildings in the area had been subjected to some measure of conversion from residential to commercial use. Very often this took the form of transforming first floors of houses into shops and offices. To be exact, eighty-six such converted buildings were noted. This process of commercialization has since been intensified further and continues to be an outstanding ecological feature of the area.

Pl. 46 (123), 49 (132), 111 (334)

Questionable as the evidence may be, estimates of land value may be taken as another dramatic evidence of the accelerating transformation of the area. Information on land value is available for the short period between the late 1950s and early 1960s.[12] Since the estimates are based on the actual number of transactions, nothing can be inferred about land values in areas where no sale of property has occurred—such as the central business district. The data nonetheless provide an indication of the spread of transactions throughout the city. It is clear from the three stages surveyed by Miss Hearst that Ras-Beirut, and Hamra in particular, is the area in which maximum land values have been registered. An estimate of L.L. 400 ($130) per square meter or more seemed to have been the prevailing rates in central Hamra. This is definitely a conservative figure.[13] In one specific instance known to the writers, a parcel in central Hamra was sold for L.L. 1,050 ($350) per square meter in 1960. Further interviews with a few land owners in the area indicated that land values continued to increase in subsequent years until the June War of 1967. Such a high land value can naturally be seen as a by-product of the keen competition for available land and the expected demand for floor space. Commercial establishments, which were invading the area in this period, are obviously more capable of bidding for high-rent premises, and thus began to absorb additional floor space constructed in central Hamra.

The ecological transformation of Hamra becomes all the more apparent when one considers two further attributes of the intensity and scale of urbanization: density and land-use patterns.

Density: From Farm Houses to High-rises

Despite the rapid urban development Hamra has witnessed over the past twenty-five years, the area does not depart markedly from the prevailing population densities in the metropolitan region of Beirut. Compared to densities in European and American central cities, however, the density of Hamra is high.

The gross density of Hamra (i.e., total population in relation to total surface of the area) is 244 persons per hectare. This is almost identical to the estimated average population density of Beirut in 1964. Except for the extremely high densities observed in some camps and bidonvilles in the peri-urban areas (2,000 or more per hectare), the range of densities in Beirut proper is not very wide.

Net density (i.e., total residential population in relation to total residential floor space) is a more refined measure of the intensity of urbanization. It is also

---

[12] Data on land value was obtained by Wendy Hearst on the basis of official taxable land values involved in real estate transactions. Data quoted from Miss Hearst's Master's thesis, Department of Geography, Durham College, University of Durham, 1966.

[13] Registered rates in the cadastral department are often underrated to avoid excessive taxation levied on real estate transactions.

an appropriate index of the quality of housing and the general standard of living within the area. Net density has been expressed here as residential floor space per person, and as the number of persons per room. On both these indexes the area reveals relatively low density. The residential floor space per person is estimated at 27 square meters, and the number of persons per room is 0.7.[14]

No comparable reliable figures on net densities are available for other areas of Beirut. The Hamra densities, however, seem considerably lower than Churchill's estimates of 1954 for Beirut (about 1.4 persons per room) and certainly much lower than the estimates of Jane Hacker for Amman (2.6 to 5 persons per room) or other estimates for Cairo and other comparable cities in the region.[15]

Another dimension of density is the physical structure of the area as manifested in the intensity of the utilization of land. The first visual impression one gains of Hamra—and perhaps not altogether an incorrect impression—is of a highly dense and compact urban area not unlike many other central cities: an incessant flow of cars and pedestrians, congested traffic on sidewalks and parking lots coupled with narrow streets flanked by blocks of perpendicular concrete structures erected directly at the street limit. All this contributes to the impression of an exploding metropolis that can only expand by eating up breathing space.

Such visual impressions can be easily documented by the proportion of surface in relation to parcel area, built-on and traffic space, and other such measures. As shown in Table 1, Hamra is undoubtedly a highly urbanized area in physical terms. A few of these physical features should be underlined.

Of the total surface of Hamra only 24% is traffic area, and the rest is private property in the form of parcels. Some of the implications of this feature for the quality of urban life and the scope of future urbanization are quite clear. By almost any standard 24% is a low proportion to allow for the effective absorption of traffic and parking in a densely urbanized area. This also implies that Hamra is virtually a "closed" area in that any further expansion demanding more accessible additional space must be provided by demolishing or converting already existing structures.

This becomes even more apparent when we consider the parcel structure and the plot ratios. As much as 42% of the total parcel area is built on, yielding a plot ratio of 0.42. This is a high ratio by any standard comparable to prevailing rates in American and European central cities. Not only does Hamra suffer from a high plot ratio but the parcel size is also small, averaging 612 square meters per parcel. This is no doubt an expected by-product of rapid urbanization in a laissez-faire economy accompanied by excessive speculation in real estate. While the cadastral map of 1930 showed a total of 275 parcels, the number increased to 671 in 1955 and dropped slightly to 658 in 1967. This drop reflects a

[14]   The total residential floor space is estimated at 497,000 square meters, of which 30% is allotted for hallways, entrances, staircases, and the like. This leaves 348,000 square meters as net residential floor space. Moreover, if the average room size is calculated at 20 square meters, this yields a total of 174,000 rooms or 0.7 persons per room.

[15]   Charles Churchill, *The City of Beirut* (Beirut: Dar el-Kitab, 1954), p. 21; Jane Hacker, *Modern Amman* (Department of Geography, University of Durham, 1960), p. 88.

tendency toward an increasing scale in recent construction which has involved pooling of small parcels into larger building sites. This has also involved a transformation in the character of real estate ownership: from individual to corporate property. With the increase in large-scale construction and speculation in real estate, it has become correspondingly more difficult for individual entrepreneurs and owners to retain their hold on property or to command any

TABLE 1. PHYSICAL CHARACTERISTICS (HAMRA)

	Units		Total areas in category	Surfaces percentages		Floors	
	Number	Average Size		gross	net	percentage	Ratios
A. Total surface	-	-	531,960	100	-		
Traffic area	-	-	129,190	24	-		
Parcel area	658	612	402,770	76	100		
Not built-on			231,230		58		
Built-on			171,540		42		
B. Buildings	833	206	171,540		100		
Plot ratio							0.42
C. Floor space	3,262	270	879,230			100	
Non-residential	2,000	159	318,959			36	
Residential	4,543	123	560,271			64	
Floor ratio							2.18
Height ratio							5.11

Note: All areas are in square meters
Plot ratio = Built-on area ÷ Parcel area
Floor ratio = Floor space ÷ Parcel area
Height ratio = Floor space ÷ Built-on area

effective control over the entire process of financing and planning the massive construction projects Hamra has witnessed lately.

Another aspect of physical structure contributing to high density is the number, character, and location of buildings. Two marked features stand out in this respect as decisive factors: first, the rapidly increasing demand for floor space generated by the inflow of new urban groups seeking residential space and the simultaneous invasion of commercial establishments and professional institutions. The waves of Palestinian migrants after 1948 and the political instability in neighboring Arab countries must have, among other factors, intensified the already existing demand. Second, the traditional mode of establishing dwellings in clusters and compact neighborhoods has also contributed to the density and proximity of residential units. This explains perhaps why Hamra, unlike many other newly-emerging areas, has assumed a structure closer to the model of a "vertical" city than to the "horizontal" pattern common in residential areas of Europe and the United States.

This vertical pattern of growth is readily seen in a height ratio of 5.11 (i.e., the total floor space divided by the total built-on area, see Table 1). This, in effect, means that the built-up area corresponds to an average level of five floors.[16]

TABLE 2. DISTRIBUTION OF BUILDINGS AS TO NUMBER OF FLOORS (HAMRA)

| No. of Floors | 1952 | | 1967 | |
	Number	%	Number	%
1-2	316	55	331	40
3-4	191	33	190	22
5-6	64	11	125	15
7-9	3	1	165	20
over 9	0	0	24	3
Total	574	100	833	100
Average floors/building		2.6		3.9

Sources: Floor count undertaken by Charles Churchill for the City of Beirut, 1954; and Land-use Survey of 1967.

As shown in Table 2, not only has there been a dramatic increase in the number of floors from 1,494 in 1952 to a total of 3,263 in 1967, but the change in the distribution has been even more striking. While only 12% of the buildings in 1952 consisted of five floors or more (with 1% over seven floors), the proportion of high-rise buildings leaped to 38% in 1967 (with 23% over seven floors). It should be noted that this impressive increase in modern high-rise apartments has not completely displaced some of the traditional house forms which were in style until the end of World War II. As shown in Table 3, Hamra continues to sustain a significant number of farm houses and suburban mansions or villas.

TABLE 3. BUILDING TYPES, 1967 (HAMRA)

Building type	Number	%
Farm houses	66	8
Traditional villas	46	5
Emerging apartment houses (walk-ups)	232	28
Modern high-rises	183	22
Total	527	63

*Of a total of 833 buildings in Hamra, 527 were clearly identified as to type and style. Accordingly, percentages do not add up to 100.

[16]   The height-ratio should not be confused with the average number of floors per building.

47. A graceful suburban villa sternly resisting the invasion of high-rise apartments.

48. Another graceful variety of a suburban villa. Like many of its type, it is unfortunately beginning to give way to a more intensive form of urban residence.

49. The intersection of Abdul Aziz and Bliss streets in 1970. A perfect example of vertical sorting and heavy centralization (e.g., many doctors' offices concentrated in this area just across the street from the University Hospital).

50. The final stages of Hamra's urbanization: the invasion of high-rise commercial and office buildings.

Insofar as the style and form of a building contributes to the urban character of an area, it may be meaningful to consider briefly some of the characteristic features of the prominent building styles prevailing in Hamra. Since these building types made their appearance at different points in time in the urban development of the area, they may be taken as milestones marking the different stages of urbanization. Only a few of the prominent features of each type will be identified. The four types described here in no sense exhaust the variety and diversity of building forms. But together they account for 63% of all existing houses in the area. The remaining 37% could not be clearly classified in any one distinct group.

Since Hamra, like the rest of Ras Beirut, was at one time predominantly an area for small-scale garden farming, it is not surprising that farm houses marked the early phases of urban development. What is remarkable is that despite the increasing scale and intensity of urbanization, this form of simple dwelling still contributes 8% of the total number of buildings. In both style and construction, farm houses comply with an almost rudimentary and uniform pattern that is easily identifiable. The typical farm house is a square, flat-roofed, one-story Pl. 43 (122) building constructed with the traditional sandstone blocks quarried in the area. It rarely exceeds a floor space of more than 300 square meters, and occasionally it sports a fountained garden plot.

The suburban villas, which marked the second stage of urbanization, are the typical coastal two- or three-storied, red-tiled houses with elaborate façades and decorative railed stairways and balconies. Unlike the farm houses which were Pl. 44 (122), evenly scattered in the entire region, there are evidences that most of the 45 (123), suburban villas made their initial appearance along Bliss Street and other areas 47-48 (131) adjoining the university. In both structure and style, these villas reflect the relatively more privileged socio-economic origins of their inhabitants, who mark perhaps the first truly urban group settled in the area. As will be shown later, this group also marks the appearance of the newly emerging urban middle class that was to become the dominant socio-economic group in the area. Despite the differentiated ethnic and religious background of these mobile groups, they were all invariably drawn into the area by the opportunities generated by the growth of the university. Their residences, in one way or another, reflect a rather modest but comfortable style of living. The villas are often spacious, with walled garden plots and well-tended patios.

Unfortunately, and one cannot but lament their passing, these picturesque villas are becoming scarce relics in the urban ambiance of Ras Beirut. Despite concerted efforts made to preserve them, they have had to give way to a more intensive utilization of urban land.[17] While in 1952 the two- and three-storied houses contributed 54% of all buildings in the area, their share in 1967 dropped to 30%. In effect, this has meant the disappearance of 64 such houses in a span of 15 years.

While farm houses and suburban villas continued to be the predominant form of dwellings until the end of World War II, the increasing demand for floor space

---

[17] Attempts to rescue worthy structures are being made by the Association for the Protection of Sites and Old Buildings in Lebanon.

51. Hamra District of Beirut showing from foreground to background the evolution from traditional villas to emerging apartment houses (walk-ups) to modern high-rises. (Photo: H. Conway Zeigler.)

after 1948 ushered in a new and more intensive form of urban residence. The emerging apartment house evolved as a successive building type to cope with this increasing demand for living space. With regard to structure, the emerging apartments were in many respects a by-product of prevailing building forms. In some instances, they were simply conversions of older houses. Accordingly, they retained some of the spacious quality of the urban villa, along with open balconies and stairways, though the floor space of residences decreased. However, they differed in one significant respect. With a range of four to seven floors, the apartment house marks the first appearance of a vertical residence.

Because the emerging apartment house corresponded with the construction boom in the 1950s, it has continued to be the largest single group of house type in the area. Twenty-eight percent of all houses belong to this category. The sharp increase in density of built-up area between 1945 and 1955 demonstrates further the contribution made by this house type to the rapid urbanization of Hamra. The total floor space probably tripled in this decade. With the invasion of apartment houses, the physical character of Hamra underwent radical transformation. For the first time the area began to assume an uneven skyline. Walled gardens, agricultural plots, and alleys lined with cactus hedges began to disappear.

Thus far, the demand for residential space had been met either by constructing on free parcels or by remodelling already existing buildings. By the mid 1950s, as the scale of urbanization increased, a more intensive utilization of scarce land was resorted to. Blocks lined with buildings along the street were filled in by new constructions on parcels already built on. Moreover, the process of demolishing existing buildings and pooling adjoining parcels became more pronounced in real estate operations preceding new constructions.

This last phase of urbanization was marked further by three significant developments: first, the continuing pressure for utilizing empty space because of the sharp rise in land value and speculation in real estate. Second, the invasion of commercial establishments along with the persistence of unmet demand for residential space. Third, the innovation in building techniques, along with the necessity for comprehensive planning, resulting in large-scale construction and corporate financing.

The modern high-rise apartment or office building was the inevitable outcome of the combined effect of the above factors. Towering structures in reinforced concrete with glittering glass façades and prefabricated aluminum frames began to overwhelm the urban scene. Hamra, finally, began to display some of the universal features of large-scale urbanization.

The modern high-rise, which now accounts for 22% of all buildings and 57% of the total floor space in the area, does not diverge much from the standardized and uniform high-rises encountered in almost any growing metropolis. Typically, they have eight to ten floors and occasionally fourteen, with elevators rather than walkups and open stairways and concierges to replace walled gates. The basic attribute of spaciousness of the traditional urban house has entirely disappeared. Two or more apartments are now squeezed on a floor. Gone also are the open balconies and the shuttered windows. Instead, buildings assume an almost faceless façade, particularly those in the modern commercial centers.

Pl. 50 (132)

With the advent of the high-rise, this final stage of urban transformation has made possible a much more intensive use of space. As much as 580,000 square meters of floor space has been added since 1955, and consequently Hamra can now claim a very high floor ratio of 2.18. This is in line with ratios observed in most large metropolitan centers. But since only sixty-four parcels remain unbuilt, accessible land reserves have declined to 51,000 square meters. In other words, Hamra is approaching the saturation point in intensity of urbanization. Only 10 to 15% new floor space can be added if the present plot and floor ratios are to prevail.

This development has also been marked by a significant transformation that will continue to change the urban quality of the area. Hamra has begun to lose its exclusive residential character. Except for a few modern high-rises, residential units have to share floor space with invading commercial activities.

Mixed Land-use Patterns

The physical features just outlined in terms of density, intensity of land utilization, and variety of building types which marked the rapid urbanization of Hamra have left a definite impact on the land-use pattern observed in the area. Inasmuch as the area is in a state of ecological transition and the competition for scarce land and floor space has been generated by varied groups of land users, a highly mixed land-use pattern and a curious configuration of urban functions is displayed.

Nowhere is this feature more striking than in the apparent diversity of functions and activities that a typical high-rise building attracts. It is not unusual to find a predominantly residential building housing a variety of household units (ranging from single-men's dwellings to furnished apartments to full-fledged households) together with a curious mélange of commercial, recreational, and institutional functions. It is quite common, for instance, to have the basement of a building utilized as a discotheque, bar, or nightclub, or possibly a garage or warehouse; the ground floor as a movie house, sidewalk cafe, restaurant or snack bar; the first few floors as bank and financial premises, executive and administrative branch offices or foreign companies, marketing research outfits, insurance companies, transportation and airline agencies, professional offices side by side with beauty shops, Swedish massage institutes and fashion shops; and the upper floors as residential units, penthouse apartments, and roof gardens.

Pl. 46 (123), 49 (132)

In contrast to this variety of functions sheltered in high-rises, the land-use pattern of the free space around buildings is rather simple and uniform. Such space is used mostly for storage and parking. While traditional garden farming has virtually ceased to exist, one still finds a few inhabitants who cultivate their gardened plots in the shadow of high-rise buidlings.

This pattern of vertical sorting and absence of areal-functional specialization, as several observers have remarked, is common—especially in older parts of non-Western urban areas.[18] Hamra in some respects complies with this pattern. It departs, however, in the sense that it is a newly urbanized area and that it re-

[18]   See Gerald Breese, *Urbanization in Newly Developing Countries*, pp. 116-117; and Robert Marsh, *Comparative Sociology* (New York: Harcourt, Brace and World, Inc., 1967), p. 188.

veals an appreciable degree of areal specialization along with mixed land-use patterns. This is not unusual for an area characterized by a state of rapid flux and transition.

Despite rapid urbanization and the massive influx of commercial and institutional activities, Hamra continues to retain its original character as a predominantly residential area. As shown in Table 4, 62% of floor space is used for residential purposes. In some respects this belies the outward impression Hamra generates as a busy center for commercial and recreational day- and night-time activities. This impression is not altogether incorrect since nearly 40% of the total floor space is used for non-residential activities. Of these, retail uses—such as retail stores, restaurants, hotels, service stations, travel bureaus and branch offices of banks—account for 18% of the total floor space.

The share of office use is even smaller. Offices occupy only half the area utilized by retail activities. Under this general category we classified activities such as manufacturers' sales offices, wholesalers, agents, brokers, business services, contractors, professional offices, and offices of international organizations.

Finally, other non-residential activities comprise mainly institutional uses such as schools, hospitals, churches, mosques, and welfare organizations along with government offices. Altogether these account for 11% of the total floor space.

The striking absence of industrial uses of land should be noted. As little as 1,800 square meters is devoted to industrial activity, and certainly not of the heavy or large-scale variety. The "industrial" activities in Hamra are devoted to workshops of carpenters, plumbers, furniture makers, and the like.

TABLE 4. LAND USE SUMMARY (HAMRA)

Area	Square meters	%
Surface area		
Streets	109,074	23
Parcels	370,926	77
Total	480,000	100
Parcel area		
Not built-on	218,818	59
Built-on	152,108	41
Total	370,926	100
Floor space		
Residential uses	497,462	62
Retail uses	142,820	18
Office uses	73,157	9
Other: institutional, administrative and industrial	88,996	11
Total	802,435	100

*The figures do not correspond to those of Table 1 since land-use measurements are based on grid-cell analysis for 90% of the area under study.

A more precise expression of the areal balance is given by the ratio of non-residential to residential floor space. Here, as well, Hamra reveals a high ratio of 0.61 (i.e., 61 square meters of non-residential for every 100 square meters of residential floor space). This apparent mixed land use can be qualified further by considering variations of the non-residential to residential ratio over the grid cells.

As is clearly shown in Table 5, only a very slight proportion of the cells are exclusively residential or non-residential, while the remaining 86% are mixed in character. It should be noted nonetheless that 45% of all cells are mixed but predominantly residential.

Grid-net analysis also suggests that there is a considerable degree of clustering of non-residential activities, notably office use, and that a certain degree of areal specialization seems to be emerging. This is all the more remarkable given the mixed land-use character and relatively small size and compact quality of the area.

TABLE 5. NON-RESIDENTIAL AND RESIDENTIAL FLOOR SPACE (HAMRA)

	Ratios	Number of grid cells	%
Completely residential	0	6	8
Mixed but predominantly residential	0.01-0.3	34	45
Mixed and approaching balance	0.31-1.0	21	27
Mixed but predominantly non-residential	1.01-3.0	11	14
Non-residential	10.0 or more	3	4
Total		75	98
Median ratio	0.21		
Average ratio	0.61		

THE SOCIO-ECONOMIC PROFILE OF HAMRA

What has been the impact of this swift urbanization on the socio-economic character of the people Hamra has been attracting? Has the intensive process of urbanization—marked by increasing population density, mixed land-use patterns, and ecological and spatial differentiation—been reflected in any uniformities or differences in the socio-economic composition of the population? Only a few selected results can be briefly presented here.

Types of Households

The type and age of household, the nature of the family, the form or duration of the lease of rented residential units, and the length of residence in Hamra may be expedient indicators of the degree of urbanization. Among other things, they provide us with some hints as to the settled and transient nature of the population, and the extent to which residents of Hamra are beginning to manifest attributes of anonymity, impersonalization, and weakening of kinship ties often associated with urbanism as a way of life.

Though a large proportion of the households interviewed (78.1%) may be considered as normal family units consisting of parents, children, and occasionally extended kin, there is still not an altogether insignificant number of households that are not composed of families in this strict sense of the term. As shown in Table 6, nearly 22% of the households consist of single-men's dwellings, joint apartments of unrelated members (mostly students or colleagues sharing furnished or rented flats), joint apartments with related members (as is the case with brothers and sisters), or other families or individuals in transit who take up residence for a short duration of time.

As anticipated, only 2.6% of the households are extended families. This is not at all surprising given the scope and nature of urbanization of Hamra and the shifting character of its population. To a considerable extent, these are some of the older families who settled early in Hamra and have not moved since.

TABLE 6. TYPE OF HOUSEHOLD (HAMRA)

Household	Number	%
Normal family	416	78.1
Single apartment	48	9.1
Joint apartment: unrelated members	37	6.9
Joint apartment: related members	21	3.9
Members in transit	6	1.1
Family in transit	5	0.9
Total	533	100.0

The impact of urbanization may also be seen in the proportion of households who own their dwellings, compared to those living in rented houses or flats. In this respect, Hamra displays some highly urban attributes. As shown in Table 7, only 15% of the households are living in houses which they own. This is a considerably lower proportion than Churchill's findings for a sample of total Beirut, where ownership of buildings was achieved by a quarter of the households surveyed in 1954,[19] and is additional evidence of the growing transient and marginal character of the Hamra population. This is also apparent by the significant number of households 12.8%—who rent their houses on a monthly basis. The monthly rent, in effect, implies residence in furnished apartments—a form of urban housing which has been burgeoning extensively in the area.

---

[19] Charles V. Churchill, *The City of Beirut*, p. 20.

TABLE 7. OWNERSHIP OF RESIDENCE AND TYPE OF LEASE (HAMRA)

Ownership/Lease	Number	%
Ownership	80	15.0
Lease/yearly	385	72.2
Lease/monthly	68	12.8
Total	533	100.0

The New Middle Class

Apart from some of the common household features and demographic composition of the population—such as low dependency ratio, low fertility, and a predominantly young and active population—Hamra also displays some homogeneous socio-economic attributes. In terms of both occupational and income distribution, the emerging pattern is one of relative homogeneity, with little or no sharp socio-economic differences.

Despite the relatively large proportion of students (34.6%) and housewives (21.3%), nearly one-third of the total population is economically active. Of these, as shown in Table 8, more than one-third are professionals and semi-professionals; 26.2% are proprietors of large or small business firms; 23.3% are clerks; and nearly 5% are officials and executives. Only 3.9% are semi-skilled or unskilled workers. So the district is overwhelmingly white collar in its occupational structure, composed mainly of professionals (probably more salaried than self-employed), independent business, employees, clerks, and executives. Expectedly, Hamra draws an insignificant number of blue-collar or manual workers. A larger proportion of the manual workers, nearly 7% of the active population, are skilled craftsmen such as tailors, hairdressers, photographers, and carpenters.

The occupational composition of Hamra marks a significant departure from Churchill's socio-economic survey of Beirut. While only 9.7% of the households in his sample were professionals and semi-professionals, Hamra attracts a professional base of nearly 34% of the active population.[20] This is also significantly larger than Berger's estimate of the proportion of professionals of all the middle class in urban Egypt. While not more than 19% of the middle class in Egypt were professionals, the proportion is nearly 40% for the Hamra population.[21] Hamra also attracts a much larger base of people in clerical occupations than Beirut in general. Clerical occupations accounted for only 6% of the economically active in 1954. Now they comprise nearly one-quarter of the employed population of Hamra. Interestingly, the middle class of Hamra and the urban middle class of Egypt are almost identical in the proportion of clerks

---

[20]   Ibid., p. 50.
[21]   See Morroe Berger,"The Middle Class in the Arab World," in *The Middle East in Transition,* ed. W. Z. Laqueur (London: Routledge and Kegan Paul, 1958), p. 64.

in private and government offices. In both groups, they are numerically preponderant and contribute 26% of the composition of the middle class.

TABLE 8. OCCUPATIONAL STATUS (HAMRA)

Economically Active Population	Number	% of total population	% of active population
PROFESSIONALS	155	8.0	24.0
Doctors, engineers, pharmacists, lawyers, professors, teachers, judges, dentists, social scientists, etc.			
CLERKS	150	7.7	23.3
Clerical workers, secretaries, salesmen			
SMALL BUSINESS	118	6.1	18.3
Retailers, dealers, agents, proprietors of repair shops, and personal services			
SEMI-PROFESSIONALS	69	3.6	10.7
Pilots, technicians, accountants, intepreters, hostesses, nurses, decorators, journalists, publishers, artists, and entertainers			
LARGE BUSINESS	51	2.6	7.9
Bankers, industrialists, managers, contractors, proprietors of large business			
SKILLED CRAFTSMEN	44	2.3	6.8
Tailors, hairdressers, carpenters, photographers			
OFFICIALS, EXECUTIVES	31	1.6	4.8
Government employees, heads of sections, army officers, employees of embassies			
SEMI-SKILLED	18	0.9	2.8
Cooks, barbers, drivers, foremen, policemen			
UNSKILLED WORKERS	7	0.3	1.1
Daily laborers, office boys, peddlers			
INACTIVE POPULATION			
Students	673	34.6	
Housewives	414	21.3	
Unemployed	56	2.9	
Retired	35	1.8	
Rentier	7	0.4	
Infants	109	5.6	
No Answer	6	0.3	
Total	1,943	100.0	

The almost total absence of an industrial or working-class component from Hamra must be noted. While it accounts for more than 20% of the gainfully employed of Beirut's heads of households,[22] it is nearly non-existent in Hamra.

This numerical preponderance of white-collar and middle-class occupations is another manifestation of the growing dominance of corporate and modern bureaucratic structures within the Lebanese economy. It also highlights the changing and transitional nature of the occupational composition of the Hamra population and the role it plays in absorbing and generating new skills and occupations. Apart from the continuing proliferation of professionals, Hamra has doubtlessly been instrumental in attracting careers—such as pilots, hostesses, interpreters, decorators, journalists, publishers, artists, entertainers, public relations experts, market analysts, and other relatively new semi-professional skills and occupations. The change is not only numerical. It must have had a profound effect on the character and quality of the occupational structure. As Hamra attracts an increasing number of foreign establishments and institutions, as firms merge and corporations become more dominant, free entrepreneurs, independent professionals, and craftsmen are inclined to become salaried employees. The small shopkeeper can no longer compete with the bourgeoning supermarkets and shopping centers; independent professionals—particularly doctors—become part-timers in university hospitals or join a collective clinic or medical center; architects and engineers become consultants or associates of construction and real estate development firms.

This has not meant, however, the obsolescence or extinction of some of the traditional skills or conventional walks of life. Hamra still sustains a relatively sizeable number of small shopkeepers, retailers, proprietors of repair shops, and skilled craftsmen who tend their trade as a self-employed class.

This apparent coexistence of traditional and modern occupations and skills, though not unique to Hamra, must nonetheless be underscored. Among other things, it provides further evidence of the dualistic character of its occupational structure and the viability of its mixed economy. Market analysts, systems engineers, and public relations experts still coexist with the self-employed middleman or traditional brokers. Supermarkets have not as yet displaced the small shopkeeper or the grocery store. Nor have shopping centers for ready-made clothes and mass-produced shopping goods driven the tailor, carpenter, or traditional blacksmith out of business. In much the same way, the traditional money lender and idle rentier still coexist with bankers, heads of investment firms, and real estate agents. Finally, eating stalls and street vendors continue to derive a viable existence despite the proliferation of self-service restaurants and sidewalk cafes. In short, much like the mixed character of its land use pattern, Hamra continues to display a dualistic and mixed occupational structure.

Despite the diversity in occupations and skills, Hamra is unmistakably a middle-class area. Indeed, if professionals are to be included within the middle class, then nearly 88% of the active population may be considered middle class

---

[22] Churchill, op. cit., p. 50.

in character. As shown in Table 9, professionals and semi-professionals are the major components of the middle class. Nearly 40% of the middle class are professionals. This is a sizeable proportion by almost any standard, and does, as already mentioned, depart markedly from the composition of the Egyptian urban middle class or that of Beirut in general. The presence of the American University of Beirut and associated institutions have been doubtlessly instrumental in attracting and sustaining such a large professional base. In this sense Hamra is more akin to a university town or a college neighborhood than to a typical urban community. Over and above the 34.6% student population, a large proportion of the economically active are, in effect, associated in one way or another with the university. At least 50% of the total population is directly attached to the university without mentioning the subsidiary and sundry institutions and services that must have emerged in response to the growing needs of a university community. This is one further evidence that the university has been a fundamental and not merely an incidental factor in the urbanization and growth of Ras Beirut; or at least it is doubtful whether Hamra and its adjoining areas could have developed at the same pace without the presence of AUB.

TABLE 9. COMPOSITION OF THE MIDDLE CLASS (HAMRA)

Occupation	Number	% of Active Population	% of Middle Class
Professionals	155	24.0	27.3
Clerks	150	23.3	26.4
Small business	118	18.3	20.8
Semi-professional	69	10.8	12.2
Skilled craftsmen	44	6.8	7.8
Officials and Executives	31	4.8	5.5
Total	567	87.9	100.0

The proliferation of new professional skills is significant in more than a numerical or quantitative sense. Professionals—whether salaried or self-employed—are not only the carriers of new skills; they are also the shapers of new ideas and opinions. Professors, editors, journalists, along with writers and artists, are the architects of ideologies and new styles of life. They are the intellectual elite, and all intellectuals—conservative, liberal, or radical—are part of the new middle class.

The preponderance of professional, technical-managerial, and clerical employees and the consequent diminution of merchants and business groups indicates the emergence of a new middle class. Among other things, it signals the gradual decline of the propertied entrepreneur, the free professional, the independent merchant, the shopkeeper, and the rise of the dependent employee and the salaried clerk. This bourgeoning middle class is new in at least two fundamental ways: First, occupation rather than property or inherited wealth is increasingly becoming the source of one's income and class situation. If anything, this is one indication that achievement criteria are beginning to displace ascriptive considerations which so far have been traditionally instrumental in determining social rank and social mobility in Lebanese society. Second, it is new in the sense that it is more of an employed than an employing or self-employed class. Though at no point perhaps in the socio-economic history of Lebanon has the middle class ever been an employing class, certainly a larger proportion of professionals and semi-professionals were more self-employed than they seem to be today.

Though the data at hand do not enable us to assess the exact proportion of free versus salaried professionals, the general composition of the middle class prompts us to suggest that it consists more of people who work for someone else and to a lesser extent of a self-employed class. Except perhaps for the entrepreneurial class of small businessmen and skilled craftsmen, which together comprise 28.6% of the middle class, the bulk are engaged in salaried occupations.

The "employing" segment of the middle class must be considerably smaller. Certainly, the capacity or potential of professionals, small businessmen, semi-professionals, and skilled craftsmen to employ any sizeable number of the economically active is naturally limited. In this sense, compared to the role its counterpart played in the West, the middle class is perhaps still economically weak.[23] But in no sense should this detract from its vital role as a carrier of new skills, ideologies, and styles of life. And this is certainly more relevant to its role as an agent of modernization.

A cursory review of the income distribution of households confirms the impression that Hamra is a relatively high income area, a feature which should prompt us to qualify some of the foregoing remarks concerning the economic weakness of the middle class. The employing power of the economically active may be limited, but they are definitely enjoying pecuniary rewards commensurate with their occupational status and a level of income disproportionate to other socio-economic groups in Beirut. With an average monthly income of more than L.L. 1,225 ($400) per family, the earning potential of the average household in Hamra is at least double that of Beirut as a whole.

Sketchy as they seem, the socio-economic features outlined above can still lead us to advance a few broad inferences about the nature and character of the middle class:

1. The economically active population of Hamra—which is predominantly a middle-class population—may not possess the economic powers often associated with the middle classes of more advanced societies. Nor does it possess some of the social privileges and inherited wealth of the more established families. It does, however, possess two attributes which have been associated with the rapid urbanization of the area: a high earning potential and a style of life germane to the spread of new ideas and patterns of behavior. Naturally, the fact that the new middle class is drawing high salaries is not as important as its role of carrier

---

[23] Morroe Berger considers this feature an inherent weakness of the middle class in the Arab world. See "The Middle Class in the Arab World," op. cit., pp. 65-66.

of new ideas and careers relevant to modernization. It is nonetheless "new" in both senses: that it is salaried and that it has been an effective agency of modernization.

2. Despite increasing urbanization and the proliferation of white-collar employees and salaried occupations, this expanding middle class is not entirely an employed class. Because of the survival of some measure of dualism in the socio-economic system and the mixed character of its land use, Hamra continues to display a mixed occupational structure.

As shown earlier, not an insignificant number of small businessmen and skilled craftsmen continue to tend their trade as self-employed entities. It also seems unlikely, even under an accelerated pace of urbanization and large-scale commercialization, that this dualism in the occupational structure should entirely disappear in the near future.

3. Because of the survival of traditional and communal attachments, the middle class remains relatively diffuse and amorphous as a social group. It still lacks the cohesion and self-consciousness which characterized the growth and nature of the middle class in other societies.[24] This is not unusual for a society which continues to be sustained by primordial affinities.[25] Class identity in such societies is not usually as intense or meaningful as kinship and confessional consciousness. No doubt, the scale and scope of urbanization will ultimately dilute part of such traditional attachments. Presently, however, this has not taken place on any significant scale. Evidence will be subsequently furnished to demonstrate that urbanization in Hamra has not so far eroded kinship and traditional loyalties. In this sense, the weakness of the middle class in Lebanon may be seen in much the same perspective as the weakness of political parties, ideological groups, and other rational and secular instruments of a nation-state.

Religious and Ethnic Composition

The relative socio-economic homogeneity of Hamra in terms of class, income, and occupation should not be taken to mean that the population displays little differentiation in its ethnic and religious composition. Despite its outward uniformity, Hamra continues to be a "mosaic" of composite sects and varied national groups.

Insofar as 72.8% of the sample household heads surveyed belong to Christian sects, then the religious composition of Hamra departs markedly from the

[24] The heated debate between Amos Perlmutter and Manfred Halpern is quite instructive on this point. Although the polemics is concerned with the role of the new middle class in Egypt, it is theoretically relevant to the present argument insofar as both parties probe into the cohesion and self-consciousness of the middle class and its implication for modernization. See A. Perlmutter, "Egypt and the Myth of the New Middle Class," *Comparative Studies in Society and History* 10, no. 1 (October 1967); and M. Halpern, "Egypt and the New Middle Class: Reaffirmations and New Explorations, "*Comparative Studies in Society and History* 2, no. 1 (January 1965): 97-108.

[25] One of the authors has elsewhere explored some of the implications of such traditional ties for the political system and industrial development in Lebanon. See, Samir Khalaf, "Primordial Ties and Politics in Lebanon," *Middle Eastern Studies* 4, no. 3, (April 1968): 243-269; and Samir Khalaf and Emilie Shwayri, "Family Firms and Industrial Development: The Lebanese Case," *Economic Development and Cultural Change* 15, no. 1 (October 1966): 59-69.

Two aerial views of Beirut. 52. (opposite)Low air view from the seaside. 53. (above)Low air view of the high-rise apartment buildings and the wide boulevard along the coastline near the Pigeon Grotto. (Photos: Pan American World Airways.)

total population as a whole. Since historically the coastal urban population of Lebanon has been predominantly Muslim, this imbalance in the sectarian distribution becomes all the more striking. That 31.7% of the Hamra population should be Greek Orthodox is not in itself surprising given the historical role this religious community has played in the commercial activities of Beirut in general. The relatively high proportion of Protestants reflects further the impact of the university and the alien character of the population.

The cosmopolitan and mixed character of the population is also readily apparent in the ethnic composition of Hamra. Less than half of the residents are Lebanese; the remaining are a composite of Palestinians, Armenians, Europeans and Americans, Syrians, Egyptians, and other Arab nationals.

This mixed ethnic and religious composition of the population is not in itself significant if these differences were not reflected in varying patterns of residential segregation and other variations in socio-economic status and patterns of behavior. To mention a few, type and size of household, visiting patterns, ecological mobility, literacy, economic participation, the proportion of women in the labor force, and evidence of secularization all seem—in varying degrees—to be associated with the ethnic and religious background of the inhabitants.

TABLE 10. RELIGIOUS AND ETHNIC COMPOSITION (HAMRA)

Religious breakdown	Number	%	Ethnic Breakdown	Number	%
Greek Orthodox	169	31.7	Lebanese	240	45.0
Sunni Muslim	107	20.1	Palestinian	73	13.7
Catholic	91	17.1	Armenian	44	8.2
Protestant	75	14.1	Other Arab	42	7.9
Maronite	53	9.9	European	33	6.2
Druze	13	2.4	American	28	5.2
Shiite	11	2.1	Syrian	27	5.1
Jews	6	1.1	Egyptian	25	4.8
Others	6	1.1	Others	21	3.9
Undetermined	2	0.4			
Total	533	100.0	Total	533	100.0

Persistence of Traditional and Communal Attachments

The city, as has been repeatedly observed, represents socially a relatively unusual form of human association: a large, densely concentrated aggregation of heterogeneous individuals living for the most part under conditions of anonymity and indirect social control. Social contact is temporal, segmental, and generally impersonal. By virtue of such segmental relationships and participation in impersonal and contractual groups, urbanites, it is often asserted, "hang together by the slenderest threads."[26] In conformity with the classic tradition in sociology,

---

[26] E. Gordon Erickson, *Urban Behavior* (New York: Macmillan, 1954), p. 304.

some of the descriptions of the modern urbanite, as Oscar Lewis has aptly put it, read like another version of the fall of man.[27]

While there is undoubtedly a large measure of truth in such portrayals, they have nevertheless described the rural and urban worlds as extreme poles of life, a description which hardly fits some of the outstanding features of urbanization in Beirut or Hamra in particular. Such polar typologies and ideal type constructs—a tempting and powerful tradition which still occupies a peculiar place in the folklore of sociological theory—must be modified if they are to correspond with the realities of urbanization and the nature of urban groups in Beirut.

Preliminary results regarding visiting patterns, ecological mobility, type of household or residence, character of social relationships with other groups in the neighborhood, and permanence of residence all seem to reveal an appreciable degree of intimacy, integration, and survival of traditional attachments. Even the inhabitants' justifications for living in Hamra or their choice of a particular residence reflect the mixed urban character of the community and the role it has come to play in assimilating rational and traditional considerations. It is also indicative that Hamra continues to display mixed land-use patterns and that the area is clearly emerging as a self-sufficient unit. Much like a preindustrial medieval town, an appreciable number of Hamra residents live, work, shop, play and pray within the constricted radius of half a square kilometer. In other words not only does Hamra serve the conventional multi-urban functions, it also seems to satisfy man's craving for some measure of intimacy and identity and his aesthetic impulse for certain standards of style and popular culture.

In short, the Hamra population has not begun its "descent to anomie." Tentative as the nature of the evidence is, it may still be suggested that urbanization in Beirut thus far has not been associated with a large measure of decline in kinship or weakening of traditional ties and communal attachments. Nor has it created a depersonalized and atomized society. One may perhaps conclude that the intensity and increasing scale of urbanization has not been accompanied by a proportional degree of urbanism as a way of life.

---

[27] Oscar Lewis, "Further Observation on the Folk-Urban Continuum and Urbanization," in *The Study of Urbanization*, ed. P. H. Hauser and L. F. Schnore (New York: John Wiley, 1965), p. 501.

5

The Socio-Economic Evolution of the Inhabitants of a Desert City: The Case of Omdurman

by Karol Krótki

IN April, 1970, it was announced that the Imam al-Hadi al-Mahdi was killed on the Ethiopian border leading a revolt against the government of Khartoum. The announcement was made by General Jaafar al-Nimeiry, leader of the government of the Republic of Sudan. A few days earlier, al-Nimeiry had been prevented from landing at Aba Island, headquarters of the followers (the *Ansar*) of the Imam. Nimeiry also had to quell a revolt in the Widno Bawi quarter of Omdurman. In this manner, a chapter in the history of Sudan—and of Omdurman—may have come to an end.

Omdurman was laid out and built as a modern and "model" African city by the Khalifa (successor) of the celebrated Sudanese Mahdi Muhammad Ahmad, who was the great grandfather of the recently killed Imam. After the conquest of Khartoum by the Mahdist forces and the death of Gordon in 1885, the then main city was abandoned and Omdurman was built on the other (western) side of the White Nile. At its center stood the white gleaming tomb of the Mahdi. Fourteen years later, in 1898, at the time of the reconquest, the tomb was desecrated and Kitchener's soldiers threw the Mahdi's bones into the Nile. Yet, the tomb itself has retained its holy character and has continued to be the aim of pilgrimages.[1] Since then, the city has changed very little, and until very recently, Omdurman remained a city typically African, completely untouched by any Western influence. Only Kano, on the other side of the continent, and on a comparable scale, can claim such a distinction.

---

[1] "Pilgrimage to Mecca was declared unnecessary, Omdurman and the tomb of the Mahdi being held to be sufficient for the faithful," from K. M. Barbour, *The Republic of the Sudan: A Regional Geography* (London: University of London Press, 1961), p. 14 "... the most outstanding architectural feature of Omdurman ... was the Mahdi's tomb where ... three sons of the late Mahdi received innumerable pilgrims," from F. Rehfisch, "A sketch of the early history of Omdurman," *Sudan Notes and Records*, no. 45(1964), pp. 35-47; "... the Khalifa made frequent use of the *hijra*, which had now come to mean in practice the enforced visit of a tribe or individual notables to Omdurman," from P. M. Holt, *The Mahdist State in the Sudan* (Oxford: At the Clarendon Press, 1958).

Old and New Cities in Sudan. 54. The façade of an abandoned Turkish warehouse in Suwakin (once the major port of Sudan) contrasted with . . . 55. (below) A major street in Port Sudan, developed in the early years of the twentieth century.

THE PRIMACY OF OMDURMAN

In the classical sense[2] a city becomes a primate city for a number of reasons, and once it achieves ascendancy over others it gains an impetus which is self-sustaining. Such a city has two or three times the population of that of its next size neighbor. Whether we label Omdurman a "primate city" depends on whether we lump it together with Khartoum and Khartoum North.[3] Each of the three occupies one of the three parts of land formed by the junction of the White with the Blue Nile. Communications between Omdurman and Khartoum as well as between Khartoum and Khartoum North are easy, and many people live in one of the three towns and work in or go to school in another. It is natural to think of them as one socio-economic organism, which could be called Greater Khartoum, with Omdurman the major shareholder.[4]

It has been suggested that the degree of primacy of a city is associated with It is the greater: six characteristics.[5]

(a) the smaller the densely inhabited part of the country;
(b) the lower the average per capita income and the greater the service monopoly of the city;
(c) the greater the dependence of the economy on exports;
(d) the more marked its colonial past;
(e) the greater the degree of dependence of the country on agriculture;
(f) the faster the growth in national income.

It would appear that Greater Khartoum, and with it Omdurman, confirm each one of the hypotheses, though hypotheses (a) and (f) require a word of explanation. Both depend for their validity on limiting their application to the riverine areas stretching both south and north of Omdurman and particularly to the always rich and fast-expanding cotton-growing Gezira. This limitation is justified by the undeveloped communications network, by the sparse population density of the rest of the country, by the low involvement in money exhange of much of the economy, and by the vastness of the country and remoteness of many of its regions.

---

[2] M. Jefferson, "The law of the primate city," *Geographical Review*, no. 29 (1939), pp. 226-232.

[3] The ratio of the population size of Omdurman to the next largest town, when Omdurman is taken alone, ignoring Khartoum and Khartoum North, works out at 2.2 and at 4.7 when the three towns are taken together. See Department of Statistics, *First Population Census of Sudan 1955/56: Town Planners' Supplement*, prepared by D. B. Climenhaga (Khartoum, 1960), Table 9.19. The primacy of the world's metropolitan areas with over 1,000,000 population, measured through the same ratio, varied in 1955 from 16.3 to 1.0. See Arnold S. Linsky, "Some generalizations concerning primate cities," *Annals of the Association of American Geographers* 55 (September 1965): 506-513; and reprinted in Gerald Breese, ed. *The City in Newly Developing Countries* (Englewood Cliffs: Prentice-Hall, Inc., 1969), pp. 285-294.

[4] Such lumping of neighboring cities into one conurbation for the purpose of assessing primacy is apparently an accepted procedure. See Saigon-Cholon, Lille-Turcoing, Tokyo-Yokohama, Osaka-Kobe, Essen-Dortmund-Duisberg, and Katowice-Zabrze-Bytom, in Linsky, op. cit.

[5] Arnold S. Linsky, "Some generalizations concerning primate cities," *Annals of The Association of American Geographers* 55 (September 1965): 506-513; and reprinted in Gerald Breese, ed., *The City in Newly Developing Countries* (Englewood Cliffs: Prentice Hall, Inc., 1969), pp. 285-294.

HISTORY OF OMDURMAN

The history of modern Omdurman truly begins with the arrival of the armies of the Mahdi in 1884 to close the ring around Gordon and his forces in Khartoum. What history there was on this patch of land prior to this event has been described on a few pages of print.[6] It is not known with certainty prior to 1884 whether the place was inhabited at all or whether it was just the name of an area (in two instances it was thought to be the name of a tribe). On his arrival the Mahdi found a fort, called Fort Omdurman, under the command of a Sudanese soldier loyal to Gordon, Farajallah Pasha Raghib, in charge of some 240 troops. Farajallah Pasha surrendered to the Mahdi with Gordon's permission and Khartoum fell a few days later. After some weeks, a few months at the most, of hesitation the Mahdi decided to move his capital across the river to the gravelly plain north of Fort Omdurman, but he allowed those who so desired to remain in Khartoum. Not so his Khalifa and successor: He insisted that he be joined by all loyal followers in Omdurman, and Khartoum became a ghost city. Its stones were used to build Omdurman and the tomb of the Mahdi.[7]

The pilgrimage to Mecca was declared unnecessary and the tomb of the Mahdi took the place of reverence and affection by the faithful. It is not possible to say what contribution this made to the growth of Omdurman, but the Khalifa's wish to have tribal representatives at hand in order to keep them under surveillance must also have been an important element in the growth of the new city. The interest in the new administration and what it had to offer, plus the chance of protection in times of famine and unrest, must have also lured further immigrants.

Beginning as a captured fort with a few hundred soldiers, then serving as a large military encampment for the armies of the Mahdi, the town grew in a few years into a large city stretching from five to twenty kilometers, depending on the period of the report and the estimate of the writer. The population fluctuated, depending on the season of the year (the Gezira already demanded seasonal labor), the vagaries of the Khalifa's policy with regard to friendly and hostile tribes, and his desire to supervise them closely. The population soon reached 120,000,[8] and then probably stabilized at 150,000.[9] In the then prevailing conditions of town planning, the urbanistic results of that type of accelerated growth must have been nothing short of appalling. In any case, there is little doubt that the growth *at that time* was fast.

After the reconquest in 1898, the population dwindled rapidly. The Khalifa's armies left with him after his defeat at the battle of Omdurman. The groups

---

[6] F. Rehfisch, "A sketch of the early history of Omdurman," *Sudan Notes and Records*, no. 45 (1964), pp. 35-47.

[7] The Khalifa's motives were political in the narrow sense of internal power play. It is erroneous to say that "Omdurman across the Nile . . . was built . . . to replace Khartoum when the latter was burned down." John Gunther, *Inside Africa* (London, 1955), p. 232.

[8] C. Rossignoli, *I miei Dodici Anni di Prigionia in Mezzo ai Dervisci* (Mondovi, 1898), quoted in Rehfisch, op. cit.

[9] J. Ohrwalder, *Ten years' captivity in the Mahdi's camp* (London, 1892).

brought to Omdurman by the Khalifa as hostages or tribal representatives drifted back to their homelands. A few years later, the population was estimated by relatively shrewd observers at 46,000.[10] It grew at a moderate pace to reach 100,000 during the Second World War (see Table 1) and some 115,000 ten years later[11] (a slow rate of growth when compared to that now expected from under-developed countries). Indeed, there are good reasons, as will be indicated later,

TABLE 1. HISTORICAL ESTIMATES OF POPULATION SIZE
OF SUDAN AND OMDURMAN

Year	Sudan[a]	Omdurman	Sources for Omdurman
1881	8,750,000	-	
1888	-	120,000	Rossignoli, 1898
1890	-	150,000	Ohrwalder, 1892
1898	1,250,000	-	
1904	2,000,000	46,000[b]	Gleichen 1905, pp. 1 & 47
1917	3,600,000	-	
1921	-	d	
1926	-	76,000	c
1935	5,697,000	-	
1943	-	104,000	c
1944	-	106,000[e]	c
1951	8,764,000	-	-
1956	10,259,000	114,000	Department of Statistics, 1960, Table 9.19

[a]There is an obvious paucity of data and also a bewildering variety. The various sources are given in Karol J. Krótki, *Estimating vital rates from peculiar and inadequate age distributions (Sudanese experience)*, Ph.D. diss., Princeton, University, 1960, pp. 427-428.

[b]"Very many houses are now (1904) deserted . . ."

[c]Typescript reports (very fragmentary) of local counts.

[d]There was an unofficial count, in or about 1921, but so far no absolute figures have come to light, only proportions for some characteristics.

[e]The 1944 enumeration was tied to wartime rationing. Prior to the enumeration the ration strength of the town was 113,000. Some of this overestimation might have remained in the enumerated total.

why Omdurman has experienced this sluggish growth and why the pattern is unlikely to change. Data made available after the last census show that Omdurman is likely to lose its major share in the primacy of Greater Khartoum, if it has not already done so.

THE TRIBAL COMPOSITION

Six writers, prisoners at the time, have left reminiscences of the Khalifa's Omdurman. As such they are perhaps not the most impartial observers. (Further-

[10] Lt. Col. Count (Late Director of Intelligence, Sudan Government and Egyptian Army, and Sudan Agent), *The Anglo-Egyptian Sudan*, ed. Gleichen, Cairo, vol. 1 (London, 1905), p. 47.

[11] In forty years (1904-1944) the population increased by 130%; in the next twelve years (1944-1956) it increased by 8%. The change in pace on a semi-logarithmic scale is quite dramatic. On the other hand, the estimate for 1944 is a possible overestimate as indicated in footnote (e) to Table 1.

more, at least one of the books was in all probability edited by the chief of British Intelligence in Egypt, at that time engaged in what would now be called anti-Khalifa war mongering.) However this may have affected their outlook, all five writers vie with each other in listing the tribes living in Omdurman during the Mahdiya. The later the period to which the description refers, the longer the list of tribes. Eventually, most of the tribes of the Sudan and all of the tribes of northern Sudan must have been represented in the town. The hijra[12] was used as an excuse for near-compulsory and compulsory visits by tribes and their leaders to the Khalifa, and the immigrants were virtual hostages.[13] There is apparently no quantitative estimate available of the tribal composition of Omdurman during the Mahdiya. Some of the forced transfers to Omdurman must have been more notable for their "news" value than for their numerical contribution to the growth of the town. The fate of the Ashraf, the relatives of the Mahdi, who were allowed to scheme against the Khalifa only for a short while in Khartoum, before they were forcibly transferred to Omdurman, is such an example. His own kith and kin among the Rizaygat, Habbaniya, and particularly among the Ta'aisha, were moved on his orders. He was motivated as much by policy consid-erations (being unable to impose his will by other means) as by tribal loyalties.

It is not possible to estimate how far this motley group of tribes was swept back during and immediately after the reconquest, but certainly the composition of the population changed after the reconquest. Three tribes suffered particularly bitterly under the Khalifa: the Kabbabish, the Shukriya, and the Jaaliyin. It was said that they became "practically extinct." The more reliable data from the First Population Census of Sudan 1955-56 confirm this impression with regard to the first two. But the Jaaliyin, in 1956, were the largest single tribe, comprising almost two thirds of all the Arabs or one third of the whole town.

After the reconquest, Omdurman was filled with Northerners, specifically with the Nubiyin, because their services were in demand on account of their high literacy levels. They provided recruits for the army of clerks and middle level officials required to service the machinery of the new government. Later, the British in power were to promote from among them a high proportion of the first senior Sudanese officials. There was hardly a family of prominence in the districts North of Omdurman which would not have a base of some kind or another in Omdurman, and the more affluent had a town house. However, as years went by, the qualitative superiority of the Nubiyin was not accompanied by increases in numbers. Thus, the available data, as usual in fragmentary form, show that the proportion of Nubiyin in Omdurman declined from 33% about 1921[14]—through a proportion still to be established in the unpublished census of

---

[12]   The original hijra was the emigration of the Prophet Muhammad and a small band of followers from Mecca to Medina in 622, a date that served to mark the beginning of the Muslim calendar. By extension, the notion of a hijra, meaning "to follow a religious leader," has been adopted by later millenarian movements in Islam, such as the Sudanese mahdiya.

[13]   P. M. Holt, *The Mahdist State in the Sudan* (Oxford: At the Clarendon Press, 1958), p. 141.

[14]   F. Rehfisch, "An unrecorded population count of Omdurman," *Sudan Notes and Records*, no. 46 (1965), p. 39.

1944—to 14% in 1956.[15] It is possible that with the spread of education, however limited, the Nubiyin monopoly of service in the government became less exclusive.

Another notable group in Omdurman are the Negroid Southerners. They are distinct in every respect from the Northerners and are sociologically a typical minority group. From about 4% around 1921 they increased to about 6% in 1955, a not very marked increase considering the improvement in communications which took place in the meantime. The seven thousand Southerners living and working in Omdurman are a highly mobile group: their age and sex structure suggests that they must be arriving in large numbers and in age selective groups.[16] If in spite of this age structure their total in the town does not increase, it must be because they leave almost as frequently (having earned, presumably, enough for whatever they were aiming at in Omdurman). It would thus appear that there is a sharp dichotomy in Omdurman between the convinced city-dwellers, who would actually be averse to the suggestion that they go back to the country, and the temporary in-migrants who never contemplate staying in Omdurman. This dichotomy seems to be much stronger than in some other African circumstances "where people are not certain yet whether to entrench themselves in the city or work for the day when they will go back to the land, or who have already made up their minds that eventually they will do so."[17] The likelihood of the Southerners staying permanently in Omdurman is small: partly because of the disturbed political situation, somewhat unfavorable to them, but also partly because of the continuing social climate, in which they have to survive. Two recent observers report that the Southerners in Omdurman are still being looked upon by the host majority as ex-slaves or descendants of slaves, treated accordingly, and called by some related term.[18]

Two other colorful groups in the town are the Westerners (from Darfur) and the West Africans, 5% and 2% respectively in 1956. They are popularly believed to be making their way for years on end to Mecca and back. A fair proportion is suspected to like Sudan so much that they stay for good, or at least for long periods of time. However, the main stream of these semi-religious, semi-economic migrants bypasses Omdurman. It flows probably further south through the Gezira on account of Gezira's providing work in the cotton fields.

[15] Department of Statistics, *First Population Census of Sudan 1955/56: Town Planners' Supplement*, prepared by D. B. Climenhaga (Khartoum, 1960), Table 9.15.

[16] With more reliable data than those available for Omdurman, it was possible to show that a particular type of urban age-and-sex structure is indicative of the temporariness of rural-urban migration. From Karol J. Krótki, "Temporariness of Urban Migration Estimated From Age Distribution in Large and Small Towns of East and West Pakistan," *Proceedings of the Pakistan Statistical Association*, no. 11 (Lahore, 1963), pp. 115-126 and four graphs. This is so when census after census gives a town a surplus of the young adult males who somehow never age. Judging from the urban growth and the prevailing fertility, they also make no contribution to urban fertility. Obviously, they come, soon go away, and their place is taken by others similarly motivated.

[17] Ezekiel Mphahlele, "African City People," *East African Journal* 1 (June 1964): 3-10.

[18] F. Rehfisch, "A Study of Some Southern Migrants in Omdurman," *Sudan Notes and Records*, no. 43 (1962), pp. 50-104; and P. F. M. McLoughlin, "Economic Development and the Heritage of Slavery in the Sudan Republic," *Africa* 32: 355-391.

The bulk of the population, but still less than half, are Arabs narrowly defined, i.e., excluding such groups as the Nubiyin, the Beja, the Darfurians, and the like. It is probable that this proportion will continue to rise, the proportion of the Nubiyin is likely to continue declining, and the proportion of Southerners will not become significant, as a result of the reasons already discussed. Then there could be operating the sheer momentum propelled by tribal support of one's own kith and kin.

Whether there is a subtler influence in the realm of assimilation is uncertain. On the one hand, the influence of the Arabic language seems to be strong. Although less than half of the population of Omdurman reported themselves in 1956 as Arabs,[19] as many as 97% were recorded as Arabic-speaking.[20] The relevant question in the census questionnaire referred to the language spoken as home. Mixed households (i.e., containing lodgers speaking different languages) must have reported Arabic as their lingua franca. But such an answer does not prove that the members of the mixed households lost their mother tongue. However, even if this hypothetical explanation is valid, the high percentage of Arabic speakers remains impressive. The cultural impact of Arabic must have been considerable. On the other hand, there seems to be a closing of ranks among the non-Arab tribal groups. It is as if in the strange, possibly unfriendly world of an Arabic town they had no time for their tribal particularisms and only wanted to emphasize their belonging to a larger, more powerful, better known, tribal group. It remains to be seen which of the two influences will be the stronger one in the process of assimilation and acculturation.

OCCUPATIONS

Of all the occupations listed in the 1955-56 census, the largest single occupation is that of shopkeeper—a favorite occupation among the faithful because the Prophet himself was a merchant. With shop assistants, they make up almost a fifth of the adult male members of the Omdurman labor force. In the country as a whole shopkeepers and shop assistants account for less than 3%. Even when "farmers, hunters, and fishermen" as well as "shepherds" are excluded, shopkeepers and shop assistants in the country as a whole account for only about 13% of the "non-agricultural" labor force. When all craftsmen and mechanics of Omdurman are added together they make up just over a quarter. The two groups account for almost half of the adult male labor force. The rest is spread over a wide variety of smaller occupations. Among the numerically less important occupations, there are interesting concentrations. A fifth of all non-technical professionals of the whole country live in Omdurman, but only a ninth of technical professionals—proportions consistent with the earlier suggested "drowsiness" of the town and economic non-aggressiveness of its labor force. Almost a quarter of the country's bookkeepers and junior accountants live in Omdurman. Only 67

[19] Population Census Office, *First Population Census of Sudan 1955/56: Eighth Interim Report* (Khartoum, 1957), p. 121.
[20] Ibid., p. 241.

persons reported themselves as "unemployed and beggar." The proportion in the whole country was twice as high, but even then ridiculously low. Obviously the definition did not embrace all forms of underemployment. What is important here is the similarity in this respect of the country as a whole and Omdurman. Clearly, the socio-economic changes in Omdurman are not exactly revolutionary.

The proportion of gainfully employed was lower than in the rest of the country in each of the four available age groups:[21]

		Percentage Employed in	
		Sudan	*Omdurman*
Males:	5 and over to under puberty	52.3	10.9
	Over puberty	96.5	85.2
Females:	5 and over to under puberty	6.9	1.6
	Over puberty	9.4	8.1

These proportions were lower in Omdurman in spite of the fact that the age distribution, insofar as one can judge from the fragmentary data available from the 1955-56 year census and from some earlier age distributions, was more favorable to labor force participation in Omdurman. The age distribution of Omdurman favors a high percentage of labor force participation on account of its lower fertility (which increases the proportions at adult ages) and in-migration of adult persons, including the already referred to temporary in-migration.

One is reminded of the lament of the District Commissioner of Omdurman, when he looked at the results of the (unpublished) census of Omdurman of 1944: "not a single establishment in the city of over 100,000 people employs more than twenty workers." Often, the question had been raised whether Omdurman serves merely as a dormitory center for those engaged in the industries of Khartoum. The answer has been in the negative because of the relatively slight traffic over the bridge to Khartoum. A more relevant answer might be that the whole pace of economic activity is slow and that the town of Omdurman is somehow a large parasite on the body economic of Sudan. The question then arises how one becomes an economic parasite. This journalistic phrase covers a variety of subtle phenomena. One of them is the fact that senior citizens in Sudan *like* to retire to Omdurman. Possibly for a related reason, such entrepreneurship as exists is not particularly aggressive. Surprisingly, even agriculture is slow to expand in the neighborhood of Omdurman, in spite of the increased irrigation and the next-door market for vegetables. There is some vegetable growing and a few local fruit gardens; fodder (lucerne) for milk-giving goats is reasonably profitable, but that is about all.[22] The Tuti Island at the confluence of the two Niles satisfies some part of the demand but hardly justifies the title "pearl of the Nile" bestowed upon it by Emil Ludwig in his biography of the river.

[21] Ibid., p. 1.
[22] K. M. Barbour, *The Republic of the Sudan: A Regional Geography* (London: University of London Press, 1961).

AGE AND SEX STRUCTURE

In the unofficial count of (probably) 1921 there were 87 men per 100 women in Omdurman. After the count of 1944, conducted partly as a check of the rationing system, the prestigious newspaper *El Nil* of January 9, 1945, reported that "adult females exceed the males by over 4,200 [giving possibly a masculinity ratio of 91 for all ages] but the acute marriage problem hitherto felt

TABLE 2. SOME SUMMARY COMPARISONS OF SUDAN AND OMDURMAN
IN THE FIRST POPULATION CENSUS OF SUDAN, 1955/56

	Sudan			*Omdurman*		
Population in 000s	10,263			114		
Masculinity ratio	100			110		
Percentage rural	78			NIL		
Percentage nomadic	14			NIL		
Persons per square kilometer	4			2,581[a]		
Persons per household	5			6.5		
Proportion of 1-person households	5.3			5.3		
Proportion of households with						
10 persons and more	5.8			18.8		
Proportion of households with						
16 persons and more	0.6			3.4		
		b	c		b	c
Crude birth rate	51.7	55.2	48.7	36.8	38.5	47
Crude death rate	18.5	22.0	21.3	13.3	15.0	17
Excess of births over						
death rate	33.2	33.2	27.4	23.3	23.5	30
Infant mortality rate	93.6	140.0		72.0	114.0	

[a]K. M. Barbour, *The Republic of the Sudan: A Regional Geography* (London: University of London Press, 1961), p. 97, says "over 3,000 persons" including the peripheral belt, squares, and gardens.

[b]Rates amended through a process of demographic analysis. Karol J. Krótki, "A correction to infant mortality," *Sudan Notes and Records,* no. 42 (1961), pp.53-84, which took seriously reported births of infants surviving beyond one year and deaths of persons over one year but adjusted infant deaths for underreporting by reference to numerical relationships in other countries.

[c]Rates estimated through the application of stable and quasi-stable population techniques. Paul Demeny, "The Demography of Sudan: an analysis of the 1955/56 census,"*The Demography of Tropical Africa,* William Brass *et al.* (Princeton University Press, 1968) based on several strong assumptions and a very elegant process of reasoning. If the estimate of death rates *is* too low, then the estimate of birth rates contains a downward bias and vice versa. The Omdurman column shows actual estimates for Khartoum province, as no estimates for Omdurman were made in this exercise.

can be reduced by the practice of polygamy." In 1956 there were 110 males per 100 females. The excess was all centered at adult ages, in spite of the mortality advantages enjoyed by women. Table 3 has been added to this chapter to show the difficulties of analyzing Sudanese data and the uncertainty of the conclusions.[23] The first difficulty with Table 3 is that there must have been a great deal of difference between the concept of "marriageable" in 1944 and 1956. It must have been closer to five years of age in 1944 while it was "puberty" in 1956. The large proportion of "single" in 1944 is consistent with this explanation. What is puzzling is that the number of "ever-married" males increased from 15,000 to 19,000 (an increase somewhat larger than the increase in total population would justify), while the number of "ever-married" females declined from 28,000 to 26,000. The excess of reported females over reported married males is a well-known feature of the Sudanese census. There are several contributing factors leading to this situation: polygyny is stronger than polyandry; women tend to claim married status, even if on tenuous grounds, to a greater extent than men; male mobility is higher than that of females, and consequently more males miss the net of census enumeration; and there are also other reasons.[24]   However, this feature appears particularly sharply

TABLE 3. MARITAL STATUS OF OMDURMAN INHABITANTS,
1944 AND 1956

	All Marriageable Ages	Single	Married[a]	Widowed	Divorced	% Married	% Ever[b] Married (Col. 1=100%)
	(1)	(2)	(3)	(4)	(5)	(6)	(7)
1944 males	41,251	26,746	13,386(5) [14,505]	675	439	32	35
1956 males	36,343	17,727	[18,616]		-	-	51
1944 females	44,316	16,605	15,861(14) [27,711]	9,430	2,406	36	63
1956 females	34,039	8,045	[25,994]		-	-	76

[a]Figures in parentheses show married persons with spouse absent. Figures in brackets show persons ever married.

[b]Ever married is a total of married, widowed and divorced.

SOURCE: For 1944, a typescript in the possession of this writer. For 1955, see Table 9 in Population Census Office, *First Population Census of Sudan 1955/56:* Final Report, vols. 2 and 3 (Khartoum, 1958).

[23]   The published data for Sudan, and particularly for Omdurman, are fragmentary, of uncertain validity, unreliable, and sparse. Some of the data are unpublished, particularly those coming from the 1944 count, but the tables are too bulky to be included here.

[24]   Karol J. Krótki, *21 Facts about the Sudanese* (Khartoum: Sudan, Population Census Office, 1959).

in Omdurman and is consistent with our hypothesis of Omdurman acting as a repository of widows, and of wives and mothers with husbands working elsewhere. Unfortunately, the very small number of persons married with spouses absent, as collected and reported in 1944, shakes our confidence in this explanation (Table 3, footnote a).

There seem to be two influences at work. There is in-migration of males, of which the previously mentioned Southerners are only a small portion. The in-migrants come without their wives, who are left behind in their villages; this has the beneficial result for Omdurman in that there are no bidonvilles, the curse of urban Africa. On the other hand, there is the tendency discussed earlier in this chapter for Nubiyin families to have a "headquarters" in Omdurman even if much of the economic activity is carried out elsewhere. Nomadic leaders would have a house in town much as the Jordanian bedouins do in Amman, presumably in which to keep their wives, especially the younger ones (to preserve their beauty or to facilitate their child-bearing), children of school-going age, elderly relatives, or other members of the larger family for shorter and longer visits. Almost a fifth of the households (not a fifth of the population, i.e., a much higher proportion of the population) were households of ten members or more, against 5.8% in the country as a whole. There were 3.4% households with 16 members and more against only 0.6% in the country as a whole (see Table 2). While some of the large-size households are institutional households and some may be caused by urban overcrowding, the figures are at least consistent with the observed tendency for some strata in Sudanese society to have a town house in Omdurman. They are also special types of houses, not particularly luxurious, if one can judge from averages: for the 18,000 households in 1956, there were only about 3,000 electrical connections, a slow movement on the 1,748 connections in 1944.[25]

Of the two influences described above, judging from the excess of males alone, the tendency to keep women in town seems to be weaker than the male selective migration into the town (and, shall we add, "the female selective underenumeration"). However, male selective mortality works in the opposite direction. As long ago as 1944 the War Supply Statistician reported in an unpublished document that the life expectancy at birth for men in Omdurman was 41 years and for females 45 years. One must be grateful for the rigorous segregation of sexes in a Muslim society for keeping peace among the excessive numbers of women left in town.

The proportions of infants and of children between one and four years of age are markedly lower in the case of each sex than in the country as a whole. Part of the explanation lies in a true fertility differential: the fertility in Omdurman is lower than in the country as a whole (see Table 2).

---

[25] In the statistical yearbook for 1956 a figure is given for all three towns together. It has been apportioned to Omdurman by reference to an earlier report giving electricity data for each of the three towns separately. This procedure has probably the effect of overestimating the growth in Omdurman.

CROSS-ROADS OR BACKWATER?

The Khalifa moved over to Omdurman because he felt closer to the deserts of the west and did not want to be cut off from them by the river in case of **attack** by hostile gunboats which could appear with little notice. There he built his forts to protect the town from the unfriendly river and kept his back open to the deserts. There are no more hostile gunboats on the river today, but the open Nile is small consolation as a means of transport. Such steamers as operate do so at a loss or have to stop short of reaching Omdurman when the river is low. Much of the profitable traffic has been skimmed off by the lorries (trucks) plying on the west bank of the river over the Bayuda Desert to Dongola. It is actually a surprisingly comfortable trip for a seasoned traveller, but the high cost of transportation and the limited economic opportunities of the Dongola area are such that no large-scale economic growth can be expected from this direction. The deserts further to the west might still be neutral or even friendly, but it is said that only the chewing tobacco grown south and west of El Fasher can stand the expense of the journey and still sell at a profit.

The nomads from Jizzu grazing[26] (one year in three) and those who were fortunate to find the luscious grass near the Meidob hills and in the Wadi el Howar might bring their animals for sale and take back with them in exchange grain, sugar, tea, and cloth. But all this is a small trade on which no big metropolis is likely to be built. The large meat-camel caravans for Egypt (there is no camel market worth speaking of in Sudan) go directly to Egypt, most of them over the Road of the Forty Days,[27] without the assistance of Omdurman merchants. The Eastern nomads, mainly the Rashaida, also go directly to Egypt. The Gezira nomads, Kawahla and Husseinat, might sell an occasional sheep, usually over-fat, and buy in exchange tea, sugar, and thread.

The big developments have missed Omdurman altogether. There is no railway siding and no airport of commercial significance. The new railway opening the distant west from El-Obeid was built as a continuation of the old railway which avoided Omdurman already forty years ago.[28]

Khartoum is no longer the foreign city or the city of the foreigner. The Sudanese moved in about seventeen years ago in force. The university is placed here and nearly all Government departments as well as the provincial headquarters. Successful coups d'état take place in Khartoum while they fail in Omdurman. There is no economic base in Omdurman and no longer powerful political groups.

---

[26] Jizzu grazing is possible in one year out of every two or three when rains have fallen in the waterless area on the Libyan border. It is quite a sight when the shiny, prancing, fat horses (in the absence of water they are limited to camel milk, while camels find the refreshing qualities of jizzu grass sufficient) return to their tribal areas; it takes superior feats of horsemanship to restrain them.

[27] The Arbayin Road was so-called because it took a caravan forty days to reach the Nile and the first markets in Egypt from the camel breeding areas of Darfur. It was an arduous road, but direct, and if public order prevailed, it enabled the camel caravans to avoid the rapacious intermediaries of Omdurman.

[28] The budding and the future trans-African trade from Port Sudan to Wadai beyond Sudan's Western Frontier will follow the rail and also miss Omdurman.

Some of the population estimates available for Sudan and Omdurman have been summarized in Table 1. The meteoric rise of the city during the Mahdiya was followed by the devastation immediately after the reconquest. The reasonably rapid increase in the first decades of this century was not continued in the middle of the century. Placed against the background of the changing socio-economic structure of the town, its demographic history, including the most recent history, makes a consistent picture: today the town does not grow much by in-migration; the turnover of its labor force is not contributing to population growth; the natural growth of its population is less than that in other parts of the country; its tribal composition is changing from the overbearing and powerful to the generally insignificant and unnoticeable; and its labor force has changed from being the back-bone of the Khalifa's arsenal into small merchants satisfied with a small turn-over.[29]

[29] Not even the sheil trade, this blessing and curse of rural Sudan, is much in evidence. The sheil are non-usury loan arrangements of mortgaging the next crop. There are not many crops to mortgage in Omdurman and its area.

ANNOTATED BIBLIOGRAPHY

Arkell, A. J., *A History of Sudan to A.D. 1821.* University of London: The Athlone Press, 1955. Good for the earliest history of Sudan. The book deals with the pre-history until 1821, when Ismail Pasha with the Egyptian Army, almost effortlessly, took over the various kingdoms still existing in the area of central Sudan and their monarchies collapsed. It is interesting and relevant to note that of the five references in this book to Omdurman all are archaeological. Omdurman did not exist until the Mahdi and Khalifa, the latter in a huff, moved his capital from Khartoum.

Climenhaga, D. B., "First Population Census of Sudan 1955/56. Final Report." *Town Planners' Supplement,* vol. 1. Khartoum: Department of Statistics, 1960. This handsome volume of over 300 pages contains much data of socio-economic significance for the 68 towns of Sudan, including Omdurman. Further valuable tables with statistical data for Omdurman in 1955/56 can be found in the three volumes of the final report from the census and in the Eighth Interim Report.

Davis, Kingsley. *World Urbanization 1950-1970,* vol. 1 (basic data for cities, countries, and regions). Population Monograph Series, No. 4, Institute of International Studies. Berkeley: University of California, 1969. In the consideration of urban phenomena, the "dominance" of the principal city and the various ways of measuring it are of particular importance for international comparative studies. The index used in this chapter was a two-city index. For a recent use for a four-city index see Davis, 1969, pp. 242-46. The indices, whether two-city, or four-city, or ten-city, are highly correlated. For a critical consideration of the related concept of "overurbanization," see Sovani, 1964.

Dugmore, A. Radcliffe. *The Vast Sudan.* London: Arrowsmith, 1924. Travelogues vary in quality depending on the interests of the writer, his powers of observation, and his ability to render impressions in writing. But they also depend on how recently the trip was made: the more recent the less interesting. However, even the most journalistic and superficial report will contain something of interest. As an example, the adventures of a photographer will contain confirmation of the racial admixtures of Omdurman (e.g., Dugmore, 1924, p. 59); an indication of the urbanistic problems (ibid., p. 58); and quite a gem in the form of a photograph of the Mahdi's tomb (ibid., facing p. 64) in its dilapidated state in the early twenties, that is, before its rebuilding was encouraged by colonial authorities.

Henderson, K. D. D. *The Making of Modern Sudan: The Life and Letters of Sir Douglas Newbold.* London: Faber and Faber Ltd., 1953. The life and letters of a British civil servant, who spent most of his mature life in Sudanese service, rising from the most junior administrative position to the most senior, "a true blue" (Newbold was a Scholar of Oriel at Oxford), who came to rule the "blacks." The biography is interesting and relevant: It shows the unimportance of the principal towns in the vastness of the country, and is an example of the lack of affection of the British rulers (and many senior Sudanese) for urban life.

Hill, Richard. *Slatin Pasha.* London: Oxford University Press, 1965.

Holt, P. M. *The Mahdist State in Sudan, 1881-1898.* Oxford at the Clarendon Press, 1958. This work of a British historian is based largely on the original archives of the Mahdiya, most of which were hitherto unused by researchers. On publication of the book, an immediate and comprehensive change in the prevailing and traditional ideas about the Mahdist state took place. There is much information about life in Omdurman, though all of it is scattered and tangential to the main theme of Holt's work. Reviewing a new edition, *The Times Literary Supplement* of 15 January 1971, p. 59, has this to say about the book: "It is Professor Holt's achievement that we now take for granted this picture of late nineteenth-century Sudan."

————. "The Source materials of the Sudanese Mahidiya." *Middle Eastern Affairs* 4(1958): 107-118.

Linsky, Arnold S. "Some Generalizations Concerning Primate Cities," *The Annals of the Association of American Geographers* 55 (1965): 506-513.

Ohrwalder, J. *Ten Years Captivity in the Mahdi's Camp, 1882-1892.* London: Sampson Low, Marston, 1892. There are also several translations. For the earliest Omdurman, the Omdurman under the Mahdi and his Khalifa, there are six memoirs by European prisoners of the Khalifa: Rudolf Slatin, the Austrian-Jewish Governor of Dar Fur Province appointed by General Gordon, turned Moslem, later Inspector-General of Sudan, friend of kings; Fathers Josef Ohrwalder and Paolo Rossignoli, priests from the Catholic missions in the Nuba Mountains; Ibrahim Pasha Fawzi (Slatin was only a Bey at the time of the captivity), commander of the Egyptian troops taken prisoners at the fall of Khartoum; a humble Italian by the name of Giuseppe Cuzzie; and a German trader from the Polish town of Poznan named Karl Neufeld. Every one of the memoirs provides rich anthropological and sociological detail of the life in the strange capital of the Khalifa, but if a choice must be made, Slatin's or Ohrwalder's memoirs are probably the most rewarding. However, Holt (1958) has shown quite convincingly that the two books were edited by Wingate, at the time chief of British Intelligence in Egypt and author of what would be called nowadays a war-mongering book against the Mahdist state. Both memoirs are written from memory. They are, nevertheless, valuable, particularly when corroborated with other materials. In any case, Slatin must be read with caution. One historian (Theobald, 1951) thinks that Slatin repaid ten years of generous hospitality with a scurrilous book, while another historian (Hill, 1965, p. 41) thought that "Slatin's hatred of the Mahdist regime was founded on twelve years' humiliation under its yoke."

Omar, Zein M. "First Population Census of Sudan 1955/56. Final Report." In *Town Planners' Supplement*, vol. 2. Khartoum: Population Census Office, 1960. This handsome companion to volume 1 contains 68 town plans and the plan of Omdurman with the boundaries of census divisions indicated to facilitate comparisons with any other areal data that might be forthcoming.

Von Slatin, Rudolf C. *Fire and Sword in Sudan.* London: E. Arnold, 1896. There are various editions, abridged and full length; also translations into German, French, Italian, and Arabic and probably into other languages.

Sudan Notes and Records

The forty-eighth volume of this sturdy annual appeared in 1967. Before, it had appeared twice a year. We hope that it will continue to appear even if delayed. It is a mine of data and information on things Sudanese. It is not possible to give a complete citation of all references to Omdurman in the *SNR*, but the following list might serve as examples of the kind of subjects dealt with in the annual.

48 (1967):33-61	translation of parts of Rossignoli, 1898
46 (1965):33-39	Rehfisch: "An Unrecorded Population Count of Omdurman"
45 (1964):35-47	Rehfisch: "A Sketch of the Early History of Omdurman"
43 (1962):50-104	Rehfisch: "A Study of some Southern Migrants in Omdurman"
42 (1961):52-84	Krótki: "A Correction to Infant Mortality"
35 (1954): 75-90	Sandison: "Problems of Low-cost Housing in Sudan"
34 (1953):281-285	Kenrick: "The Need for Slum Clearance in Omdurman"
31 (1950):65-81	Zenkovsky: "*Zar* and *Tambura* as Practiced by the Women of Omdurman"
30 (1949):39-46	Zenkovsky: "Marriage Customs in Omdurman"

Sovani, N. V. "The Analysis of Overurbanization." *Economic Development and Cultural Change* 12 (1964):113-122.

Theobald, A. B. *The Mahdiya.* London: Longmans, Green and Co., 1951.

Trimingham, Spencer J. *Islam in Sudan.* New York: Oxford University Press, 1949. Much information on the socio-cultural structure of the northern Sudanese with frequent bearing on life and its slow change in Omdurman.

56. Sheer population expansion has often left parts of the old madina seriously overloaded even though most of the population increase has been absorbed by the new modern sectors. This photograph shows one of the more important lower-class and lower-middle-class suq areas in Tunis, Tunisia. The mosque of Sidi Mahrez (*ca.* 1675) can be seen at the end of the street. (Photo: Lewis Ware.)

Contrasting "desert traditional" and "desert modern." 57. An aerial view of Riyadh, Saudi Arabia, showing traditional styles in center and foreground. Note the charming open courtyard in the foreground. (Photo: John Witmer.) 58. (below) The governmental ministries lining the four-lane Al-Wizarat Avenue leading to the airport. (Photo: Aramco.)

6

Kuwait: A Case Study

by Saba George Shiber

NOT far from the ancient seats of civilization—indeed not far from ancient Babylon, Nineveh, Persepolis, and Baghdad—a new Arab city has been built during the past two decades to add one more chapter to the saga of urbanization. This is New Kuwait: an extraordinary urban phenomenon strangely wedded to Old Kuwait.

THE SETTING

Many people, in their enthusiasm about the masculine and speedy development of the new city of Kuwait, tend to forget, if not disparage, the old city. The new city is undoubtedly a startling machine that has been assembled in an astonishingly short period of time. Yet, to a sentient student of urban affairs, the old city of Kuwait is, itself, a magnificent creation of man.

Located on Kuwait Bay, the old sea-oriented city of Kuwait is eight square kilometers in area. It was surrounded until 1954 by a mud-wall hurriedly built during Ramadan, 1918, in defense against incipient battle. The wall had four major gateways—Jahra, Naef, Shaab, Sabah—plus a small North gate. All these gates led out into the endless desert. Perhaps the outstanding urban characteristic of Kuwait today is the severe contrast between what *was*—the compact old town—and what *is*—the distended new town. Perhaps here, more than in any other place or time, diametrically opposed urban (and architectural) genres co-exist. The old town was compact, its typical dwelling a courtyard house (centripetally-oriented), its scale human. The new town straddles nearly twenty times the old area, its typical dwelling the house-in-a-lot (centrifugally-oriented), its scale that of the very large car. The old city was a cellular, "patio-city" strung around main pedestrian traffic arteries producing an urban pattern as "organic" as can be imagined. The visual prospects of Old Kuwait were simple. Urban aesthetics derived from spatial tension and release, from suqs

Pls. 63-64 (174)

Pls. 26-27 (79)
Pls. 57-58 (167)

This chapter is reprinted from the author's *Kuwait Urbanization* (Kuwait: privately printed, 1964), with appropriate updating.

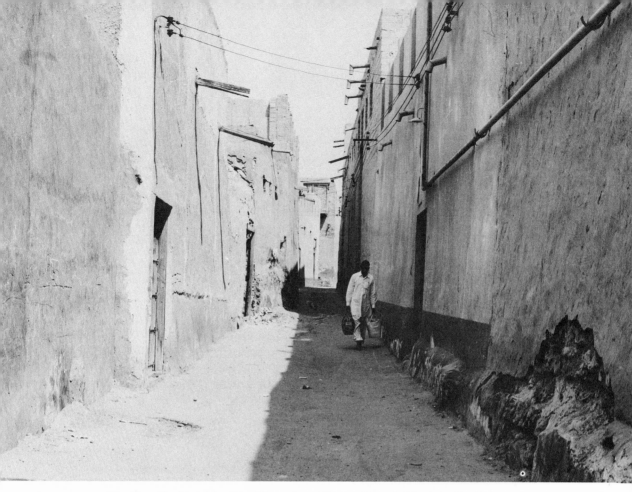

59. Kuwait. Street in the old section. (Photo: Kuwait Municipality.)

60. Hofuf, Saudi Arabia. Market day in the Suq. Comparable to Old Kuwait, Omdurman, and other desert Arab cities. (Photo: Aramco.)

and "midans" (squares) and from the domes and minarets of mosques. The old port served as a link with the outside world, and a colorful setting, or atmosphere, of "business" characterized the old waterfront. Here shipping, dhow building, and an "outside" type of social life, on a human scale, existed. Approaching the city by the sea or desert route one could see, in the distance, a typically Islamic desert Arab city. Although large parts of Kuwait have, in one way or another, changed radically, there are still quarters in Old Kuwait that have not been disturbed, giving one a true picture of the pre-oil urban state of affairs.

The old city was like a huge apartment house, its bazaars a huge department store, its alleyways and streets an interesting network of "highways." Its courtyards were centers for family socialization, industry, and relaxation. A balance had been achieved—the sort of balance of the medieval city—between man and man, man and God, man and nature, and man and his antagonists: the sea, the desert, the heat, the absence of fresh water, the harsh sandstorms. This was the urban and social setting as oil bombarded both city and man with a plethora of problems. Oil revenue increased from 1948 till it is, at the present time, estimated at over $800,000,000. The impact of revenue on the urban and social landscapes has been meteoric, radical, ruthless. It has all but obliterated in one hectic decade nearly all physical and social landmarks of the past. Industrious sedentariness became agitated urbanization, the latter fast becoming metropolitanization, regionalization, and cosmopolitanization.

The "mono-metropolitanization" of Kuwait occurred with lightning speed—setting, quite probably, a record in large-scale desert urbanization. As if with a vengeance, the compact and narrow areas of yore yielded to the distended and agoraphobic vistas of the new. Where there were a few cars in 1948, there are over 114,000 today. Space, cars, villas, highways, and large buildings replaced the intimate vista, the courtyard, the domain of man, the human scale. The car became glorified till now it is urban master.

Pl. 61 (171)
Pls. 65-66
(184)
Pl. 67 (191)

So significant is the advent of the car—especially the large and powerful car—on the urban scene of Kuwait that it is hard to comprehend the scope and scale of the new spaces in streets, parking areas, and undesignated areas its advent forced on Kuwait. It could be stated that Henry Ford's invention probably contributed more to the urban revolution in general—and to the urban revolution of Kuwait in particular—than wars, politicians, scientists, and social scientists. The automobile needs gasoline. Kuwait supplies the world market with large quantities of gasoline. With the revenue from its only exportable commodity, Kuwait has become, if not the highest, at least one of the highest, users and consumers of automobiles and gasoline per capita of population of any other society in the world. This is a cardinal factor that must be constantly borne in mind when the subjects of changing social mores and urbanization in Kuwait are broached. That the car has been the dominant factor of planning the city is, at one and the same time, the forte and liability of Kuwait's planning to date.

61. Safat Square, Kuwait, demonstrating the "advent of the car." (Photo: Ministry of Guidance and Information, Kuwait.)

62. Modern villas in Kuwait. The individual houses express an outward-looking extroverted style. Nevertheless, traditional Arabo-Muslim notions of private housing survive, at least in part, in the fairly high wall, which gives a sense of self-containedness to each plot, and, in the absence of sidewalks, a sort of no-man's land between houses and the street. (Photo: Kuwait Municipality.)

PAST AND PRESENT

Writing about aspects of Kuwaiti society, a well-informed Kuwaiti has stated:

> Unlike most Arab societies, Kuwaiti society was a compact, united, and classless society. Classes in the economic (Western) sense or the social (Oriental) sense never existed in Kuwait. The whole population—to all intents and purposes—constituted one big family. Even the wealthier members of society could not, and did not, attempt to separate themselves from the rest. This aspect could be attributed to many factors:
>
> 1. The size of the city of Kuwait, the country's only urban center.
> 2. The very small size of the population restricted one's circle of friends and companions.
> 3. The absence of non-Arab influence in Kuwait rendered the class concept incomprehensible. In other parts of the Arab World, classes existed due to foreign influence (from the Turks, the French, and other nationalities).
> 4. The absence of agriculture and, therefore, land ownership.
> 5. The nearest Kuwait had reached to developing a class system was at the peak of the pearl-diving era. But the decline of diving prevented its further development.
> 6. Due to tribal connection, coupled with tribal pride, even the poor elements of society refused to allow money and property to be a dividing factor.
> 7. Money had no place in considering marriage questions. Some families associated with less superior tribes, who accumulated wealth, tried to link themselves with superior tribes by marriage, but failed to do so. Hence, a class system, with all its traditions and conventions, never developed in Kuwait.

One encounters in Kuwait a decidedly unusual Arab, an Arab who, more like the Englishman, has developed an insularity of character mixed with a versatility of attitudes and actions. The Kuwaiti Arab fought the desert on one side, the sea on the other, and explored the depths of the sea in yet another direction. He is a desert-farer, a seafarer, a deep-sea diver, and a trader all in one. Having had to withstand the rigors of both desert and sea, in addition to the rigors of climate, the Kuwaitis had developed a discipline—an *esprit de corps* and a group feeling hard to encounter elsewhere.

A fair idea about the sea-faring and pearl-diving prowess of Kuwait can be gained from information supplied by a reliable Kuwaiti historian who has stated that, by the end of the nineteenth century, Kuwait boasted a merchant fleet of one hundred and fifty ships and that, by the early part of the twentieth century, thirty thousand men working with eight hundred ships engaged profitably and industriously in pearl-diving.[1]

To fight desert and sea the Kuwaitis built the unusual city of Kuwait on the inward side of the peninsula forming the Kuwait Bay. It was here that the winds, passing over the bay, cooled off a bit before they hit the mainland. At this point too, the sea was generally calm for the seaworthy ships the Kuwaiti built and which he still builds even to this day.

Old Kuwait is a unique urban form. Perhaps the truest Arab desert city type, it represents unmistakably how "necessity is the mother of invention." It had a bow-shaped rubble wall around its perimeter protecting it from the attacks of both man and the scorching sandstorms. Kuwait was sea-oriented; it faced Iran

---

[1] Hussein, Abdul-Aziz, *Muhadarat 'an al-Mujtama' al-'Arabi bil-Kuwait* [Lectures on Arab Society in Kuwait] (Cairo, 1960).

and Iraq and developed contacts with India and the Far East, and it is only relatively recently that the Kuwaiti Arab began meeting his Arab brethren from the West.

Not only was the city strategically located, oriented, and protected, but the internal anatomy of the city was so formed as to satisfy the needs of everyday life. The town was compact, with the necessary interstices for fresh air, shade, circulation. It is a masterpiece of the type of organic planning that grew as a solution to basic problems and needs.

The houses that the Kuwaitis built evolved also organically out of the requirements of a harsh environment. They answered social mores, climatic conditions, and the availability of building materials. There was no pretension about their design. Simple and dignified, they were built close to each other, protecting one another from sandstorms and heat. Built generally to produce a courtyard, they became the entity around which the social life of the Kuwaiti family revolved. The simplicity of the walls and their thickness, the use of woodlogs for roofing, the size and location of windows, the embellishment of doors and windows still command the attention of the sensitive eye as it is harrassed by the garish and obsequious imitation of "modern" architecture recently imposed on Kuwait.

Old Kuwait, like so many of its sister Arab towns, *is* an organic city. Its structure, seen from the air, is visually astounding. There is beauty in its overall form, logic and science in its diversifed parts, and interest in the quality and diversity of its architectural patterns. Infinite variety of prospect exists within the entity that is the city. Every space, every narrow street, every form grew, over time, to answer specific needs. And as the city grew and became ramified, it became the expression of a culture: of a sea-faring, desert-daring, pearl-diving, patriarchal society, governed and guided by the main driving force of the Arab: the religion of Islam.

Through Islam, architecture gained the mosque, a form of great architectural beauty. The play on dome and minaret, on the enclosure and release of space and on the use of Arabesque features for decoration can be seen throughout the old city of Kuwait. Approaching the city from either desert or sea, the minaret provided the contrapuntal element that helped to mellow the generally horizontal features of the site by providing vertical landmarks rising over the predominantly one- and two-storied city.

Until the mid-1950s, Old Kuwait was a pristine Arab town. It was light brown in color, congregated in a strategic area, and surrounded by a crenellated wall from sea to sea. Vestiges of the old wall may still be seen at four points around the city, providing interesting vistas into the newly rising sections within the old city. One can also see some trees growing around the old gates of the city, as well as along the central strips of the new broad city streets, a witness to the indefatigable efforts of the government to introduce greenery into the city.

The old city walls have been torn down and, in their place, a "green-belt" will be nurtured over the coming years. (This reminds one of the hundreds of medieval European city walls that yielded to the pressures of industrialization.) The desert yielded to a vast street system which divided the outlying areas into

63. Old Kuwait in foreground and to the right. High-rise buildings of New Kuwait in the background.

64. "Moderate-income" housing, Kuwait. (Photo: Ministry of Guidance and Information, Kuwait.)

neighborhood units. Instead of the old, narrow, winding alleys, one sees today ringroads, double-carriageways, and radials. Even the old city yielded to the new street system, and the network became one that encompassed and joined old and new. Hospitals, schools, government buildings, industrial areas, mosques, and housing spread in the old city and throughout the sections of the new city. Whereas there were only around 90,000 people living in Kuwait around 1950, today there are around 400,000. And whereas in 1955 there were a handful of cars in Kuwait, there is today a staggering number of cars in relation to the population.

Kuwait has been in general luckier than most other booming Arab cities. To a large extent, it depended on a modicum of science in the ordering of its physical urban affairs. It spent generously on roads, schools, hospitals, and housing. It spent generously to attract technicians from all over the world to man its expanding amenities and administrations. It followed an enlightened policy of facilitating the entry of people willing to participate in the building of New Kuwait. It spent generously to build Government administrations. It spent generously on consultants, experts, and contractors. It cannot be denied that, in an era of unlimited boom, the Kuwaiti Government acted as wisely as could be expected or anticipated during a situation of pressure, changing concepts, and augmenting problems, and in an environment plagued with physical harshness and a motley group of newcomers inveigled to the scene by the prospects of fast profit.

One feels sanguine enough to believe that the responsible authorities in Kuwait recognize the importance and urgency of writing the second chapter of Kuwait's development—a chapter that can only be written by the collaborative effort of the various government ministries as they draw on science, planning, and modern economic thought to act as the guidepost of development.

THE HOUSING PROGRAM

In many parts of Kuwait, people pressed for housing built all types of shelter indiscriminately. A large portion of the unguided and uncontrolled housing was built *without* municipal sanction. As a result, areas outlying the fringes of Kuwait, as well as the many villages surrounding it, exploded in unplanned fashion, thereby interposing obstacles to sound planning.

Faced with what seemed to be insuperable difficulties, I submitted a detailed report to the Municipal Council, entitled "Towards a Comprehensive City Planning and Housing Policy in Kuwait." The report, dated November 27, 1961, stated in part:

. . . housing is a serious social, political, economical and aesthetic proposition. It is neither a contractor's pastime nor an architect's exercise in geometry. It is a field with many basic and serious ramifications. How the housing problem in general, and aspects of it in particular, is solved will have a great bearing on the net social, visual, economic, and physical shape of things to come on the Kuwait urban-regional scene.

Kuwait faces at present many programs of housing that are not, so far, coordinated or articulated on either general conceptual grounds, on social conceptual ideas, or on physical dispositional distribution. To date, no comprehensive urban-regional schema exists to guide the type, distribution, and standard of housing; neither does a schema of graduation of housing type and quality exist. Nor is the place of work, the availability of transportation or the desired future shape of the city of Kuwait taken into consideration when a scheme comes up for action or verification. The most that may happen is that it is referred to PWD (Public Works Department).

Today, housing subsidy to low- and even medium-income groups is the entrenched policy of many governments. Housing agencies, departments, authorities, boards, commissions, or ministries exist to execute government policy in the design, erection and management of public housing developments. Subsidized housing is the policy of the Government of the Kuwaiti State. Being on the threshold of a new housing era, the Kuwaiti Government is in no position—time-wise or even money-wise—to improvise or experiment with public housing. For, this field has grown in recent times to be an institutionalized, complex, ramified, and vital field with a large body of knowledge associated with it. And Kuwait has its own indigenous and local characteristics and problems that must enter the overall picture to require a modulation of the known dynamics of housing to fit the particular circumstances. There is Kuwait's climate and local building materials; there is the existing and particular urban fabric and social structure; there is the particular and unique economy and the demographic dynamics; there are the cultural-ethnic characteristics and the landscape features—among a million and one other subtleties, complexities, and characteristics—that *must* enter the picture in the synthesis and evolution of a housing program, in building it, managing it, and making it a *human environment* instead of merely a *dormitory assemblage* of monotonous and soulless buildings.

For it well behooves Kuwait—as it seriously becomes engaged in a ramified and graded public housing program or a housing program based on varying degrees of subsidy geared to the different income strata of its population, as well as becoming concerned with demograph—to consider the following points seriously:

1. Public housing, though a duty of government, is not merely the physical construction of dwelling space to house people. It is a far more significant philosophic, social, physical, and economic endeavor.

2. It is essential for the Kuwaiti Government to set up an independent ministry or authority, preferably in conjunction with a ministry harboring Town and Regional Planning, and to require it to discharge the duties of survey, study, design, erection, and management of a comprehensive Housing Program.

3. Such a ministry or authority must have an assured annual budget, and its chief executive must be directly responsible only to the Minister of Finance and Economy in the elaboration and discharge of policy. Informal, but specific and close, liaison must be established with such ministries as Social Affairs, in which the Housing Census Unit is lodged, as well as with the municipality and the Housing Department. In the reorganization, consolidation, and creation of new departments, the housing function must receive special attention for authority, placement, and responsibility within the overall governmental fabric.

4. A housing survey dealing with existing housing conditions and housing shortages must be scientifically conducted to obtain an accurate documentation of housing units, their type, intensity of occupancy, structural and sanitary conditions, and distribution on a city-wide and country-wide basis. This survey must be supplemented with demographic statistics, as well as with statistics dealing with the sex and age composition of the population, its migratory characteristics, its income-levels, its occupations, its space-requirement indexes, and the like.

5. A five-year housing policy must be evolved and budgeted for, this being an act of the legislative body of Kuwait that cannot be remanded by a change of Government officials, in order to assure continuity of program, financial backing, and a stable, phased tempo of construction.

6. Capable town planning, housing and architectural experts, as well as capable social scientists, statisticians, and economists must be recruited to study and analyze the statistical housing and demographic picture as a preliminary step in the evolution of the actual housing programs and their distribution within the region of Greater Kuwait.

7. No public housing should be approved until definite justification is ascertained for its social, economic, and architectural validity by the permanent team of experts attached to, or advisory to, the housing ministry or authority.

8. The importance of the technical aspects of housing design—from the choice of site to the choice of building materials—must never by underestimated or discharged lightly. In a program of recurrence, concepts of mass production must be applied to effect accumulative economies when total volume is considered.

9. Any housing program must be geared to a *masterplan* of city and region; that is, it must be chosen to fit an envisaged urban and regional factor. Matters such as the place of employment of the housing residents, commuting distance to and from work, shopping, educational, recreational, and spiritual facilities as well as proximity to present or future public utilities, must all be thought of as essential to, and concomitant with, the overall housing program.

10. Too many housing developments in and around Kuwait have been built that are so dysfunctional, bleak, poorly executed, poorly maintained, and mislocated on the urban and regional landscape that they call for alarm. The repetition of such housing must be prevented.

11. The Kuwaiti Government must introduce serious town and regional planning training, as well as training in the fields of housing design, financing and management in its university missions abroad, for these are fields that grow daily in importance and urgency in a fast-growing state, while the training that is taking place in them is, for all purposes, insufficient.

12. Housing programs must be envisaged as positive tools in the execution of national policy dealing with population movement, industrial and agricultural trends and patterns, and the raising of the physical and spiritual standards of living of the citizens and residents of the State of Kuwait. *Rational communities*, and not projects of dormitory assemblages, must be the aim of housing subsidized by the Government of Kuwait or built directly by it.

13. The Kuwaiti Government must be on guard against quick, commercial, and package-deal solutions when this or that housing need arrives. It should particularly heed the broader, the more ramified, and the more comprehensive aspects of housing.

14. The proper location of sites for *any* housing program the government undertakes to finance and build must be given due scientific and town planning study.

Varying the Type of Housing Unit

Any discussion of housing is incomplete without reference to the absence, so far, of a balanced, harmonious, and varied admixture of the different known types of housing. Strange physical-architectural phenomena characterize the present residential areas of Kuwait. The neighborhood units contain, 100%, the single-house type of residential unit as do the villages generally. The remaining areas, particularly those in the Hawalli-Nugra-Salmyya residential complex, contain the multi-family type of dwelling going up in height sometimes to four stories. This dichotomous segregation of housing type may have had some strong justifications in the past. However, it would seem inadvisable to continue designing neighborhood-units on the basis of only the single-house type at the expense of the exclusion of *all* other types, as well as allowing building to create radical dichotomies in overall residential zoning or distribution.

Pl. 62 (171), 64 (174)

A report submitted by the author to the Municipal Council—entitled "Various Building Types for Limited-housing" (dated April 7, 1962)—served to highlight this problem:

If Kuwait continues to grow according to the pattern of the 750 and 1,000 square meter plot, it will become even a more tremendously extended city than it is at present. This is not only uneconomical but it is not conducive to social interaction and the conservation of valuable urban land.

In the case of building lots for limited-income housing, this probably becomes even more accentuated, especially in view of the daily increasing demand for lots for limited-income houses.

It is therefore necessary to reconsider the question of single plots for limited-income housing and to think seriously about the use of land in more imaginative and frugal ways. This can be done by using *row-houses*—two or two-and-a-half stories high—and *apartment houses*—three to four stories high. Not only will this type of housing conserve land, but it will provide the urban designer with more opportunity for creative layouts befitting to the unique climate and conditions of Kuwait. One can be this means create courtyards and commons, shaded areas and enclosures.

It has become customary practice in contemporary planning to inter-mix the different building types—single-house, row-house and apartment-house—in such ways as to create a physically and socially balanced community. There will be for a long time to come a need for varying building types for the different income-brackets of the Kuwaiti community, and an inter-mixed community would come closer to realizing a balanced community, as well as effecting economies in the use of land, the provision of streets and public utilities, and the creation of more adequate open areas for public use.

The three-storied walk-up apartment house should be seriously considered as a building type for limited-income groups within the bounds of the old city. In this area of the old city, it is expected that considerable land will become available for rebuilding purposes. Parts of it could be allocated to housing limited-income families in functional, simple, three-storied walk-up apartment-houses.

In the remaining parts of the city the row- or terrace-house is certainly worth exploring as a means for housing limited-income families. With the use of the row-house through proper design one can conserve the building area allocated, *per plot and family*, and using the effected economy in land and street surface for public and recreation areas.

Still better, when a large-scale scheme for housing is under consideration, one would do well to use the three types of building—single, row and apartment—in ways, means, and proportions to meet the needs of the various income-strata of the population to be housed.

In this way one will achieve many types of economy as well as an amelioration in urban prospect. For the indiscriminate use of the single-house—especially for the low-income brackets of the population—is not the most economical, desirable, and aesthetic proposition. It is worthwhile for the municipal authorities of Kuwait to give their attention to mixed types of housing.

AGRICULTURE

The approach to the problems posed by agriculture in Kuwait must be one that is scientific, imaginative, and comprehensive. It must receive the undivided and unstinting study and support of the authorities, for it is a sector of endeavor that is doubly important in the situation Kuwait faces.

Organic and scientific agriculture in Kuwait must be fostered, developed, and bolstered for the following reasons:

1. To mellow the harshness of the climate by changing, if not the *climatic*, at least the *micro-climatic* characteristics of the city region.

2. To create shaded areas and a better visual prospect within the city and beyond it.

3. To ameliorate the monotonous visual prospects which will, no doubt, be immeasurably enhanced by a concerted landscaping effort in the public and private areas of the city and its immediate region.

4. To shield against and attenuate the severity of the sandstorms by a scale of agriculture commensurate with an expanded concept of city and region.

5. To serve as a basic source of fresh vegetables and produce.

6. To propagate alfalfa and serradella on a large scale to support a livestock industry, as well as helping to produce a year-round prospect of greenery.

7. To promote agricultural employment, which, in turn, will foster a segment of a population usually dependent on agriculture.

The advantages accruing to Kuwait from a concerted, limited, but comprehensive effort in agriculture are legion. No doubt the difficulties faced by such an effort are tremendous. But, for the state to possess sounder prospects for the climatic, visual, and alimentary aspects of the problem must be scientifically approached and tackled.

Efforts to Date

The efforts of the government have been worthy of attention, and are commendable, but they are still on an experimental scale that does not contribute, *regionally*, to the vitality of the city-state. Certainly, the government is generous in its concerted effort to plant trees in the city, but this is only one facet in a comprehensive approach, if agricultural development on a far deeper and far wider scale is envisaged.

Flowers and lawns have been planted; large circles have been converted into pleasant parks; gardens, in many cases, are well tended; even a small livestock and poultry farm "industry" is in existence. And private companies have been set up on a commercial basis to prove that success is possible and assured for agriculture, horticulture, dairy farming, and so on. If approached on a scale commensurate with the demands of the situation and employing the full resources of the government to finance a comprehensive agricultural effort, surprising successes lie ahead.

Water

From times immemorial water has been known to act as a cogent magnet for urbanization. Thus, the Nile and Tigris-Euphrates areas have supported civilization for over five thousand years because of the presence of water, and the area that is Kuwait today has been eschewed, except for limited and negligible urbanization, due to the scarcity, if not absence, of fresh water.

A noted Quranic passage states: "Verily we have made from water every living thing." Water *has* played an important role in the history of the Arab. Even today, one knows of the bedouin's search for water and his almost instinctive "smell" of it. He has been able to survive in the harshness of the desert only by seeking out rare sources of water and with the aid of his camel—the "ship of the desert."

What water *can* do to Kuwait may be even more significant and dramatic than what oil has done, for without a permanent, dependable, and ample supply of fresh water, a sound agricultural program in Kuwait would be very difficult. To establish an extended agricultural effort solely on the basis of water distillation is, economically, also a dubious proposition from a long-range point of view. A permanent and economical supply of fresh water must be sought, and the Government of Kuwait has been unstinting in its efforts to discover or develop new sources of fresh water.

The condition of the desert may well be changed as a result of the discovery in 1962 of large underground bodies of water under the Rawdatein and Um-el-Eish areas. The Rawdatein aquifer is now known to be forty-five square kilometers in area and over fifty feet in depth. The Um-el-Eish aquifer is forty square kilometers in area and over thirty-five feet deep. By simple mathematics, one can gain an idea of the millions of gallons of water stored under the Rawdatein and Um-el-Eish areas, and one can gain an insight into what this volume of water, scientifically and judiciously used, can do to Kuwait City as well as to other parts of the state. As more detailed hydrological surveys of Kuwait are undertaken, many new "lakes" may be discovered that have been formed by the seepage of rain water.

Since the discovery of the Rawdatein and Um-el-Eish aquifers, the dynamic Ministry of Electricity has expanded the capacity of the present water distillation at Shuwaikh and is erecting a large water distillation plant in the Sheibe industrial area. A water supply network for Kuwait is under study and the Planning Board is, at the present time, conducting studies into the best way to approach the Shatt-el-Arab scheme.[2] This all indicates that the water situation in Kuwait is receiving the cardinal and concentrated attention of the Government and that it is safe to assume that the most serious problem facing Kuwait—namely the water shortage—is on the way to a permanent and viable solution. This being the case, the importance of the role agriculture and allied activities must play from here on is basic. Therefore, it is wise to lift the hitherto two-dimensional role of agriculture to one of multi-dimensionality and comprehensiveness and to expand its scope from one of limited city horizons to one of city-regional scope.

Not far from Rawdatein and Um-el-Eish, towards the Iraqi border, fresh-water wells of a capacity to support small settlements of four to six hundred persons can be speedily, easily, and economically bored. The soil in those areas has a lower salinity content than the areas of Kuwait City because they are, at present, dressed up with trees and greenery. The gas at the well of the Kuwait Oil Company at Rawdatain is just as useful as that at Ahmadi, and any advantages existing in the Sheibe area prompting the promotion of industrialization there, exist, perhaps just as suitably, economically and strategically, in the Rawdatein and Um-el-Eish areas. The urbanization of bedouins vitally concerns the state at the present time. A masterplan of regional development and settlement is in order—indeed demanded—by the confluence of cogent promotive factors of settlement, power

---

[2] Since Mr. Shiber wrote this, the following developments have taken place in Kuwait's water distillation and distribution: The total capacity of the units at Shuwaikh is now 18 million imperial gallons per day (MIGPD). In July 1961, a new distillation plan at North Shuaiba industrial area was put into operation, providing 5 MIGPD. It is one of five units to become operative in a year's time, yielding a total of 25 MIGPD. The present plant at South Shuaiba produces 9 MIGPD. Kuwait's present consumption of potable water is 25 MIGPD. Its future availability is estimated at 52 MIGPD. Kuwait's main water distribution system is already under construction and the entire system is scheduled to be completed by early 1974. The Shatt-el-Arab scheme studies and proposals are still being carried out though often delayed by political and/or technical considerations. (Mr. Victor G. Shiber, the author's brother, kindly gathered this information from the Kuwait Ministry of Electricity and Water.)

development, industry, and agriculture. A viable constellation of self-contained "settlement-units" could be developed that would provide good, secure, and productive living for many people. Settlements and agricultural estates can easily be brought into being. Moreover, large recreation and wildlife areas can be promoted by judicious water usage and protection. Kuwaitis can build agricultural, hunting, and recreation estates to be used for holidays, over the weekend, and so on. One knows of Safwan, for example, as an agricultural area. The same can be done in the general area of Rawdatein and Um-el-Eish as well as, in the distant future, in many other areas.

Tree Planting and Landscaping

No urban critique can ignore the vital element of planting and landscaping. There is a commendable and concerted effort to landscape and beautify Kuwait despite the antagonistic natural features such as poor soil conditions, excessive heat, and limited quantities of water. The agricultural-horticultural-landscaping effort warrants due pride in Kuwait, although deeper studies and better designs could capitalize on, and optimize, the overall benefits that must accrue from this effort. Like urbanism and architecture, landscaping must be functional and organic before being decorative, and, in Kuwait especially, it must be tuned to the compulsions governing urbanism and architecture. The Government Farm, Salwa Garden, Ahmadi planting, the planting in Dasman Palace and the Palace of H. E. Sheikh Abdullah el-Jaber, all demonstrate the benefits of concentrated planting in a habitat such as Kuwait's. In conjunction with planting and landscaping, the building of fountains is a necessity in Kuwait. And landscaping must depend heavily on inexpensive, lightweight shade-making devices, much more than used hitherto. Too much planting effort has been wasted in wrong areas instead of being geared to mollifying and beautifying the inhabited and frequented urban spaces. Indeed, a fact to ponder, along with similar situations in city planning and architecture, is that *not one* single landscape architect has ever been employed in Kuwait to date.[3]

Vegetational texture, like landscaped planting, is a spatial component in the overall spatial field and, thus, a determinant of urban formation. Natural or landscaped planting, as horizontal and vertical urban textural differentiators, are of increasing importance to the urban mosaic. Nor can planting *forms*—level, serrated, tall, short, clumpy—be underestimated as maskers of urban forms or as elements in silhouette, line, base, and parallax. Thus, when landscaping is referred to, its instrumentality as a modeler of space and volumetric regulator should be adduced, rather than the geometric artistry ordinarily associated with this field. This tenet is of basic applicability to the unique circumstances of Kuwait.

[3] The situation is now changed somewhat. At present the Kuwait Municipality employs one university graduate in landscape architecture. A second is currently on leave, pursuing postgraduate work in the same field. Major landscaping schemes have been commissioned to international consultants as part of a proposed Master Plan for Kuwait. (Mr. Victor G. Shiber has kindly gathered this information from the Kuwait Municipality.)

Untapped Resources

The Arabian Gulf and Kuwait Bay are rich in fish resources, and still no one has yet thought about fish as food for cattle, for example, as the Arabs of the Gulf did several centuries ago and which is, today, a procedure used routinely in many places in the world. The menhaden variety of fish could be used as fertilizer too.

A species of coastal plant, called mangrove, is known to grow along the water's edge in many places in the world that share with Kuwait its harsh characteristics. Still, not a seedling of mangrove has yet been introduced along the Kuwaiti waterfront.

Alfalfa is known to be the most tolerant type of plant to desert soil and is a top-grade plant in its tolerance to saline soil; it is known to hold the soil particles (and is thus good protection against sandstorms), changes the micro-climate, is excellent fodder, and can be rotated in monthly cycles. It tolerates brackish water well, provides a green prospect, and, yet, tons of alfalfa clog up the old port because alfalfa is still imported instead of being planted locally. Desert bushes and weeds can be propagated by sowing the desert with seeds. Kuwait has many helicopters, and yet not one seed has ever been dropped over the desert.

Land reclamation is a known science. If the soil is poor, it is fertilized; if it is saline, it can be "washed" or leached by either super-saturation with fresh water or by surface or sub-surface washing, flushing, and draining. That is why man has devised canals, underground perforated tile canals, and so on. To date, no flushing, leaching, or washing has been undertaken. Have the agriculturalists of Kuwait ever used "alginure" that could condition the harsh soil of the desert? Soil and flora classification are well-known sciences, yet who is engaged in Kuwait in this science, to date, seriously and scientifically?

The painting of desert sand surfaces by Aramco in the Eastern Province of Saudi Arabia is, by now, an accepted procedure to reduce the nuisance of the sandstorm and to enable wind and nature to work for man, just as windmills have been put to work for man. Sand dunes are hewn or cut down by a judicious "zebra-type" painting of the desert sand. No efforts in this direction have yet been attempted in Kuwait.

Many other fields are indicated as vital sectors for study and research to challenge the desert. For instance, no efforts have been expended in the conservation of the bushes of the desert, in harnessing the winds, or in the proper husbandry of the land. No research has been made in the probability of using a type of petro-chemical substance to spray the sand expanses with in order to hold the sands from flaring up into sandstorms. The prevention of the harrowing and harassing sandstorm begins at the source: at the Iraqi-Kuwaiti border. This, as well as water, soil, and other allied problems, must be faced and challenged in a concerted, scientific, and comprehensive manner.

Developing a Scientific Approach

For all this to be efficiently accomplished, the agricultural function and its place in the government *must* come up for scientific and organizational scrutiny in order to capitalize on these, as yet, untapped resources in Kuwait. What Kuwait needs, at this juncture of agricultural reappraisal, are more agricultural scientists and researchers, not merely field technologists.

In the old days, and by virtue of the necessity of survival, the Kuwaitis developed and lived in green areas, vestiges of which one can still discern despite the vast concrete and asphalt urbanization. In their primogenial status, Jahra, Salmyya, Fintass, Fahaheel, Abu-Halaifa—looked upon regionally before the automobile changed the scale of the region—were a chain of green settlements along Kuwait's waterfront. They are starting points, if one were to enlarge the horizons of his thinking, to an expanded outlook on agriculture. From these points agricultural effort could start, expand, and radiate till a useful and badly-needed mantle of green is spread out from these points of origin. This can be done if a masterplan is projected for agriculture by agricultural master-planners working as a team and given the unflinching support of all that science and finance can provide.

TOWARD A MASTER PLAN OF KUWAIT

The unguided growth of Kuwait *beyond* the so-called planning area came as a surprise to all responsible planning authorities and officials, engineers, and architects after mosaics of aerial photography conducted in October, 1960, arrived in Kuwait. What was revealed was spread and sprawl, ribbon development, mixture of uses, wastage of land: a dishevelled urban portrait that hid, beneath it, the germs of urban disorder. To me, the urban situation loomed as a catastrophe and as unnecessary, wasteful spoliation. I became convinced that all possible forces in executive power, talent, and the law *had* to be mobilized as one mobilizes to face an emergency, to save the day for augmented Kuwaiti urbanization.

From the very first day I started working in Kuwait (June 15, 1960) I had formed a general idea about what the planning maladies *then* facing Kuwait consisted of, as well as about the broad framework within which the corrections must be made in order to enable the broad structural framework of the future urbanization to be realized. In the realization of this master-conception, I did not have the sympathy or support of my immediate planning staff, who were too busy with the insignificant and immediate minutiae of planning to realize that ordering the broad lines of the physical affairs of the city was all-important. I was, however, fortunate to have the sympathetic ears and open minds of several key members of the Municipal Council who, more and more, granted me their unqualified support at those critical junctures when planning decisions had to be made.

From the beginning, I was oriented in my planning paths by several guideposts I had early set for myself as targets. Some of the factors that dictated the need for a unified treatment or master-plan follow:

1. *The functional interdependence* of the parts within Kuwait, while transcending conventional visual limits, demanded an integrating idea at the basis of which is rationality and the will to order. This warranted overall planning.

2. *The natural unity* of the regional configuration of Kuwait (a platform on which the urban mantle is spread) is a *de facto* unity, demanding its assimilation in urban configuration as a desirable design goal. Topographic accents and nuances

65. Aerial view of Kuwait showing public park and major hotels in the foreground. Note the major broad boulevard winding through the city. Old Kuwait is dwarfed in the distant background. (Photo: Kuwait Municipality.)

66. General view of Kuwait with the Shuwaikh neighborhood in the foreground. (Photo: Kuwait Municipality.)

may not only attract the actual locus of specialized types of urban settlement, but may serve to inspire new developments based on the natural beauties of the region. The unified sculptural geomorphology of the region demanded a new type of development and a unified treatment.

3. *The kinetic element* of urban progression is enhanced visually if the chronology of seen objects is *unifiedly,* even though cinematically, designed. Principles of harmony, rhythm, integration, surprise, interest, tension and release (known to the musician, conductor, novelist, cameraman) must be geared to the human being's need for variety in the cajolement of eye and ear, thus demanding composition of urban settlement on a continuous scale.

4. *The critical need for municipal expansion* beyond the political, or arbitrary, to natural boundaries may not be a cause for unified design on a large scale, but a result of the same factors that demand the treatment of evolving settlement as a plastic sculptural unity. Annexation of urban land to urban centers is a common practice by which financial solutions to urban problems are sought.

5. *Kuwait's potentials* were not only commensurate with the type of overall planning I envisaged, but were so unique they demanded statesmanship in planning above all to capitalize on their benefits.

Thus, notwithstanding its trans-visual spread, Kuwait, by absorbing regional geomorphic form, had to be functionally and visually organized so that it could be a composite of the diversiforms of its infra-natural and man-made parts. The stronger the topographic character and natural content of the region, the more natural will be the overall form-movement of the city. Unlike its predecessor, now Kuwait loomed as a unity on a regional scale made up of entities of varying spread, set in the unifying circulatory system. Through design, emergents could be arranged so as to realize such architectural qualities as may be deemed aesthetically desirable.

I gathered my thoughts into a general policy statement dated February 20, 1961, and entitled, "Kuwait: Year 2000 A. D.: Toward A Curvilinear City," which was circulated to the planning staff and presented to the Municipal Council. The following are excerpts from the statement:

A city must derive form, shape, and structure as much as possible from geography, topography, philosophy, and ecology. These four sources of inspiration in city formation and growth contain perhaps all the necessary factors that must be taken into account in city formation. Thus, *geography* contains determinants such as climate—an important factor that begs for careful scientific and aesthetic treatment in the overall projection of city growth as it does in architecture. *Topography* involves important elements such as the nature of the site and the waterland situation if this exists. Conformance and due regard to topography (which means surface land configuration as well) is an elementary principle in town growth and site planning design. *Philosophy* is a more tenuous determinant than either geography or topography for its compulsions lie more in the social, spiritual, and aesthetic realms than in the tangible, physical, and tactile ones. *Ecology* involves basic relationships between organisms (of which man is the most sophisticated) and the habitat or environment.

It has been a rare feat in the march of cities to successfully coordinate geography, topography, philosophy, and ecology in their formation, evolution, and expansion. There have been, however, towns that have grown *organically;* that is, in conformity with the compulsions and determinations of the foregoing elements. The medieval city is considered to be one such type and the typical Arab town—of which Old Kuwait is a classic example—is another.

As one studies closely the general and original dispersion of population in what is today considered "Greater" or "Metropolitan" Kuwait, one would discover easily that this area has grown so fast as to encompass the original, germinal nuclei of population settlement. A process of *conurbation,* or *coalescence,* has happened and is still happening. Broadly speaking, the original settlements have been Jahra (an oasis slightly removed from the sea due to the presence of fresh water in that locale), Old Kuwait (originally called *Koot,* meaning an arsenal or fortress), Salmyya (ad-Dumna, Ras al-Ard, al-Bida), al-Fantas, Abu-Halaifa, Ras al-Mangaf, Fahaheel, and Sheibe—all settlements that were attracted by the waterfront. The hinterland, or desert, was deliberately eschewed, and rightly so, because proximity to the water proved a more rational place of settlement . . . .

In 1951, when the plan of Kuwait was prepared, comprehensive city and regional planning had long superseded mere paper or street planning, and this advocated type of master-planning is not "crying over spilt milk" but, rather, a warning that the continuation of the present trends of sporadic urban "addification" and "stratification," improvised as this or that city need arises, must be immediately stopped. Though the physical damage done to Kuwait—micro- and macrocosmically is serious, some repairs are nevertheless possible on the microcosmic level, such as the reorientation of planning thought in the CBD (Central Business District); but on the macrocosmic scale the city must be encouraged to take on a *linear growth-motion* along the coastline. From Salmyya to Abu-Halaifa that *is* still possible. And, if the type of excrescenses that are fast loading the western flank of the city are checked (cemeteries, stockyards, leprosarium, contractors plots, prison, quarantine station, etc.), the same remedial action may be possible in this area too.

The future shape of Kuwait can be made curvilinear with residential development forming the first layer of growth on the land side of the *grand-corniche.* Within this arc-shaped and broad development will be the heavy urban facilities: airport, industries (especially as the need for them grows by the day), public institutions, etc. The city would then look something like a linear, coastal city: a rational, functional, economical, comprehensive, and commodious conceptualization.

This type of urban projection and conceptualization will require a major policy decision on the part of Kuwait's authorities; a major reorientation of the present developmental libido; a major review of presently accepted concepts of land acquisition; and a refurbished concept in municipal city structure and administration. The municipal authorities of Kuwait *can* pave the way for the future growth of Kuwait along these broad lines when it is realized that the alternative to contemporary, comprehensive regional planning is day-to-day improvisations, an aggregate of urban inconveniences, a greater loss in wealth and the wastage of the opportunity to create a new urban idiom in house-and-garden, in street-and-building. In short, a new type of desert city, blessed with unlimited space opportunities, wealth, and the pecuniary attraction of first-class technical help can, and *must,* be created.

On January 12, 1962 I submitted a report to the Municipal Council of Kuwait entitled "Urgent Long-range Master-highway Network for the Kuwait Region." Excerpts of my translation of the report from Arabic follow:

Looking at a regional plan of the Kuwait area and its vicinity, that brings into focus the area west of Jahra and south of Ahmadi, enlightens one as to the future shape of this fast growing metropolis which one would like to call *Kuwaitopolis* for easier reference.

Looking at Kuwaitopolis reveals many important facets about an area that has exploded in a series of ringroads and radials to become at least twelve times its original area of settlement, from the advent of oil and during the past twelve years. One sees in broad outline something resembling a *double-humped camel* pointing its hump to the Arabian Gulf and the Kuwait Bay: the camel seated with Asheirij its neck and head and the Ahmadi-Fahaheel complex its tail.

The line roughly between Jahra and Ahmadi constitutes the base of the kneeling camel. The area covered by the profile of the camel is a large desert area, with the regions of the two humps the already urbanized areas. The villages of Fantas, Abu-Halaifa, al-Mangaf, Fahaheel and Sheibe constitute its sloping back.

One foresees this large region, within the next fifty to sixty years, to be the "Greater" or "Regional" Kuwait area. It is in this light that one *must* view the region *today* to assure for it a main regional structure. Such a structure would prevent any misdirected growth from happening along the main circulatory system. In the short-term development of Kuwait, during the past ten or twelve years, many impediments to logical growth have occurred to create major urban problems. The repetition of such mistakes must be foreseen *today*, and steps must be urgently taken to assure for Greater Kuwait an unimpeded growth in the years ahead.

In order to make this growth possible, the approval of five major traffic arteries or routes must be made as soon as possible because they are crucial to Kuwait's future . . . .

These five major roads are the *bases*—the structure—of future Greater Kuwait. They are essential for assuring steady flow, access, and linkages; any delay in their adoption, *in principle*, may provide the opportunity for immovable impediments growing up in their proposed paths. With these as the main arteries of future Kuwait, one can base the future land-use study on general and broad categories: *residence, recreation, transportation, industry*, and so on. Their adoption will assure a dispersive traffic pattern in the future and will aid the spread of traffic as uniformly as the major traffic magnets will permit. . . .

This general "Greater Kuwait" highway network must be speedily approved in principle. After that a general land-use study must be made for the land areas affected by this network. And the planning jurisdiction *must* be enlarged from the presently artificial limits to encompass the natural area extending from beyond Jahra to the west to the Neutral Zone to the south, thereby bringing in under one overall planning jurisdiction the south-western part of the State from Jahra to the point of inflection of the boundary of the Southern Neutral Zone along the boundary of the Neutral Zone to the Arabian Gulf. If an arrangement can be reached whereby coordinated planning can be achieved South of the Neutral Zone along the coast of the Arabian Gulf, this step would achieve many planning advantages of a long-range nature.

In another report, entitled "Comprehensive Master-plan for Kuwait" (dated December 27, 1961), I wrote:

What is needed for the preparation of a comprehensive master-plan for Greater Kuwait is more than the employment of just one or two planners or experts. What is needed, first of all, is a *Central Planning Board*, commission or authority, the span of knowledge and control of which would cut through all government ministries. The Central Planning Board must encompass in its membership experts in the major allied fields of city and regional planning, and they must, as much as possible, represent the major government ministries in order to act, at the same time, as the unifiers—the coordinating agents—between themselves.

Second, this board must have a capable secretariat for handling the necessary administrative, legal, and correlative functions. In addition, it must have a full-fledged technical staff of planners, architects, engineers, statisticians, economists, sociologists, analysts, and industrialists.

Third, the Central Planning Board must have knowledge—the kind of knowledge that is assembled scientifically and not by hearsay or guesswork. It must have either under it directly or in some way attached to it the Central Statistical Bureau, or Census Unit, of the Government. Without the essential bureaucracy, the most that can be expected is schematic and ad hoc planning, the type of which Kuwait is not only replete with but which, indeed, has characterized it during the past six to seven years despite the great credit due to the building of such a major urban complex.

For the preparation of a master-plan for Greater Kuwait, one must also have at hand the basic urban data that are commonly collected by means of what is called a "planning survey." The planning survey, actually, is constituted of many surveys, the most essential of which, in the contemporary planning dogma, are the following:

1. *Mapping Survey.* All types of maps are needed, at various graphic scales, for the preparation of a master-plan. These maps must depict existing buildings, streets, contour lines, and natural characteristics and features.

2. *Aerial Survey.* A basic planning tool, it is already being made available after the aerial photography survey conducted in October, 1960. Additional airphoto information is currently

being asked for. Indeed, being small in area, Kuwait State must be covered in detail by aerial photogrammetry, and air-photo interpreters must be retained.

3. *Traffic Survey*. This is needed by the planner in order to be guided by the picture of traffic flow, volume, distribution and patterns . . . The traffic survey helps in projecting traffic volume and load into the future in relation to projected overall land-uses.

4. *Population Survey*. The information collected by the Census Department of the Ministry of Social Affairs and Labor must be analyzed in order to provide the planner with a true picture of population composition, density, and distribution. What is the use of census information if it is not disseminated to the concerned authorities who should, in turn, use it constructively for planification and design? Demographic projection must be based on future immigration policies and government policies in both the public and private sectors.

5. *Land-Use Survey*. This must be conducted soon to provide the planner with an exact picture of the manner in which *all* land in the city-region is currently being utilized. From it the planner must be able to spot areas of land-use malfunctions; it also aids him in preparing the zoning map (and ordinance) through which a master-plan is commonly effectuated. The industrial and oil-use land in the Sheibe complex must receive priority.

6. *Condition of Buildings Survey*. This gives the planner a true picture of what building, or group of buildings, are standard or sub-standard and guides him in his studies for the allocation of slum-clearance or redevelopment areas and for the need of future building as well as for expropriation outlays and priorities.

7. *Community Services Survey*. This type of survey locates all land and improvements thereon used for public purposes. It will show schools, hospitals, mosques, parks, cemeteries, fire stations, police stations, and the like. These must then be tested for adequacy against present and projected population figures.

8. *Land-Use Survey*. This basic tool of the planner is helpful to give an indication of what his proposals will entail in terms of expropriation money, as well as aiding in the gearing of budgeting for land acquisition.

9. *Land-Ownership Disposition Survey*. This shows what land is to be expropriated, what land is in public ownership, and what land is in private ownership.

10. *Current Projects and Pending Projects Survey*. This will document for the use of the city-regional planner the fluid state of urban affairs, so that he may be guided in his long-range planning.

11. *Particularistics Survey*. This will indicate all unusual features of the area to be taken into account in future planning.

Obviously the new planning must be of a broad as well as of a deep scope, bringing under the span of planning every allied and related activity of government. Kuwait's future is unique. To optimize future results and returns the caliber of the staff charged with planification must be high. Kuwait has set the precedent in many basic fields of endeavor in the Arab world. It can set the precedent in overall, comprehensive, and scientific state planning.

In the Arab world, generally, planning—where it has been operative—has not been applied on the basis of data collected and analyses made as much as on the basis of guesswork and arbitrariness. In the field of city planning, planning has likewise been more the result of the quick lines and strokes of men often remotely removed from the essence of the scientific method and, consequently, many serious functional, aesthetic, and economic casualties on the metamorphosing Arab urban scenes have been inflicted.

TOWARD A THEOREM OF URBANIZATION

From the foregoing documentation, analysis, and critique, as well as from the relative magnitude and speed of the Kuwait urbanization, many conclusions can be adduced. This urbanization has, by all standards, been a unique one in the history of urbanization by virtue of the unique conditions in which it happened.

Urban formation may follow primarily functional dictates irrespective of visual results, or it may be a result of the conscious fusion of functional and visual determinants. The latter approach is more comprehensive because it places equal emphasis on aesthetic and functional considerations. Isolated, generic observations of actualities or obvious causalities are deficient, as, for example, the interaction of form and function in urban formation. Moreover, attempts to isolate theories about as universal and dynamic a process as urban formation, based on either the observation of fact, the fecundity of imagination, or limited hypotheses, lead to universally inoperative, or partially operative, theories of urban formation. And such general descriptions as "the form of cities" or "theory of city form" miss the cardinal precepts on which urban formation must be predicated because, by their ambitious generalizations, they fail to account for the *comprehensive* interplay of functional and non-functional determinants in the never-finished symphony of formation.

Theorem of Urbanization

To account for the many decisive variations of urban development, variables may be set up in a dynamic equation, which is called here, "theorem of urban formation." This theorem is modulated, in time, by the incidence and activity of universal urban forces. The application of "active urban universals" in the theorem of urban formation is a more comprehensive approach to the prediction, within the limitations of predictability, of urban formations from which *may be* adduced possible form patterns and/or non-patterns.

This theorem may be stated thus: Given active *urban universals* (factors that should influence urbanization rationally), *urbanization* and *urban forms* may be delineated with certainty. Corollary to this are the following points:

1. A theoretical and ideal-type urbanization might be expected by design if the theorem of urbanization functioned in a rational context.

2. Subject to this logic, urbanization is independent of materials of construction and style of architecture since the definition of aesthetic, functional, and behavioral space is largely independent of detailed articulation but is formed by geometric-plastic planes.

3. For any past, present, and future time it is possible, in the present and within broad limits, to explain, design, and project urbanization.

Obviously, this theorem and its corollaries may be challenged, because it is impossible for an ideal-type urbanization to keep a simultaneous pace with change. Thus, the active element per se is dynamic and subject to vitiation by any change in planning principle. The lag, or discrepancy, between a succession of active universals lies at the core of urban contradictions and enigmas. In addition, the term "human" connotes some ingredients of irrationality. Thus, the main variants of the universals are period and people.

Therefore, the foregoing theorem must be modified to read thus: *Given active urban universals, urbanization, and thus urban forms, may be broadly ex-*

plained, predicted, and designed in direct proportion to the predictability of change and the mode of incidence of the rational factor.

This dynamic theorem explains why most urban scenes are, and may continue to be, patchwork mosaics of emergents and groups of emergents often displaying unconcealed physical convolution. It also explains why, were an urbanization to be spatially conceptualized within the harmonious interplay of the universals, the *convolution,* irrevocably correlated to dynamicism, would likely continue to transpire, as a comic commentary on man's urban handiworks; they would either incorporate the idiosyncracy of an individual by inevitable sequential obsolescence, or be the composite idiosyncracy of the group whose actions are similarly susceptible to the inevitablity of obsolescence. Thus, the vision and creativity of the urban architect must harness all types of urban contrasts as harmoniously as possible.

Final Considerations

The existence or absence of planning directives may help in a functional ordering of form, but does not necessarily guarantee to offset the many inevitable hierarchies of urban contraposition.

Thus, a platonic idealism vis-à-vis urban formation is likely to be frustrating, were the ranges of beauty, aesthetics, and form not as elastic as they are and were man's aesthetic judgment immune from emotional and, it may be added, romantic tinges. Functional urban principle will effect a lesser dependence of urban aesthetics on what man designs than on what nature does to the resulting forma-tion. (Herein lies one of the main reasons why landscaping in Kuwait *must* receive particular, scientific attention.)

Where urban beauty is unattainable by sensitive and exacting differential design, nature must perforce enter the urban scene to temper man's failings. This entry harbors hopes for urban beauty. This beauty may be optimized if emergents are consciously harmonized for optimum elegance and sightliness with man-made and natural space, and if the exciting evolving forms in architecture and engineering are not spent, isolatedly, without optimum harmonious co-relationship to augment their singular beauty . . .

Perhaps the weakest link in the chain of urban formation is an aggressive creativity in design. It is suggested that urban design education be scrutinized for content to discover whether the future urban architect does get an intimate understanding and a feel of the static-dynamic urban determinants examined in this study. For it is by aggressive manipulation of these determinants that vivid, interesting, aesthetic urban environments are discoverable. Such design must be further attuned to the vicissitudes and meanings of *time* in urban formation, where many time spans obtain, each requiring comprehension and attention.

Historic Time. It demands a philosophy and perspective of change, whereby the old and the new are harmonized and contrapuntally treated. This does not advocate an archaeological congelation of the past in the present but a dynamic,

67. Major shopping street in modern Kuwait. (Photo: Ministry of Guidance and Information, Kuwait.)

68. Modern apartment building in downtown section of Jiddah, Saudi Arabia. Note the lattice-work shutters added in two cases for privacy. One may question whether these modern, Western balconies accord with either the harsh sun and heat of the environment or the cultural preferences of the buildings' inhabitants. (Photo: Aramco.)

overall, and localized relation of the present to the past. This represents a slow but continuous thread of change.

Planning Time. Planning time may be considered a subdivision within historic time. Being a relatively speedier process (25-30 years), time-span must be handled so that the inevitable design-in-time process does not introduce comic and avoidable anomalies in space and scale but that change, occasioned within planning time, is accommodated as harmoniously as possible.

Progression Time. It demands a synchronization of the parts to the whole in relation to the kinetic component of vision in terms of *coups d'oeil* of urban features.

Modular Time. Day, night, and seasonal modulations are proposed as short-range, long-range modular considerations whose maximization is possible by sympathetic acknowledgment in design.

That there is no paucity of possible urban forms but, rather, a prolific reservoir of pleasing forms in consonance with the active urban universals must lead to the belief that, where such forms are not capitalized upon in the construction of the urban environment, the fault must lie either in those sectors of human endeavor that retard, if not obstruct, the enactment of the best potentials of man-made creation or in the design capacity of those entrusted with creation, or in *both*.

The results of countering urban ugliness by large new developments, the danger of achieving "the sanitary age" by "antiseptic design" in regimented monotony, is the danger that confronts urbanism today. Can this tendency towards what may be called a sterile urban aesthetic be avoided?

CONCLUDING THOUGHTS

Whatever the future of the cities of man may be, man is building cities or expanding them madly. And, unless man blows himself up, cities will certainly continue to grow at an accelerating rate to catch up with the spiralling population explosion.

The significance of contemporary urban planning must lie in the deeds made for the citizen. It must lie in the spiritual, social, cultural, and educational . . . not in the marble or marble-clothed monuments, memorials, and other clichéd antics of city beautification. To be magnificent and marvellous the city must be so *socially*.

City planning today is, first of all, a serious human outlook. Second, it is strategy in the use of land and the building dispositions that take shape over it. Third, it is the use of science, economics, sociology, and modern finance and administration in building and running a city. And throughout, the silken thread of art, architecture, and aesthetics—in short, *beauty*—ties the disparate parts and phases together and knits them into a harmonious unity.

To lift the architectural-aesthetic content of the environment, the content of the cultural component must be uplifted. A relationship of close reciprocity exists between the two. The value of the art aspects of the urban environment depends on, and revolves around, the values the society chooses to set as its preceptual and ideological targets, and how sincerely it complies with them.

Part III
COUNTRY PLANNING

7

Evolution of Concepts of Housing, Urbanism, and Country Planning in a Developing Country: Morocco, 1900-1972

by Jean Dethier

THE following essay is deliberately schematic. No attempt has been made to write the contemporary history of urbanism—and even less of the city—in Morocco. The central aim is to propose several modest themes for the sake of a dialogue, or to provoke a necessary debate as soon as possible, on a subject which one scarcely talks about in spite of its importance.

Architecture and urbanism are powerful factors conditioning the individual. They are especially important because one is always under the influence of his environment even though he may not always be conscious of it. It might be said that during the colonial period, Western imperialism was in this way able to insinuate itself into the Third World by utilizing radical methods of de-personalization, or at times by more subtle but even more dangerous means.

The anthropologist Lévi-Strauss and the sociologist Pierre Bourdieu have demonstrated the mechanism of this refined system of alienation. They have explained how missionaries or the civil or military authorities of colonialism utilized urbanism and housing to uproot traditional values and, even more, to "pacify," stupify, and annex the Bororos in Brazil and the Kabyles in Algeria. If indeed there existed a "colonial urbanism" to support colonization, there exists now, no less, methods adaptable to the new process of "neo-colonialism."

Before the colonial powers established themselves in colonized countries, the so-called "underdeveloped" countries had created cities and traditional architecture of a great quality. In this regard, the countries of the Near East possess an exceptionally valuable architectural patrimony, but one which often remains unknown or despised. The colonial situation in effect destroyed or falsified the values and introduced considerable confusion of spirit. It is thus that certain

69. Fez, Morocco. Gate and fountain of the caravanserai Nejarin. Note the "fret" design in stone and plaster, and intricate geometric and floral design—quite typical of Moroccan and North African architectural decoration. (Photo: Office National Marocain du Tourisme, Rabat.)

countries of the Third World continue to copy indiscriminately those Western concepts which are most harmful to their psychic, cultural, and economic integrity.

To stop this unhappy state of affairs it is necessary to break the vicious circle by:

1. analyzing the process used to "colonize" the minds and countries of the Third World in matters of urbanism and housing,

2. denouncing the harmful methods and theories,

3. rehabilitating the perennial values of the cultural, architectural, and urban tradition in each of these countries,

4. studying new ways which will associate in a realistic and harmonious fashion a modernized tradition with the teachings of multiple contemporary experiences.

The Western model is not universal, and it has already caused sufficient damage. New means of action for urbanism and housing which permit the abolition of the system of mental, technical, and economic dependence on the rich countries and which favor the flourishing of the Third World into authentic new cultures must now be found. In this way urbanism and architecture will have rediscovered the true role which they have lost for several generations.

As a guide in this situation, the Moroccan case seems to be especially interesting for several reasons: first, because a great number of admirable examples of the urban role and tradition growing out of the popular spirit, ancient or modern, still exists; second, because during the French presence (1912-1956) a great number of different urbanistic and housing doctrines were applied, ranging from the most subtle in their neo-traditional paternalism to the most radical in their authoritarian technocracy; finally, because independent Morocco has resolutely decided to put forward a new realistic strategy well-adapted to its own resources and aspirations.

1906–1926

Since the beginning of the twentieth century, various European countries have tried to settle in Morocco. France aimed to set up a coherent network of territories in North Africa, where she had already "possessed" Algeria since 1830 and "controlled" Tunisia since 1881. In 1907, different pretexts gave the French Army the opportunity to penetrate into Morocco, and military settlements were established on the eastern plateaus and at Casablanca in the west. On both sides of the territory, the machine was at work. Immediately following on the heels of the Army came a new kind of people—pioneers, adventurers, and settlers.

Creation of Interest

From 1907 to 1912, "numerous acquisitions of land were made and enthusiastically encouraged by the consuls of every nationality in order to establish their individual interest and give their respective governments rights over the Sherifian Empire" whose final fate had not yet been decided by the colonial powers. "Land acquisitions made at random without any prior study were particularly disastrous in Casablanca: the city will always show the indelible mark of its

Fig. 8. Sketch Map of Morocco.

chaotic origin and will never really get rid of it. Casablanca was composed almost entirely of plots laid out haphazardly . . . Frantic speculation took place, everybody picturing his own plot as the center of the future city."[1] Prices increased and the frantic rush of private interests accelerated. In 1910, the German company Mannesmann acquired huge plots in areas of potentially high real estate value, especially in Mohammedia. In 1912, the French company Hersant did the same thing. Just before the creation of the French Protectorate it seemed likely that in the years to come a "policy of non-interference" would extend to every city in order to satisfy without delay the desire of foreigners for immediate benefits.

Policies and Town Planning

In 1912, when France officially established a Protectorate over Morocco, Marshal Lyautey was nominated both as "Résident Général" and head of the army. He had

[1] Henri Prost, in *Urbanisme*, no. 88 (Paris, 1965), pp. 12-13.

full power and intended to use it, particularly for the realization of his conceptions as a town-planner. He was later to say, "I have always had two passions—policies regarding the natives and town planning." His concern for town planning was revealed in 1897. "It was in Madagascar that I first understood the beauty of the *urbs condita* when I saw with a father's eye the small town of Ankazobe, whose plans I had drawn on that very ground."[2]

Thanks to his personality and convictions, the Moroccan cities were well taken care of. He was perfectly aware of the errors in town-planning made in other French colonies. He knew, for instance, that town planning in Algiers and in other Algerian towns had been disastrous, because every town-planning action was under the jurisdiction of the Ministry of War. . . in Paris! In Morocco, Lyautey wanted to express clearly his own style of government, which could not be dissociated from an energetic program of action in cities.

Centralization

Lyautey soon made three personal decisions which were to have considerable effect on the entire organization of the country and on the nature of the national network of cities and communications.

First, he ordered the transfer of the political capital from Fez to Rabat. The insecurity still prevailing within the country induced him to avoid geographic isolation. In further justification he observed, "as the starting point of seven big natural routes which open out like a fan in every direction, Rabat is wonderfully well situated as an administrative capital."[3]

Shortly thereafter, he created a new, modern harbor at Casablanca, 90 kilometers south of Rabat, destined to become the economic metropolis of the country and one of the largest harbors in Africa.

In addition, in 1914 Lyautey decided to create *ex nihilo* a new city in the estuary of the Oued Sebou in the fertile plain of the Gharb, 45 kilometers north of Rabat. This artificial urban center which initially satisfied the military requirements was to become a flourishing civilian town. This was the city which was to bear his name, Port Lyautey (now Kenitra), until independence.

As for the new town of Mohammedia—located between Casablanca and Rabat—its expansion and the operation of its harbor were in the hands of private capital. In short, right from the beginning of the Protectorate, a series of settlements had been concentrated on the Atlantic coast. The furthest distance between these four localities was 130 kilometers. Half a century later, this "string of towns along the coast" was to attract half of the urban population of the country and one-eighth of the total population within an area of less than 1% of the whole of Morocco.

The first steps that Lyautey took toward centralization caused the center of Morocco to gravitate toward the Atlantic. The traditional system of regions and regional capitals was replaced by a new, modern order evolving around two poles

---

[2] See Pierre Lavedan, *Histoire de l'urbanisme* 3 (Paris, 1957): 190.
[3] Maréchal de Lyautey, *Textes et lettres*, 4 vols. (Paris: Plon, 1957).

consisting of an administrative capital (Rabat), an economic capital (Casablanca), and various satellites.

Town Planners for the Protectorate

Once these major decisions had been made, Lyautey sought town planners to plan the cities where European populations would be concentrated.

Among those recruited was Henri Prost, who arrived in Morocco in December 1913, with a one-year contract. He was destined to stay ten years. In 1910, Prost had won the prize at an international competition held in Belgium for the planning of the harbor and the city of Antwerp.[4]

Prost became Lyautey's official town planner and was assigned a considerable task—the creation of the new cities of Casablanca, Rabat, Meknes, Fez, Marrakech, Sefrou, Taza, Ouezzane, and Agadir. Improvisation was ruled out. Lyautey had already given much thought to the kind of program he wanted, and he imposed from the start three rules to be scrupulously followed in every case.

1. *Separation of madinas and European quarters.*

The first rule was that *new European quarters to be built must be separated from the old madinas in order to protect the autonomy of each.* Some people took this as evidence of his intention to enforce segregation. Others, on the contrary, saw in it a great respect for the habits of Moroccans, and a desire not to interfere with their traditional organization of cities. The 1925 edition of the *Guide Blue* for Morocco offered the following explanation, which seems to reflect official thinking: "The experience acquired in Algeria and Tunisia suggested the use of an excellent principle concerning the preservation of the old Moroccan cities. European quarters were built, as far as possible, away from the Moslem cities, in order to preserve the striking originality of the latter and the kind of life to which their inhabitants were accustomed."[5]

The coherence of the traditional Moroccan cities obviously fascinated Lyautey, who, for a military man, was exceptionally aware of the cultural and artistic aspects of cities. He probably realized, too, that it was politically advantageous to protect native culture. No doubt Lyautey sincerely wished to avoid defacing the madinas, as had been the case in Algiers. In a letter written on January 2, 1922, he reminds us that the protection of native cities had always been "one of [his] major concerns."[6]

Prost tactfully interpreted Lyautey's imperative insistence on a separation, so as not to create a sort of "no man's land" between two civilizations. In Rabat, for instance, one can proceed from the European quarter to the madina as naturally as one proceeds in Western cities from the old quarters to the new ones. On the other hand, "the European sector of Kenitra is separated from the native section by a military strip (covering an area 500 meters wide and 1,200 meters long)."[7] This is because the plan of this town was the only one conceived by the military before the arrival of Prost.

---

[4] *Urbanisme,* no. 88 (Paris, 1965), p. 13.
[5] Guide Bleu, *Maroc* (Paris: Hachette, 1925), pp. 71-72.
[6] Maréchal de Lautey, *Lettres et documents* (Paris: Plon, 1952), vol. 1.
[7] Guide Bleu, *Maroc,* p. 238.

2. *Protection of the cultural heritage.*

The second important rule in Lyautey's town planning project was the *protection and improvement of the most representative urban sites and ancient monuments of Moroccan history and of traditional architecture.* This choice was complementary to the first. Within the framework of the Protectorate, Lyautey wanted to protect the cultural heritage. As early as 1912, he created a *Service des Beaux-Arts et des Monuments Historiques* with the purpose of preserving and restoring venerable architectural units. He often intervened personally, with great determination to rescue the heritage of Moroccan culture, which he held in high esteem, and often asserted views considered very progressive for the times. Rather than enforcing administrative measures to protect a single monument (which could in the future be surrounded by new buildings detracting from its beauty), he preferred to "consider the totality of a quarter as an historical monument not to be touched in its lines and aspects."[8] In 1920, he was advocating town-planning concepts which were to be applied internationally only in the 1960s. Thanks to his paternal and watchful protection, Moroccan cities can still be proud of the remains from their past. Particularly remarkable are the walls surrounding the cities. Some people, however, interpreted the decision to maintain walls around madinas as a strategic measure, intended to facilitate the control of the native populations when trouble arose.

3. *A new style of town planning—for Europeans.*

Lyautey's third rule consisted in *applying to the new cities the newest and most elaborate principles of town planning.* The first two rules were mainly "protectionist"; it was only in this third that Prost had a chance to show his creative talents. At the time these modern cities were constructed, working conditions varied according to three factors: (1) possibilities of acquiring the necessary land; (2) topography; and (3) occupation of the land by preexisting (old and new) buildings or districts. In Meknes, Fez, and Marrakech, the location of the new city was determined by the situation of the suburban lands, which either belonged to the *makhzan* (state) or were the properties of *Habous* (religious foundations). Under these circumstances, it was possible to avoid speculation by the gradual, controlled sale of huge plots; and the advantage of their being sold directly or auctioned at a moderate price was counterbalanced by the obligation which lay on the purchasers to put their land to good use according to every requirement of the Administration and the relevant urban project. This insured in a positive way the coherence of the new cities.

These properties, however, were often two or three kilometers away from the old madina. Thus, in these three cities, the situation of the available land confirmed or stressed the initial will to separate the two communities.

Fez and Marrakech were two important and traditional capitals in comparison with which the rising European quarters appeared merely as small dependencies located at a prudent distance from the madinas. In order to reassure the foreign minority groups, important military camps were situated within a short distance of

---

[8] Lyautey, *Lettres.* Letter of December 13, 1921, concerning the protection of the Oudahias Quarter in Rabat.

the European quarters, such as Camp Gueliz at Marrakech and Camp Dar Mahres at Fez. On the other hand, in Meknes as well as in Rabat, the new city was initially of the same importance as the madina. The two entities balanced.

Rabat: Urban harmony

In Rabat, both cities lie side by side and at first sight make up a visually harmonious whole. There existed outside of the madina of Rabat various ancient monuments or buildings standing alone in fields or orchards—for example, a large mosque, the palace of the Vizier, Bab Rouah, the Hassan Tower, and the Chellah, an ancient Moslem necropolis encircled by remarkable ramparts. Around these historical witnesses located within the natural expansion area of the city, Prost planned with imagination and skill the organization of the new city center and its main administrative and residential districts. His well-conceived plans were gracefully adapted to the sites and requirements of the preexisting buildings, which thus became noticeable and well-integrated points of the new city. Prost had in mind the refinement of the asymetrical compositions of the Middle Ages and the Baroque era, and he approached town planning as a cultured man, as an aesthete. Rigidity and abstract planning were carefully avoided in favor of a varied and graceful layout allowing for a gradual discovery of perspectives, sites, and buildings. No pompous monumentalism, no military systematization. In Algeria, by contrast, the new cities and the settlement centers had been "designed" by army officers according to the Roman tradition. But Lyautey remained violently opposed to such architectural and urbanistic stiffness. He hated stereotyped formulas and plans, and railed against the use of ready-made formulas imposed without regard for circumstances; for architectural mediocrity—particularly that of military and public buildings—infuriated him.

Casablanca: a Huge Jigsaw Puzzle

Rabat is without doubt Prost's greatest achievement; but in Casablanca, on the contrary, he did not accomplish much. He opposed the speculators whose interests had already left their mark and had conditioned the city. "The French authorities are faced with the problem of having to deal with a city which has already undergone a fantastic rate of growth according to private needs and initiative. The idea is no longer to create something new but to try to harmonize what already exists within the broader framework implied by the final [sic] French settlement."[9] Prost further explained that "cutting into such an important and parcelled out city in full prosperity, to alter its orientation and reorganize its basic elements (the harbor and railway station), is a difficult operation which can be solved only by special laws."

Legislation Comes to the Rescue of the Town Planner

These sorely needed laws were rapidly passed and enforced. First the "dahir on urban planning" of April 16, 1914, was "an instrument adapted to the necessity of

---

[9] Extracted from the report of the Director of Political Affairs addressed to the Resident General on June 18, 1945.

acting quickly in order to forestall too rapid a growth of the cities." [10] The goal of this first modern town-planning law in Morocco was to create for a whole city or for various districts an expansion and development plan which would determine the width, direction, and layout of streets; the location, dimensions, and disposition of gardens, parks, squares, and open spaces; and the various obligations to be fulfilled in the interests of public safety, hygiene, traffic, and aesthetic considerations. Thereafter no construction could be undertaken without a permit from the authorities.

In 1914, there was no such legislation even in France. (It would be introduced five years later.) Morocco, meanwhile, served as a trial run, a huge field for experimentation. To complete this law, the "dahir on the associations of urban landowners" was approved on November 10, 1917. It aimed at facilitating a rational reclamation of plots belonging to various landowners within certain areas affected by development operations (sanitation, for instance), for, undeniably, the former process of expropriation had been inadequate and ineffective.

Community Interest versus Individual Interests

Despite these legal implements, the urban plan devised for Casablanca was not bold enough. "Prost's predictions, which seemed to have been warranted by the uncertainties of the period, were in fact constantly outrun by the events. The authorities themselves, still in the throes of organization, could not effectively follow, control, and direct the often unpredictable development of the mushroom-town." [11] Prost had not foreseen the colossal nature of Casablanca's growth in the followng decades; one had to admit that nobody had predicted such an expansion. Even so, he organized the center, attended to the most important issues, and established the essential administrative bodies of the city. All this was to be outpaced by an irresistible wave of profitable individual ventures which together made up a vast and incoherent magma.

Rabat and Casablanca—the two largest cities in the country—make an interesting confrontation thanks to their geographical proximity and to their differences: on one side we have urbanism, as opposed to rampant urbanization; the clash of a city of "men" against an agglomeration of "businessmen"; a harmony of community against individual speculation.

Urban Planning and Egocentricity

The plans for every new city were made as if the Protectorate were to be eternal and, in particular, as if only the European population were bound to grow. With few exceptions, the Moroccans were confined within the walls of their old madinas, and no plans were made to provide them with new districts. The disastrous consequences of this carelessness and urban-egocentricity were felt as early as the 1930s. There are, however, some remarkable exceptions to this rule. The Administration of the Habous is a traditional religious foundation whose organization was modernized following the 1913 dahir intended to secure

---

[10] Preamble of the Law.
[11] Report of June 18, 1945, to Resident General.

immediate and practical use of the massive funds available for it. The Habous thereafter became an important semi-official body able to invest in the construction of buildings which might be planned by the state. It was in this context that between 1915 and 1930 the first modern developments of native Moroccan housing were conceived, such as the Habous quarters in Rabat, Meknes, and Casablanca (the latter by far the most interesting in its conception and dimension).

An Exemplary District: The "Habous Quarter" in Casablanca

From the very beginning of the Protectorate, the old madina was explosively overpopulated. It was thus decided to build, on the southern outskirts of Casablanca, a new community in order to absorb and attract the excess Muslim population arriving in droves from the country. The first nucleus of this "native district" was called the "Habous quarter," and it was viewed as an autonomous entity within the large city. In fact, this exemplary district remains today one of the major testimonies to the architecture, urbanization, and housing of the 1920s. It is also the symbol of a certain "social action" of the Protectorate apparently undertaken in order to please and accommodate a growing new social class.

The "Culturalist" Approach

In her book *Urbanisme: réalités et utopies*,[12] Françoise Choay notes two opposite trends in the development of ideas about the modern city—the "culturalist" and the "progressivist" approaches. The first approach has been followed (since the "pre-urbanism" of the eighteenth and nineteenth centuries to the "urbanism" of the twentieth century) by Ruskin, William Morris, Ebenezer Howard, and, more recently, Camillio Sitte, Unwin, Patrick Geddes, Mumford, and others. The "progressivist" approach is represented in the twentieth century by Tony Garnier, Gropius, Le Corbusier, and the architects belonging to the CIAM.[13] In Morocco we can notice, between 1920 and 1950, this same divergence of theories but more grotesquely expressed. Prost, together with Lyautey, led the "culturalists," and the Habous quarter stands as this movement's manifesto. Françoise Choay notes that France has not known in the twentieth century any follower of this culturalist movement while there are numerous examples in Anglo-Saxon countries. It is interesting to note that the transfer of French urban architects to the Morrocan context immediately provoked their adopting the "culturalist" teachings. They accomplished several works of international value still little known in architectural or urban planning circles. The Habous quarter, therefore, deserves to be carefully analyzed for it is a perfect illustration of the tendencies of an era and a region.

A Neo-Traditional Urbanism for . . . Moroccans

The Habous quarter was conceived as a truly urban entity, very precisely delimited, whose uniformity of style contrasts with the heteroclite buildings erected later on

---

[12] Françoise Choay, *Urbanisme: réalités et utopies* (Paris: Le Seuil, 1965).

[13] "Congrès Internationaux d'Architecture Moderne," a movement founded by Le Corbusier whose members drafted the "Athens Charter."

its outskirts. This coherent quarter was envisaged as a small suburban town three kilometers from the harbor). Its surface area was reduced but the site was densely occupied. Strongly inspired by the organic image of the traditional Moroccan madina, the planning of the quarter combined an impressive series of neo-traditional visual and aesthetic effects with the technical advantages of the modern city (such as garbage disposal, water and electricity supply, and sewers). This successfully synthesized the traditional organic aspect with a discreet but efficient modernism. All symmetrical or geometrical forms were avoided. Before conceiving any plan, the architect Albert Laprade made numerous drawings and surveys of the madinas of Fez, Salé, Rabat, and Marrakech in order to determine the sources of inspiration. The results of his research were published, and the book is today regarded as one of the best graphic documentations about traditional urban architecture.[14] Everything in the Habous quarter shows this knowledge of and admiration for the old local environment. However, the result was not—as in Europe, with some "culturalists"—to revive a dead past, since the Moroccan madinas in the twentieth century are still urban bodies of medieval type in full activity. It was rather an effort to retain the "image" of an outdated past. One cannot even say that this implies "a flight from the insurmountable obstacles of the present" on the part of the planners since the same team simultaneously created "new cities" for Europeans whose program conformed with the criteria of modernism.

Casablanca's "New Madina" Townscape

In this urban landscape, there is no hint of monotony, prototypes, or repetitive standards. The public buildings and community facilities assume the greatest qualitative and visual importance. These are numerous and are carefully integrated into the texture of housing units: no trace of monumentalism in the Western style (such as the isolation of a significant building by open spaces). Public areas (streets and squares, galleries and malls, lanes, and small squares) have been handled with a care and a refinement exceptional for the twentieth century. The variety and nuances of their highly differentiated outlines are equalled only by the prodigious diversity of contrasted space and volume offered for the appraisal of the passer-by.

The abundant ornamentation skillfully alternates with the unadorned masses and the empty and occupied spaces of a sculptural but familiar architecture. Everything is devised so as to transpose (or rather to keep alive) the multiple semantic expressions of the traditional urban life.

This urban quasi-theatrical "scene setting" produces a diversified succession of enclosed and intimate spaces and creates, at least for Europeans, a "psychologically reassuring climate" that stimulates interpersonal relationships.

But the life and success of this area are particularly well expressed in the intense activity encouraged by its numerous socio-cultural facilities—two mosques, one hammam, one funduq, one qaysariya, coffee shops, several suqs and other shops, all amounting to more than a hundred commercial establishments. All these establishments are remarkably well placed among the different housing units from which they can not be visually, materially, or socially dissociated. The emphasis is

[14] Albert Laprade, *Croquis* (Paris: Vincent Féal, 1954).

always on the communal and social aspects of the city. By contrast, the houses appear modest, but they are provided with real urban comforts, including individualized spaces in well-conceived buildings that are adequately equipped. There is an effort in every building or house to blend architectural individuality with traditional ornamentation. From the planning stage, craftsmanship was seen as an integral part of the architecture. It is not merely a decorative "superimposition" (as it became later), but a real desire and an opportunity to restore to architecture an ornamental value which by then had disappeared in Europe. Prost himself observed that he was "lucky to find in Morocco a decorative art still living in spite of its having remained constant for centuries . . . so architects have assistants who create for them conditions similar to those of their colleagues in the great centuries of art."[15]

Urbanism as "Psychic Pacification"?

All this town planning and preoccupation with urbanism seems politically significant. Was it not the very expression of the concept of "protectorate" transposed into architecture? What was the object of such thorough and elaborate work? Did the architects not act, in this colonial context, patronizingly? We could perhaps apply to this kind of achievement the critical vocabulary used in the 1960s by some Moroccan intellectuals to qualify the colonial action of the Protectorate. Was not this urbanism an attempt at "cultural recuperation," at "ideological manipulation through colonial human sciences"? Was it not an attempt at "psychic pacification"? Was not this environment designed to "petrify the contemporary development of a national culture" by the fostering of an "excessive fascination for the past"? Did they not try to emphasize certain traditional cultural forms pre-selected for their so-called "harmless" aspect in order to "reduce Moroccans to a non-intellectualized expression of their own culture"?[16]

These questions are always valid. However, the achievements of the Protectorate—and others similar to it—were considered in the 1930s as the perfect example of the type of urbanism to be extended to colonies everywhere.[17] And they required huge investments, extensive work over a long period of time, and all said and done, concerned only 5,000 inhabitants (in other words, less than 1/300 of the population of Casablanca in 1970).

Inspired by the Habous quarter, or its genetic model—the madina—other planners conceived various "cities" for workers designed to provide lodgings for Moroccans working at some important factories. In Casablanca, we have the "COSUMAR" and "SOCICA" quarters; in Bou-Jniba and Khourbiga, the units of the "Office Chérifien des Phosphates." Most of these quarters are surrounded by walls broken up by only a few points of access. Did this correspond to a neo-traditional sense of aesthetic or to a desire to "trap" the working class?

---

[15]   *Urbanisme*, no. 88 (Paris, 1965), p. 29. Architecture predominates as the artistic medium because of the reluctance in most Muslim countries to reproduce human forms; hence, the paucity of sculpture and painting.

[16]   L'Association pour la recherche culturelle, *Souffles*, no. 12 (Rabat, 1968), pp. 3-9.

[17]   Jean Royer, *L'Urbanisme aux colonies et dans les pays tropicaux* 1-388 (La Charité-sur-loire: Delayance, 1932); 2: 124 (Paris: Les Editions d'urbanisme, 1935).

Achievements

The achievements made from 1910 to 1920 can be summarized as follows: The districts reserved for natives were few in number but their conception required most of the talents, creativity, and spirit of the French architects and town planners. On the other hand, quantitatively speaking the essential effort of urbanization, equipment, and urban planning was devoted to the extension of strictly European cities.

Nevertheless, these achievements brought considerable praise to France at the "First International Congress on Urbanism in the Colonies" held in Paris in 1930. It was solemnly declared that "the Moroccan experiment now was, thanks to Lyautey's and Prost's efficient collaboration, regarded as an authoritative example, listened to and respected by every large colonial nation."[18]

"Among all the North African countries and perhaps among all the colonies, Morocco was at the head of the urbanist movement. Morocco had the good fortune to be governed by a man who had full power and who combined, in this capacity, artistic insight and a gift for action. He was the soul of this work."[19] Lyautey's aim was to plan and build cities in accordance with his program of political organization.[20]

"Urbanism was introduced in France thanks to colonial urbanism."[21]

1926–1946

Reflux of the Pioneers

In the last years of the 1920s, France witnessed the return of politicians and architects who had introduced in Morocco the first options and methods of modern urbanism. It was to be another twenty years before men of action returned to Morocco to confront the problems of urbanization. The time between these two periods was devoted—until the War—to the circumspect administrative applications of the numerous plans Prost had conceived. Until 1926, all these plans were zealously defended by Prost himself, and even by Lyautey, who never hesitated to intervene personally.[22] When they both left, the towns were under the control of civil servants who had never been involved in the creative process of the plans. If the administrative machinery—which was weak at first—was then working smoothly, the spirit of innovation was soon missing. The memory of Lyautey and his team led their successors to follow prudently their initial options, but they had neither the energy nor the ability necessary to adapt them to the new conditions.

And conditions were changing rapidly. The economic crisis which shook the world was first felt in Morocco in 1931. It caused, in particular, a sharp decline in agricultural prices. The selling price of a hundredweight of wheat, which was 133 francs in 1930, had fallen to 60 francs by 1935. The income of the farmers

[18]   Ibid.
[19]   Ibid.
[20]   Ibid.
[21]   Ibid.
[22]   Lyautey often intervened personally, both to establish an important priority and to assure himself that a project was carried out correctly down to the last detail.

70. Casablanca, Morocco. Close-up of houses in bidonville, 1967. (Photo: Direction de l'Urbanisme et de l'Habitat, Rabat.)

71. Casablanca, Morocco. Bidonville and new squatters' housing project (background) on the outskirts of the city. (Photo: Direction de l'Urbanisme et de l'Habitat, Rabat.)

dropped brutally, showing a decline of 60% from 1930 to 1933. Thereafter, rural depopulation increased as a new myth appeared, that of finding a job in town, and an income to support families still as large as ever. But in towns, the situation had also deteriorated. Artisans, for example, who represented a third of the urban population, were deeply affected by the closing of their export markets, while they also had to compete with imported products. There ensued a sharp rise in unemployment, and a massive increase in the towns of an enormous resourceless population which upset an already precarious balance. The rural elements brought an ever-increasing proletariat into the towns, and three main housing phenomena appeared: the bidonvilles; the *douars* or "clandestine settlements"; and the over-population of the madinas.

Convergence of the Uprooted in the Madinas

The uprooted fellahs tried to settle mainly in the towns in which they had family contacts. Because the Protectorate had not planned or built "new Moroccan districts," the native population was still confined to the old madinas. It was in these that the first waves of farmers tended to congregate. The density of the population in these old districts rapidly became "abnormal," then "alarming," and finally "critical": 1,200 to 2,000 people to the hectare. Aside from the sanitary and psychological dangers presented by these human conglomerations, this phenomenon also progressively drove the well-to-do to abandon the traditional districts. This rupture of the old social balance of the madinas caused the creation of proletarian or sub-proletarian ghettos, enclosed within the walls of the old city. Ultimately, the Moroccan bourgeois and the European were to establish themselves on the other side of these walls.

Rise of Bidonvilles

The overpopulated madinas could no longer absorb the continuous flow from the country. As a result, hamlets and urban douars rose at the periphery of the towns. They were built from materials retrieved from the wastes of the urban civilization: bits of lumber, corrugated tin sheets, tar paper, oil drums and cans. Henceforth, the shantytowns were to surround the towns like an additional city belt. Taken unawares by this unexpected development which bothered the good conscience of the citizenry, the town authorities launched operations to regroup the small bidonvilles into larger ones, supposedly easier to control. Systematically conceived on a grid pattern of a military type, these clusters of shacks were located on municipal or privately-owned lots carefully chosen at a distance from the "normal" zones of habitation. Colorful expressions were chosen to designate the blighted areas: "plague of the towns," "a cancer," "a scandal," "a shame." This vocabulary shows the prejudice established from the start against this type of habitat. For a long time, the authorities and the press aimed to break down the shantytowns in order to "free the towns" from this "unbearable plague." The first large Pl. 70-71 (210) shantytowns appeared in Casablanca in the 1930s; in 1940, their inhabitants numbered 50,000. Then the numbers escalate—1950: 100,000; 1960: 160,000; 1970: 250,000.

Clandestine Proliferation

The massive influx of new city-dwellers (or neo-city dwellers) gave some landowners the opportunity to speculate, because the migrants did not know the existence of laws prohibiting the sale of any non-improved lot. They did not even know that the acquisition of a lot required a title. Taking advantage of these facts and of the housing shortage, certain bourgeois acquired at the periphery of cities lots of varying size which they illegally subdivided into minuscule lots and sold at outrageous prices to the peasants who still had some money. These operations were conducted without the knowledge of municipal authorities (thus the name "clandestine lots") or with their tolerance, as was the case, for example, for the district known as the "new madina" in Casablanca.

The whole organization of these lots went against the most elementary rules of hygiene, urbanism, equipment, and construction. Once these districts were up—without there being any hope to restructure them in the future—overpopulation there became even more critical than in the old madinas. In shoddily-made houses, without any aeration, light, or space, it was common to find twenty-five or thirty-five people living in six rooms. If the town authorities had not been duped at the beginning of the operation, they often were at the end; for in theory the buyers of the lots had to present a plan of the house to the proper authorities in order to obtain a permit to build. When this administrative procedure was followed, it very often proved of no avail, because the concept of the house was so modified and "densified" during or after the construction that the finished house bore little if any resemblance to the original design. We shall see that these abuses became more widespread in the following decades, because the municipalities were understaffed in qualified technical personnel.

The multiplication of these problems—overpopulation of the madinas, bidonvilles, and clandestine lots—frustrated the plans conceived by Prost ten years earlier. A few town authorities took some random initiatives on the local level, attempting to solve the problem of the bidonvilles, always the most glaring and eye-catching problem. Thus, for example, in 1938 at Mohammedia (formerly Fedala) the construction of a new madina was decided upon, supposedly to guarantee the transfer of the bidonvilles and the elimination of the slums. But these programs were sporadic and very rare.

Second Wave in the Thirties

In 1939, the Moroccan towns were submitted to a new and massive influx: that of Europeans fleeing from the imminence of war. This sudden migration upset once more the housing situation and increased the urban concentration. In order to furnish housing of one type or another the state forced house-owners to put part of their houses at the disposal of the newcomers. This measure discouraged private investment in the building industry and made the situation worse. In an attempt to solve the situation on its own, the state created the "Office Chérifien de l'Habitat Européen" (OCHE) in 1942. The title of this first official organization reflects the main preoccupations of the Protectorate at this point—to insure the establishment of foreigners in the best possible conditions. One is reminded of the phrase of Albert Sanavet: "The salvation of France lies in the colonies."[23] It is interesting to note that in roughly the same period the Istiqlal party published its manifesto and Moroccans were given the right—in theory—to join labor unions. In 1944, the first claims for national independence were made. Since the beginning of the economic crisis, the concentration in the towns or in the fringe of society in the bidonvilles of an enormous mass of uprooted Moroccans had permitted the progressive crystallization of nationalist feelings.

It was in Casablanca, the economic metropolis and the largest city in the country, that the general crisis of the towns and of the housing situation appeared at its most glaring. In the beginning of the 1940s, the unrest was felt very strongly: "Everything must be tried to fight against the formation of a native proletariat."[24] The author of this quotation added: "I think that it is necessary to draw, without any delay, a plan of native urbanism in keeping with the development of the Moroccan population." Another author declared: "The most critical problem of the last years, and the one which is the most urgent to solve, is that of the organization of large districts of native housing. The European quarters, surrounded . . . by non-planned clusters of houses (i.e., bidonvilles), are threatened by asphyxiation [sic] . . . . One cannot hide the fact that now out of a population which is over 500,000, the number of settled natives is getting close to 400,000, and that number can only increase."[25]

The Prefecture of Casablanca and the General Secretariat of the Protectorate sensed the unrest, and, in 1944, they hired an architect-urbanist as a temporary consultant to advise them concerning the measures to be taken in the near future. The resulting "Courtois plan" was the first such plan for a Moroccan town which provided a large district of housing for the Moroccans. This plan surprised the public by its scope, and, more precisely, by the quantitative and qualitative importance it gave to "native urbanism." The project was strongly supported by the Director of the "Political Affairs of the Protectorate," who deemed Casablanca an "urban monstrosity," and considered that the "moment had come to reopen that wound," and moreover, that it would be "dangerous to wait any longer."[26] An enormous appropriation to implement the plan was requested, but no action followed.

Public unrest may have provoked the changes introduced in 1944 to the structure and the objectives of the "Office Chérifien de l'Habitat Européen" which had been founded two years earlier. Indeed, a more neutral name was adopted—"Office Chérifien de l'Habitat" (OCH). The office was henceforth divided into two sections: one responsible for the needs of the Europeans; the other, more active, responsible at last for the needs of the Moroccans. For these, the OCH undertook at first operations to re-house the bidonville dwellers: 700 families at Rabat in the Douar Debbagh (in the cité Yacoub el-Mansour) and 3,000

[23]   Quoted by Jean Royer in *L'Urbanisme aux colonies.*

[24]   C. Sanguy, "Reflexions sur le problème de l'habitat indigène à Casablanca," *Maroc Medical*, no. 265 (Rabat, 1946).

[25]   André Pauty, "Casablanca et son plan," *Revue de Geographie du Maroc*, no. 3-4 (Rabat, 1945), pp. 4-7.

[26]   Report of June 18, 1945, to the Resident General.

in a section of Mohammedia (known under its old name of Fedala el-Alia). They had to transfer the inhabitants of the slums from their bidonvilles to "improved noualas," inspired by a type of habitation current in the country but adapted for the town and built in series by the government.

Little Action, but a "Model"

On the other hand, the OCH undertook the building of the "model city" of Ain Chock in Casablanca (15,000 inhabitants) and of the "new madina" of Mohammedia (5,000 inhabitants). To counterbalance the unassuming appearance of the districts of noualas, more spectacular and dramatic projects were initiated where architecture still held its own. Their creator, Antoine Marclusio, had succeeded Prost as "architect-in-chief to the *Residence Générale*." On the urbanistic and aesthetic levels, these two showplaces are interesting. The district of the Habous and the city of Ain Chock are separated by two kilometers and a span of twenty years; during this time the different methods of tackling the problems have changed. If the influence of traditional architecture remains in evidence at Ain Chock (patios, blind façades, houses at two levels grouped in compact clusters), the modernistic influence of cubism and the "Bauhaus" is also apparent. The interpretation of the ancient madina is less "literal" and more "open." We have here combinations of Occidental and Muslim principles rather than a simple modernization of the idea of the madina. For example, all the streets, even the secondary byways, are open to cars. In fact, the "second generation" Moroccan districts (conceived by public officials) reflect an effort to break free from the main characteristics which had given a rather typed aspect to the district of the

Pl. 72 (217)   Habous. As for the city of Mohammedia, it represents one of the rare attempts made by the Protectorate to promote at the same time an architectural environment of value and technological methods of simple construction engaging the often underestimated resources of a new semi-industrialized artisan class.[27]

Unfulfilled Expectations and Remedies

But the expectations which the creation of 'the OCH had aroused were not fulfilled.[28] The administration, isolated from any coherent organism of planification, undertook only localized operations. It had no overall grasp of the problems caused by urban growth. Even if they were thought of as models, these cities were not able to have any influence on the fast-deteriorating situation. It became obvious that, for a long time, nobody in Morocco had seen clearly the problem of urbanism and housing. The officials were losing themselves in details, without having any method and without having any overall plan of action. To remedy this grave situation and to find solutions to the new problems, Resident-General Eric Labonne appointed in 1946 as his assistant an already well-known urban architect. In the next seven years, Michel Ecochard[29] was to put his mark on the planning of the "agglomerations" of the country.

[27]   The roofing of these houses—often the most delicate parts in them to put up—is made up of a series of bottle-like ceramic arches which overlap one another to form joined arches.

[28]   Total of housing units built for 1942-49: 2,381 European and 6,113 Moroccan.

[29]   He earned his degree in Paris in 1931 and then worked until 1943 in the Near East, first as an archaeologist and then as an architect-urbanist.

1946–1956

Balance Sheet on 30 Years of Activity

Ecochard inherited a difficult task that can be summed up in nine points:

1. In 1946, the town-planning operations only concerned the foreign population. "The new towns were initially created to satisfy only the needs of Europeans." Ecochard himself declared: "For 35 years, Moroccans had been forgotten."

2. In spite of this, Moroccan housing was provided; but being rare and precious, these operations remained marginal and dealt only with a privileged minority of the population in a few large cities.

3. Machinery was established for administration, legislation projects, and procedures. These tools, however, were already outdated and inadequate. Nevertheless, the concept of urban planning had taken root.

4. A vast traditional architectural heritage, constituting a remarkable testimony to the art and culture of the old towns, was preserved.

5. In order to preserve the urban and social integrity of the madinas, foreigners had been forbidden to settle there, but this ethnic and aesthetic protectionism had not prevented these madinas from becoming the overcrowded reservations of the proletariat.

6. On the whole, urban problems had been underestimated. The authorities had been outrun by the tremendously quick growth of the towns. Except for a few cases, nothing had yet been done to solve the problems of the proliferation of squatters and bidonville dwellers.

7. What is more, only towns had been attended to, leaving aside the fate of the rural communities or the small towns in between city and countryside. Similarly, such laissez-faire form of "planning" had facilitated the mushrooming of towns along the coast, sometimes monstrously, without any effort to balance their growth with the rest of the country. Thus far, there was no trace of regional planning.

8. Casablanca became an "urban monster" which drained the principal economic resources of the country: 65% of the industrial activity; 80% of the economic transactions. "Casa" represented abusive centralization. It was a gigantic metropolis growing out of control. It was an "urban texture" torn by the race for easy and immediate profit; unchecked laissez-faire town planning and "profitable chaos."[30] It was a gigantic checkerboard, a terrain of 180 kilometers—an area equivalent to that of the city of Paris—where undeveloped plots blocked by all-powerful speculators alternated with full developed areas, everything achieved at random whether illegally or officially. In 1950, in distributing its 650,000 inhabitants, Casa stretched out its urban magma over 20 kilometers. This resulted in ridiculously high expenses in management, maintenance, and equipment.

9. Although the Moroccan urban population amounted in 1920 to merely 10%, in 1950 it had grown to 25%. In Morocco the expansion rate of towns has been five times faster than in France at corresponding periods of their histories (10% in 1700; 25% in 1850). Within 30 years, then, Morocco had gone through an

---

[30] An expresion first used by Lewis Mumford in *The City in History* (1961).

amazingly rapid urbanization as compared to France, who had worked out her own over a span of 150 years.

Ecochard coped with the situation by organizing a strong team completely converted to his ideas. In 1949 he created the "Service de l'Urbanisme" coupled with a new "Service de l'Habitat."[31] These two complementary agencies were ultimately integrated in one (central) technical national body: the "Direction des Travaux Publics."[32]

Taking Lyautey's idea of a "Maroc utile,"[33] Ecochard tackled these problems on a national scale or at least in a way to embrace all of "useful Morocco." His first goal was to restrain Casablanca's unbridled growth and to bring about industrial decentralization in favor of towns such as Meknes, Safi, Agadir, Marrakech, Kenitra, Rabat-Salé or even smaller towns like Beni Mellal, Sidi Sliman, Berkane. All the plans of urbanism conceived from 1948 for these towns (and many others) included a large industrial area. These praiseworthy proposals concerning decentralization did not, however, succeed in cutting down the strong attraction that Casablanca exerted on the industrialists as well as on the masses. The concentration of factories and workers in Casablanca has in fact increased considerably since 1950.[34]

Balance of Urban and Rural Environments

Besides being aware of the impact of industrialization on urbanization, Ecochard also understood the interaction of rural environment and town planning. He was the first in Morocco to emphasize the creation of "villages-centers," agreeing with Le Corbusier that "it is impossible to deal with urban planning without first dealing with rural areas." From 1945 on, the rural landscape changed as land was cleared, plantations established, a road network created, and the first irrigation canals introduced. Simultaneously, a new type of built-up area appeared which was no longer the traditional village (the douar) but not yet really a town. These new rural centers crystallized around the administrative centers, the suqs,[35] or around the crossroads of regional routes.

The new plans transformed the old hamlets into market towns[36] and the market centers into towns.[37] Ecochard wanted "to give the rural centers the opportunity of a healthy development in the future."[38] He wanted to create a

---

[31] Circonscription de l'Urbanisme et de l'Habitat (CUH).

[32] In existence up to 1967.

[33] It consists essentially of the agricultural plains of the West and Center, that is to say, the general triangle marked by the cities of Kenitra, Fez, and Agadir.

[34] Casablanca remains the economic center, but industries have proliferated elsewhere, viz., a chemical complex at Saffi; various textile factories at Fez and Temara; several sugar refineries in Gharb and Tadla; factories producing building materials at Agadir, Temara, and Safi; a factory for assembling refrigerators at Marrakech; a cellulose factory in Gharb; a pharmaceutical factory at El Jadida; etc.

[35] Weekly markets traditionally organized in the open air at the center of a tribal territory.

[36] For example, Sidi Slimane and Sidi Yaya in the irrigated area.

[37] For example, Beni Mellal and Khemisset. The former benefited from its proximity to the irrigated region of Tadla, and the latter, in a non-irrigated region, benefited from its proximity to the major road between Fez and Rabat.

[38] R. Fornichon, "L'Aménagement des campagnes marocaines," *L'Architecture d'aujourd'hui*, no. 35 (Paris, 1951), pp. 29-31.

72. Mohammedia, Morocco. Part of the new madina built during the years 1939-51 by the Office Chérifien de l'Habitat. (Photo: Office National Marocain du Tourisme, Rabat.)

73. Experimental apartment project for Muslim families in Casablanca, Morocco, in 1952. Architect: Sturder. (Photo: Direction de l'Urbanisme et de l'Habitat, Rabat.)

temporary substructure between the starting points and the arrival points of the rural exodus. Among the 200 rural centers which already existed in Morocco, in different stages of development, 50 benefited between 1947 and 1950 from development plans and equipment. "The immediate object of this equipment was to locate as closely as possible to the sites suitable for production, in particular those industries dealing with agricultural produce which often tend to settle near the big urban consumption markets."[39]   Moreover, housing problems proved to be less acute in these centers than in the towns, "local resources often helping to keep down the costs of construction. A problem did exist, however—that of preventing housing from being too scattered (the spontaneous choice of a still largely rural population) for that would raise the costs of the substructure to a point where no further progress would be possible."[40]   Through advocating or practicing industrial decentralization, Ecochard initiated the first attempt at regional reorganization and development in Morocco.

Restructuring of Towns and their Regional Positioning

When faced with the delicate problem of Casablanca, Ecochard envisaged its future expansion in terms of its regional context. He wished to break away from "the ridiculous concentric inflation" of the metropolis (object of so much speculation) and induce a vast and well-balanced linear development along the coast. He also sought to connect Casablanca and Mohammedia (41 kilometers away), thus forming an urban complex sufficiently large and well-structured to absorb in the years to come the millions of new inhabitants who, according to the demographers, would inevitably arrive. Here again, Ecochard revealed his adherence to the theories of Le Corbusier in his application of the rational scheme for a "linear industrial city."[41]

Ecochard's disciples held to this view when they introduced in 1965 a development scheme for the littoral urban axis. The aim was to control the growth of a coastal megalopolis covering 130 kilometers, from Casablanca to Kenitra, taking in Salé, Rabat, and Mohammedia. This grandiose vision, considered utopian at the time, proved later to be highly realistic, and there is today a return to this approach.[42] But the influence of Le Corbusier can be most markedly felt in the conception of urban planning and housing in which the imperative recommendations of the new bible of urban planners, the "Charter of Athens,"[43] have often been scrupulously enforced.

The Arrival of the "Progressivists"

Whereas the previous generation had followed the views of the "culturalists," the young Ecochard team [44] was to adopt rigorously the instructions and the attitudes

---

39   Ibid.

40   Ibid.

41   Le Corbusier, *Les Trois Etablissements humains* (Paris: Editions de Minuit, 1954).

42   Maroc, Ministère de l'Interieur, DUH, CERF, *Nouvelles Reflexions pour l'aménagement de l'axe urbain littoral* (Rabat, 1969).

43   Congrès International Architecture Moderne, *La Charte d'Athènes* (Paris: Editions de Minuit, 1957).

44   In 1950, the principal architects on the team were: Mas, Aujard, Pelletier, Mauret, Duru, Delarozière, Godefroy, Riou, Deneux, Marozeau, Nespola, Henneton, Chapon, Bazot, Degez, and Hodil.

of the "progressivist" movement. And from this time, the accomplishments of these two schools could be clearly seen confronting, or rather competing with, one another in the main cities. Quantity replaced quality as a priority in the race for achievements. The idea was no longer to create model towns or native districts but mass housing, satellite towns, housing units, networks, and housing cells. Doctrines were changing as was the language, which was no longer that of the *architecte honnête homme* or the "generalist," but was becoming the monopoly of the enlightened specialist with his own esoteric jargon.

Pl. 73 (217)
Pl. 74 (223)

Increasing but Sketchy Activity in the Field of Urban Planning

To establish more orderly towns, plans were henceforth to advocate strict zoning, and delicacy was abandoned in the battle against urban chaos. The city was now to be expanded by the addition of specialized sectors, often separated from one another by open "green" spaces—often overrun with grazing sheep or goats and filled with litter—or by wooded areas which diluted the urban atmosphere to the point of destroying it completely. The "Charter of Athens" formulated that there were four essential urban functions which should be clearly expressed: "(1) work, (2) movement, (3) housing, and (4) the opportunity to cultivate one's body and one's mind." The plans reveal a concern for a network of roads (often excessively complex) for vehicles rather than one designed properly for pedestrians. The "traditional" street, in which all manner and means of communication (material, visual, social, semantic, and auditive, for example) were spontaneously mingled, was now banished in the name of progress.

The progressivists did not draw their inspiration for a new urban model from the traditional madina; they followed a world-wide tendency to back adamantly all that is modern, while rejecting any possible contribution that the past and tradition might have to offer.

Satellite Cities: Athens in Morocco

The progressivists were, however, deeply interested in the future, and one of their primary concerns was the expansion of towns, which proved to be indispensable during the two decades that followed. They proceeded to extend urban centers by constructing peripheral "satellite towns"—such as the cité Yacoub el-Mansour at Rabat and the cité Sidi Bernoussi at Casablanca—with a view to their being, at least in theory, autonomous units. Their population capacity (40,000 to 50,000), their facilities, and their structure were dictated by the inevitable "Charter of Athens" or by its imperative results. This rigorous planning process led to a dispersal, an "atomization," of the town into a series of distinct entities—abstract areas dissociated from the vital structure of the city center. This purist attitude to urban planning, doubtless intended to give the Muslim population the opportunity to enjoy "space, sunshine, and greenery" in their working area, led only to an oppressing and constricting new paternalism.

In order to bring into being these "neighborhood units," Ecochard persuaded the state to purchase vast expanses of land in areas adjacent to the towns. This is one of the numerous positive aspects of his unfailing energy. The land reserves thus acquired between 1946 and 1953 were considerable, and a large section of these estates were still available in 1971, thanks to his intelligent and far-sighted policy.

In Favor of Quantitative Housing

On these vast estates Ecochard launched his multiple projects for reasonably priced housing destined for the so-called lower-income section of the Moroccan population. [45] The main object here was to put on the market a sufficient quantitiy of living quarters to encourage the resettlement of bidonville inhabitants and ease the population pressure on their districts. Always behind this thinking about lower-class housing lurked the idea of a single human type. Whether for the rural (e.g., the village of Haddada, near Kenitra) or the urban milieu (e.g., the cité Takadoum, at Rabat), for the coastal towns of the south or for the built-up areas on the eastern plateaux, the prototype remained the same: all regional particularism was rejected. Theoretical uniformity was supposed to reduce the multiple aspects of society—geography, ways of life, ethnic groups, climate and materials to a single denomination: the schematic image of the Moroccan standard. And for this "modern Moroccan" the panacea of the "8 x 8 meter cell" was conceived with its indissociable network, often appropriately referred to as the "Ecochard network" ("la trame Ecochard").

Standard Housing for the Average Citizen

After various experiments and tests, Ecochard decided on a system of plots of 8 x 8 meters, allowing for the suitable organization of "two habitable rooms necessarily facing the south and the east, a kitchen, and a central courtyard."[46] Thousands of examples of this cell were reproduced in many towns. The repetitive juxtaposition of these living quarters was "organized in the style of a honeycomb in order to utilize the maximum of wall space and to cut down on the surface area of roads and public services."[47] These cells were intended to offer a temporary solution and to give way in years to come to the construction of vertical apartment blocks.

From 1947 to 1953, Ecochard and his team undertook to build houses for Moroccans on 9,500 acres of land. This immense national system of satellite towns, networks, and 8 x 8 cells[48] was built with a view to housing a population of 1,500,000 inhabitants.

Efficacity and Authoritarianism

It was a considerable effort, especially in comparison with the insignificance of what had been achieved between 1912 and 1947. On the quantitative front, therefore, an ambitious program had been launched with the aid of ample funds. On the qualitative side the picture was less happy. What appeared to be a systematic juxtaposition of identical housing units brought with it a depressing sense of monotony and inflexibility, a feeling of repressive urbanization. Re-

---

[45] But the most difficult problem remained unsolved in 1970, namely, that of providing appropriate housing to families earning less than 200 Moroccan dirhams (40 U.S. dollars) per month (i.e., about 50% of the urban population).

[46] A model established after experimenting with different kinds of cells.

[47] Michel Ecochard, "L'Habitat de type marocain," *L'Architecture d'aujourd'hui*, no. 35 (Paris, 1951), pp. 32-35.

[48] In addition to several rare variants in vertical housing in which an attempt was made to integrate the traditional element of the patio.

pression was also in effect where the living quarters themselves were concerned; since each unit was conceived by the technicians according to a "comprehensive scheme," the occupant was obliged to adapt his way of life to its requirements. It was forbidden to modify it in any way. Improvements were not allowed since the building was, in theory at least, temporary. Its development could be brought about only according to the plans conceived by the architects, and any intervention on the part of the tenant was considered as an act of vandalism, of incomprehension, or, at best, the work of an ignorant person. Behind a veil of democratic terminology, the authoritarian attitude of the architects and town-planners was manifest.

Achievements of a "Trouble-Maker"

Even if Ecochard's methods seem too schematic or oversimplified, they have a distinctly social tendency. As a left-wing man of action, he managed to provide the underprivileged classes with much-needed housing and facilities.

But his fierce opposition to the determined laissez-faire approach of the factory owners and real estate "promoters" and speculators caused him to lose his position in 1953, three years before Morocco became independent. His successors were left with a clear-cut situation: possibilities of decentralization; an active policy toward low-cost housing; considerable land reserves; up-to-date and broadened legislation; new ideas in urban planning; and an impressive series of plans, both general and detailed, for a multitude of built-up areas and in particular for Casablanca.

Ecochard left behind him a team well-trained in his teachings, and the leader of these men was to be, up to 1966, Pierre Mas.

1957–1967

Independence in 1956 modified only very gradually these theories, and the work patterns began to be affected even later (1968). From 1957 on, however, the "Service de l'Urbanisme" was directed by young Moroccan architects, with the help of numerous European colleagues. Furthermore, they had all been trained abroad. For many years Ecochard's theories prevailed; eventually, they were to be questioned, modified, and ultimately forgotten. Most of the urban development plans had been made before independence to cover a theoretical period of twenty years. They also had to conceive plans for the ten northern towns restored to Morocco by Spain in 1956.

As early as 1957, the Government allocated to the "Circonscription de l'Urbanisme et de l'Habitat" (CUH) considerable funds (an average of 45 million dirhams a year), specifically to finance housing programs which were more diversified than in the past. The ability of a large part of the populaton to "auto-construct" had so far been considerably underestimated. Furthermore, the public had become accustomed to a quasi-systematic intervention of the state to solve housing problems. The tendency, consequently, had been to encourage passivity of both the private sector and the general populace whose building energy was, however, obvious in towns as well as in the country.

"Auto-Construction" in the Middle Classes

In order to cope with this initial inertia, a new principle in low-cost housing was established shortly before independence. On state-owned land, only the development of substructure (sanitation, water supply, and sewers) and the distribution in plots of 70 to 120 square meters were undertaken. In order to finance the purchase of these plots and the construction of the houses (according to a compulsory formula), loans for a period of ten to fifteen years were granted at the rate of 3 or 4% by the "Banques Populaires" amounting to 45,000 dirhams at the most. However, there were two requirements:[49] the prospective owner must make a personal downpayment of 10 to 20% of the total investment and [50] have a regular job. The monthly income of the head of the family had to be between 200 dirhams and 250 dirhams; but 50% of the urban population had a monthly income of less than 200 dirhams, so this solution to the problem, though "economical," did not affect the lower classes but rather a new middle class and particularly the civil servants.[51] This project, which for the first time required personal participation, was very successful.[52] But the demand still remained much greater than the supply, which, from 1956 to 1965, amounted to 12,300 lots, thereby affecting at least 75,000 people. The total amount of loans granted over this period was 125 million dirhams.[53]

A different form of this system was tested in Marrakech for one thousand lots under the name of the "beaver system" ("systéme castor") by analogy with an animal that builds its own housing. Beside the equipped land, the CUH provided woodwork shops, various building elements, and—what was then an innovation—technical assistance on the building sites. The future dwellers were supposed to do the building themselves under the technical supervision of the state, and the expenses for this assistance were to be paid back within ten years.

Construction of Dwellings by the State

Since 1947, the state had been building houses to rent; from 1956 to 1965, more than 32,000 so-called low-cost dwellings were constructed with rents amounting to 6% of the building costs (30 to 50 dirhams a month). More than 160,000 town-dwellers were housed either in these districts of one- or two-family houses, or in the increasingly numerous apartment blocks. This concept of vertical housing, imported from Europe, was indiscriminately extended by the state to the entire country. These apartment blocks often appeared poorly integrated into the urban landscape and ill-adapted to the technical resources of the country and the Moroccan way of life. These often oppressively banal apartment blocks were sometimes looked upon as the symbol or even as the source of a certain

---

[49] In accordance with the *dahir* of November 5, 1962, these loans are granted by the *Banque Populaire*; formerly, they were granted by the *Caisses Regionales d'Epargne et Credit*.

[50] Wage earners must have been employed for a minimum of 18 months; others must have had uninterrupted service in their profession for a period of three years.

[51] For civil servants of a certain rank (i.e., "titularistes") no time period of employment was required to qualify for the loans.

[52] For example, the program of 1,089 building lots achieved in Rabat at the cité Youssoufia, facing the bidonville of Douar Doum.

[53] Maroc, Ministère des Travaux Publics, *10 Ans d'Independence* (Rabat, 1967), p. 94.

74. Casablanca, Morocco. Low-income housing project of 1952 following the principle developed by Michel Ecochard, the French architect. (Photo: Direction de l'Urbanisme et de l'Habitat, Rabat.)

75. Low-income housing development project in Casablanca, Morocco, in 1964, following the principle of the *trame sanitaire améliorée*. The shops are in the center. (Photo: Direction de l'Urbanisme et de l'Habitat, Morocco.)

acculturation. In spite of the obvious constraints on traditional family life, these pseudo-European apartment blocks were probably considered by their occupants as an outward token of prestige or emancipation.

Peripheral Housing Development

These various housing types (building plots, apartment blocks, and houses of different kinds) were to be found in the low-cost housing areas located on the outskirts of the towns, such as the cité of Youssoufia at Rabat and the cité Tabriquet at Salé. The clustering of people from different income brackets was supposed to avoid social segregation. Other characteristics of these new housing developments were:

1. Integration into the group of residences of an elaborate system of collective facilities (sometimes built before the houses)—schools, mosques, public baths, dispensaries, markets and shopping centers, streets and parking lots.

2. Grouping of these public buildings around a framework intended to structure the district and serve as the center of its economic and social life, in reaction to the dreariness of the "8 x 8 network."

3. Search for a diversified urban landscape: the creation of perspectives, variety in types of open spaces, streets, and architectural disposition, and the introduction of small public parks.

But "while giving a clear conscience to the collectivity scheme, the action of the state concealed the real problems. Today one has to admit that the efforts of the state to follow a social trend affected only a privileged minority who had stable jobs if not administrative positions."[54] Overbalancing a few spectacular achievements was the failure to solve the most difficult problems, such as insufficient housing for the very low-income classes and lack of control over town development.

Various solutions were tried from 1962 on, such as the "improved sanitary facilities" ("trame sanitaire améliorée"). The time, however, for theoretically attractive ideas or arrangements was over; a solution financially workable on a large scale had to be found. Once again, "architecturally speaking, it was necessary to lower standards."[55] The reduction in rents was essentially due to a lowering in housing quality: the units were to be smaller and more elementary. On a plot of forty to fifty square meters (equipped and fenced), the state would build a room of 12 square meters and include a toilet and a water faucet. The dweller was allowed to build for himself a second room and, in theory, maintain a patio. Examples of such improved quarters are Sidi Othman in Casablanca (2,561 dwellings) and Kenitra (984 dwellings). From 1962 to 1965, almost 9,000 housing units of this type were completed in seven towns. If in the course of these operations architectural concern disappeared, at least there was an effort to provide this type of housing with a minimum of public facilities.

Pl. 75 (223)

    [54] Maroc, Ministère des Travaux Publics, CUH, *Nouvelles reflexions pour une politique d'urbanisme et d'habitat* (Rabat, 1964), p. 1.
    [55] As noted by Ecochard in relation to his 8 x 8 networks in *L'Architecture d'aujourd'hui*, no 35 (Paris, 1951), p. 9.

As with so many other projects, this one should theoretically have led to an absorption of the bidonvilles. But the objective has in fact remained utopian since the average rate of growth of the bidonvilles (7%) is itself higher than that of the towns (5%).

To conduct operations directly concerning the bidonvilles, still simpler procedures were resorted to. Here, where the income of the dwellers was ridiculously low, the problem was to establish some order and to insure an absolute minimum of hygiene. That was the aim of the operations known as "sanitary networks" ("trames sanitaires"): a few public toilets and public water facilities, a rudimentary sanitation system, and eventually a few street lights, installed on an open site. The remainder of the area was to be geometrically divided into small lots of 35 square meters. On this primitive substructure, the shacks of former bidonvilles (deemed too unsanitary or ill-placed) were to be relocated, together with new huts or noualas. In fact, these new areas are nothing more than bidonvilles materially restructured by the state; but at least they benefitted from a suitable location (which was not always the case with the unplanned bidonvilles). An attempt was also made to integrate these officially recognized bidonvilles into the structure of the new low-cost housing development, such as the Tabriquet quarter at Salé.

Was the bidonville to be officially recognized by the authorities and considered—along with other types of housing—a normal, legal district open to improvement? That point had not yet been reached. But circumstances and a more realistic (and not sentimental) view of the problem has gradually led the authorities to review their a priori judgments. The bidonville has always been regarded as a phenomenon which was against the law—marginal, abnormal, horrible, and un-desirable. The bidonville has always been considered a blight to be suppressed or pushed away as far as possible. But it was unthinkable that it could be transformed and improved. In the insane hope of sentencing it to death, its growth was thwarted and its organic life sterilized. The state, fully aware of what it was doing, prevented the inhabitants from having an adequate living area[56] and from having security of tenure. John Turner clearly demonstrated in the studies he did in Chile[57] the absurdity of refusing to employ the enormous mass of human resources pent up in the bidonvilles toward a progressive improvement of the standards of housing. Yet no one admitted that shantytowns were an inevitable and normal step in the urban development of a country where the rate of rural depopulation is very high, the income of the inhabitants very low, and where the demand for real estate far exceeds the supply. This is not to say that bidonvilles have to exist forever. Indeed not. But the bidonville dwellers must be granted the psychological and material opportunities that will enable them gradually to trans-form their own houses or districts.

This problem now affects one million people, spread out over the various urban or semi-urban bidonvilles of the country (one-fourth of the urban population). The

[56] In the bidonvilles the lots varied between 20-45 square meters; a normal house would require a minimum of 70-80 square meters.

[57] John Turner, "Peuplement Urbain non reglementé: problèmes et politiques," *Revue Internationale du Développement Social*, no. 1 (New York: United Nations, 1969), pp. 125-149.

passive authoritarian approach must be replaced by active encouragement and by the proper guidance, calling upon individual initiative, "auto-construction," and community development. This process has been slowly implemented from 1969 on.

A New Strategy for Employment and Development

Beginning in 1961, certain points of this doctrine were applied on a large scale in Morocco by a new state agency called "Promotion Nationale." It was not so much an administrative body as a practical developmental philosophy adapted to the needs of the Third World. Paradoxically enough, most underdeveloped countries suffer at the same time from widespread underemployment of their human resources and a generalized under-equipment. In the rural areas of Morocco, moreover, the situation was aggravated by constant and large-scale land erosion. The task of the Promotion Nationale was to take up that challenge. The originality of the method decided upon lay in that it employed for useful and profit-earning works a floating population of unskilled manpower; it gave the manpower a basic education and a professional training on the side. For a nominal pay [58] the formerly unemployed, organized in teams, carried on the job of equipping the country and, at the same time, they learned a trade. The enterprise was enormous; the results often impressive.

In the first year of operation (1961), fifteen million working days were divided between 6,000 workers on hundreds of sites. This undertaking cost 63 million dirhams, and 91% of this budget went towards the paying of salaries in cash and in kind.[59] Of course, this construction work was devoted only incidentally to the building of houses and the development of complexes. The main object was to undertake projects which would further the agrarian economy: irrigation canals (1,800 kilometers); land clearance (5,000 acres); conservation and reclaiming of land (32,500 acres); reforestation (five million trees); maintenance; and improvement or creation of roads (16,000 kilometers). These projects mobilized 75% of the labor force gathered by the Promotion Nationale; the remaining 25% was concerned with municipal work and equipment of built-up complexes. Moreover, in order to speed up the establishment of widespread education the record figure of 1,200 classes[60] was reached by the Promotion Nationale in two months, along with primary schools and 700 teachers' quarters—the outcome of 900,000 work days. The following year saw the construction of "communal houses" (according, once again, to a standardized plan established by the Town Planning Service and consisting each of a meeting hall, a room for youths, one for women, workshops, and administrative offices) in 130 rural communities. This tremendous effort towards the provision of facilities was complemented by a specific housing program. In 1962, 375,000 work days were put in for the construction of 2,358 living quarters at Casablanca, Kenitra, and Marrakech. The

---

[58]   Each worker receives 2 dirhams and the equivalent of 2 dirhams of food a day.

[59]   Maroc, Délégation Générale à la Promotion Nationale, *La Promotion Nationale au Maroc* (Rabat, 1965?).

[60]   356 urban and 844 rural classes at a total expense of 14.5 million dirhams.

latter operation is of particular interest for it was the only one to really conform to the spirit and methods of the Promotion Nationale.

A New Attitude toward Building Development

At Marrakech, the object was to construct a new peripheral quarter (the cité Daoudiat, northeast of the urban center) consisting of 2,200 living quarters to rehouse the inhabitants of the more insanitary and overpopulated sections of the old madina[61] and those of some of the various illegal and officially unrecognized douar squatter settlements.

One of the original aspects of this operation was the introduction of a work scheme involving the recruitment of on-the-spot unemployed—for the most part, unskilled people—to undertake a vast building project. The interesting point here is that a long and complex technical operation was in fact executed by an abundant and unspecialized labor force, with, of course, qualified personnel for guidance. The technology was adapted to the means available and not vice versa as is usually the case. (The operation was comparable, on a smaller scale, to the method adopted for the construction of dams by Chinese peasants.)

The Marrakech project brought into play two hitherto neglected principles: 1) the maximal utilization of human potentialities and 2) the modernized use of traditional construction materials—in this case, earth itself. The latter point calls for a few comments.

Potentialities of the Earth

Until now in the field of housing construction, the Moroccan government had used conventional methods; for fifty years the authorities had merely imitated Europe. Even during World War II, when considerable material restrictions on the building sites were made, no effort had been made to use the resources of local materials, frowned upon as "primitive."

In the 1920s, several architects evinced a strong desire to draw aesthetic, architectural, and urban-planning lessons from the ancient madinas. But no technological inspiration was imparted at that time. The most inventive testimonies of the Moroccan tradition were mainly in the south of the country, whose military conquest was not concluded until 1934. It is, indeed, in the *ksour* of the pre-Saharan valleys that the architectural virtuosity of the people is most effectively expressed. Financial and material resources were sadly lacking in these oases; but as if in permanent challenge to the technocratic jumble of modern times, an understanding and feeling for architecture flourished here in a culture of poverty. All the buildings, from the most modest to the most sumptuous—the palaces of the caïds, for example—are constructed of earth. The occasional, but nonetheless torrential rains have not prevented them from surviving at least three generations. (Does it not seem ridiculous that we, in the twentieth century, in a country whose social structures evolve at such a pace, persist in raising solid and

---

[61] Thousands lived in the former funduqs of the madina, in which human exploitation and the absence of even the most rudimentary hygiene made living conditions especially odious.

"permanent" housing units, as though they were meant to defy the centuries?) What is more, this free and omnipresent material, the earth, does not restrict initiatives; the buildings in question are often three or four stories high; in Yemen even "skyscrapers" of ten stories have been built out of earth.

The extraordinary economy of means, along with the thermal isolation and architectural quality which earth constructions offer, was soon to fascinate a number of architects and some civil engineers. They attempted, on the experimental site at Marrakech, a first modernized adaptation of this traditional technology. The result was the widespread utilization of "stabilized adobe." On the material and technical side, the success of this venture is encouraging: in 1964 the new living quarters were rented at 10 to 12 dirhams per month. This price was calculated to cover all the costs: land, foundations, all the equipment and construction materials, and even electricity. This was indeed an achievement, for this rent is comparable to that often asked for a wretched and ill-equipped shack in a bidonville. Thus the problem of financially insolvent families could be in a few cases solved through the application of an "intermediary technology" at the service of community development. However, on the architectural side (such as the urban lay-out, the groupings of houses and public buildings, the use of space, form, aesthetic quality, possibilities of extension) the results are deplorable since, due to lack of time and personnel, a group of old plans for an "improved sanitation network" was used. Research on the architectural front had not kept pace with the technical requirements. The Belgian architect and town planner Jean Hensens, having a particular interest in this research, was the first man to suggest new ways (in 1967) for the best utilization of the potentialities of adobe. He submitted proposals for public buildings of various types, urban housing, apartment blocks, and rural or semi-urban housing. A few examples were built at Ouarzazate in 1968, according to a construction scheme much improved in comparison with the groupings of the Marrakech experiment. A number of ingenious technical devices perfected by Alain Masson[62] made it possible for a team of unskilled workers to complete in a single day two monolithic adobe houses.[63]

Toward a New Moroccan Architecture

While in the service of the Urban Planning Board, Jean Hensens and Jean Paul Ichter (and a few others from time to time) have sought to elaborate a new social architecture specifically adapted to, simultaneously 1) the economic and material resources of the country; 2) the heritage of popular art (excluding pastiche or imitations of the past); and 3) the new needs of the citizens.

A strong similarity can be seen between their attitudes here and those of Hassan Fathy in Egypt, whose village of Gourna stands out, since 1950, as an urban manifesto. In Morocco, the architects had devoted little time to research—often laborious and unspectacular—into new solutions specifically adapted to the country in which they had chosen to work. It must be said that the theoretical

---

[62] An engineer who became director of the CERF in Rabat in 1968 and of the entire technical department of the Direction de l'Urbanisme et de l'Habitat.

[63] Maroc, Ministère de l'Interieur, DUH, CERF, *La Technologie au service de l'habitat éonomique* (Rabat, 1969).

research undertaken hitherto has been rarely applied[64] or else grossly distorted.[65] Nevertheless, it is curious to note that attempts to "Moroccanize" architecture and urban planning have all been carried out by left-wing Europeans.

The Importation of "Brutalism"

All the Moroccan architects and most of their foreign colleagues established in the country have been out-and-out adepts of a style described as "international" and which more or less stood at the crossroads of the influence of Le Corbusier and of the Japanese school. It is a rigorous architecture with massive and powerful forms whose puritanism would seem to suggest austerity—but because luxurious, a false austerity.

In this somewhat rigid "brutalism" an undeniable aggressiveness emerged which occasionally produced interesting plastic effects.[66] Contrary to the whole Moroccan tradition, it is an extroverted architecture, offering no relief, no grace, and often no soul. While Morocco abounds in artists and especially in craftsmen, it is distressing to see modern architecture isolating itself in its own abstraction, refusing all dialogue with life, and particularly with decorative art. Only a few recent examples stand as an exception.[67] In the towns, the architecture of the architects too often stands out harshly as a foreign body.

The Official Style

It cannot be said that high government officials approve of this architectural style. Their preferences often lean toward copies or conservative pastiches in the Muslim style, which is the exclusive trademark of Arab urban culture. However, the official architecture of the country is, for the most part, entrusted to the "brutalists" who abuse the idea of power which the excessive utilization of concrete seems to suggest. An impressive number of buildings commissioned by the state since 1957 bear witness to this.[68] Despite the reservations that could be advanced in respect to this inflexible architecture, so often ill-adapted to its milieu, one must recognize its nation-wide unity and its quality, which is incomparably higher in Morocco than in France or Belgium, for example, where the mediocrity of official constructions is disturbingly constant. It is in Agadir that one may best appreciate this unity and the "monumental" power of the official architecture.

---

[64] As for example, the research carried on by Jean Hensens, a Belgian architect and planner established in Morocco.

[65] As was the case for the pre-Saharan new villages in the valley of Ziz and for the new quarter designed at Quarzazate by Jean Hensens.

[66] Especially evident in the work of Zevaco; notable architects working in the private sector were Demazières-Faraoui, Azagury, Riou, Tastemain, Castelneau, and Verdugo.

[67] The architects Demazières and Faraoui are the only ones, in 1971, to have attempted an integration of art and craftsmanship in their buildings. Since 1958, they have appealed to the artists of the "School of Casablanca," including Melehi, Chebaa, and Belkaya. Since 1967, their architecture has evolved toward a more sculptural, light, and nuanced style, especially suited to touristic spots, as in Tangier, M'Diq, and Azemmour.

[68] Including schools, lycées and facultés, dispensaries and hospitals, courts and administrative buildings, airports, banks, warehouses, hotels and vacation villages. Only the new mosques have been spared the appearance of this "brutalist" style.

Agadir: Earthquake and Abstraction

On February 29, 1960, Agadir was shaken by a violent earthquake, and 15,000 people were killed or injured. This city of 30,000 inhabitants, the capital of the Souss region, was 80% destroyed. The stricken Agadir became a symbol, and out of this monstrous field of ruins, a model city was raised. It stands as "a testimony to the faith and will of the people."[69]   Under the direction of Pierre Mas, the spiritual successor of Ecochard, considerable manpower was mobilized and the "Service de l'Urbanisme" team drew up the plans for organization and reconstruction. The extreme urgency of the situation led them to adopt principles—seen as classic by some, but already questioned by others—of the "Charter of Athens." The result was a dispersal of the active elements of the town over an excessively wide area (1,500 acres).

This fragmentation of the modern city, dispersed in the name of hygiene, space, and freely-moving traffic, annihilates to a great extent any feeling of being in a town with community life and animation. All effort to provide facilities and architectural effect was lost in a series of gaping, dull open spaces and abstract zones. The distances between districts and the specialized nature of the facilities of the town create a boring urban landscape which no corrective measures could eradicate.

The Rebirth of Agadir

Apart from the abstract way in which it was conceived, Agadir is nevertheless an extraordinary success. On the real estate side, a general expropriation of land necessary for a coherent reconstruction plan was made possible. For a capitalist country, this was an amazing achievement. On the technical side, praise is also due; five years after the earthquake, more than 75% of the new town had been built. Where planning and the provision of facilities was concerned, the effort was particularly remarkable; the town was provided with an impressive series of public and social services which stand out in contrast to the under-equipment of other Moroccan towns.

It is in these multiple projects that the architects of Morocco found an exceptional opportunity of expressing together, most effectively, their convictions and occasionally their talents. Agadir is an open air museum of official architecture where the usual handful of architects set the pace: Zevaco, Demazières and Faraoui, Azagury, Tastemain-Castelnau, Riou, and Verdugo. Jean Challet, the only landscape planner in Morocco, tried to soften the rigid atmosphere through a subtle planning of public squares and gardens stretching from the "central zone" to the "touristic area."

Pls. 76-77
(231)

Tourism and Urbanism

In the 1960s, the development of tourism became one of the major objectives of the government. In Agadir, and in Tangier, vast plans were made in order to develop the bay area where the first vacation club villages ("villages de vacances")

---

[69]   Speech of His Majesty Mohamed V, March 3, 1960.

76. Elementary school in Agadir, Morocco, in 1966. Architect: Verdugo. (Photo: Direction de l'Urbanisme et de l'Habitat, Rabat.)

77. Courthouse of Agadir, Morocco, in 1965. Architect: Azagury. (Photo: Direction de l'Urbanisme et de l'Habitat, Rabat.)

and new hotels were opened. Town planners tried to convince the authorities of the need for a national tourism plan and for a kind of urbanism of leisure. But in the rush of investment, the ideas of the planners were all but forgotten. Beautiful natural sites were, consequently, massacred. The Alhucemas Bay on the Mediterranean Sea, for instance, was defaced by dull buildings, unsuitably located. The hill of the Merinides, which overlooks the extraordinary site of the madina of Fez, has been forever spoiled by an excessive emphasis on touristic facilities. But through a constant warning of the danger of irremediably ruining sites (as in Spain) and their touristic potentialities, the town planners and architects occasionally succeeded in putting into operation their "salvation" plans. A good example of this is the homogeneous conception of the new thermal resort of Sidi Harazam, in the neighborhood of Fez.

The Fate of the Madinas

If the authorities insist now on a certain quality in touristic developments, they pay as yet no heed to the fate of the old madinas, which paradoxically constitute one of the principal tourist attractions. Fez is a significant example. Foreigners flock into the madina to wallow in "real exoticism" and to experience the "mysterious adventure"[70] of the "discovery" of Moslem cities. It is ironical to see rich Westerners entertaining themselves in the madinas, which have become "reservations" for an uprooted rural population and for a proletariat living in often appalling conditions.[71] With the emigration of well-to-do classes from the traditional area, the madina is on the decline—it is gradually left to itself. Its lack of facilities is aggravated by an ever-increasing overpopulation. In order to find a solution to this serious crisis in the madina, several urban planners have since 1965 devised programs of action for Marrakech, El-Jadida, Azemmour, and Fez. The program for the latter[72] is particularly remarkable for the realism and subtlety of its recommendations. It tries to improve sanitation, relieve overpopulated and unsanitary bottlenecks, create public facilities, improve the urban landscape and preserve the traditional architectural heritage, and encourage certain carefully selected and revitalized activities in the field of trade and craftsmanship. Only in Fez has the plan been partially implemented, beginning in 1967 in the district of Oued Bou Khareb, in the heart of the madina.

Ruralism

The problems of the cities are mostly due to the quantitative importance of the rural depopulation. In the hope of reducing the emigrations, a new effort was made to further the development of rural centers. A dahir of 1960 created and organized new "rural communes" in the whole country, thereby finally offering legislative and administrative support to the action of the urbanists in the rural areas.

---

[70] Expressions used in touristic literature relative to the madina of Fez.
[71] Maroc, Délégation Generale, *La Promotion Nationale*.
[72] Drawn up by Jean-Paul Ichter in Fez at the time that he was chief urbanist of the six provinces of the East and Southeast.

In 1962 a new agency was created: the "Bureau Central des Études Rurales" (BCER)[73] with the responsibility for plans and development methods. Since the word "urbanism" is by definition inconsistent with rural concerns, a neologism—"ruralism"—was brought in to designate the particulars of the new field of study. Plans could be formulated without further delay, but unfortunately in the *bled* no provision had been made to train (even in the most elementary way) those who were supposed to use and apply these plans. There were no "after sales service" or "maintenance service" for these new instruments of local planning. The "development plans" devised from 1962 to 1967 for 300 rural centers are only very rarely applied. (In addition, the choice of the centers to be provided with plans was too often arbitrary—the work of a large number of administrative bodies concerned about but not yet having agreed on the objectives.) The result has been a hazardous dispersal of the areas to be developed. At the same time, these plans are rarely enforced by local authorities, who consider them unimportant or fail to understand the implications of the decisions they had approved or simply lack the material and financial means of putting them into effect. This explains why during the annual effort to boost community development, an operation called the "Relance Communale," one can frequently see how the facilities and the funds are used in a manner contrary to the principles of the development plan. This regrettable phenomenon is mostly a result of the administrative and technical under-equipment of the rural milieu.

If the results of the research undertaken by the BCER remained often unapplied, the town-planners, on the contrary, have devised an increasingly precise theory and methodology. After the gropings of 1962, a new strategy was introduced, which from 1968 on has been widely enforced.

1968 – 1972

At the end of 1967, two important changes were introduced which directly influence all future decisions concerning urbanism, housing, and physical planning.

On the one hand, the Ministry of the Plan set limits for the options and appropriations for all the activities of the state included in the Quinquennial Plan 1968-1972. Logically enough, the productive sectors of the economy received first priority: agriculture, tourism, and education. The monies allocated to urbanism, and especially to housing, were considerably reduced. From 1956 to 1964, they had been in the amount of 54 million dirhams per year. For the next five years, the annual appropriations were only 8.5 million dirhams.

On the other hand, an administrative decision was made to transfer the services of urbanism and housing, which had been under the supervision of a technical ministry (The Public Works Administration) for the last twenty years, to the Ministry of the Interior. The first consequence of this transfer was an important loss of technical staff; however, it will permit the use of certain financial resources belonging to the local administrations.

---

[73] The BCER was successively directed from 1962 to 1968 by the architects Nespola, de Carritat, Henneton, Bauer, and Dethier. The BCER was one of the cells in Rabat of the Circonscription de l'Urbanisme et de l'Habitat.

These changes called for an immediate analysis of the situation and an appraisal of the results. It appeared that "the policies followed for several years had failed." [74] Indeed, in spite of the 60,000 dwellings which had been built, of the 12,000 lots which had been equipped in the towns, in spite of the numerous plans drawn up for the agglomerations, the housing crisis and the urban anarchy had not been kept in check. All the efforts had not been able to prevent the proliferation of the now commonplace phenomena of bidonvilles, clandestine lots, and the overpopulation of the madinas. Because of this, urban plans had remained inoperative; worse, they worked negatively, that is to say, in reverse of their options and regulations. In spite of the previous financial resources, the result could be termed a failure. [75]

Toward a New Strategy

In view of such inadequacy, a radically new way of looking at the problem and a complete review of the objectives were in order. To conceive the various elements of a new strategy, an interdisciplinary team of fifteen technicians was selected in 1969 in the "Direction de l'Urbanisme et de l' Habitat." Their task was to propose realistic means of action, taking into account the growing complexities of the needs, and the reduction of the financial resources of the state. This team was the CERF: the "Centre d'Experimentation, de Recherche et de Formation," founded and directed by Alain Masson. [76] What differentiates the ideas of Masson from those of Prost and Ecochard is, first, the will to find general solutions to the problems. The CERF team seeks to go beyond the concerns of their predecessors and arrive at a regional planning, if not indeed a general planning, for the whole country. They are also looking for solutions peculiar to the underdeveloped countries and adapted to the particular aspects of Morocco. But first and foremost, they want to be realistic.

The first change concerned housing: The state would no longer be responsible for building houses. Henceforth, the emphasis is on helping citizens build their houses themselves with the financial and technical aid of the state. The principle of "assistance to auto-construction" will be generalized in the towns and in the country.

The first problem is to offer lots for sale in quantities sufficient to fulfill the needs. For demand had always exceeded supply, a situation which worked in favor of speculators, while stimulating the creation of new "clandestine lots" and the development of bidonvilles.

In 1970 the state had at its disposal 1,800 hectares of urban land available for new districts, but a law forbids anybody—the state included—to sell lots from unimproved land (i.e., where the roads, water, electricity, and sewers have not been installed). To break this vicious circle, new legislation was passed, one purpose of which was to institute the principle of "delayed improvement." This means that people are now allowed to settle on lots which will be improved at a later date.

[74] Maroc, Ministère de L'Intérieur, DUH, CERF, *Principes d'action* (February 1969), p. 1.

[75] Maroc, Ministère de l'Intérieur, *Note Relative à la politique proposée en matière d'urbanisme et d'habitat* (Rabat, 1969).

[76] From 1965 to 1967 he directed technical research on low-cost housing at Marrakech.

Since no financial help is forthcoming from the state, the owners will have to pay for their land and their houses, and also for the future infrastructure of the district. Families having a monthly income above 200 dirhams will still be able to receive loans from banks. But for the 50% of the population having an income under that figure, the process will be different: each family will be "bound" to the municipal authorities by a contract giving the family immediate possession of the land. Then the owners will reimburse the Administration for all the sums due in monthly installments, the rate of which will be calculated on their resources. It will be a kind of forced savings, spread over a period of five, ten, or even twenty years for the most underprivileged. The monthly installments will correspond to about 10% of the family income. The capital thus accumulated will be put in a "Fund for Municipal Equipment" which will help finance other operations.

This may provide a way of restoring the bidonvilles; not as before, in a partial and authoritarian fashion, but "from the inside," by offering their inhabitants the immediate ownership of a lot for which they will pay a sum of money equal to that which they were paying for the rent in the bidonville. At first, they will transport their shacks to their new land, nothing more. But a recent analysis of the spontaneous transformations undergone in a few years in certain districts seems to indicate that the shack will be progressively improved—in five or ten years—and then replaced by a more conventional new building constructed of more solid materials. The purpose of this is to give the owners a concrete basis for the improvement of their housing. "We are ready to gamble that a complete change in the psychological frame of the bidonville dweller will cause a radical mobilization of individual energies and resources. The bidonville phenomenon is tied to the feeling of insecurity of the population. Let us give them security by giving them ownership of the land, and hope will then reappear."[77]

Having advocated this method to combat substandard housing the CERF will soon (1973?) test it *in situ* in Rabat, near the bidonville of Yacoub el-Mansour in the new quarter called "Yacoub-ouest," located between the sea and the main road to Casablanca. A first scheme for 1,250 housing plots has been ready since August 1971. The CERF is now awaiting official approval to start this important, and perhaps "historic," material and human experience.

To permit a really economic "auto-construction," the CERF also engages in various technological research that complements the previous experiences. They try to better the traditional techniques, using in the best possible way the abilities of the craftmen and employing local materials—notably "earth concrete," reeds, and plaster—in an effort to minimize the outflow of currency by curtailing the import of foreign materials.

The spreading of auto-construction of housing seems in many respects to be a welcome solution, first because underdeveloped countries have tried in vain to solve the housing crisis by other means, but above all because in these countries the large majority of the population still has building abilities. (A European family, left on its own, could not today manage to build its own house.) In the countries of the Third World, the situation is different, since many city-dwellers still have in

[77] Maroc, Ministère de l'Intérieur, *Note relative à la politique proposée en matière d'urbanisme et d'habitat* (Rabat, 1969), p. 6.

common one essential trait: ingenuity. In the country as well as in town, the traditional architecture, together with the spontaneous modern architecture, is proof that a family can, often with "primitive" means, build for itself a decent, even pleasant house.

Moreover, the direct participation of the inhabitants in the planning of their housing may lead to less stilted, less abstract districts in which the inhabitants will find the image of their own dynamism. As can already be vaguely seen in Casablanca, auto-construction may give birth to a new urban language, to a new, more stimulating and less military environment than that of the sick-looking outskirts surrounding many cities of the Western world.

Action Planning

If the old dogmas of housing have been upset, the routine of urbanism will be too. One can no longer look upon a town as an entity arbitrarily isolated from its environment for which one draws a "plan of development." Now, one has to situate each town in its context. One has to establish a hierarchy of towns, define which role will be given to the intermediary towns, and distribute the various functions accordingly. To achieve that goal, one has to have a voice in the political and economic processes, and one has to have a voice in the localization of the investments. Every single proposition of urbanism has to be completed by a program of regional development, the preparations of which are taken care of by the CERF. In this way, urbanism becomes an indispensable tool for the development of the country because it participates directly in the distribution in space of the multiple operations decided by the government.

This total approach is characterized by two types of intervention: (1) it acts to advise, synthesize, and coordinate and (2) it stimulates new initiative and provides a technical staff. Formerly, the task of urbanism consisted of imposing decisions which were often controversial. Now, urbanism takes a dynamic attitude in planning the physical improvement of the country and of its various regions.

To bring forth this new way of looking at things, the CERF is designing new plans, replacing the old plans which proved to be inadequate when the urban explosion took place. The new plans are based on a network of complementary documents: (1) *a scheme of structure and orientation* which will deal with a complete region and will propose a workable program of action for planning and equipping a territorial entity; (2) *a directing scheme* which will deal with each of the towns and define in more detail the main option of planning and equipment of that center.

As is indicated by their names, these are not detailed documents. Their only purpose is to guide and coordinate the actions of the numerous administrations which will have to carry them out in their various sectors. Moreover, they are only meant to last five years. Since the state requires an official document having the force of a law, there is a third instrument: (3) *a plan for use of the land,* drawn by districts, which defines the rules of land use, the various services and obligations, etc.

Imminent Decisions

These arrangements—together with others—were set forth in 1969 and 1970 in a *loi-cadre* concerning urban and rural planning, which was prepared by the CERF, and especially by a young French lawyer, François Perrin. The loi-cadre would replace previous laws, now completely outdated. In particular, the new law would control real estate sales in an effort to defeat—or at least curtail—speculation, which remains one of the most important stumbling blocks to urbanism and housing. But some of these new ideas have been received with suspicion or reserve. Accordingly, this loi-cadre, which should have been presented to the government authorities in the spring of 1970, was sent back to the CERF for various basic modifications, where it still is. The thinking now is that there will be two different laws: one, concerned with regional planning, should have no difficulty receiving approval, for it is concerned with general principles of rural housing; the other would deal with urbanism and urban housing. Certain observers believe that this second part of the new law has little chance of being approved (or if approved, applied) for it clearly confronts the existing political-economic system which gives scant concern to the disinherited social classes and which blocks coherent urban development with its practices of real estate speculation. However, Morocco has begun, since 1968, to implement a large program of rural planning and amelioration, certain principles of which foreshadow the method of intervention in the towns.

A Regional Program of Housing Tied to Agricultural Development

From 1912 to 1967, state intervention was essentially centered around the towns. One of the first decisions of the Ministry of the Interior, when it became in 1967 responsible for urbanism and housing, was to give priority to rural housing. In order to settle the rural populations and to slow down the emigration towards the cities, an ambitious program of village improvement was set up, a program which took into consideration the experience acquired during the last five years in that field by the BCER.

Housing is no longer thought of as an end in itself, but rather as an action which is to accompany economic development. Agriculture, and especially modern irrigation, is one of the most important resources of the economy; therefore, one must try to better rural housing while improving agriculture. The housing situation is indeed very precarious in the seven large irrigated areas of Morocco. In the northern plains, modern exploitation of the land has not been accompanied by the creation of new villages; thus the farmers' way of life is not favorable to the exploitation of their land. Farmers congregate in market-towns sometimes a long distance away from their fields, or else they live in primitive, isolated, and under-equipped hamlets. On the contrary, in the two irrigated areas of the south, in the pre-Saharan valleys, settlements have existed for centuries, but the villages (ksour) are dilapidated, over-populated, and also under-equipped. So, in the north one must create new villages or enlarge and equip some of the already existing ones; in the south, one has to renovate the ksour. The operation thus underlined is on an enormous scale; it involves 90,000 houses and half a million people.

To determine the location of the hundreds of new villages which have to be created ex nihilo in the irrigated areas, the CERF worked out, from the instant of its creation, a method of "ruralism," one of the aims of which was to set in place a hierarchy common to all these centers and to institute a clever distribution of public equipment. Thus, through these means, the regional improvement of Morocco has begun. This way of proceeding is most important, for it will enable various administrations to collaborate for the first time in a large-scale fight against the notorious under-equipment which still characterizes the rural world.

In these villages there will have to be schools, dispensaries, communal houses, and public baths; and one hopes that education, hygiene, and public health will no longer be the privilege of a minority of town-dwellers.

These villages will, of course, be "auto-constructed" according to plans drawn by the CERF and the DUH. However, to encourage these operations, and to allow the families to subsist normally during the construction, each of them is given some aid in kind. The World Food Program, an agency of the FAO, gives thirty million food rations, each of these providing enough food to feed a family of five for one day. These gifts are to help the operations of "auto-construction" not only for individual houses, but also for the participation of each and every family in the building of the equipment necessary to the village (water, sewer system, roads, public buildings). The magnitude of the improvement attempted, the will to deal with the problems "up river" from the town, the regionalization of state intervention, and the generalization of the methods of auto-construction add up to an important stage in the evolution of ideas concerning urbanism and housing in Morocco.

STATISTICS ON URBANISM AND HOUSING IN MOROCCO.

Number of cities with more than 1 million inhabitants: 1 (Casablanca)
Number of cities with more than 100,000 inhabitants: 8
Number of cities with more than 20,000 inhabitants: 25
Proportion of the urban population around 1900: 10%
Proportion of the urban population in 1970: 30%
Population of Casablanca in 1920: 20,000
Population of Casablanca in 1970: 1,400,000
Anticipated urban population in 1980: 10 million
Rate of population growth for the entire country: 3.2% per annum
Average rate of growth for the urban population: 5.4% per annum
Estimated population of the bidonvilles in 1968: 940,000
Estimated population in the bidonvilles in 1972: 1,240,000
Proportion of urban families having a monthly income between $40 and $100: 30%
Annual credits allocated by the state for housing during the period 1956-1964: $9 million
Annual credits allocated by the state for low-cost housing for the period 1965-1967: $3 million per annum
Annual credits allocated by the state for urban housing during the period 1968-1972: $1,750,000 per annum

BIBLIOGRAPHY

Only the works actually used by the author in preparing this chapter are cited. Those interested in a more complete bibliography on urbanism, housing, and cities—along with their legal, sociological, ethnographic, technical, and other problems—would find it interesting to consult the two important bibliographical studies prepared by Mademoiselle Arielle Rousselle and published respectively in 1970 and 1971. These two volumes are available from the Service de Documentation de la Direction de l'Urbanisme et de l'Habitat (8, rue de Figuig, Rabat, Morocco), and contain a total of 2,200 references to works published on these themes from 1846 to 1971.

Abbreviations used:

JOURNALS
BESM: *Bulletin Économique et Social du Maroc* (Rabat)
A & U: *Revue Africaine d'Architecture et d'Urbanisme* (Rabat)
RGM: *Revue de Géographie du Maroc* (Rabat, Faculté des Lettres)

ORGANIZATIONS
BCER: Bureau Central des études rurales
CUH: Circonscription de l'urbanisme et de l'habitat
CERF: Centre d'experimentation, de recherche et de formation

Adam, A. *Casablanca: Essai sur la transformation de la société marocaine au contact de l'occident.* 2 vols. Paris: Centre national de la recherche scientifique, 1968.

————. "Casablanca, le rôle de la ville dans la transformation de la société marocaine." *Maghreb* (1969), pp. 34-41.

————. "Le bidonville de Ben Msik à Casablanca: Contribution à l'étude du prolétariat musulman au Maroc." In *Annales de l'Institut d'études orientales,* Vol. 8, Alger, 1949-1950.

American Iron and Steel Institute. *The Agadir Moroccan Earthquake.* New York, 1962.

Aujard. *Problème du logement au Maroc.* SL.: CUH, 1958.

Auzelle, R., and Jankovic, I. "Les cités Koudiat et Saâda et le chantier expérimental aux Carrières centrales à Casablanca." In *Encyclopedie de l'urbanisme.* Paris: Fréal, 1958.

Bauer, G., and Dethier, J. *Le Ruralisme au Maroc; le rôle du BCER dans le développement des agglomérations rurales.* Rabat: BCER, 1965.

————, and Hamburger, B. *Précis de ruralisme.* Rabat: CERF, 1968.

Benhima. "La cité du Derb Jdid." *BESM*, no. 80 (1959), pp. 415-437.

————. "La politique de l'habitat urbain dans le cadre du plan quinquennal 1960-1964." *Afrique Magazine* (1962).

————, "Les problèmes d'urbanisation posés par le développement des agglomérations." *BESM*, no. 94-95 (1962), p. 30.

Chéné, Melle. *Les quatre douars de la cité Yacoub el Mansour à Rabat.* Rabat: Ministère de la Santé, 1967.

Berque, J. "Médinas, villes neuves et bidonvilles." *Les Cahiers de Tunisie*, no. 21-22 (1959), pp. 5-42.

Buy, J. "Bidonvilles et ensembles modernes: approche sociologique de 2 populations de Casablanca." *BESM*, no. 101-102 (1966), pp. 71-121.

Caqueray, G. de. "Pourquoi et comment Casablanca eut son port." *Notre Maroc*, June 1952, pp. 5-12.

Celerier, J. "Les conditions géographiques de développement de Fès." *Hespèris* 19 (1934): 1-21.

Courtois, A. "L'urbanisme au Maroc: Plans d'aménagement de Marrakech, Rabat, Ifrane etc." *L'Architecture d'Aujourd'hui*, September-October 1945, pp. 64-75.

Couzinet, P. "L'urbanisme au Maroc." *L'Architecture française*, June-August 1946, pp. 53-64.

Delaly, M. *Rabat, capital créée: Étude de géographie urbaine.* Montpellier, 1949.

Delarozière. "Où en est l'urbanisme au Maroc?" In *Compte-rendu du 5ème congrès nord-africain du bâtiment et des Travaux Publics.* Casablanca, 1953.

Delisle, St. "Le prolétariat marocain de Kénitra et l'historique de la médina." *Cahiers de l'Afrique et de L'Asie,* n.d.

Donkin, A. "The Moroccan Ksar: A Form of Completely Nucleated Settlement." *The Journal of King's College G.S.,* no. 5 (1953).

Durand, R., and Kuhn, R. "Une réalisation en très grande série d'habitat indigène économique au Maroc." *Supplément aux Annales de l'Ins. Technique de Bâtiment et des T. P.,* No. 82, October 1954.

Ecochard, M. *Casablanca, le roman d'une ville.* Paris: Editions de Paris, 1953.

――――. "Les quartiers industriels des villes du Maroc." *La Revue urbaine,* no. 11-12 (1951).

――――. "Problèmes d'urbanisme au Maroc." *BESM* 4 trimester (1951).

Ferrer, J. "L'urbanisme au Maroc." *Stocks et marchés au Maroc,* no. 23-24, November 1952.

Franchi, J. "Urbanisation d'un bidonville: Bordj Moulay Omar (Meknès)." *BESM,* 23 (1959).

Fogg, W. "Villages, Tribal Markets and Towns: Some Considerations Concerning Urban Development in the Spanish and International Zones of Morocco." *Sociological Review,* no. 32 (1940).

Forichon, R. and Mas, P. "Les problèmes de la répartition du peuplement au Maroc." *BESM,* no. 76 (1957).

Guillaud, P. *Note sur l'office chérifien de l'habitat.* Casablanca: CILM, 1950.

Hensens, J. "Urbanismes et architectures du Maroc." *A & U,* no. 5 (1967).

――――. *Rénovation de l'habitat traditionnel des vallées pré-sahariennes.* Ministère de l'Interieur, Marrakech: DRUH, n.d.

――――. *Problèmes de rénovation des Ksour et de l'habitat traditionnel des oasis pré-sahariennes.* Maroc. Ministère de l'Intérieur, Rabat: DRUH, CERF, 1970

――――, et al. *Rénovation de l'habitat dans le vallée du Draa.* Ministère de l'Intérieur, Rabat: CERF, 1968.

Hollard, M. *La croissance urbaine au Maroc.* Grenoble: Université de Grenoble, 1970.

Honnorat, J. *Étude de la démographie urbaine au Maroc.* SI, 1948.

Ichter, J. P. *Données de base pour une planification urbaine à Fès en 1980.* Fès, 1967.

――――. *Projet de couverture de l'oued Bou Khareb à Fès.* 2 vols. Edited by Maroc, Ministère des Travaux Publics, Fès: TP, IRU, 1962.

――――, and Sass, H. "Les ksour du Tafilalt." *A & U,* no. 5 (1967).

Marshall, Johnson K. "Planning in the Prefecture of Casablanca." In *Urban Government for the Prefecture of Casa.* New York: Praeger, 1969.

Joly, F. "Casablanca, éléments pour une étude de géographie urbaine." *Cahiers d'outre-mer,* April-June 1948.

Kratochvie, J. *Importance et portée de l'aménagement de l'axe urbain littoral (Casablanca-Kénitra).* Ministère de l'Intérieur, CERF.

La Casinière, H. de. "La législation de l'urbanisme au Maroc." In *L'urbanisme aux colonies et dans les pays tropicaux.* Vol. 2 (1935).

――――. *Les municipalités marocaines, leur développement, leur legislation.* Casablanca: Imprimerie de la Vigie marocaine, 1924.

――――. "Les plans d'extension des villes et l'urbanisme au Maroc." In *Où en est l'urbanisme en France et à l'étranger?* Paris: Eyrolles, 1923.

LaCharrière, J. Ladreit de. "L'urbanisme colonial français et ses realisations au Maroc." *L'Afrique française,* March 1932.

Laprade, A. *Croquis d'architecture et d'urbanisme au Maroc, en Espagne et au Portugal.* Paris: Fréal, 1958.

――――. "Une ville créée spécialement pour les indigènes à Casablanca." In *L'urbanisme aux colonies et dans les pays tropicaux.* Vol. 1 (1932).

Lavedan, P. "La création des villes au XIX et XXèmes siècles au Maroc." *Annales de l'ITBTP,* no. 8, October 1950.

Le Tourneau, R. "Implications of Rapid Urbanization." *State and Society in Independent North Africa.* Washington, D.C.: The Middle East Institute, 1966.

Lyautey, Maréchal de. "Note au sujet de l'aménagement du centre de Casablanca (1921)." In *Textes et lettres de Lyautey*. Vol. 4. Paris: Plon, 1957.

———. "Notes et directives pour la création d'une capitale à Rabat (1923)." In *Textes et lettres de Lyautey*. Vol. 1. Paris: Plon, 1953.

Mahé, Y. *L'extension des villes indigènes au Maroc*. Bordeaux: Imprimerie Bière, 1936.

Maisonseul, J. de. "Pour une architecture et un urbanisme nord-africains." *Revue d'Alger*, no. 8 (1945).

Maneville, R. "L'expérience Castor aux Carrières centrales de Casablanca." *Notes marocains*, no. 7 (1956).

———. *Prolétariat et bidonvilles*. Casablanca, 1949-1950.

Margay, G. "L'oeuvre française au Maroc. L'habitat indigène." *Maroc-Monde*, 23 November, 1947.

Maroc, Bureau Central de Études. *Pour une politique d'urbanisme et d'habitat*. SL.: BCE, 1964.

Maroc, Direction des Affaires politiques. *Notes sur les moyens juridiques, administratifs et financiers à mettre en oeuvre pour concrétiser le plan de ré-aménagement de Casablanca*. Rabat: DAP, 1945.

Maroc, Ministère de l'Intérieur. *Methodologie d'action dans les bidonvilles*. Rabat: CERF, 1968.

———. *Moyens d'action dans le milieu urbain*. Rabat: CERF, 1968.

———. *Pour un urbanisme opérational*. Rabat: CERF, 1968.

———. "Les techniques audiovisuelles au service de la diffusion des idées d'urbanisme au Maroc." *Flash DUH*, no. 3, March 1970.

———. *Pour un paysage urbain marocain. Propositions pour un tissu urbain dense de l'habitat populaire auto-constructible évolutif normalisé*. Rabat: CERF, 1970.

———. *Le sous-habitat au Maroc: analyse de la situation et strategie nouvelle d'intervention*. Rabat: DUH, 15 January 1970.

Maroc. Ministère des Travaux Publics. *Nouvelles cités d'habitat économique au Maroc (Rabat, Salé, Tétouan, Casa, Safi, etc., par Vignaud)*. Rabat: CUH, 1952.

———. *Projets de maisons économiques en béton de terre stabilisée pour le Maroc*. Marrakech: CUH, 1967.

———. *Note sur le rôle du "Bureau central des études rurales" dans le développement des agglomérations rurales*. Rabat: BCER, 1967.

———. *L'aménagement des centres ruraux dans la province d'Agadir*. Rabat: TP, DUH, 1956.

———. *Plan de résorption des bidonvilles au Maroc*. Rabat: SU, 1957-1959.

———. *Situation de l'habitat à Casablanca en 1952*. Rabat: TPSU, n.d.

———. *Note sur l'habitat économique*. Rabat: SUH, 1957.

Maroc, Promotion nationale. *Projet de résorption des bidonvilles de Settat et Marrakech. Rapport de la Commission*. SL, PN, 1961.

Mas, P. "L'urbanisation actuelle du Maroc: Les bidonvilles." *La Vie urbaine* (1951).

———. *Phénomènes urbains et bidonvilles au Maroc*. Paris: Institut d'urbanisme, 1950.

———. "Pour une planification territoriale du Maroc." *RGM*, no. 1-2 (1962).

Masson, A. *Influences occidentiales dans les villes d'Afrique du Nord à l'époque contemporaine*. Ministère de l'Intérieur. Rabat: CERF, 1970.

———. *Resorption des bidonvilles à Marrakech*. Délégation regionale de l'urbanisme et de l'habitat. Morocco: DRUH, 1965.

Mauret, E. "Problèmes de l'équipement rural dans l'aménagement du territoire marocain." *L'Architecture d'Aujourd'hui*, no. 60, June 1955.

Mokri, Si Thami, pacha de Settat. "Le problème de l'habitat rural." *Bulletin d'information et de documentation du Maroc*, March 1946.

Montagne, R. "L'urbanisme dans les villes musulmanes." *Le maître d'oeuvre de la reconstruction française*. Paris, 21 December 1945.

Montauzan, M. de. "L'organisation des villes nouvelles au Maroc. Le développement des villes nouvelles au Maroc: Casablanca et Rabat." *La Construction moderne*, 30 December 1923.

Montmarin, A. de. "Les conceptions actuelles en matière d'habitat économique au Maroc et leur application à la reconstruction du Derb Jdid à Casablanca." *Annales de l'Inst. Technique du Bâtiment et des T. P.*, no. 150, June 1960.

Morestier, H. "Les faubourgs indigènes de Rabat." *Les Cahiers d'Outre-mer*, January-March 1950.

Mourer, H. *Les problèmes administratifs de l'urbanisation au Maroc.* New York: United Nations, 1962.

Miege, J. L. "La nouvelle médina de Casablanca: Le derb Carlotti." *Les Cahiers d'Outre-mer*, July-September 1953.

———. "Les origines du développement de Casablanca au XIX siècle." *Hespèris* (1953).

Naciri, M. "Quelques exemples d'évolution de douars à la périphèrie urbaine de Salé." *RGM*, no. 8 (1965).

Nespola, H. "Kénitra, historique et analyse du développement de l'agglomération et du port et ses incidences sur l'evolution de l'économie du Gharb." *BESM*, 24 (1960).

———. "Une expérience de développement communautaire: Lalla, Minouna." *RGM*, no. 1-2 (1962).

Pauty, E. "Casablanca et son plan." *RGM*, no. 3-4 (1945).

———. "Le problème des interférences dans les villes marocaines." *Bulletin de l'Enseignement public du Maroc*, January-March 1944.

Pelletier, P. "Problèmes de la circulation dans les villes créées: L'exemple de Casablanca." *BESM*, no. 68 (1955).

———. "Valeur foncière et urbanisme au Maroc." *BESM*, no. 65 (1955).

Porquerolle, L. "L'urbanisme au Maroc." *Travaux publics et bâtiment au Maroc*, 13 November 1930.

Prost, H. "Le plan de Casablanca." *France-Maroc*, 15 August 1917.

———. *Rapport de mission d'urbanisme.* Direction des affaires politiques. Résidence générale du Protectorat français au Maroc. Rabat: DAP (1932).

———. "Urbanisme au Maroc." *Chantiers nord-africains*, February 1932.

Ratier, J. "Les problèmes du bidonville des Carrières centrales à Casablanca." Unpublished. Paris, 1949.

Rouviere. "L'activité immobilière marocaine vue à travers l'essor de Casablanca." *BESM*, no. 9 (1935).

Royer, J. "L'oeuvre de l'urbanisme Henri Prost." *Urbanisme*, no. 88 (1965).

———, ed. *L'urbanisme aux colonies et dans les pays tropicaux. Communications et rapports du congrès international de l'urbanisme aux colonies et dans les pays de latitude intertropicale.* 2 vols. La Charité-sur-Loire: Delayance, 1932 (vol. 1); Paris: Editions d'urbanisme, 1935 (vol. 2).

Tahiri, M. "Le grand bidonville de Casablanca des Carrières Centrales est en train de devenir une cité modèle." *La Vigie marocaine*, 7 December 1952.

Tarde, G. de. "L'urbanisme en Afrique du Nord. Rapport général." In *L'urbanisme aux colonies et dans les pays tropicaux* (1932).

Troin, J. F. "Marchés ruraux et influences urbaines dans l'arrière-pays de Rabat." *RGM*, no. 7 (1965).

Van Huyck, A. P. *The Moroccan Bidonville Problem.* Washington: PADCO, 1969.

Waterston, A. *La planification au Maroc.* SI.: BIRD, IDE, 1963.

Wells, A. "Low-cost Housing in Casa." *London Architectural Association Quarterly* (1969).

SUPPLEMENTARY BIBLIOGRAPHY (Anonymous Works)

"L'amélioration des conditions d'habitat des indigènes dans les villes." *Maroc*, no. 11 (1945).

"Des bidonvilles aux cités nouvelles." *Bulletin d'information et de documentation du Maroc*, 15 January 1942.

"Casablanca, grande ville marocaine." *Bulletin d'information immobilières*, July 1949.

"La charte d'Athènes et les travaux du service de l'urbanisme au Maroc." *Bulletin d'information et de documentation du Maroc*, 5 October, 1950.

"La cité de Derb Jdid." *Construire*, 17 September, 1958.

"Deux expériences d'habitat minimum évolutif au Maroc." *A & U*, no. 2 (166).

"Douars et centres ruraux." *RGM*, no. 8 (1965).

"Naissance du prolétariat marocain. Enquête collective exécutée de 1948 à 1950." *Cahiers de l'Afrique et de l'Asie*. Paris: Peyronnet, n.d.

"Lutte contre les bidonvilles." *Bulletin d'information et de documentation du Maroc*, 5 November, 1952.

"La nouvelle cité marocaine de Fès." *Bulletin d'information et de documentation du Maroc*, 20 September, 1951:

"La nouvelle cité musulmane des Carrières centrales à Casablanca." *Travaux publics et bâtiment*, 15 September, 1951.

L'oeuvre du comité interprofessionnel du logement au Maroc de 1950 à 1954. Casablanca: CILM, 1954.

"Les Plans de l'office chérifien de l'habitat." *L'Informateur colonial*, 15 December, 1947.

"Problèmes d'habitat européen hors de la métropole (au Maroc)." *L'Architecture d'Aujourd'hui*, no. 46, February-March 1953.

"Quelques particularités de la future cité musulmane d'Ain Chok (Casablanca)." *Journal général des Travaux publics et du bâtiment*, 5 January, 1946.

Rapport pour le congrès international de l'urbanisme aux colonies. Paris, Exposition Coloniale, 10-13 October, 1931. Rabat, 1931.

"Town Planning in Morocco." *Maroc-Presse* (American edition), 29 February, 1952.

"L'urbanisation et ses problèmes au Maroc." *La Vie économique*, 6 May, 1966.

"L'urbanisme au Maroc." *BESM*, 3rd trimester (1952).

"L'urbanisme au Maroc, son rôle, ses tâches." *Bulletin d'information et de documentation du Maroc*, 5 April, 1950.

"Urbanisme, habitat et ruralisme au Maroc: les objectifs et l'action du Ministère [sic] de l'urbanisme et de l'habitat." *Jeune Afrique*, July 1970.

"Les vieilles médinas et les problèmes qu'elles posent." *Bulletin d'information et de documentation du Maroc*, 5 November, 1950.

"Village marocain de Madgah (Beni-Snassen, Maroc oriental), Louis Miquel architecte." *Techniques et architecture* (1948).

8

Evolution of Spatial Organization
in the Ottoman
Empire and Turkish Republic

by Ilhan Tekeli

DURING the sixteenth century, the boundaries of the Ottoman Empire extended over the Near East, North Africa, and the Balkans. Because of its geographic location, the Ottoman Empire came into early contact with the changes taking place in the West, and, at the same time, it was the last feudal empire of Europe when industrialization began; and because it could not make the necessary adaptation to industrialization, it passed to a state of rapid decay after the eighteenth century.

Today there are about two dozen nations living within the former boundaries of the Empire which have passed through different stages of development. This chapter deals with the changes which have occurred in the spatial organization of one of these nations, Turkey, from the period of the Ottoman Empire to the present. In the analysis, the Ottoman social structure and spatial organization of the sixteenth century are taken as the reference point. Although there were important regional disparities, this study may offer a historical parallel for the experiences of other countries.

Our task will be to analyze how the settlement structure of the Ottoman Empire changed and which factors influenced this process. In historical perspective, we shall see that a change in the Ottoman settlement structure coincided with the transition to the "semi-colonial"[1] period during the nineteenth century. Later, the young Turkish Republic implemented deliberate settlement and regional development policies because of the unbalanced settlement structure inherited from the Ottoman Empire and an increasing number of ethnic problems. Although the spatial policies of the Turkish Republic were born as a reaction to the typical foreign relations of the Ottoman Empire and did show certain fluctuations in time,

---

[1] V. I. Lenin, *Imperialism: The Highest Stage of Capitalism* (New York, International Publishers, 1953), p. 10.

they remained quite stable on the whole. The essentials of the spatial policy laid down in the last two Five-Year Development Plans may be traced back to the beginning of the Republic.

SPATIAL ORGANIZATION OF THE OTTOMAN EMPIRE DURING THE SIXTEENTH CENTURY

The sixteenth century is the period when the Empire reached the limits of its expansion. The settlement organization was quite balanced and integrated within the central feudal order of the Ottoman society, bounded, of course, by the technological limitations of that period.

Land and labor were the scarce factors of production in a production pattern which was limited by the level of technology. The increase of the controlled surplus in such a pattern depended on (a) expansion in size of the cultivated land and controlled labor, and (b) a more rational use of land and labor, both of which are dependent on organization.[2]

In a feudal social system land and the size of the controlled group are expanded through conquest. As conquest itself is achieved through organization, so too is the control of the surplus of invaded areas and their integration into the existing system. An increase in organization and an increase in the size of the controlled groups led to a greater need and opportunity for urbanization. Therefore, a central authority was necessary in order to defend the position of the Empire on the main East-West road (the Silk Road), to achieve continuous expansion through conquests, and to govern a quite large urban population.

Because of the relatively stable level in the international technology of production, the establishment of central authority and supremacy depended on rationality in organization. This rationality was achieved through land tenure and military institutions[3] which developed as an interrelated harmonious system. A system of military fiefs enabled the Empire to expand its territories and the size of the controlled labor group through conquests, without the burden of supporting a substantial central army and with a minimum loss of the agricultural labor force. The military fiefs depended on the *miri* land system (domain land belonging to the sovereign power). Domain land and the state's ability to control the spatial distribution of labor through regulations, such as the *surgun* (official transfer of populations from one area to another) and those forbidding the *raaya* (subjects, in the present context, "peasants") to leave the land, made the rational use of land and labor possible. The central authority could thus maximize the surplus value it controlled with a control system.[4]

The allocation of power in an empire, such as the Ottoman Empire, which aims at increasing its power—i.e., increasing the controlled surplus through conquests—is

[2] Mübeccel Kıray, "Toplum Yapısındaki Temel Değişimlerin Tarihsel Perspektifi, Bugünkü ve Yarınki Türk Toplumu Yapısı" [Basic changes in social structure in historical perspective—Turkish social structure today and tomorrow] in *Mimarlık Semineri* (T.M.M.P.B. Mimarlar Odası), 1969.

[3] İsmail Cem, *Türkiye'de Geri Kalmışlığın Tarihi* [History of Underdevelopment in Turkey] (Istanbul: Cem Yayınevi, 1970), pp. 53-55.

[4] The question of whether or not the local control elements were hereditary is not important for the rationality of the system. Adequacy of military forces and rational use of land and labor are important.

best represented by a "center-front" model.[5] The "front" grows constantly and is self-perpetuating. In a system like this, there are important spatial problems at the "front." Not only were the fighting forces of the Empire concentrated here, but also a new mixture of cultures was formed by the planned transfer of population through exile. These societies were open to integration, very heterogenous and creative.[6] A hierarchy of control must be the basis for a central control system for an empire with a "front" like this, and a hierarchy as such must coincide with the hierarchy of spatial organization.

In sixteenth-century Ottoman society one finds a hierarchy of settlements consisting of a capital, regional centers, market cities-villages, and nomad groups. Such a hierarchy depends on the functional differentiation of cities and the relation between such cities and their hinterlands and other cities as well.

According to the economic historian Ömer Lütfi Barkan,[7] the population of Istanbul, which was 97,956 in 1478, grew to 400,000 in the period 1520-1535, thus raising Istanbul to the rank of largest city in Europe. Although the transportation and production technology of that period made the production of only a limited agricultural surplus possible, nevertheless, all the needs of a big city even as big as Istanbul could be met[8] by the excellent organization of the social system. The efficient organization of the transfer of surplus to the capital, Istanbul, and the integrated state of the Empire were the main factors contributing to the unusual growth of that city.

The existence of large groups settled[9] in Istanbul makes it apparent that despite the limited technology of the time there were no bottlenecks in obtaining a food supply for this large city. In later periods (around the seventeenth and eighteenth centuries), when food shortages began, precautions were taken to slow down the growth of the city.[10]

Istanbul was quite a differentiated city as a result of its concentration[11] of administrative, military, commercial and industrial as well as religious and social

[5] This model is different from the "center-periphery" models used in development theories. In a "center-periphery" model the integration is between a growing center and a periphery which in general is declining, whereas in a "center-front" model there is a growing, developing front.

[6] Paul Wittek, *The Rise of the Ottoman Empire* (London: Luzac and Co., Ltd., 1963), pp. 33-34.

[7] Ö. L. Barkan, "Essai sur les données statistique des registres de recensement dans l'Empire Ottomane aux XVe et XVIe siècles," *Journal of Economic and Social History of the Orient* 1 (August 1957): 20-21, 27.

[8] At this point one must remember that it was possible to transport goods to Istanbul via waterways.

[9] Among the groups settled in Istanbul were 40,000 Armenians coming from Crimea and Kefe (after the conquests of Crimea in 1475) and Bulgarians who settled in the areas between Yedikule and Topkapi and Büyükdere after the conquest of Serbia in 1520. Muslim, Arab, and Jewish groups settled in the Balat, Hasköy, and Ortaköy districts after the fall of Granada in 1492. See Osman Ergin, *Türkiye'de Şehirciliğin Tarihi* [History of Urbanism in Turkey] (Istanbul: İstanbul Üniversitesi Hukuk Fakültesi İktisat ve İçtimaiyat Enstitüsü publication no. 3, 1936), pp. 96-97.

[10] Sabri F. Ülgener, *Tarihte Darlık Buhranları ve İktisadî Muvazenesizlik Meselesi* [Crisis of scarcity in history and the question of economic unbalance] (Istanbul: İstanbul Üniversitesi İktisat Fakültesi, 1951).

[11] Some data from the seventeenth century give an idea about the size of Istanbul in the sixteenth century. When Evliya Çelebi, the well-known traveller and historian, described a procession in Istanbul, he counted about 1,100 different occupations. The people involved in these occupations were workers, merchants, craftsmen, and others who were employed by the service sector (*Evliya Çelebi Seyahatnamesi*, edited and translated by Zuhuri Danişman, vol. 2, p. 206). According to R. Mantran, in the sixteenth century more than 10,000 laborers were working in 28 public workshops, whereas in the 25,000 private sector workshops 80,000 laborers, including the employers, were working. It was necessary to allocate the agricultural surplus of Rumania, the Danube coastal regions, and most of the Rumelian Sancaks to Istanbul. See İsmail Cem, op. cit., p. 66. Cem himself is relying on information in Robert Mantran, *Istanbul dans la seconde moitié du XVIIe siècle* (Paris: Librairie Maisonneuve, 1962), p. 188.

a **Bilecik**
b **Bolu**
c **Akhisar**
d **Manisa**
e **Aydın**
f **Kasaba**
g **Gördes**
h **Uşak**
i **Alaşehir**
j **Afyon**
k **Söğüt**

l **Mudanya**
m **Keskin**
n **Kırsehir**
o **Yozgat**
p **Kastamonu**
q **Bafra**
r **Amasya**
s **Tokat**
t **Iskenderun**
u **Gaziantep**

Fig. 9. Sketch Map of Turkey.

institutions. Although both capital and frontiers gained military and administrative power, economic power and local control and organization still depended on the existence of regional centers, which were quite evenly distributed over the territory. During the sixteenth century, the population of such centers varied between 20,000-40,000 inhabitants and were located at intersections of important trade routes or at breaking points. For example, Sivas (20,000), a regional center, was located at the junction of the north-south route (Crimea, Syria, Egypt) and the east-west route (Antalya, Konya, Kayseri, Sivas, Erzurum, Tabriz); it was famous for wool and cotton textiles and especially for mohair. About 15 different types of small industrial workshops and specialized commercial shops were located in the city.[12]

The Bursa-Bilecik region was known for silk weaving. Bursa, with a population of 40,000,[13] was not only a silk market but also a warehouse[14] for buying and transporting the cotton textiles of Western Anatolia to Istanbul, Rumelia and Southern Russia and the mohair of Ankara and Kastamonu to Europe through

[12] Osman Turan, "Selçuklular Zamanında Sivas Şehri" [Sivas under the Seljuqids], Ankara Üniversitesi *Dil ve Tarih Coğrafya Fakültesi Dergisi*, vol. 9, no. 4 (1951), pp. 449-451, 456-457.

[13] H. İnalcık, "Osmanlı İmparatorluğu nun Kuruluş ve İnkişafı Devrinde Türkiye'nin İktisadî Vaziyeti" [Economic conditions in Turkey at the time of the establishment and expansion of the Ottoman Empire], *Belleten*, vol. 15, no. 60 (October 1951), p. 607.

[14] H. İnalcık, "15. Asır Türkiye İktasadî ve İçtimaı Tarihi Kaynakları" [Sources of the economic and social history of fifteenth-century Turkey], *İstanbul Üniversitesi İktisat Fakültesi Mecmuası*, vol. 15 (October 1953), pp. 51-55. See also H. İnalcık, "Bursa and the Commerce of the Levant," *Journal of the Economic and Social History of the Orient*, vol. 3, pt. 2 (August 1960), pp. 131-147.

Western middlemen. In this case one can clearly follow the correspondence of the location on the junction of north-south and east-west trade routes to the development of regional center functions.

Diyarbakir, located on the road to Trabzon-Mosul-Baghdad, had a population of 12,000[15] in 1518, and specialized in textiles and leather.

In 1520, Edirne's population reached 22,335.[16] Edirne was not specialized in any industry; yet, its population increased because of trade and the city's function as a second capital (in time of war).[17]

Geographic specialization in production takes place not only in industrial societies but also in feudal ones. The Ankara and Kastamonu areas were specialized in mohair weaving; the Konya-Afyon area in mat weaving; and the Usak-Gördes area in carpet weaving.[18] The Bursa-Bilecik area was noted for its raw silk and for weaving; Mesopotamia for its oil lamps for mosques and for its glass-wares; Manisa-Akhisar-Alasehir regions for tanning and leather products;[19] Maras for its wrought iron; Damascus for its iron works, sword manufacturing, and enamel; and Gaziantep for its footwear. Ankara was also specialized in the manufacture of caravan tools. Thus, in addition to performing transit functions on important routes, these cities, because of the geographic specialization, created commodity flows and performed commercial functions.

Such regional centers, besides specializing in one or more types of production at the interregional level, also produced goods for the consumption of their immediate hinterlands. For example, while there were 25 different guilds in Manisa,[20] the city showed geographic specialization in only one or two of these. These villages, besides their agricultural activities, also specialized in those activities which the central city was noted for. Thus the settlement areas functioned as integrated[21] production entities.[22] Geographic specialization also produced a vertical integration stemming from the local raw material: for instance, animal husbandry, tanning and leather manufacturing, footwear manufacturing; or raising mullberries, raw silk production, silk weaving; or Angora goat breeding, mohair, textiles.

---

[15] Nejat Göğünc, "Onaltıncı Yüzyılın İlk Yarısında Diyarbakir" [Diyarbakır in the first half of the sixteenth century] *Belgelerle Türk Tarihi Dergisi,* no. 7 (April 1968).

[16] Halil Sahillioğlu, "XVIII Yüzyılda Edirne'nin Ticarî İmkânları" [Prospects for commerce in Edirne in the eighteenth century], *Belgelerle Türk Tarihi Dergisi,* no. 13 (October 1968).

[17] Hasan Reşit Tankut, *Köylerimiz* [Our Villages] (n.p. 1939), pp. 12-13. Taken from Doğan Avcıoğlu, *Türkiye'nin Düzeni* [The system of Turkey] (Anakar: Bilgi Yayınevi, 1968), p. 12.

[18] The Ottomans transferred their capital from one city to another according to the direction of growth of the empire toward Europe. Söğüt, Bursa, Edirne, and Istanbul became capital cities in that order.

[19] İbrahim Gökcen, *Manisa'da XV ve XVIII Yüzyılda Deri Sanatları Tarihi* [The History of the arts of hide working in Manisa in the fifteenth and eighteenth centuries] (C. H. P. Manisa Helkevi publication, 1945).

[20] Çağatay Uluçay, *17. Asırda Manisa'da Ziraat, Ticaret ve Esnaf Teşkilatı* [The organization of agriculture, commerce, and crafts in Manisa in the seventeenth century] (1942).

[21] The Polish traveller Simeon, who visited the Ottoman Empire during 1608-1619, tells about a city called Yenipazar near Üsküp in which he observed this integration between the village and the city in the manufacture of locks. Hrand. D. Andreasyan. *Polonyali Simeon'un Seyahatnamesi* [The travel accounts of Simeon the Pole] (Istanbul: İstanbul Üniversitesi Edebiyat Fakültesi publication, 1964).

[22] Sencer Divitçioğlu, *Asya Üretim Tarzı ve Osmanlı Toplumu* [The Asiatic mode of production and Ottoman society] (Istanbul: İstanbul Üniversitesi İktisat Fakültesi publication, 1967), p. 50.

Regional centers were cultural and social centers as well. Educational, health, and social welfare services were supported by government-supervised religious trust funds. In the sixteenth century, the resources allocated for the support of such services consisted of 17% of the income of the Empire.[23] The distribution of these social service functions ran parallel to the hierarchy of settlements.[24]

This regional structure, which shows such geographic integration and specialization of production, engendered an urban hierarchy. So far we have differentiated two urban echelons: the capital and the regional centers. From documents of *nüzül*[25] (a kind of extraordinary tax levied for military campaigns) of the year 1590, it is possible to reconstruct two more hierarchical levels of settlements: those with a population of less than 10,000, such as Isparta (8,000);[26] and those with a population of less than 5,000. A fifth echelon consisted of villages integrated into this structure by means of a definite division of labor.

Since the state was the owner of the land and the peasant did not have the legal right to leave it, he had to cultivate the plot set aside for him and fulfill his social obligations. He was not free to choose which crops to grow or whether to grow anything at all. The type of crop to be raised in each region was decided by a central authority, and the product was allocated for the consumption of a certain city.

According to Ömer Lütfi Barkan, "the villages were responsible for growing the best barley or rice according to a definite plan, by share cropping. Many villages had to perform traditional duties inherited from their ancestors, such as producing alum, saltpeter, living in the area around caravanseries, and performing services for the caravanseries."[27] Thus one finds that villages also had an internal division of labor for performing non-agricultural functions in the rural area, and their obligations toward the state were not only fulfilled in kind but also in services rendered.

The average size of a village was quite large, with 500 or more houses, and a belt of such villages existed around the cities. There were also sizeable nomad groups and tribes all over the Empire, usually engaged in animal husbandry. In regions where the climate was suitable, however, their production function was twofold: animal husbandry in the summer pasture grounds and cultivation in the winter quarters. The contact of the nomad groups with the system occurred when the

---

[23] . At this point, attention must be drawn to the fact that, technically speaking, only urban groups or the highly mobile merchants benefited from these services, not the villagers who mobility was much lower because they could not leave the land.

[24] Ö. L. Barkan, "Şehirlerin Teşekkül ve İnkişaf Tarihi Bakımından Osmanlı İmparatorluğu'nda İmaret Sitelerinin Kuruluş ve İşleyiş Tarzına ait Araştırmalar" [Researches on the establishment and the functioning of Imaret centers in the Ottoman Empire with regard to the establishment and functioning of cities], *İstanbul Üniversitesi İktisat Fakültesi Mecmuasi*, vol. 23, no. 1-2 (October 1962, February 1963).

[25] Lütfi Gücer, *XV-XVII Asırlarda Osmanlılarda Hububat Meselesi ve Hububattan Alınan Vergiler* [The cereals question in the Ottoman Empire in the fifteenth to seventeenth centuries and taxes assessed on grains] (Istanbul, 1964).

[26] Zeki Arıkan, "16. Yüzyılda Isparta" [Isparta in the sixteenth century], *Belgelerle Türk Tarihi Dergisi*, no. 5 (February 1968).

[27] Ö. L. Barkan, "Osmanlı İmparatorluğu'nda Çiftci Sınıflarının Hukukî Statüsü [The legal status of the peasant class in the Ottoman Empire], *Ülkü (Halkevleri Dergisi)*, vol. 9, no. 50, pp. 102-103. Taken from S. Divitçioğlu, op. cit., pp. 14-15.

groups stopped at large cities or when temporary markets were established in summer pasture grounds.[28]   Often large nomad groups became a part of the administrative and financial system and provided an important source of income for the state. Attempts were also made to settle the nomad groups, and the nomads who settled in cities lived in separate districts.

In this spatial organization there was a special hierarchy and integration among port cities. Because of east-west trade routes, important commercial and pirate cities and ports were seen in eastern Mediterranean regions.[29]   Pirate ports of both commercial and military importance were well connected with their hinterlands, and they flourished during those periods when central authority weakened. In periods when the central authority gained power, such cities and princedoms submitted to the state, as they had in the sixteenth century. Both piratical and commercial functions, depending upon their radius of activity, required different sizes of ships and different levels of organizations, the spatial reflection of which was a hierarchy of port cities.

For the maintenance of such a specialized and integrated hierarchy, adequate means of communication and control are necessary. The increase of integration within the technological limits of the era could only be achieved through organization. In order to measure the degree of integration, the intensity of commodity flow and communication must be know.

The empire's important trade routes and military campaigns involving large armies required an efficient transportation organization. In 1564, the mayors (*kadis* or *qadis*) of ten cities in Bulgaria were ordered to deliver 150,240 sheep to the army at Belgrade for a military campaign.[30] During a campaign to the East, 40,000 *irdep* of wheat, 50,000 irdep or barley, and 20,000 irdep of beans were transported from Egypt to Tripoli and Damascus. Provisions were then transported from Tripoli to Birecik and from there to Baghdad via the Euphrates River. The provisions consisted of 99,000 camel loads, which were roughly the equivalent of 30,000 tons. Such heavy transportation took place not only in wartime but also in peace. In 1610, a caravan going from Baghdad to Basra consisted of 943 loads, or some 1,100 transport animals. Such a caravan was capable of carrying a load of about 300 tons,[31] and its length would be around three kilometers, which gives an idea of the size of service organizations they required at the resting points. Between Kayseri and Sivas (a distance of approximately 200 km.) alone there were 24 caravanseries.[32]

Security on the roads was provided by the *derbent* organization. The derbents were organized as villages or *timars,* and the members of the derbent were

---

[28] Faruk Sümer, "XVI Asırda Anadolu, Suriye ve Irak'ta Yaşayan Türk Aşiretlerine Umumî Bir Bakış" [A general glimpse at the Turkish tribes living in Anatolia, Syria, and Iraq in the sixteenth century], *İstanbul Üniversitesi İktisat Fakültesi Mecmuası,* vol. 2, nos. 1-4 (October 1949, July 1950).

[29] Maurice Aymard, "XVI. Yüzyılın Sonunda Akdeniz'de Korsanlık ve Venedik" [Venice and piracy at the end of the sixteenth century], *İstanbul Üniversitesi İktisat Fakültesi Mecmuasi,* vol. 23, nos. 1-2 (October 1962, February 1963).

[30] Ahmed Refik, *Türk İdaresinde Bulgaristan 973-1255* [Bulgaria under Turkish administration 1565-1839] (Istanbul, 1933), p. 8, also see pp. 9-11.

[31] Halil Sahillioğlu, "Bir Tüccar Kervanı" [A trading caravan], *Belgelerle Türk Tarihi Dergisi,* no. 9 (June 1968).

[32] Osman Turan, op. cit.

responsible for the maintenance and repair of roads.[33] Parallel to this network of roads, there developed a communications system based on horseback messengers.

The shifting of the moveable factors of production labor also demonstrates the degree to which the system was integrated. The surgun, as well as being a means for achieving the best land-labor equilibrium, was also a means for ensuring the integration of newly-conquered areas into the empire by resettlement and colonization.

Population groups from integrated areas of the empire were resettled in newly-conquered areas, and population groups from the newly-conquered areas were resettled in integrated ones. In 1461, after the conquest of Trabzon, two surgun movements in opposite directions took place. On the one hand, people from nearby Muslim Turkish cities (Amasyan, Tokat, Samsun, Bafra) were transferred to Trabzon, and timars were distributed to *sipahis* coming from different places but mostly from Albania; on the other hand, part of the local population of Trabzon was transferred to Istanbul, and most of the former Christian sipahis were exiled to Rumelia.[34]

The shifting of the location of the mobile factor of production sectors is seen not only in agriculture but also in other production sectors. Construction works which created a temporary demand for skilled labor also depended on shifting the location of labor.[35] With the help of a central documentation system, it was possible to specify the number of laborers with specific skills, name by name. At extraordinary times, a great portion of the empire could send construction foremen and laborers to certain areas and thus the financial burden could also be spatially distributed.[36]

So far we have analyzed some of the spatial organization data indicating the degree of integration of the spatial structure of the empire in the sixteenth century. We must not forget that this integration was bounded by existing technology. The fact that a central administrative structure could penetrate such a vast area given the limited technological possibilities of the period reveals that this integration was

[33] Derbent villagers, like the raaya, could not leave the derbent. The only difference is that the derbent villagers were exempt from some taxes in return for the services they rendered. Cengiz Orhonlu, *Osmanlı İmparatorluğu'nda Derbend Teşkilâtı* [The Derbent organization in the Ottoman Empire] (Istanbul: İstanbul Üniversitesi Edebiyat Fakültesi publication, 1967), pp. 8-31, 47-55, 95-100.

[34] The word surgun, as currently used, involves the concept of punishment, whereas in the Ottoman Empire surgun was a planned adaptation process in spatial organization for achieving the best land-labor equilibrium as well as a means for ensuring the integration of newly-conquered areas into the empire by resettlement and colonization. Since the raaya could not leave the land, we cannot expect the adaptation to changes in spatial organization to be achieved through voluntary migration. Only when the Ottoman order began to decline and it was no longer possible to control the raaya did migration become a means of adaptation. However, at periods when voluntary migration was not possible, adaptation was achieved through forced transfer of population. See Ö. L. Barkan, "Osmanlı İmparatorlugu'nda Bir İskân ve Kolonizasyon Metodu olarak Sürgünler" [Forced migration as a method of settlement and colonization in the Ottoman Empire], *İstanbul Üniversitesi İktisat Fakültesi Mecmuası*, nos. 1-4, 11-15 (October 1953-July 1954), pp. 209-137.

[35] In 1583, 600 workers from Mytilene and Yörüks from Tekirdağ were brought to Istanbul in order to perform construction work. Ahmed Refik, *Türk Mimarlari* [Turkish Architects] (Istanbul: Hilmi Kitapevi, 1937), pp. 111-114.

[36] Ö. L. Barkan, "XVI ve XVII Asırlarda Türkiye'de İnşaat İşçilerinin Hukukî Statüsü" [The legal status of construction workers in Turkey in the sixteenth and seventeenth centuries], *Sosyal Siyaset Konferansları*, fourteenth book (Istanbul, 1963).

based on a very delicate balance. Within this delicate balance local areas and regions were able to preserve their relative autonomy, although to different degrees.

The most pervasive form of control exercised by the central organization over the empire is seen in the taxation system. The documents related to taxation reveal that the relation of the capital with the states _(eyalet)_ was not at all uniform. The empire had 39 states and within these states there were 176 _sancaks_ and _livas._ More than 100 different taxation codes were issued for the states and sancaks of the empire.[37] This shows that even at the sub-state level, the type of control applied by the capital was differentiated.

With the appointment of sipahis to new timars after the conquests, ownership of the timar tended to become hereditary. When a timar owner died, the _dirlik_ (literally: "means of livelihood," a general term for any grant from the Sultan to provide a living for the grantee) was usually given to his son;[38] moreover, after the conquest, most of the local _beys_ could keep their land.

There was another informal control relation in the empire which included vast territories where total integration could not be achieved due to limited technology. The _Ahi,_ a guild system, controlled production technology and set the necessary regulations. In most cases, the Ahi also had administrative and control functions. Control regulations were set by Ahi Baba, supposedly related to the Ahi Evren Dynasty, who lived in Kırşehir, and the apprentices were accepted according to his regulations.[39] In Istanbul another leader, Zeydi Hindi, established regulations. Informal control relations could not be established over the empire, and a special central organization was required.

As a result, we can now describe the spatial organization of the empire by asserting that it consisted of regions which, although isolated, in essence were quite integrated, given the limited technological possibilities of the time, and which preserved their autonomies and showed a distinctive hierarchy among themselves. Although there were important geographic disparities among them, they did not show marked differences of development.

SPATIAL ORGANIZATION IN THE SEVENTEENTH AND EIGHTEENTH CENTURIES

The loosening of the social structure of the empire during the seventeenth and eighteenth centuries was reflected in its spatial organization. The integrated spatial organization of an industrial society could not materialize, because the society did not make the transition to an industrial mode of production. Several hypotheses can be put forward to explain this failure. They may be categorized in three groups.

---

[37] Şinasi Altundağ, "Osmanlı İmparatorluğu Vergi Sistemi Hakkında Kısa bir Araştırma" [A short investigation regarding the taxation system of the Ottoman Empire], _Ankara Üniversitesi Dil ve Tarih Cografya Fakültesi Dergisi,_ vol. 5, no. 2 (1947), p. 190.

[38] Cengiz Orhonlu, _Osmanlı İmparatorluğu'nda Derbend Teşkilâtı,_ pp. 36-37, and Ö. L. Barkan, _Ülkü (Halkevleri Dergisi),_ vol. 8, no. 58 (1937) and no. 59 (1937), pp. 295, 414, 420.

[39] Franz Taeschner, "İslam Ortaçağında Futuvva" [Fatuvva in Medieval Islam], _İstanbul Üniversitesi İktisat Fakültesi Mecmuasi,_ no. 15 (October 1953-July 1954).

The *first group* explains the failure to industrialize in the differences in the internal dynamics of the Ottoman social structure. These differences are basically threefold:

1. According to the arguments based on the hypothetical existence of an "Asiatic" mode of production,[40] the existence of a central despotic authority prevented industrialization.

2. Another reason is the "hegemonia paradox." In an empire which overexpands, effective control weakens and a substantial military apparatus becomes necessary. The structure eventually collapses under its own weight. Aspects of this hypothesis may be traced back to Ibn Khaldun.[41]

3. Another hypothesis is that the empire was dominated neither by a central authority nor by the feudal system,[42] and this situation was an obstacle to industrialization.

The *second group* seeks the reason in the internal dynamics of the European countries and their interrelations:

1. As a result of the geographic discoveries, the European countries obtained the first accumulation of capital from their new colonies. It was this accumulation of capital which helped them in their transition to the capitalistic stage.

2. Another explanation is based on the production technology of northwestern Europe. The introduction of horse-drawn plows in the tenth and eleventh centuries (at the time oxen-drawn plows were being used in the Mediterranean area) and the substitution of wheat in place of rye led to an increase of the surplus accumulating in the hands of the merchants.[43]

The *third group* is based on the type of relations the Ottomans had with the Western world, and thus this explanation is based on the external dynamics of Ottoman society: Capitulations and the hindrance of development by Western countries led in one sense to the colonization of Ottoman society. This reason may be valid for the period beginning with the end of the eighteenth and extending through the nineteenth century; yet, it is not an adequate explanation when applied to the seventeenth and eighteenth centuries. In this period, it could have been only a complementary factor.

The second group of hypotheses are quite acceptable as far as they go. There remains, however, the question of whether the Ottoman failure to industrialize can be attributed solely to a higher rate of development elsewhere. Did not perhaps the internal dynamics of the Ottoman society play a decisive role in delaying the development? Explanations given in the second group do not give sufficient attention to this problem. We can only assert that the "hegemonia paradox" and the failure of local groups and the central authority to maintain systematic control

---

[40] Sencer Divitçioğlu, op. cit., for a discussion on "Asiatic" mode of production, see pp. 6-26; for the "despotic central authority" (*ceberrut devlet*),see p. 63.

[41] For a more economics-oriented interpretation of the "hegemonia paradox" in the Ottoman Empire, see İdris Küçükömer, *Duzenin Yabancılaşması* [The alienation of the system] (Istanbul: Ant publication, 1969), pp. 41-42.

[42] Niyazi Berkes, *100 Soruda Türkiye İktisat Tarihi* [Turkish economic history in 100 questions] , vol. 1 (Gerçek Yayınevı, 1969), p. 115.

[43] Mübeccel Kıray, op. cit.

78. Istanbul, Turkey. View of Istanbul with the Yeni Valide Mosque, Galata Bridge, Galata, the Golden Horn, and the Bosporus. The image of Istanbul as an imperial capital and port is powerfully conveyed in this picture. (Photo: Atila Torunoğlu.)

79. Istanbul, Turkey. Yeni Valide Mosque in background and Galata Bridge on right. This perspective captures the sense of majesty and magnitude expressed by so many of the major mosques and public buildings of the former Ottoman imperial capital. (Photo: Pan American World Airways.)

prepared a suitable environment for foreign forces eventually to dominate the Ottoman Empire (by the nineteenth century) and, in the process, prevent industrialization.

Certainly, developments in Europe after the sixteenth century affected the empire by limiting its expansion, and simultaneously, the empire ceased to represent a center-front model.

In order to maintain its expansive military posture against Europe, the empire henceforth kept a large army. The permanent *janissary* army, which numbered 12,000 in the sixteenth century, rose to 200,000 excluding cadets *(acemioglans)*,[44] in the eighteenth century. As a result, the military fief system lost part of its importance and state expenses increased. The change in the trade routes during the Age of Discovery caused a decrease in the income of the empire, and rising state expenses forced changes in the land tenure system. The appointment of central government officials *(kapikulu)* for the administration of timars and *zeamets* was reduced, and timars and zeamets (form of land grant) were sold to local lords by *mukataa*. As a result, the autonomy of local control groups increased.[45] During the period 1530-1580, the population of Anatolia increased 40-50%.[46] But the increase of population and the change in the land tenure system[47] disturbed the resource-population balance. Since the expansion of the empire also slowed down, this balance could not be retrieved through surguns. At the same time, the technology remained constant, so the balance could not be reset.

This led to the *Celali* revolts. The raaya revolted against the new local control system of country notables or *ayans*. Although the central authority supported the public revolts against local lords,[48] the latter triumphed in the end. And at the beginning of the seventeenth century, as a result of increasing exploitation, most villages were deserted, for the raaya had fled.

The ayans strengthened their control by hiring and supporting bandits. Although public uprisings and brigandage existed to a limited extent in the eighteenth century, documents show that after the second half of the eighteenth century, the brigands were controlled by ayans, and struggle among ayans was substituted for public uprising and brigandage. The ayans won further autonomy by a legal agreement with the central authority in 1808.

At the end of the eighteenth century, only two provincial centers were under the complete control of the capital or palace. The rest of the empire was indirectly

---

[44] İdris Küçükömer, op. cit., p. 54n., and İsmail Cem, op. cit., p. 140.

[45] Çağatay Uluçay, *18. ve 19. Yüzyıllarda Saruhan'da Eşkiyalık ve Halk Hareketleri* [Banditism and popular movements in the eighteenth and nineteenth centuries in Saruhan] (Istanbul: Berksoy Basımevi, 1955).

[46] Ö. L. Barkan, "XVII. Asrın İkinci Yarısında Türkiye'nin Geçirdiği İktisadî Buhranların Sosyal Yapı Üzerindeki Tesirleri" [The influence on social structure of the economic crises undergone by Turkey in the second half of the seventeenth century], *İktisadî Kalkınmanın Sosyal Meseleleri* (Istanbul: Ekonomik ve Sosyal Etüdler Konferans Heyeti, 1964).

[47] The change in the control system initiated a parallel change in the agricultural crop pattern. Since animal husbandry did not require close control, most agricultural land was turned into pasture (İsmail Cem, op. cit., p. 149).

[48] Mustafa Akdağ, *Celâlî İsyanları (1550-1603)* [The Celali revolts] (Ankara, AU DTCF publication, 1963).

administered through the channels of local authority. [49] Although local autonomy increased, the provinces never achieved complete independence.

The raaya, more exploited than ever, began leaving their land. These unemployed masses migrated to cities and especially to Istanbul, where the population rapidly increased. According to the historian Inciciyan,[50] the population of Istanbul already exceeded a million people at the end of the eighteenth century. Other sources give 873,000 as the population of 1850, and it was becoming more and more difficult to supply food for the city. Toward the end of the sixteenth century, measures were taken to slow down the migrant flow to Istanbul.[51] A decree was issued to turn back the incoming groups on their way to Istanbul and to send back the unemployed to their original residence.[52] When urbanization gains momentum without concomitant industrialization, a city cannot always provide enough employment for incoming groups. Thus, certain occupations appeared; for example, the *tablakars,* who resemble the peddlers of today. (In the eighteenth century measures were taken to prevent the increase of the tablakars.)[53] Also, the existence of the unemployed and low-income groups caused the appearance of low-quality housing resembling the shantytowns (gecekondu) of today.[54]

There was also migration to the other large cities and regional centers. Edirne, for example, which covered 350 hectares toward the end of the fifteenth century, grew to 850 hectares toward the end of the seventeenth century.[55] The population of Edirne was 22,335 in 1520, yet in the eighteenth century there were 20,000 households (or nearly 100,000 people).[56] Even if this number may be considered too high, other sources verify that the city had more than doubled.

In these growing cities the production structure was increasingly coming under the influence of Western goods. For example, in an annual fair in Bursa in the eighteenth century, inferior quality textiles from France, England, the Netherlands, and Venice imported through the Izmir port were sold and also exported to the Orient. The Western merchants were now buying primarily raw materials from Turkey;[57] for example, after supplying Istanbul and Aleppo textile works, about

---

[49] Doğan Avcıoğlu, op. cit., p. 33.

[50] P. G. İnciciyan, *XVIII Asırda İstanbul* [Istanbul in the eighteenth century] (Istanbul: İstanbul Fethi Derneği publication, 1956), p. 14.

[51] Rukiye Bulut, "18. Yüzyılda İstanbul" [Istanbul in the eighteenth century] *Belgelerle Türk Tarihi Dergisi,* no. 3 (December 1967), pp. 30-32.

[52] A good indication of the heavy immigration at that time: Evliya Çelebi mentioned that there were close to 80,000 bachelors in Istanbul (*Evliya Çelebi Seyahatnamesi,* edited and translated by Zuhuri Danişman, vol. 2, p. 26).

[53] İbrahim Sivrikaya, "18. Yüzyılda İşportacılıkla İlk Mücadele" [The first struggles with street hawkers in Istanbul in the eighteenth century], *Belgelerle Türk Tarihi Dergisi,* no. 13 (October 1968).

[54] Orhan Erinç, "250 Yıl Önce İstanbul'da Gecekondu Sorunu" [The shantytown problem in Istanbul 250 years ago], *Belgelerle Türk Tarihi Dergisi,* no. 12 (September 1968).

[55] Gündüz Özdeş, *Edirne İmar Plânına Hazırlık Etüdü* [Preparatory study for the restoration plan of Edirne] (Istanbul: İstanbul Teknik Üniversitesi Mimarlık Fakültesi Yayını, 1951), pp. 23, 28-29.

[56] Halil Sahillioğlu, "XVIII.Yüzyılda Edirne'nin Ticarî İmkânları" [Prospects for commerce in Edirne in the eighteenth century], *Belgelerle Türk Tarihi Dergisi,* no. 13 (October 1968).

[57] The accumulation of precious metals in the West increased the prices of the raw materials, so it was difficult for the Anatolian handicraftsmen to compete with Western buyers, who could afford higher prices (Niyazi Berkes, "Azgelişmişliğin Tarihsel Nedenleri" [The historical reasons of underdevelopment], *Yön* (21 October 1966).

3,000 *kantars* [58] of Bursa silk remained for export. Even so, at least 2,000 looms were still working in Bursa.[59] Good quality Ankara mohair was not then sold to Western merchants. Ankara's annual production was up to 20,000 rolls of camlet and mohair. In this period, trade with Western countries was organized through their consulates.

In the meantime, although the influence of the West was becoming stronger, regional centers were growing rapidly. They still maintained their production functions and were able to make regional controls more effective than before.

Since local autonomy now increased and central power weakened, more capital could be accumulated locally.[60] and more surplus could remain in the locality where it was produced. This fostered the growth of regional centers, but the capital was suffering from shortages in grain supply.[61] Increasing taxes coupled with the pressure of the ayans also affected the smaller settlements. The villagers, abandoning their villages in valleys and on roads, took shelter in places safe from the tax collectors. Toward the end of the sixteenth century, this loosening of the central authority and abandoning of the villages resulted in important changes in the geographic appearance of Central Anatolia. In the eighteenth century, the break-up of the rural settlement pattern caused cultivation to be abandoned in many places. Those who took shelter in the mountainous areas[62] became shepherds, breeding enough animals to maintain themselves.[63]

In order to stop the brigandage[64] of increasing nomad groups and to resettle the abandoned areas, the empire had to make certain changes in its settlement policy. Beginning in 1691, nomad tribes were settled in abandoned areas. The aim was to reconstruct the vacant areas, to open them to cultivation once again, and to terminate the struggles between nomad tribes and settled groups.[65]

---

[58] 1 kantar is equal to 56.5 kg.

[59] Halil Sahillioğlu, "18. Yüzyıl Ortalarında Sanayi Bölgelerimiz ve Ticarî Imkânları" [Our industrial regions in the middle of the eighteenth century and their commercial prospects], *Belgelerle Türk Tarihi Dergisi*, no. 11 (August 1968).

[60] In Bursa, one rich man's wealth varied between 250,000 and 300,000 gold coins. This roughly amounted to one-ninth of the total budget of the empire. The state, which expected to collect 1,500 purses of gold from Bursa for internal loan, could only collect 100 purses (Halil Sahillioğlu, op. cit.). We can thus draw the conclusion that there was an accumulation of local capital due to the weakening of the central power.

[61] In Istanbul there was a scarcity in all the important consumption goods. For example, providing wood for the winter had become quite a problem. According to a decree issued in 1803, ports on the Black Sea coast were ordered to send 450,000 cartloads of wood to Istanbul. Many decrees were issued in the eighteenth century for the solution of such shortages. See Halil Kutluk, *Türkiye Ormancılığı ile İlgili Tarihî Vesikalar, 1487-1923* [Historical documents concerning forestry in Turkey, 1487-1923] (Istanbul: Tarım Bakanlığı Orman Genel Müdürlüğü, 1948).

[62] About two-thirds of the Ankara villages were completely abandoned. In Bacı county only 5 out of the former 38 villages, and in Haymana county 10 villages out of 80, remained (İsmail Cem, op. cit., p. 162).

[63] Necdet Tunçbilek, *İç Anadolu'nun Ekonomisi Hangi İstikamette Geliştirilmelidir?* [In what direction should the economy of inner Anatolia be made to progress?], Istanbul, 1962, p. 9, taken from Doğan Avcıoğlu, op. cit., p. 31.

[64] Çağatay Uluçay, *Saruhan'da Eşkiyalık ve Halk Hareketleri* [Banditism and popular movements in Saruhan], pp. 80-81.

[65] Cengiz Orhonlu, *Osmanlı İmparatorluğu'nda Aşiretlerin İskân Teşebbüsü, 1691-1696* [The attempt to settle tribes in the Ottoman Empire, 1691-1696] (Istanbul: İstanbul Üniversitesi Edebiyat Fakültesi publication, 1963), p. 5.

Although no important changes took place in the communication and transportation technologies, increasing insecurity caused a decline in central control. Insecurity and declining commercial activity reinforced each other—insecurity causing a decrease in commerce, and the very fall in the flow of commodities heightening insecurity. The changing balance in income and expenses necessitated a revaluation of expenses, and thus a decrease in the allocation of funds to charitable services, such as *imaret*. This naturally affected the facilities offered on the roads, and many caravanseries were left to decay.[66] Thus in this period, the integrated structure of both the interregional and regional levels loosened, the interconnection among the parts decreased, and the system became ready for a new type of integration.

In this period, we also see the appearance of nuclei within the system which in a subsequent period played an important role in the integration of the system with foreign countries. Among these we can mention the organization of foreign trade through the consulates, the organization of the religious and educational institutions of the West, and the granting of capitulations.

SPATIAL ORGANIZATION IN THE NINETEENTH CENTURY
(Semi-Colonial Period)

In the nineteenth century, Europe was already industrialized and searching for new markets, and a consequence was that foreign influence increased in the empire. It is obvious that the empire, which was forced to become an open market after the 1740 capitulations and especially after the 1838 Anglo-Ottoman Trade Agreement, could not achieve the transition to an industrial mode of production within the matrix of such foreign political relations. With the 1838 Trade Agreement, the empire did in reality become an open market, and the production activity in Ottoman cities rapidly declined. In Bursa, the number of silk-weaving looms, had been as high as 2,000 in the eighteenth century, fell to 45 in 1845. While more than 25,000 bales of wool had been processed and exported from Ankara, in 1836 less than 5,000 bales were processed.[67] Moreover, after 1850, Western commercial and industrial capital began to pour in. Industries processing the first stage of raw materials were established, especially in the port cities, bearing clear witness to the increasing foreign influence rather than to the development of a national industry. The establishment of such industries necessitated the control of natural resources; the land law passed in 1858 allowed private ownership of land, and this meant abandonment of the land tenure system which had been the basis of the Ottoman order. It is now known that this law had important repercussions and paved the way for foreign influence. To facilitate the passage of this law, foreign powers extended credit to be used in cadastral applications. An 1867 law gave foreigners the right to buy land.[68] With the establishment of the "Council of the Public Debt"

---

[66] İsmail Cem, op. cit., p. 171.

[67] Alfred Bonne, *State and Economics in the Middle East: A Society in Transition* (London: Routledge and Kegan Paul, 1960), p. 231.

[68] In return for Ottoman debts, the British tried to colonize the Empire by buying land (c.f. Austin, *Underdeveloped Resources in Asia*, London, 1878, p. 28). The Germans pursued similar goals in the construction of the Baghdad railroad (Tevfik Çavdar, *Osmanlıların Yari Sömürge Oluşu*) [The Ottoman transformations into a semi-colony] (Istanbul: Ant publication, 1970), p. 45.

in 1881, the control of Ottoman resources by foreign powers gained in status and reached its peak.

The decline of industry, the opening of the resources of the empire to Western markets, and the change in traditional trade routes and functions led to important changes in spatial organization. The Anatolian cities thus lost the production activities and geographic specialization they had achieved in the sixteenth century and became trading centers assuming collective and distributive functions. As the empire became an open market for Europe, a new transportation system responding to the needs of the Empire's new status was born. This determined the appearance of new cities as well as the decline of others.

The most important characteristic of the cities that grew in this period was their location at the breaking points of the new transportation network. The commercial activity opportunities offered at these points encouraged their growth. Mersin, where there were a few houses in 1852, had forty years later a population of 21,756. Izmir, which was administratively tied to Aydın, became the province center in 1851. The population of Izmir rapidly increased up to 250,000 before the First World War,[69] and as a result, the city became the second largest urban center in Anatolia. On the other hand, the population of Bolu, which was a trade and cultural center, fell from 20,000 in 1836 to 8,000 in ten years. When the Black Sea coast was opened to trade, Trabzon, a coastal city, developed and Tokat, and internal center, declined;[70] later, the opening of the Suez Canal contributed to the lessening of importance of Trabzon due to changes in the Persian Trade route.

The railway network penetrated into the hinterlands of the ports to connect the two. The network's tree-like pattern is evidence of the colonial structure. This form is clearly visible in the Izmir-Aydın, Izmir-Kasaba (1868), Mudanya-Bursa (1892), and Damascus-Hama railway lines. The hinterlands where the railways penetrated were openly controlled by foreign countries. The railway system could not be internally connected due to the resistance of the foreign powers who wanted to delineate areas of influence for themselves. Growth of an internal transportation system and the delineation of areas of influence for foreign powers became identical. The Baghdad railway is a well-known example of this situation.[71] The Ottoman government was careful in preventing one foreign power taking over another foreign power's area of influence.

The typical settlement pattern of the era consisted of separate regions each under the influence of a certain foreign power, which controlled a port and a railway track connecting the hinterland to that port. The ports were not the only breaking points; the terminations of railway tracks served this function as well.[72]

[69]   Emin Canpolat, İzmir, Kuruluşundan Bugüne Kadar [Izmir, from its foundation to our day] (Istanbul: İstanbul Teknik Üniversitesi, Mimarlık Fakültesi, 1953), pp. 53, 65.

[70]   Tuncer Baykara, "19. Yüzyılda Anadolu'nun İktisaden Çöküşü ve Bugüne Etkileri" [The economic decline of Anatolia in the nineteenth century and its effects on the present], Belgelerle Türk Tarihi Dergisi, no. 25 (October 1969).

[71]   M. E. Earle, Turkey, The Great Powers and the Baghdad Railway: A Study in Imperialism (New York: The Macmillan Co., 1924), passim, especially 120-146.

[72]   This statement is inspired by William Alonso's theoretical analysis of the structure of transport costs and trans-shipment points. See his "Location Theory," Regional Development and Planning, eds., J. Friedmann and W. Alonso (Cambridge, Mass.: Massachusetts Institute of Technology Press, 1954) pp. 84-88.

At such points, collection systems based on a preindustrial level of technology were organized, and cities such as Afyon were able to preserve their importance. Cart drivers controlling 100 or more carts[73] were commonplace.[74]

The settlement scheme maximized the dependence of the region on external factors; and a concentration of educational and other social facilities organized by the foreign power dominated the area and helped to strengthen foreign dominance and influence.[75]

The importance of port cities lay in their ability to perform the collection function even without railways. A hierarchy was formed among ports since sea transportation was relatively easy. Goods were sent from small ports to large harbors on traditional small vessels and were exported from there. Because of the characteristic growth of the transportation network, this structure necessitated the formation of big harbor cities, such as Salonica, Istanbul, Iskenderun, and Beirut, in order to achieve interregional flows and relations. The organization of traditional transportation was integrated with the railways wherever tracks were paved, and the main trade routes were changed. Both caused a decline in the organization of traditional transportation and therefore created important problems. To assist the people faced with starvation in Ankara, Kırşehir, Yozgat, and Sivas (20,000 died in Keskin and 4,000 in Ankara villages), 1,700 sacks of food were sent from Izmir to Ankara. Of these, only 680 reached Ankara in 20 days and 680 sacks could be transported by 200 army mules brought to Izmir for this purpose.[76] These examples show a decline of the traditional transport system, as compared to those extending in the sixteenth century.

It was not only the pattern of transportation networks which prevented regional economic integration. The customs system was also developed so as to prevent this integration. After the 1838 Trade Agreement, a foreign merchant paid a 5% duty on the goods he sold in the empire, whereas an Ottoman merchant paid a 12% duty for the goods he transported from one province to another.[77]

Pls. 78-79 (254-255)

Because of Istanbul's Western orientation, its acceptance of a Western type of administrative institutions, and its increasing harbor functions, the population of the city continued to increase. Although its population reached 1,200,000[78] in 1903, Istanbul was only the tenth largest city of Europe. In fact, the city was closer to the West than to the empire. For instance, it was easier and cheaper to import wheat to Istanbul from Europe than from Anatolia. In 1911, 21,331 ships visited the harbor with a total tonnage of 20,169,000. Annual tonnage fell to 4,500,000 in 1927.[79] If we consider that even in 1960 the total load carried on both national and foreign ships in all Turkish harbors was 8,200,000 tons,[80] we

[73] While camels could carry 300 kilos, water buffalo carts (*kağnı*) could carry loads up to 1,600 kilos.

[74] E. Banse, *Auf den Spuren der Baghdad Bahn* (Weimar: A. Duncker, 1913) pp. 132-138.

[75] Tevfik Çavdar, op. cit., pp. 84-109.

[76] *Türk Ziraat Tarihine bir Bakış* [A glance at the agricultural history of Turkey] (Istanbul: Publication of the First Rural and Agricultural Development Congress, 1938).

[77] Doğan Avcıoğlu, op. cit., p. 52.

[78] Curtis, William Eleroy, *The Turk and His Lost Provinces: Greece, Bulgaria, Servia, Bosnia* (Chicago, London, 1903), p. 102.

[79] Ahmed Hamdi, *İstanbul Limanı* [The port of Istanbul] (1929).

[80] *Ulaştırma (Deniz Ulaştırması)* [Communications (maritime communications)] (Ankara: State Planning Organization, 1964).

80. Istanbul, Turkey. Beşiktaş Mosque and in left foreground the clock tower of the Dolmabahçe Palace. The merging of old and new, indigenous and foreign, is not a matter of "yesterday" in this part of the world. Note in the Beşiktaş Mosque the use of Western-style windows and towers, and in 81.(below) the even more complete Western borrowing in the nineteenth century Dolmabahçe Palace.(Photos: Pan American World Airways.)

realize the empire's degree of dependence on the foreign world. Because Istanbul had such weak ties with its hinterlands, consumption goods became scarcer in the second half of the nineteenth century.[81] In other cities which could not import wheat from abroad due to the inadequate condition of the transport system, especially in the villages, many died of starvation in bad harvest years.

In this system of economic relations, certain social classes allied themselves with certain foreign powers. Increasing exploitation provided new economic opportunities for local minority groups. The Levantine class, more inclined to identify with Western civilization, was able to serve as a commercial intermediary, thereby gaining new power. The social pattern was also reflected in the urban scene, as a dual structure developed in the cities. On the one hand, the districts in which the elite minority and the rich lived and in which entertainment and cultural facilities were concentrated (like the Pera district in Istanbul and the Punta district in Izmir) were copied from the West. On the other hand, Turkish Muslim districts preserved their traditional urban identity and mode of life. In 1879, two separate municipalities existed in Izmir, and the port, the trolley cars, and the gas and electric services were run by foreign companies.

The relations of the empire with the West resulted in a decline of the economic life of the Central Anatolian cities. These cities became conservative centers opposing the Westernization movements as represented by the mode of life in the Western port cities.

Within this pattern of relations, the empire had to make at the same time changes in the agricultural production system in order to preserve its position as the raw material market for the West. Britain tried to organize cotton cultivation in Turkey; the Germans initiated the irrigation project for Cumra Valley in order to supply cargo for the Baghdad railway; and, around 1911, 15,073 villages in Anatolia were cultivating tobacco. [82]

After the contact of Ottoman society with the West, the economic structure and social stratification under the influence of foreign forces showed a development parallel to the changes in the spatial organization. Many technological developments were imported from the West, but their use was controlled by the suppliers and therefore integration in the spatial organization of the country could not be achieved. The country was divided, therefore, into several areas of influence, each integrated to a foreign power.

Port cities rapidly grew at the breaking points of this new integrated system, and Central Anatolian and Eastern Anatolian cities rapidly lost their importance. They began to decline, developed defense mechanisms against Westernization, and became conservative structures; and interregional dis-equilibrium replaced the traditional Ottoman system.

In all the regions in which capitalism had developed a market economy—like Rumelia, Marmara, Ege, and Cukurova—the feudal structure weakened, whereas Eastern and Southeastern Anatolia still kept parts of their feudal structure.

---

[81] Oya Sencer, *Türk Toplumunun Tarihsel Evrimi* [The historical evolution of Turkish society] (Istanbul: Hobora Kitabevi, 1969), p. 40.

[82] İsmail Husrev, *Türkiye Köy İktisadiyatı* [The village economy in Turkey] (Istanbul: Kadro Mecmuasi Publication, 1934), p. 35.

The central administrative structure adopted from the West and the development of a communications system depending on contemporary technology could not remedy the imbalance resulting from radical changes taking place at the very foundations of the system. In 1864, there were 76 telegraph offices; in 1908, the telegraph network covered most of the empire, but even this network was not under the complete control of the central government. Before the First World War, six European countries had separate post offices in Istanbul.

We must differentiate between interregional dis-equilibrium in a disintegrated and unbalanced structure and the unbalanced but integrated structures of the West, where industrialization is achieved through market mechanisms. In the latter, there is a relationship among the sizes of urban concentrations as a result of integration. The problem is one of internal dynamics.

The interregional dis-equilibrium of the Ottoman society at the end of the nineteenth century was due to the disintegration of the internal structure and subsequent integration of each region into different foreign economies in different degrees. This is a dis-equilibrium born out of the external dynamics of the system and resulting from international imperialistic relations.

But in the nineteenth century, a reaction began against the socio-economic and spatial structure of the empire, and the people began to oppose foreign colonization. Such reaction shaped the ideology of the political movements of subsequent periods.

CHANGES IN SPATIAL ORGANIZATION DURING THE REPUBLICAN ERA

We can consider the spatial organization policy of the Republican era as being a reaction to that of previous eras. A basic characteristic was the reaction against the imperialistic foreign relations of the Ottoman Empire and the desire to change them, and it led to important changes in its spatial organization. In this section, we shall seek the origins of the specific policy applied in this period.

The Republican era can be studied in four periods, each characterized by different policies of economic development. Between 1923-1929, the liberal period, development was by the private sector utilizing internal resources; "etatism" was applied in the period 1930-1946; the period between 1946-1960 was again a period of liberal economy; and after 1960, an era of planned economy began. In all these periods no matter which policy predominated, the mixed economy always existed, and the policy of the spatial distribution of public investments always remained quite stable. The relative importance attached to the private sector determined the differences in the location of urbanization in different periods.

In the period between 1923-1946, when the intensity of reaction to the results of the Ottoman social structure remained constant, the significant national objectives from the point of view of spatial organization were: modernization, abolition of the Ottoman image, reduction of imperialistic influences to a minimum, protection of a national industry, and the development of Anatolia. These were the criteria for choices in the spatial organization of the Republican era.

The first spatial problem of the Republican era was that of resettling a rural population of 400,000 refugees coming from Greece. It is known that a population of 741,000 had been settled by 1929; this involved the resettlement of more than 5% of the total population.[83]   After the War of Independence, 800,000 Greeks migrated from Turkey, and during the exchange agreement 150,000 more went to Greece.[84]   The main consideration in the resettlement of this population was to make them productive as quickly as possible; so the refugees were settled in newly vacated areas. This exchange of refugees did not have an important impact on the spatial organization structure, although it did create differences in the size of the settled population and some differences in land use. Post-war demographic policy encouraged the rapid increase of population, but the government did not encourage family planning until 1960.

Four Policies

The Republican era can be summarized in terms of four main policies,[85] each a reaction to the Ottoman order:

1. The transfer of the administrative and cultural center from Istanbul to Ankara.

2. The transformation of many provincial centers into modern administrative and cultural centers, thus introducing and initiating social changes to their hinterlands.

3. The construction of a railroad network to cover the country and thus replace the former "tree form," and the development of highways to support the railways.

4. The location of large public industries in small Anatolian towns.

The transfer of the capital from Istanbul—which had been the capital of Byzantium for more than 1,000 years and of the Ottoman Empire for more than 500 years—to Ankara[86] was not only born from a desire to continue the image of the War of Independence (between 1920-1923) and to locate the government in the heart of Turkey, in Anatolia; but it was also a revolt against the way of life of the Levantine class of Istanbul who identified themselves with the West. Behind the competition of Ankara with Istanbul there was the desire to create a new bourgeoisie of a Republican character that would counter the Levantine groups of Istanbul.

Placement of the country's decision-making functions in Ankara was the most important factor in causing self-perpetuating growth; concentration of higher educational functions also furthered the development of Ankara. Within the new

Pls. 82-83 (266-267)

---

[83]   *İskân Tarihçesi* [History of settlement] (Istanbul, 1932).

[84]   Cevat Geray, *Türkiye'den ve Türkiye'ye Göçler ve Göçmenlerin İskânı* [Turkish out- and in-migration and the settlement of migrants] (Ankara: Siyasal Bilgiler Fakültesi, 1962), pp. 3-4, 48.

[85]   M. D. Rivkin, *Area Development for National Growth: The Turkish Precedent* (New York: Praeger Special Studies, 1965), pp. 48-74.

[86]   This was the first example in the world of the transfer of a capital from the largest city to a smaller inland city. The example has been repeated in several countries. Moreover, it is a very early example of the successful creation of growth poles through a regional settlement policy.

82. Ankara, Turkey. View of the modern city, business district and residential area in the foreground; the old city in the distant background. (Photo: Atila Torunoğlu.)

83. Ankara, Turkey. Gecekondu (squatters' settlements) around and in the citadel. The modern city is in the background. (Photo: Atila Torunoğlu.)

system, the tensions created between Istanbul and Ankara were soon dissolved and Ankara was integrated into the system.

Provincial centers were to be developed as cultural centers from which reforms could penetrate the hinterland. This was how the Western mode of life, perceived differently in the Republican period, was to be introduced. The Republican bourgeoisie was going to be born. The "people's houses" (*Halk evleri*, local cultural centers) are the result of such a program and thought. Besides modernizing society, the people's houses were to provide for the cultural integration of a disintegrated society inherited from Ottoman times.[87] Thus, Anatolian provincial centers were used as contact points in introducing social change, and they became a means to destroy the conservative centers established in the former period.

The slow rate of urbanization also made the municipal efforts toward the "beautification" of cities possible. The reconstruction of Ankara became an example for such activities in other cities. An important part of the green areas and parks in the cities were built in this period.

The major policy of this era in the field of transportation was that of railways. The main objectives after the War of Independence were the repair of tracks destroyed in the war, nationalization of tracks held by foreigners, and construction of new railroads. The main reason for insistence on this policy resulted from the bottlenecks met with during the First World War and then during the War of Independence.[88] Railway policy was not implemented according to a definite program. Main lines in Central Anatolia in the East-West direction formed a network, and this network was tied to the port cities. A highway system was then developed to support the railways.

The fourth settlement policy, the location of industry in the interior, drew the most criticism. The policy could now be implemented because of the improvement in the railway network, thus illustrating the internal complementarities of the four policies. The major issue was not the choice of location but whether development would be realized by the public sector or by the private sector.

The factories established had other aims than just production. One aim was that a factory should be a focal point of social change in the area; another was that it should encourage the development of the private sector and thus initiate self-sustaining growth. Before discussing whether or not the aims were realized, we must consider whether it is realistic to expect the fulfillment of these goals.

Since the profits of these factories were sent to their central offices and from there distributed to new investment areas, the factories could only have indirectly developmental effects on the areas through the consumption activity of the workers. So we must direct our analysis to both forward and backward linkage effects. Because most of such factories produced final consumption goods (for instance, textiles and sugar), they could stimulate the production of raw materials such as sugar cane, but the factories could not be expected to attract other

---

[87] R. D. Robinson, *The First Turkish Republic* (Cambridge, Mass.: Harvard University Press, 1963), pp. 37-92.

[88] Murat Ergun, *Bir Demiryolcunun Kurtuluş Savaşı Hatıraları* [Memoirs of a railwayman concerning the War of Independence] (Istanbul, 1966).

industries. There are no substantial sociological studies showing the effect such factories have had in introducing social change to their surroundings, and although their isolation from their environment and the restriction of their social services to small groups would serve as limiting factors, there is reason to believe that they were not without an impact.

In addition to these four settlement policies, another important policy influencing spatial organization was that of encouraging a population increase. This policy was considered rational in the first years of the era because of the low density and the possibilities for opening new areas to agriculture. Health programs were implemented to support the policy, such as that of malaria eradication—one of the most successful campaigns in the world—which turned the study of water and land resources into a marsh-drying project (e.g., the drying of Cellat Marsh) rather than irrigation and energy production. The study of resource development remained limited and could not be realized despite important investment allocation.[89] The rate of urbanization was quite low because agricultural land was still available, mechanization was not widespread, and industry in small cities had not yet reached a critical size. This was more in line with the policy of holding rural population in the agricultural areas.

At the end of this era we can see the change in many structural factors of the previous era. Special care was given to Central Anatolia in an attempt to remedy interregional disparities, but Eastern Anatolia remained neglected. The rates of growth of Istanbul and Izmir were below the rate of increase of the total population and the total urban population. On the other hand, Central Anatolian cities, led by Ankara and Eskisehir, grew rapidly[90] —the result of a spatial organization during this era which was oriented toward achieving an interregional balance.

After the Second World War, there was a change in the economic development policy. The policy of development by the public sector with the use of internal resources was abandoned, and development was to take place by using foreign aid and through the private sector. Although there was not a great change in the shares of the public and private sector of the economy, the system of relations was changed. A policy of development through agriculture, rather than industry, and increased emphasis on infrastructural investments was chosen. This new policy had important effects on spatial organization, such as the expansion of agricultural land through mechanization and the shift of priority from railway to highway investments.

Beginning in May, 1949, tractors arrived through the Marshall Aid Program. In accordance with the recommendation of the U. S. Military Aid Organization in 1947, a large highway investment program was undertaken by the General Directorate of Highways (the Directorate had been established with the guidance of the U. S. Public Road Administration). In 1948, the Iskenderun-Erzurum road was

---

[89] Of the 100 million Turkish pounds allocated in 1929 to be spent in 12 years, only 12 million Turkish pounds were spent eight years later. Ahmet Demir, *Türkiye İç Sularından Faydalanma* [Taking advantage of internal waters of Turkey](Ankara: Siyasal Bilgiler Fakültesi, 1963).

[90] Ruşen Keleş, *Şehir ve Bölge Plânlaması Bakımından Şehirleşme Hareketleri* [Urban development from the point of view of city and regional planning] (Ankara: Siyasal Bilgiler Fakültesi, 1961).

Fig. 10. Turkish cities A.D. 1935.

Fig. 11. Turkish cities A.D. 1965.

Fig. 12. Turkish cities A.D. 2000.

The rapid increase in size and number of communities qualifying as "urban" in Turkey is illustrated by these three maps, two historical and one conjectural. The map of urban communities of Turkey in the year 2000 was prepared by population projection techniques. It was assumed that the national population will grow from its present 36 million (1970) to 76 million by the year 2000; that the proportion of the population living in rural communities will continue to decline approximately as in the past; and that recent rates of growth of particular communities, as well as historical patterns of city growth in Turkey, in general, are indicative of which communities will grow more than others. Unanticipated economic, administrative, and demographic developments will undoubtedly intervene and require modification of the projection in many details. Nevertheless, the general pattern of urban Turkey in the not distant future may well emerge approximately as sketched here. (Courtesy: Frederic C. Shorter.)

built for military purposes. This road program did not take into consideration the integration of highways and railroads. In the first years it had an encouraging effect on the railway freight but later the unplanned competition caused an economic crisis among the railways. Agricultural mechanization[91] achieved with the assistance of foreign aid not only increased cultivable land but also caused the unemployment of an important portion of the labor force. Population growth and agricultural unemployment combined with an improved highways system resulted in a rapid urbanization. Rapidly growing rural-urban contacts strengthened the market economy in the south and west coastal regions, and increased urban-rural integration.

[91] *Türkiye'de Zirai Makinalaşma* [Agricultural mechanization in Turkey] (Ankara: Siyasal Bilgiler Fakültesi, 1954).

In a period when more importance was attached to infrastructural investments rather than to productive investment, priority was given to the development of water resources and highways. The water resources development program emphasized the building of dams[92] rather than irrigation. The increased allocation of infrastructural investment meant a decrease in the share of industrial investment coming from the public sector. Although industrial investments in the public sector decreased generally, their allocation to Central Anatolia continued as a political maneuver to secure votes. The importance of port cities increased once again (like Istanbul and Izmir), and Western and Central Anatolian cities with a population of 50,000 continued to grow, whereas urbanization remained quite low in Southern and Eastern Anatolia.

After the Revolution of 1960, which occurred at the end of an inflationist era, there was a return to the policy practiced during the first years of the Republic. Again the question of interregional balance gained importance, and for the first time developmental priority was given not to Central Anatolia but to Southeastern Anatolia. With the return to power of the Democratic Party, as the new Justice Party, the policy of the First Five-Year Plan was soon changed and a Second Five-Year Plan was developed from it. The policy of using urbanization as a means of development gained importance along with the policy of interregional balance. After the Second World War, and despite the impact of the 1960s, the social and economic structure continued expressing the same characteristic and decisive influence on the formation of the spatial organization. The only change brought about during this period was the encouragement of urbanization in the east.

CONCLUSION

It is important to consider the question of changes in the spatial organization in historical perspective. Such an approach aids in clarifying the more significant variables of the system. When the Turkish historical experience is studied from the viewpoint of changes in spatial organization, the decisive variables are the level of technology, the basic institutions of social structure, and the external relations of the system. There is a one-to-one correspondence between the changes in the external relations and institutions and the changes in the spatial organization. Of several variables, only technology remained constant in the sixteenth, seventeenth, eighteenth, and even in the nineteenth centuries. Changes in the social institutions in the seventeenth and eighteenth centuries and changes in the matrix of foreign relations also had their divergent impacts on the spatial organization. Only in the twentieth century did changes in technology, foreign relations, and social institutions converge as mutually-interacting variables.

What is the theoretical relevance of the above discussion? Where do the present location theories fit into such a framework? Location theories, it might be argued, consider the variables mentioned in the foregoing paragraph as constants. And, as a

---

[92] Between 1953-1962 about 60% of the investments of the state water works department went into dam building (Ahmet Demir, op. cit.).

result, the solution to problems using these theories cannot go beyond increasing efficiency in a given system. When the question is that of planning structural changes in the society, present location theories and analysis techniques will not suffice. It is necessary, therefore, to develop a macro-location theory establishing the links between basic social institutions and spatial organization. The independent variables of such a theory will be population, technology, and institutional arrangements.

GENERAL BIBLIOGRAPHY

Avcioğlu, Doğan. *Türkiye'nin Düzeni* [The system of Turkey]. Ankara: Bilgi Yayınevi, 1968.

Bonne, Alfred. *State and Economics in the Middle East: A Society in Transition.* London: Routledge and Kegan Paul, 1960.

Çavdar, Tevfik. *Osmanlıların Yarı-Sömürge Oluşu* [The Ottoman transformation into a semi-colony]. Istanbul: Ant Yayınları, 1970.

Earle, M. E. *Turkey, the Great Powers, and the Baghdad Railway.* New York: Macmillan, 1924.

Eldem, Vedat. *Osmanlı İmparatorluğu'nun İktisadi Şartları Hakkında bir Tetkik* [A study on the economic conditions of the Ottoman Empire]. Ankara: Türkiye İş Bankası Kültür Yayınları, 1970.

Hershlag, Z. Y. *Turkey: The Challenge of Growth* (2nd revised edition). Leiden: Brill, 1968.

Karpat, K. H. *Turkey's Politics: The Transition to a Multi-Party System.* Princeton: Princeton University Press, 1959.

Lewis, Barnard. *The Emergence of Modern Turkey.* London: Oxford University Press, 1961.

Mears, Grinnel Eliot. *Modern Turkey.* New York: Macmillan, 1924.

Mustafa, Akdağ. *Türkiye'nin İktisadî ve İçtimaî Tarihi* [Economic and social history of Turkey]. Ankara: Türk Tarih Kurumu, 1959.

Rivkin, M. D. *Area Development for National Growth.* New York: Praeger, 1965.

Robinson, R. D. *The First Turkish Republic.* Cambridge, Mass.: Harvard University Press, 1963.

Taner, Timur. *Türk Devrimi ve Sonrası, 1919-1946* [The Turkish Revolution and its aftermath, 1919-1946]. Istanbul: Doğan Yayınları, 1971.

Uzunçarşılı, İ. H. *Osmanlı Tarihi* [Ottoman history], vol. 3. Ankara: Türk Tarih Kurumu, 1954.

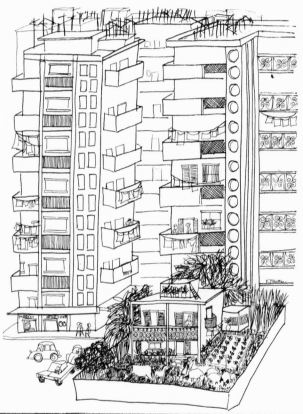

Fig. 13. Varieties of juxtaposition between old and new, indigenous and imported in the modern Near Eastern City. (Drawings by Kathe Tanous, courtesy of Aramco World Magazine.)

Part IV
THE CULTURAL HERITAGE
AND AESTHETIC FACTORS

9

The Care of Historic Monuments and Sites in Turkey
by Cevat Erder

ONE mark of man is his concern for the preservation of the past, especially as symbolized by its monuments. Twentieth-century man is not exceptional in his care of historic monuments. A few examples from ancient history may indicate how naive perhaps are our present conceptions of the past.

In seventh-century B.C. Nineveh, Sennacherib showed his dedication to the conservation of an historic environment, if not human life, when he proclaimed that property owners along the Great Royal Road were responsible for the preservation of its appearance. Anyone found guilty of altering its form was to be hanged from the roof of his house.[1] Although the ancient Greeks did not go to this extreme, they left evidence of their dedication to the protection of monuments in their sanctuaries. Pausanias records the Temple of Hera at Olympia as still standing after 800 years of continuous use, during which time it had been repeatedly renovated.[2] He also describes how in the same sanctuary architectural elements that had survived from the house of Oinomaos were exhibited in an especially interesting manner. Just as in the open-air museums of today, they were arranged on a pillar and surrounded by a rectangular structure.[3] An equally advanced approach is recorded by Plutarch, who claims that the ship in which Theseus was said to have returned with the Athenian youths was carefully preserved until the time of Demetrius of Phalerum by periodically replacing each unsound plank.[4]

Official regulations to ensure the care of cultural property did not become common in Europe, however, until the early nineteenth century. Most recently, the notion that historic monuments should be preserved has been extended to embrace

[1] British Museum No. 124800.
[2] Pausanias, *Description of Greece*, Book V, XVI, 1-8.
[3] Ibid., V, 20.
[4] Plutarch, *Lives*, I, I.

"not only the single architectural work but also the evidence of a particular civilization, a significant development, or an historic event."[5]

In Turkey the concept of the historic monument has been restricted to the nineteenth-century sense of a single structure of historic value. In the past few years, however, we have witnessed in Turkey a growing awareness by the public of the value of preserving historic sites, and architects and planners are beginning to realize the importance of their preservation. The concern of this paper, therefore, will focus on Turkey's care of monuments and sites both in the past and present, and the prospects for salvaging traditional quarters in urban centers.

THE OTTOMAN LEGACY AND PRECEDENT

Turkish cities are still rich both in individual works and in whole quarters that remain much as they were a century or two ago. These cities became unintentionally centers for the conservation of the works inherited from a great variety of past civilizations. From the time the Seljuqs first entered Anatolia one finds a surprising survival of previous monuments. The present towns of Central Anatolia which formed the Seljuq stronghold testify to these rulers' care for and integration of pre-existing architecture into their own culture.

The Ottomans continued this tradition, as may be observed in Istanbul. One need only recall those ancient landmarks of Constantinople which happened to outlast the Latin occupation. They may still be found in their original sites, although standing often unnoticed and with none of the tourist fanfare one expects in the West. The Ottomans also added from their campaigns to these monuments of the capital. After the Mohaç Campaign in 1526, Ibrahim Pasha transported the statues of Artemis, Apollo, and Hercules from the square of the Budin palace to Istanbul and had them erected in the Hippodrome before his palace.[6]

Most instances of conservation, however, occurred quite by accident. Raymond Matton in his study of Rhodes quotes Cottu's apt description written in 1844: "Everything remains standing at Rhodes as it was since the day when the Grandmaster and his brothers abandoned the island. The Turk has destroyed nothing, built nothing. He came, seated himself on his carpet with his pipe which he has smoked for centuries."[7] Churches, however, were regularly converted into mosques, usually by adding a minaret and whitewashing the interior. We are indebted to this method of concealing wall decorations for the unwitting preservation of many fine works of art, such as the striking eleventh-century Byzantine frescoes which have survived at Ochrid. In most cases, however, the Turks moved into existing structures and kept them in use. Their very disinterest in the physical transformation of their environment proved a guarantee for the

[5] II. International Congress of Architects and Technicians of Historic Monuments, *Venice Charter*, Article 1 (1964).

[6] Turğut İşiksal, "Tarihî Eserlerimizin Yağma edilmesine ve Kaçırılmasına Ait Örnekler " [Examples of the plundering and stealing of our historical works], *Belgelerle Türk Tarihi Dergisi*, no. 4 (January 1968), p. 28.

[7] Charles Cottu, "L'île de Rhodes," *Revue des Deux-Mondes*, t.v. (March 1844), quoted in Raymond Matton, *Rhodes*, Collections de l'Institut Français d'Athènes (1966), p. 68.

survival of cultural property. Even in the late nineteenth century, when the "sick man of Europe" was approaching his final hour, another traveller reported that "when the Turks occupied the Eastern Empire the destruction of antique monuments was already three-quarters accomplished .... The Turks who are neither intolerant nor inclined to vandalism have not destroyed, they must be granted this justice, a single famous monument." [8]

During this last period of the empire, however, the Sultan or members of the administration began either openly to use monuments in the diplomacy of the Near Eastern question or politely disregard their disappearance when this was expedient. The rich acquisitions of European museums date to this period. At the same time, however, the Turkish public became concerned with the fate of their historical monuments to the extent that payment to the European powers with antiquities occasionally had to be handled with delicacy.

The oldest evidence of public intervention is a letter dated 1799 from an official of the Porte to Sultan Selim III. The former suggests that the gift of a sarcophagus requested by the British Ambassador should not be made directly because of the public opposition its removal might occasion, but, instead, should be first taken to the palace and then transferred to the ambassador at a "convenient" place. The Sultan's seal is affixed to the request and in his hand is the note, "let it be brought to the palace and have them come here to fetch it." [9] One need only recall the French-English-Ottoman triangle of that year to understand the diplomatic significance of this gift. The reaction of educated Ottomans, however, somewhat brightens this dismal picture of the loss of antiquities. In 1846, Istanbul's first official museum was opened, and in 1868, the first decree governing the administration of museums was passed. The architects who sketched and executed the designs for the additions to the archaeological museum from 1892 to 1908 applied the latest techniques in contemporary museum display. [10] In the 1880s, the first school of archaeology and museum science opened, but it disappeared after only a few years of operation. Legal efforts to define and control antiquities may be traced to the "Antiquities Proclamation of 1869." [11] The proclamation defines cultural immovables, states the rules for obtaining permission to excavate, and establishes the division of finds between the state, property owner, and excavator. All these archaeological interests flared up and just as quickly died, as did so many other Ottoman causes of the time. As Turkish national consciousness grew in the late nineteenth and early twentieth centuries so did the idea of preserving national cultural property. It only received partial attention, however, during these long years of war and struggle for a national identity.

---

[8] Reinach Salomon, "Le Vandalisme Moderne en Orient," *Revue des Deux-Mondes* (1883), pp. 154-155.

[9] Hattı Humayun Tasnifinde 15.015 sayılı belge [Document No. 15,015 according to the Imperial Decree classification]: T. Işiksal, op. cit., pp. 30-31.

[10] "The New Turkish Museum of Antiquities," *The American Architect and Building News* (October 15, 1881), pp. 179-180.

[11] Ahmet Mumcu, "Eski Eserle Hukuku ve Türkiye" [The law of ancient works and Turkey], *Ankara, Üniversitesi Hukuk Fakültesi Dergisi* 26, no. 3-4 (1969): 66, 70.

MODERN TURKEY'S CHALLENGE TO THE PAST

Ironically, the danger to historic monuments in Turkey, particularly to Seljuq and Ottoman structures in urban areas, dates from modern times. Over a period of nine centuries first the Seljuqs and then the Ottoman Turks had enriched the cities of Turkey with a religious, civil, and domestic architecture which achieved a distinct synthesis of indigenous and introduced elements. Most of these structures responded to the everyday needs of their society, and many were under the control of the state as a pious foundation. When fascination with the West—and its technology—first began over a century ago, its influence on the historical environment was limited. Later, with Turkish nationalism and then with the Republic, rejection of the Ottoman heritage virtually became a creed. Monuments such as baths or markets, which had functioned unchanged for centuries, were neglected or replaced with "superior" modern structures. Entire historic centers within cities were destroyed to make room for new roads and a more modern transportation system.

The new architecture, too, reflects the opposing trends: one, a search for a national architecture synthesizing Turkish and international styles or adapting these to local conditions; another, an indiscriminate adoption of international architecture. Kemaleddin Bey and Vedat Bey were among the first to search for a national architecture; and Sedat Hakkı Eldem, in the 1930s, attempted to reconcile international architecture with Turkish styles and materials.

Since World War II, the search for a national architecture has been all but abandoned.[12] Experiments with a Turkish synthesis are scattered and barely noticeable among new structures, which are indistinguishable from those going up in Beirut, Munich, or Kansas City.

Pl. 2 (16),
82 (266)

Social changes are also important in bringing about the demise of whole quarters and many monuments, although in this era of planning it becomes increasingly difficult to differentiate between self-propelled social evolution and induced change. Until the twentieth century, Turkish cities functioned as they had since Byzantine times. With the structural changes inherent in modernization, the physical patterns of cities altered. Traditionally, cities had been composed of units or districts that were administratively self-governing and characterized by the primary social relationships associated with small settlements. Each district was responsible for the upkeep of its own mosque, baths, and other public buildings and monuments. This system languished and consequently so did the monuments. Rather than improving upon the existing system or proposing an innovative solution, modern city planners simply stamped Western patterns on the Anatolian landscape. These conformed neither to the needs of a vanishing society nor to the emerging functions of a modernizing one. Roads are a telling example. Planners eliminated winding streets and drew rectilinear networks to replace them; dead-end streets were forbidden and existing dead-end streets were opened.[13]

---

[12] Tuğrul Akçûra, "Architecture et Urbanisme en Turquie," *L'Architecture d'Aujourd'hui*, no. 140 (1968), pp. 89-91.

[13] K. A. Aru and C. Erder, "Tarihî Miras ve Modern Dünya" [Historical heritage and the modern world] *T.M.M.O.B., XII. Devre Çalişma Raporu* (Ankara, 1966), Folio: 802.

84. Pamukkale, Turkey. A rear view of one of the present motels that covers ancient hot springs at the very center of the city's historic monuments. (Photo: Cevat Erder.)

The implications of the foregoing changes for historic monuments and sites become evident when one realizes that 70% of Turkey's major settlements are completely or partially located on ancient sites. Of Turkey's ancient sites, about 2,120 have been identified by their classical names, and perhaps one quarter rank as major ancient cities. Drastic alterations in the urban landscape destroy not only monuments above the ground but also many that lie unexcavated. While architects have completed and implemented over half of the plans for the 1,500 cities and towns eligible for master plans, organizations protecting antiquities have made little progress.

The High Commission for Monuments, founded in 1951 and composed of fourteen scholars and experts, is overtaxed and hopelessly involved in the details of solving the daily problems affecting individual monuments. The *Vakıflar* (Foundation for Pious Endowments), in charge of monuments once belonging to the Ottoman State and now to the public, has been generally successful at preserving the monuments in its charge, although legally one would expect the Department of Museums and Antiquities to be the more active and competent.[14] To this list of organizations concerned with monuments may be added the Ministry of Tourism and Information, the Parliament's Administration of National Palaces, the Ministry of Reconstruction and Resettlement, the Ministry of Public Works, and the municipalities. But these offices act independently of each other, and their activities are not coordinated with the planning offices.

Turkey has reached a critical crossroads; an effective solution must be found or most of her cultural heritage, of interest to Turks as well as to the world, will be irrevocably lost. On the one hand, officials interested in the economic prospects of tourism are at last making funds available and thus care possible. In the First Five-Year Plan, about \$12.5 million were marked for the care of monuments alone. In the current Second Five-Year Plan, the amount has been raised to about eighteen million. An informed public is also making private resources available. In 1967, *Milliyet*, a prominent national newspaper, initiated a national campaign which raised \$365,000 to salvage monuments to be flooded by the Keban Dam and to record previously unexcavated höyüks; donors ranged from the Turkish government to companies and elementary school children. On the other hand, physical change is taking place at an accelerated pace. Population growth and a rural-urban shift have caused most cities to double or triple in size, some only during the past ten years; this has not been tempered by a concurrent appreciation for the quality of the environment. Moreover, plans for preservation have focused on capturing the immediate attention of the tourist rather than seeking long-term solutions of distinction.

*   *   *   *   *   *   *

Pamukkale, ancient Hierapolis, is a prominent example of the disastrous results which such an exaggerated emphasis on tourism may produce. Hierapolis is one of

---

[14] A. B. Kunter, "L'Aspect national des fondations pieuses turques (Vakoufs)," *Vakıflar Dergisi* 2 (1956): 293-297; A. H. Berki, *Vakıflar, Cihan Kitaphanesi* (Istanbul, 1941), pp. 239-241.

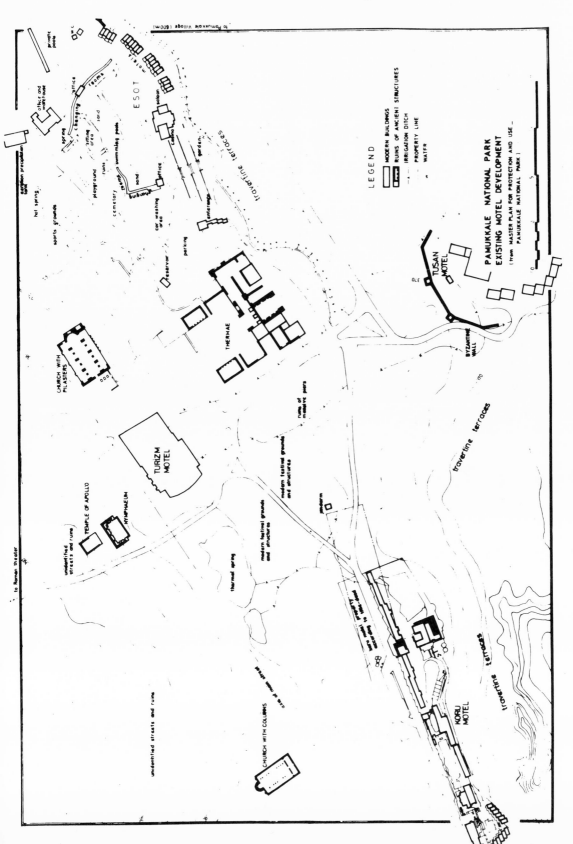

Fig. 14. Plan of Hierapolis (Pamukkale National Park) today showing the spread of motels and tourist shops over the antiquities. (A Master Plan proposing the removal of all modern construction has been prepared by the National Park Service.)

the most impressive natural and historic sites in Turkey. Located some 100 miles inland from the Aegean, the ancient city commands a lush green valley from atop travertine cliffs eroded by natual sulfur springs into fantastic layers of dazzling white. This was a favorite spa and religious center of antiquity. The ancient monuments, such as baths, theater, cemetery, and basilicas are clearly visible spread out along the cliffs in a fine state of preservation. Others are being brought to light and restored under the direction of Professor Paolo Versone.

Pl. 84 (281)   In the early 1960s private entrepreneurs and the government fastened upon Pamukkale as an unexploited tourist center of particular promise. Aided by government credit, entrepreneurs and even the municipality began constructing a series of unsightly motels directly on the ancient site. One surrounded the hot springs of the ancient baths; others extended along the travertine terraces, rechanneling the natural flow of water into artificial pools and a carwashing area for hotel guests. Once water ceased cascading over the cliffs the natural erosion and whitening process was halted. If this continues the "mountain of cotton" will soon be no different from the surrounding hills. Much is still to be learned about the ancient settlement, but the new motels and tourist shops built directly on the old city have interfered with the work of the archaeologists.

Fortunately the public[15] and the government have gradually come to recognize their error. A recent plan prepared by the National Park Service proposes transferring the motels to the valley, rechanneling the springs, restoring the travertine terraces, and eliminating the modern road that slices the cliffs.[16] In this instance, perhaps, we shall be successful in rectifying our mistakes, but only at a great cost.

*   *   *   *   *   *   *

The combined staffs of the Department of Antiquities and the Vakıflar consist of some fifteen architects and engineers and twenty technicians—too few to properly oversee the many sites which are under their control. Now additional funds and the tourist objective have brought unforeseen destruction in the form of faulty restoration. The funds allocated annually must be spent during that year. Since available manpower permits only a limited number of projects to be executed, the restoration is so to speak maximized for each structure. In one case, this has involved the total rebuilding of a Seljuq mosque with new materials from only the foundations and a partial minaret. Based on unsound evidence and inappropriate historical documentation, the results may be a misleading fantasy. In certain cases where original stones are still in situ, the restorers have discarded them and have gone through the expensive process of having new ones cut.

Promise for Immediate Improvement

In spite of this record of stops, starts, and cultural loss, I am convinced that the next five years hold promise for radical progress in the care of historic centers. An

---

[15]   İsmet Gürses, "Pamukkale'nin Dramı," [The Drama of Pamukkale] *Türkiye Turing ve Otomobil Kurumu Belleteni*, January, 1966, pp. 4-5.

[16]   Millî Parklar Dairesi, *Pamukkale Millî Parkı: Uzun Devreli İnkişaf Planı* [Pamukkale National Park: Long Term Improvement Plan] (Ankara, 1969).

informed public is growing; funds are being made available; and the government is involved. The remaining obstacles are ineffective organization and lack of technical personnel. The former can be solved only by the government itself; the latter is being confronted by, among others, the Middle East Technical University (METU) through the training of graduate architects in conservation, through seminars for professionals, and through the introduction of new recording and analysis techniques.

Since the university program is intended to serve as a regional center and to benefit other Near Eastern countries, it may be worthwhile to review the objectives and accomplishments of its first five years. The program in conservation opened in 1965. It offers the first regional training for architect-restorers; previously they had been trained "on the job" through a costly and time-consuming system of apprenticeship. Students collaborate with the government offices during the two-year period of the master's program and thus immediately offer their technical services. They in turn gain valuable field experience. These are restoration projects of actual monuments or historic sites, and subjects are selected from those on the priority lists of the Vakıflar and Department of Antiquities. Departmental field work fulfills academic requirements and contributes to pressing conservation problems. For instance, one departmental survey initiated the International Keban Dam Salvage Project, and the findings were published in *Doomed by the Dam* [17] Another survey of residential architecture in a well-preserved Ottoman town, Göynük, has been published, and its recommendations for conservation are being applied by the town's population. [18]

The people of Göynük demonstrated that townspeople are far more aware of their architectural heritage and ready to take a stand for its protection than many in Turkey had realized. When planners in the capital drew a modern highway through the heart of the old town, they succeeded in implementing only the first part of their proposal. The Göynük people saw the scale of a whole neighborhood destroyed and refused to permit further construction. Such action against the decisions of a centralized bureaucracy requires determination. Neither city plans nor preservation projects can be accomplished without the support of groups such as this.

The introduction of new recording and analysis techniques ranks with the preparation of architect-restorers in importance. Since the majority of monuments remain unrecorded and many will be destroyed before intervention is possible, it is vital that those remaining be catalogued immediately. Such a project is inconceivable with the classical methods of measured drawings, and attention to even a select few is beyond the capabilities of the total Turkish staff.

Architectural photogrammetry by means of stereoscopic photographs can accomplish in a single month architectural surveys over one hundred times as extensive as those carried out employing painstaking measurement methods. [19] Moreover, it frees the architect from the task of preparing routine drawings to that

---

[17] Department of Restoration, Middle East Technical University, *Doomed by the Dam* (Ankara, 1967).

[18] Department of Restoration, Middle East Technical University, *Göynük: A Town in a Timber Region* (Ankara, 1970).

[19] Cevat Erder, "The Role of Photogrammetry in Surveys of Works of Art Endangered by Extensive Public Works," *International Council of Museum and Sites* (Paris, 1968), pp. 95-98.

of actively participating in the preservation of monuments for which only he is qualified. The initial financial investment for equipment is heavy, but the equipment pays its own way in only six months of full operation.

The METU program has put into operation a photogrammetry laboratory and field service. It is intended to train both students and government officials in its use, to serve as a research center, and to stimulate its adoption by offices concerned with conservation.

In conducting surveys, priority must be given to those monuments and sites immediately threatened with destruction by public works. Simultaneously, areas liable to be endangered in the near future should be identified, and more thorough building surveys should be carried on without the pressure of competing construction activities. Accurate and detailed recording of vast areas, such as the quarters of old Ankara now being leveled for a new medical school, is within the realm of possibility through the use of architectural photogrammetry.

While this discussion may have unintentionally left the impression that preservation of old quarters and urban modernization are mutually exclusive, this is not necessarily true. A creative compromise between restorer and planner is feasible where the juxtaposition of new and old can be effective. The restorer must be ready to admit the constraints imposed by modern technologies; he can also use the same technologies to enhance the quality of living in an old center and to prolong the life of its structures. The planner, in turn, must be aware of the long-term financial and cultural investment that lies in an old center. For instance, the continuous cultural investment in the Blue Mosque-Topkapı Palace quarter of Istanbul has made it one of Turkey's most successful examples of area preservation. It required, however, little large-scale planning or restoration. It was, rather, the still intact legacy of centuries of uninterrupted Byzantine and Ottoman rule from those strategic heights. Authorities wisely decided to prevent the intrusion of modern concessions and to maintain a green belt about the mosques, Haghia Sophia, Saint Irene, and the Topkapı Palace. The extensive area is kept as an open-air museum and park overlooking the Bosporus. Here, at the very heart of Istanbul, is a place where city dwellers can relax and visitors can truly sense the power that once overlooked Asia Minor, the Marmara Sea, and the Bosporus. Few cities can boast so many historically significant buildings. Nevertheless, a planner must be receptive to an evaluation of the center from an architectural point of view and to methods of refunctioning the old structures. Taken individually, the buildings may be historically insignificant, but as a unit they become a witness to the life styles and ideals of another age. The volumes and spaces associated with the streets, squares, and symmetry of façades compose an architectural whole. Once this is broken by the insensitive intrusion of a modern scale and pattern the individual structure may become worthless and the former human scale may disappear.

BIBLIOGRAPHY

1. Early works which have shaped the thinking of those working in the conservation of historic monuments today:

Dvorȁk, Max. *Katechismus der Denkmalpflege.* Wien: Verlag von Julius Bard, 1918.

Riegl, Alois. *Der moderne Denkmalkultus, sein Wesen und seine Entstehung.* Wien: W. Braumüller, 1903.

Ruskin, John. "The Lamp of Memory." In *The Seven Lamps of Architecture.* New York: Bryan, Taylor and Co. 1894.

Viollet-le-Duc, Eugène Emmanuel. *Dictionnaire raisonné de l'architecture Française du XIe au XVI siècle.* Paris: A. Morel et Cie., 1868- 1874. (Section on restoration.)

2. The experience of various countries in preserving historic monuments and quarters:

Barbacci, A. *Il restauro dei monumenti in Italia.* Roma: Ist. Poligrafico dello Stato, 1956.

Briggs, Martin S. *Goths and Vandals: A Study of the Destruction, Neglect and Preservation of Historical Buildings in England.* London: Constable, 1952.

Clemen, Paul. *Die deutsche Kunst und die Denkmalpflege.* Berlin: Deutscher Kunstverlag, 1933.

Fedden, Robin. *The Continuing Purpose: A History of the National Trust, its Aims and Work.* London: Longmans, Green, 1968.

Hosmer, Charles B. Jr. *Presence of the Past: A History of the Preservation Movement in the United States before Williamsburg.* New York: G. P. Putman, 1965.

Leon, Paul. *La Vie des Monuments Français: Destruction, Restauration.* Paris: Ed. Picard et Cie., 1951.

Perogalli, Carlo. *Monumenti e metodi di valorizzazione: Saggi, Storia e caratteri delle teoriche sul restauro in Italia dal medioevo ad oggi.* Milano: Libreria editr. Politecnica Tamburini, 1954.

Zachwatowicz, Jan. *Protection of Historical Monuments in Poland.* Warsaw: Poloniz Publishing House, 1965.

3. Contemporary reference books on the theory and principles of architectural restoration:

Annoni, Ambrogio. *Scienza ed arte del restauro architettonico.* Milano: Ed. Artistica Framar, 1946.

Bonelli, Renato. *Architettura e Restauro.* Venezia: Neri Pozza Ed. 1959.

Ceschi, Carlo. *Storia e Teoria del Restauro.* Roma: Ed. Bulzoni, 1970.

Clifford, Henry Dalton, and Enthoven, R. E. *New Homes from Old Buildings.* London: Country Life Limited, 1954.

Crema, Luigi. *Monumenti e Restauro.* Milano: Ceschina, 1959.

Dvorȁk, Max. "Gedanken über Denkmalpflege." *Kunstgeschichtliches Jahrbuch der K. K. Zentral Kommission,* IV, Beiblatt für Denkmalpflege, pp. 211-214.

Grassi, Liliana. *Storia e Cultura dei Monumenti.* Milano: Societá Editrice Libreria, 1960.

Historic Preservation Today. Williamsburg: The University Press of Virginia, 1966.

Rains, Albert and Henderson, Laurance G. eds. *With Heritage So Rich: A Report of a Special Committee on Historic Preservation under the Auspices of the United States Conference of Mayors with a Grant from The Ford Foundation.* New York: Random House, 1966.

4. Guides to the administrative and legal aspects of protecting monuments and sites:

Brichet, R. *Le régime des monuments historiques en France.* Paris, 1952.

Brown, G. Baldwin. *The Care of Ancient Monuments: An Account of the Legislative and other Measures Adopted in European Countries for Protecting Ancient Monuments and Objects and Scenes of Natural Beauty, and for Preserving the Aspect of Historical Cities.* Cambridge: The University Press, 1905.

Gieski-Zeller, Heinrich. *Der rechtliche Heimatschutz in der Schweiz.* Aarau, 1910.

Grisolia, M. *La tutela delle cose d'arte.* Roma: Soc. ed. del Foro Italiano, 1952.

Parpagliolo, L. *Codice Delle Antichità e degli Oggetti d'Arte.* Roma: Libreria dello Stato, 1932.

5. Books on the life of cities which have affected current approaches to the treatment of historic urban quarters:

a) General works:

Lavedan, Pierre. *Histoire de l'Urbanisme.* Paris: Henri Laurens, 1959–1966.

Jacobs, Jane. *The Death and Life of Great American Cities.* New York: Vintage Books, 1961.

Mumford, Lewis. *The City in History: Its Origins, its Transformations and its Prospects.* New York: Harcourt, Brace and World, 1961.

———. *The Culture of Cities.* New York: Harcourt, Brace and World, 1938.

Sitte, Camillo. *Der Städtebau nach seinen künstlerischen Grundsätzen.* Wien, 1889.

b) Practical applications in the treatment of historic urban quarters:

Giuliani, A. *Monumenti, centri storici, ambienti.* Milano: Taburini, 1966.

Providence, City Plan Commission College Hill: *A Demonstration Study of Historic Area Renewal Conducted by the Providence City Plan Commission in Cooperation with the Providence Preservation Society and Dept. of Housing and Urban Development.* 2nd ed. Providence, 1967.

Ward, Pamela, ed. *Conservation and Development in Historic Towns and Cities.* Newcastle upon Tyne: Oriel Press, 1968.

6. Important international meetings and decisions which have influenced the care of historic monuments and sites in many countries:

Congrès International des Architectes et Techniciens des Monuments Historiques. *Chartre de Venise.* Venice, 1964.

Conseil de l'Europe. *Conservation active des sites, monuments et ensembles d'intérét historique ou artistique dans le cadre de l'aménagement du territoire. Rapport.* La Haye, 1967; Strasbourg, 1967.

Council of Europe. *The Preservation and Development of Ancient Buildings and Historical or Artistic Sites.* Strasbourg, 1963.

ICOMOS. *Colloque (2ème) pour l'étude de la conservation de la restauration et de la réanimation des ensembles historiques.* Tunis, 1968.

———. *Monuments et Société. Actes du Colloque ICOMOS.* Leningrad, 1969.

Lavachery, H., and Noblecourt, A. *Les Techniques de Protection des Biens Culturels en cas de Conflict Armé.* Paris: UNESCO, 1954.

Le Corbusier. *La Charte d'Athènes: Avec un discours liminaire de Jean Giraudoux.* art. 65-70. Paris: Editions de Minuit, 1957.

7. Recent discussions in Turkey on architectural and site conservation:

Erder, Cevat. "On the Training of Architect/Restorers for Turkey," *Momentum* 5 (1970): 25-31.

———. *Tarihi Çevre Kaygısı* [Consideration for historical sites]. Ankara: Middle East Technical University, 1971.

Frodl, Walter. "Anıtlar, Bakım ve Onarımları" [Monuments, their maintenance and repair], *Akademi,* no. 5, March 1966.

Kuban, Doğan. "İstanbulda Tarihi Çevrenin önemli kısmı ortadan kalkıyor" [A considerable portion of historical sites in Istanbul is disappearing], *Mimarlik,* no. 24 (1965), pp. 20-21.

———. "Modern restorasyon ikleleri üzerinde yorumlar" [Comments on modern restoration principles], *Vakıflar Dergisi* (1969), pp. 341-356.

Ülgen, Ali Saim. *Anıtların Korunması ve Onarılması* [Preservation and repair of monuments], Ankara: Maarif Matbaasi, 1943.

8. Periodicals that regularly publish articles in the field:

The Architectural Review
Bollettino d'Arte (Ministero della Pubblica Istruzione)
Deutsche Kunst und Denkmalpflege
Historic Preservation
Les Monuments Historiques de France
Monumentum (ICOMOS).
Österreichische Zeitschrift für Kunst und Denkmalpflege
The Town Planning Review
Urbanistica
Vakıflar Dergisi

85. Amman, Jordan. Partial view of the city around the Roman amphitheater in the foreground; a good example of the incorporation of old monuments into later urban development. (Photo: Pan American World Airways.)

10

Muslim Cities: Old and New
by Richard Ettinghausen

It seems only natural that when one is considering at greater length problems pertaining to urban planning and urban prospects in the Near Eastern city, one wishes also to consider the problem of the artistic interrelationship between old and new parts of towns and cities in that vast and important area. It seems likewise appropriate that one should call for the opinion of an art historian who has made the Near East his special field of interest and research.

However, such an undertaking at once encounters some basic difficulties. As our usual way of thinking moves nowadays in closed circles and our university studies are therefore departmentalized, it is altogether difficult to find a professional who is equally familiar with the problems of the old madinas and of the new towns. Our research is either oriented toward the traditional—be it with regard to history, religion, literature, art, or society—or toward the issues of modern urban life, approached from the point of view of the sociologist, anthropologist, architect, or city planner. Besides, the art historians who have studied traditional Near Eastern cities up to the time of their contact with the West are concerned primarily not with town planning, but with major monuments— mosques, madrasas, castles, palaces, mausoleums, hammams, and even gardens. These monuments—often renovated and remodelled—have had varied histories, and they are usually of a complex nature. To reconstruct the plans and elevations of the various buildings, to study their decoration, to read the inscriptions, and to relate these monuments to historical sources was, and many times still is, a major task for the handful of scholars working in this field. There was, and is, comparatively little interest in the functional nature of a monument, let alone of a larger area and hardly ever of the city as an organic whole. We can, for instance, make some general statements about madrasas, suqs, and khans, but here again only when they were studied as historical buildings. In other words, we have so far dealt with the static aspects of the buildings as such; but we have not yet had time (nor developed an interest) to study the development of the functional nature of the monuments and to perceive them as growing organs, nerve centers, and arteries within the larger civic body.

86. Tripoli, Libya. The coexistence of different ages. Arch of Marcus Aurelius and Ottoman-style minaret separated by modern street. (An Exxon photograph.)

87. Aerial view of the old quarters of Damascus, Syria. In addition to revealing the great use of inner courtyards and suggesting a narrow, labyrinthine street pattern, this photograph also emphasizes the desirability of a "total milieu" approach to the preservation of historical monuments and architecturally interesting old buildings. The several fine structures in this picture (e.g., center foreground) cannot simply be "sealed off" from the surrounding environment. (Photo: John Witmer.)

88. View of Cairo with its citadel as seen from the minaret of the Ibn Tulun Mosque. (Photo: Sir Archibald Creswell.)

89. Old Jerusalem, Aerial View. (Photo: Pantomap Israel Ltd.; reproduction by special permission.)

We should state at once that there is no such thing as a general, standard form of the traditional Muslim city, just as there are now emerging many different versions of new towns, growing spontaneously or specifically planned according to theoretical concepts. As to the shape of the ancient town, it may in this connection be worthwhile to point out that, for instance, in certain cities the most conspicuous feature is the *Qal'a* or citadel, on a promontory within the city, such as we find in Aleppo, Damascus, Jerusalem, Cairo, Delhi, and Granada. But there are other important cities in which this feature is minimized or lacking entirely, as in Isfahan, Tunis, Fez, and Cordova. Another characteristic is the accessibility of the main mosque, which can be found in the old quarters only by those who are familiar with the general layout of the many crooked streets; other mosques are on big squares and dominate the urban setting, as is the case in Isfahan or Istanbul. But these more conspicuous buildings do not necessarily have to be from more recent centuries, as we have only to mention the Dome of the Rock and the Aqsa Mosque in Jerusalem, which are among the oldest Islamic monuments, to point out that even an ancient shrine can be of great prominence within the heart of the city. Another point to be made in this connection is that there is a good deal of variety not only in the physical aspects of mosques, but also in their number. In such ancient cities as Cairo, Isfahan, and Istanbul, they are numerous; on the other hand, such large cities as Teheran and Kabul have comparatively few, and considering their enormous expanse, the same observation can be made about Delhi and Lahore.

Nevertheless, everybody senses that even in spite of this variety there are certain features which distinguish traditional Near Eastern towns from those of the West and leave no doubt that we are in such a place, should we by any chance land in one from an airplane on a nonscheduled stop.

Having referred to this diversity, it seems appropriate to focus our attention on the specific problem, namely, the nature and special aspects of the ancient and the modern towns, because only when we are aware of their character and salient features can we hope to establish whether or not there exists any physical or organizational relationship between them. Here it seems, of course, natural to speak of the inhabited towns and to leave out the vast ruins of earlier civilizations, particularly Roman ones, which are to be found near the present towns but which are no longer inhabited (or only by squatters) and thus represent no real urban aspect that should be considered for the questions of relationship between the old and the new.

If we wish to delineate as succinctly as possible the basic situation, we might as well start with a popularly held image of the old towns: It appears as a unit which through its (often-preserved) surrounding walls and towers is compact and even constricted within the space given to it. Within this area the streets never run straight but in crooked, turning fashion without providing any long-range views to specific monuments or displaying the individual houses along it in any conspicuous, inviting manner. Within the townscape, there is hardly any planned visual articulation by means of squares or wide streets. Indeed most of the streets are (as in Old Fez today) very narrow and often of such a nature that they are not suitable for wheeled traffic and thus can be used only by pedestrians, horsemen, and pack

Pl. 88 (292)

Pl. 89 (292)

Pl. 4 (20)

animals. The suqs, the shops and places of work for artisans, are small, narrow, and dark and are aligned horizontally, one next to the other, without any provision for an extensive display of merchandise. Close to this arrangement of one- or two-storied houses and shops are the major monuments, particularly the mosques, whose location is indicated only by a gateway; this is often ornamented by stone carvings or tile work and occasionally by framing towers, but there is little indication of the nature, character, and size of the building beyond it. We can speak of a front, but there is rarely a full-scale façade. The whole town—mosque as well as private houses—seems to be turned inward on itself.

Fig. 15. Plan of Qazvin in the sixteenth century.
(Drawn by Donald N. Wilber.)

By contrast, the modern city is expansive, and there is no limit to it as it encroaches more and more on the countryside. Its streets are straight and wide, and they are created not only for wheeled traffic, but for rapid transportation by motor vehicles. The lines of buildings are interrupted from time to time by more spectacular structures, which are often also the viewpoints of converging streets and wide squares. Their character is totally different from those of the old town because instead of the mosques, madrasas, mausoleums, and entrances to the bazaars, we now have city halls, radio stations, hospitals, schools, and railroad stations, as well as ministries, office buildings, and even department stores and apartment houses. They are all distinguished not only by their size and vertical organization, but also by the special treatment of their façades, which stress their intrinsic importance, demonstrate their size, and very often invite one to enter.

The concepts of these two urban conglomerations strike us at first as being diametrically opposed. Seeming to be so different, it is difficult to imagine how any of their features could be interrelated. In view of this disparity, it is all the more essential to find any possible connection between old and new towns or evidence of similar attitudes, as this might then serve as the basis of a fruitful interrelationship for now and the future.

In view of the necessities of modern life, its tremendous demands and pressures, it is appropriate to pose as a basic question whether there are indeed historical and artistic reasons to preserve the old city, especially as so much seems architecturally undistinguished. Although it is for the time being a place of residence for much of the population, it seems also to represent an incumbrance to modern progress and to be a potential slum area. Indeed there is little doubt that the old city represents to the forward-looking citizens, especially the youth, an expression of old-fashionedness which is entirely out of keeping with modern trends. Thus, it follows that the buildings and the whole structure of these ancient towns embody not only the times gone forever, but actually an *ancien regime* which has been overcome, often by force or a *coup d'état*, and superseded by a more progressive and up-to-date *Weltanschauung*. This applies in general terms to the buildings of the Qajar Period in Iran and even more specifically to numerous and often very conspicuous structures of the Ottoman Period in Turkey. However, the latter country should give us some hope, since more than in any other country we find there a growing number of scholars who appreciate the monuments of their past, be they Seljuq or Ottoman, and are seriously studying and restoring them.

Quite irrespective of the aesthetic values involved, two considerations underline the positive value of the old towns. First, it is clear and generally agreed that the cultural development and the whole efflorescence of the Islamic civilization is based on life in an urban milieu, as it was the congenial setting for its many activities. Indeed, without this particular ambiance, all the great theological, philosophical, historic, poetic, and scientific works would probably not have been written, because life in small towns, and certainly in villages, was on the whole not conducive to large and diversified intellectual production. Secondly, in the present period of adjustment to the demands of the present technological age, most of the nations of the Near East feel themselves to be at a developmental disadvantage, and, therefore, like to remind themselves that there were periods of great accomplishments in their past when the cultural roles were reversed. Architectural monuments and works of art, unlike philosophical or literary works, require no translation from a native language to that of a Western nation. Understandable in themselves, they serve as witnesses for past achievements and stand as promises for new ones to come. In this respect, it does not matter that those buoyed by what these ancient monuments represent are not too specifically cognizant of the nature and quality of this achievement; the very existence of the monuments is enough to bolster the morale of these nations. In other words, these monuments are, so to speak, the basis of national self-confidence and promise of the potential for future achievements. These factors are probably even more important than another which is often quite rightly put forward: that these monuments, in all their glory, are true national assets and therefore represent an economic value, especially from the point of view of tourism.

Were one to forego this positive attitude and sacrifice these old towns and their monuments to the god of progress and modernity, a great hiatus between the present and the past would be created. Even worse could happen, since many of the traditionally-oriented people would feel out of place in a modern town, and their creative ability be impaired, all of which would lead to an alienation of the people from their own country and civilization. This has not only cultural implications—because a nation so disturbed could more readily become further unsettled and prone to violent revolutionary change. As a matter of fact, there is evidence for such an assumption. Nor is this a purely Near Eastern occurrence, as the wartime destruction of major old parts in certain cities in Germany has in conjunction with other changes led to a cultural decline.

Beyond these general considerations, this reservoir of ancient monuments is essential, because it represents the artistic norm to which the nations concerned will eventually revert and adjust themselves once they have overcome the often all-too-hasty and not fully thought-out change-over to the mid-twentieth century patterns conditioned by Western concepts. Such reorientation and renascence have always been an aspect of human development, both West and East, but in each and every case it was necessary to return to something still existing. This does not mean that these old monuments and decorations will eventually be slavishly copied or even paraphrased; yet they represent at least a well-tested and congenial form of national expression, developed at high points of the past history and therefore eminently suitable to serve as models and inspiration.

We could well imagine that for this preservation of the best of the national or regional life style the presence of ancient towns on the order of Rothenburg, Carcassonne, Venice, and Williamsburg would be most helpful. That this full-scale preservation is possible is shown by the existence of certain Near Eastern "shrine cities," of which Jerusalem or Mashhad, Qumm, Konya or Moulay Idris (in Morocco) are telling examples. Other old city monuments of great historical and artistic significance, like Cairo or Fez, have fortunately been largely preserved. It would be of inestimable value if, with government support, such expressions of national genius could endure to inspire future generations.

The second basic question to be posed is whether there have been in the past other total changes in the urban development which are similar to the ones we are witnessing today and if so, what the consequences were. In fact, two such momentous changes occurred, but the results were in each case quite different from each other.

Historically, the first was the impact of Hellenistic and Roman civilizations on the vast area between Morocco and Iran. Whatever the systems of dwelling and public buildings in these regions had been—and they can nowadays be mostly reconstructed only by archaeological investigation—they were not based on a grid system of wide streets fit for vehicular traffic, open squares with porticoes, columned temples, and tiered theaters, Impressive as these ruins are, they apparently made little impression on the native population and were ultimately rejected by it as foreign bodies. Many of these old and often ruined buildings served as quarries to later generations of builders. We can only speculate about the reason for this negative attitude. It seems that there was no self-identification of the indigenous people with these creations, whose functions, shapes, decorations remained alien to them. Being in their eyes devoid of an understandable purpose and lacking any beauty to which they could relate, these monuments could not be admired or, eventually, integrated.

Quite different was the effect of the arrival of the Arabs and Islam in the Near East. Although the event and its consequences over several centuries are still insufficiently known, certain aspects are clear to us. Let us take Iran as an example: a court-centered, aristocratic society was superseded by a more egalitarian one in which the rising middle class of merchants and artisans played an ever increasing role. Hence the architectural requirements were obviously of another nature; specifically, the houses of divine worship, the palaces, and the funerary monuments were different. Even the building material changed from rubble set into mortar to brick. This transformation was initiated by a minority, which only later, owing to religious conversions, turned into a majority. The same radical transformation took place in Egypt. Such a major Egyptian Muslim monument as the Mosque of Ibn Tulun, finished in 879, is "Egyptian" only owing Pl. 90 (299) to its location in Cairo; it is un-Egyptian in every other respect—specifically, in its layout, shape of its minaret, building material, and forms of decoration. It is difficult to assess how such foreign importations became so easily naturalized, so that no odium of alienness taints them. It may very well be that the novel types of building were readily accepted throughout the Islamic world because they satisfied basic needs.

The general adaptation of the architectural layout of the madrasa is another example of this ready assimilation. It is usually a four-eyvaned structure which is entered by a portal leading into or close to an open hallway directed toward a court; on each of the three sides of this court are similar open halls, the eyvans, which are used as classrooms, while areas between the eyvans contain the rooms of the students. This is basically an Iranian house form, since in Eastern Iran in the eleventh century domestic buildings were first used as schools. What is surprising is the fact that this purely regional, restricted, type of architecture was quickly accepted everywhere in the enormously extensive Islamic world, in nearby Iraq as well as in distant Morocco. The difference is only in secondary aspects: in the building material, the proportions, the interior organizations, and the forms of decoration, or lack of them. While the ready acceptance of the hypostyle mosque, which is related to the Arab house, in particular the Prophet's house, may be

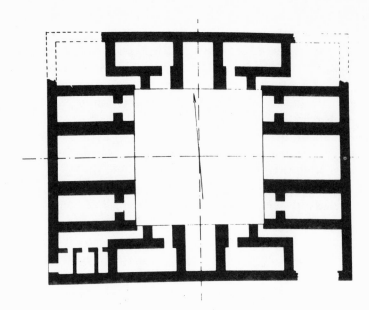

Fig. 16. Rayy, Iran. Plan of a Seljuq Madrasa.
(Drawn by Andŕe Godard.)

explained by the overwhelming pressure of an "imperial" power and its official religion, the adoption of the madrasa well beyond the realm of the Seljuqs, who had first fostered it, indicates a close, all-Muslim cohesion and interrelationship which influenced each region and created an integrated civilization with only local variations.

Pl. 91 (299)
Pl. 92 (301)

The implications of these historical facts for present-day planning are obvious. To give just one example: a non-indigenous, novel architectural type, such as an airport building, introduced into the Near East, does not have to be built in an alien or bland international style; it can be built according to local custom and be decorated on its exterior and interior in the spirit of regional traditions; such a structure can easily become an attractive building for native and foreigner alike. It would have the added advantage of fitting into the historical landscape, in spite of its novel function and alien origin.

The case is, of course, much easier when the new building is traditional, as it would be in the case of a mosque. The experiments of combining modern building concepts and technology with traditional shapes and local decorative features have therefore often been successful. An example of such a successful combination is the mosque which has recently been built on the campus of Teheran University. Here the purely imitative approach, which in the West has led to neo-Gothic cathedrals and college buildings or colonial churches and banks, has been happily

Pl. 93 (301)

avoided, and the result is neither a sterile copy nor a hodgepodge of styles, but twentieth-century Iranian.

90. Cairo, mosque of Ibn Tulun, A.D. 879.

91. Typical Mamluk Madrasa: Cairo, madrasa of Sultan Inal (1453-60), west liwan and south side. (Photo: Sir Archibald Creswell.)

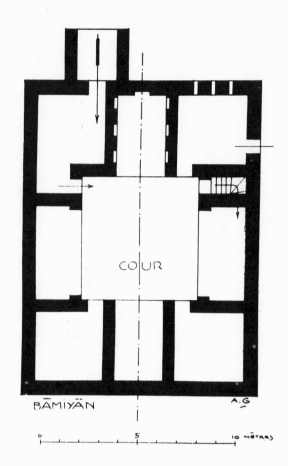

COUR

BĀMIYĀN   A.G

0   5   10 MÈTRES

Fig. 17. Bamiyan, Afghanistan. Plan of a private house.
(Drawn by André Godard.)

Another case in point are the mausolea. Ever since the ninth century, such monuments, be they secular or religious, have filled specific needs and are an important aspect of the townscapes, although they are also to be found in or near villages. In modern times, mausolea have become chief national monuments dedicated to the memory of the founder or reformer of a modern state; but contemporary and even classical literary figures have also been honored in this fashion. Modern mausolea run the whole gamut from the traditional to the purely modern, and there are also cases which combine both. The tomb of the founder of Pakistan, the Qaid-i Azam, Muhammad Ali Jinnah, the result of a large in-Pl. 94 (303)ternational competition, is traditional and follows closely Indo-Muslim mausolea from medieval times. This seems only appropriate, because Jinnah wanted to create in the Indian subcontinent a modern state which would be outspokenly Muslim. The opposite is represented by the mausoleum of Atatürk in Ankara. He wanted to get away from Islamic tradition, so his mausoleum is symbolically non-Islamic and in a modern Western idiom. Still, Mustafa Kemal was called Atatürk, "the Father Pl. 95 (303) of the Turks," and he personally showed his strong sense of Turkish history by, for

92. Typical Safavid Madrasa: Isfahan, Madrasa-yi Mader-i Shah, courtyard and sanctuary, 1710-11.

93. Modern mosque using traditional features and techniques: the mosque on the campus of Teheran University by Aziz Farman-Farmayan, built in the mid-1960s.

instance, endowing the Turkish Historical Society (Türk Tarih Kurumu) in Ankara. But as far as one is aware, there is nothing specifically Turkish in the structure of his mausoleum. Thus, striking as it is, it expresses only one aspect of the personality of the founder of the Turkish Republic. A median attitude is followed by the tomb of the Reza Shah in Rayy, near Teheran. Its basic features are in the Iranian

Pl. 96 (304)

tradition, being a towerlike structure with a ceremonial entrance gate and a covering flat dome. It is, however, built in a modern style. This fits the ideas of the former Shah, as he wanted to be a modern ruler, and his state a twentieth-century Iran.

In those instances in which a grateful country wishes to honor the memory of one of its earlier sages or poets by building or rebuilding a mausoleum dedicated to him, it is natural that the architect select an early style for the basic concept of the new monument. In the best example this did not mean that one is now faced with an archaistic monument based on antiquarian research. As the new mausoleum of

Pl. 97 (304)

Avicenna in Hamadan proves, the traditional aspects are evident in the general shape and salient features; yet, the secondary aspects are novel and the technique is that of the twentieth century. Some of these new national monuments belong therefore to the best integrated combinations of the old and the new, which apart from historic considerations can be acclaimed for their creative spirit.

*   *   *   *   *   *   *

As a by-product of this discussion, it has become apparent that, contrary to first impressions, there exist connections between the ancient monuments and those of modern times and that the two forms of urban architecture are not always too dissimilar. Now, we wish to discuss certain misconceptions which have impeded a proper understanding of early architecture. It can be shown that certain attitudes and features which we associate with a modern approach to art existed already in past centuries—at times even in the early Middle Ages—and yet they are not generally associated with classical Muslim art. An awareness of this relationship might therefore help break down the mutual distrust between the old and the new and provide a basis for the desired rapprochement.

Cliché number one wants us to believe in an unchangeable East. Here we are, of course, not concerned with tribal customs or life styles and practices, but with various artistic manifestations. From this point of view, it can be stated that art does not only vary from country to country but it does so also from century to century. These differences in style are so pronounced that a monument above the simple, popular level, even though it may be without an inscription, can usually be dated within fifty years. There is a world of difference between a fifteenth-century mosque of Bursa and a sixteenth-century imperial mosque of Istanbul. Indeed, nothing shows the variety of Islamic art so much as the fact that there are at least four widely different forms of the mosque, not counting less common forms, especially those developed in such marginal areas as Kashmir, Indonesia, and China. The forms are the Arab hypostyle mosque; the four-eyvaned Persian mosque with its large sanctuary dome; the single-domed Ottoman mosque with attached half domes; and the triple-domed hypostyle Mughal Mosque of India. Of course, there are further subdivisions of each type according to plan and decoration, but all this

94. Mausoleum of the Qaid-i Azam in Karachi. (Photo: Government of Pakistan.)

95. Mausoleum of Atatürk in Ankara. (Photo: Government of Turkey.)

96. Mausoleum of Reza Shah Pahlavi in Shah Abdul-Azim near Rayy. (Photo: Government of Iran.)

97. Mausoleum of Ibn Sina (Avicenna) in Hamadan, by Hoshang Seyhoun, built *ca.* 1954. (Photo: Government of Iran.)

certainly suffices to destroy the idea of the monolithic character of a never-changing art.

Cliché number two wants us to believe that there is no planning within an Islamic city. This idea is based on the crooked lanes and the lack of open spaces that characterize many of the old towns. However, every visitor to the Maydan-i Shah, the Royal Square in Isfahan, is familiar with the bold layout of the vast open square around which four major monuments are placed; in at least two instances they are (or were) in turn the key points leading to important quarters behind them. Nor is this the only case of early seventeenth-century planning in that city, because Chahar-Bagh Avenue, leading to one of the magnificent bridges over the Zenderud, runs in a straight line and is also laid out according to a master plan which, again, runs counter to the general idea of nondescript buildings everywhere and a compulsion for curving streets. Another example of spectacular planning is the Registan in Samarkand, in which three important monuments from the fifteenth to the seventeenth century are coordinated on three sides of the square. Other instances of a skillful layout of buildings which have an interrelation are the *külliyeh* complexes in Istanbul with their large mosques, madrasas, libraries, bath houses, soup kitchens, hospitals, fountains, and other public structures. This is not even an imperial development of the sixteenth century, since the külliyeh goes back to buildings in Iznik and Bursa of the fourteenth and fifteenth centuries. Even these cities do not provide the earliest examples of city planning. Indeed, one of the boldest is the layout for eighth-century Baghdad: a large ring-shaped outer unit of four quarters separated by four major gates, with the mosque and palace in the center of a huge open area. Still another case of early Muslim town planning is the city of Raqqa, which was laid out in the form of a horseshoe. It is true that these early concepts were not followed through, or at least nor kept up, and in particular Baghdad lost all semblance of its former scheme. Nevertheless, the fact that it was so conceived, and that later on, in the sixteenth and early seventeenth centuries one finds several bold attempts at town planning, show that the widely held image of a jumbled-up Muslim town does not universally apply. Indeed, it must be remembered that even when we have crooked lanes, in every instance the private houses, mosques, madrasas, and the other buildings aligned along them are always built around a formal rectangular court. This alone shows that a sense of clarity and orderliness permeates the concept of the madina, a fact which is not surprising considering that throughout the centuries this whole region produced a considerable number of distinguished and even famous mathematicians. Here another related point should be made: that the syndrome of the "crooked lanes" does not imply "disorganization" in civic matters. Speaking in the most general terms, one can say that the suq usually represents the main artery and urban axis from which secondary side streets with other shops and ateliers branch off and that close to it are the khans and other important buildings. Around this area are the residential districts. Minorities have their own quarters with their own places of worship and civic needs, and altogether there is a definite pattern of urban organization.

Cliché number three postulates that traditional Muslim architecture is obscured by too much ornamentation and that the luxuriant designs are usually minute and densely applied. It is believed that they can hardly please the modern mind, which

Fig. 18 (306)

Figs. 19-21
(307-309)

Fig. 22 (310)

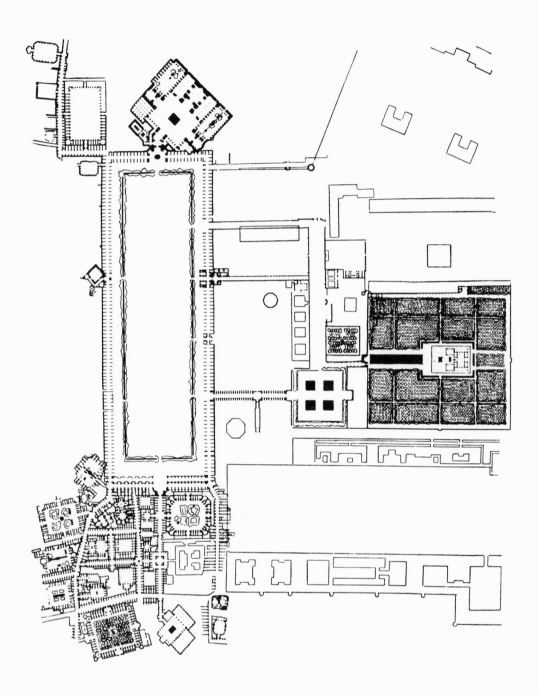

Fig. 18. Plan of the Maidan-i Shah, the "Royal Square" in Isfahan. (Drawn by E. E. Beaudouin.)

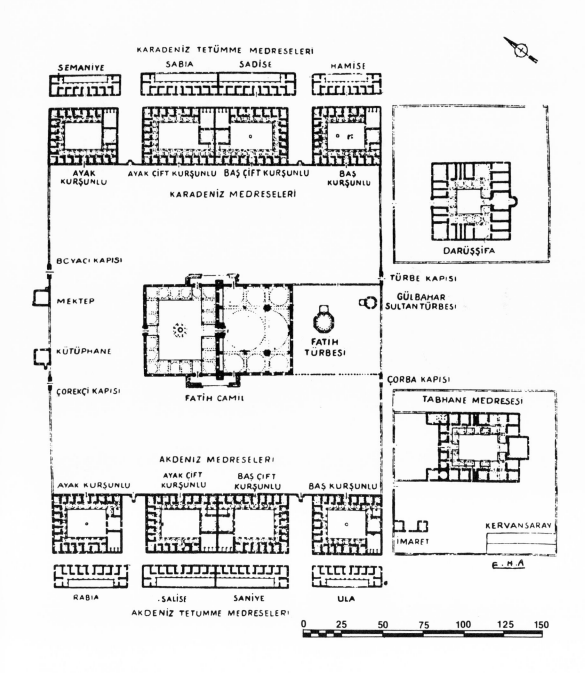

Fig. 19. The Külliye of Bayazid II in Edirne with mosque (built in 1484-1488), hospital, insane asylum, medical school, charity kitchen, bakeries, and management buildings. (Drawn by Cornelius Gurlitt.)

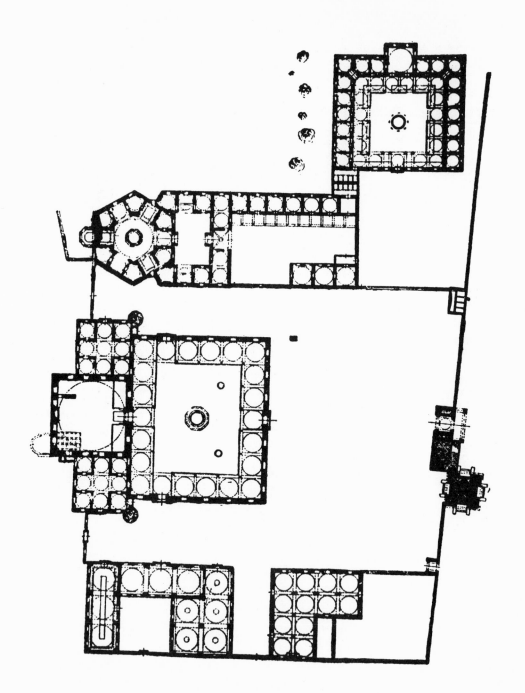

Fig. 20. The Külliye of Mehmet II in Istanbul with mosque, madrasas, mausoleum, library, school, hospital, and medical school. Mosque built in 1767-1771; the other buildings, slightly earlier or later. (Drawn by E. H. Ayverdi.)

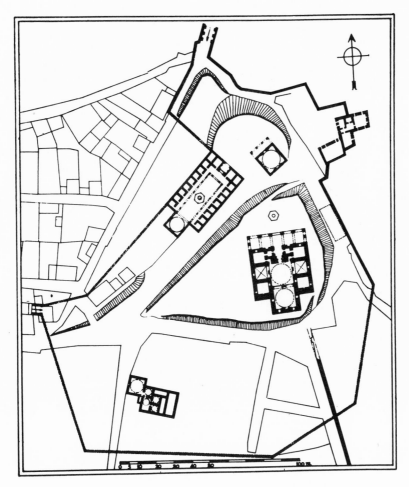

Fig. 21. The Külliye of Bayazid I Yıldırım in Bursa, 1398-1403, with mosque, madrasa, mausoleum, palace, fountain, charity kitchen, bathhouse, and aqueduct. (Drawn by Albert Gabriel.)

finds greater satisfaction from the sight of uncluttered surfaces or from designs of a rather limited scope. This concept is, however, derived only from rather late creations of Muslim art which represent a stage of artistic decline. This image is particularly evoked by eighteenth- and nineteenth-century Turkish architecture with ornately-carved stone and stucco decoration and panelled woodwork and by the nineteenth-century Qajar buildings in Iran with garish tilework on the outside and all-too-elaborate mirror- and stucco-work on the inside. Or the concept is based on the polychrome tile patterns and stucco work executed in the last period of Muslim Spain, in the fifteenth century, and then still further elaborated in the sixteenth and seventeenth centuries in North Africa. The image of overdone decoration has become further entrenched by the impression made by recent Persian carpets, which often copy designs of the sixteenth and early seventeenth centuries in a dry and sterile fashion and which lack the subtlety of color arrangements that distinguished the earlier ones.

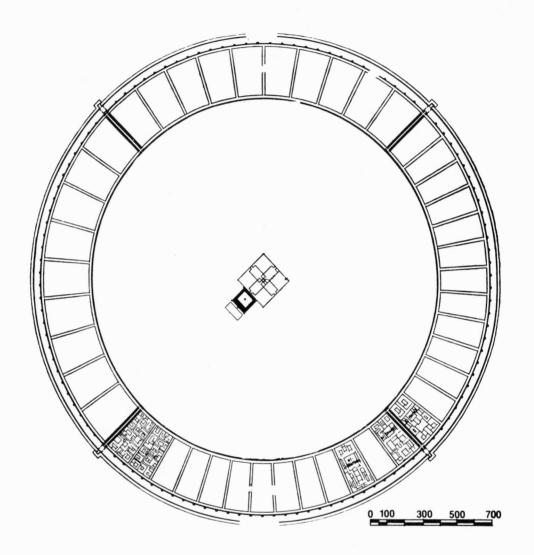

Fig. 22. The Circular City of Baghdad with the Palace of the Golden Gate (or Green Dome) and the Great Mosque in the center. Founded by al-Mansur in 762-766. (Drawn by Ernst Herzfeld.)

There are, however, many buildings which demonstrate a clear understanding of the bold use of geometric shapes to create a monumental impression by the superimposition or the juxtaposition of the component parts. Superb examples are the dome chamber of the Great Mosque in Isfahan, of the late eleventh century, or the Rabat-i Malik of about the same period. No modern architect could find fault with the way in which the large undecorated shapes are combined and brick is used to create a vibrating surface texture. Still other buildings which come to one's mind are the tall star-shaped tomb tower called Gumbad-i Qabus of 1006 or the extra-ordinarily audacious ninth-century minaret of the Great Mosque of Samarra, whose outside spiralled ramp forms a giant corkscrew and whose shape reminds one—I daresay favorably—of Frank Lloyd Wright's much acclaimed Guggenheim Museum built eleven hundred years later. And as to monumental starkness in a building—produced by gigantic bare brick walls interrupted only by the enormous half-circular protrusion of a plain mihrab and two simple doors—there is in all the world's architecture, old and new, hardly any parallel to the Mosque of Ali Shah, called the Ark, in Tabriz, built in 1310-20. Nor are these just early examples without later successors. All the great Turkish mosques of the sixteenth and seven-teenth centuries, and even the lesser ones in the provinces, combine cubic forms with domes and half domes whose exteriors are composed of undecorated, beauti-fully cut stone. The plain whitewashed architecture of North Africa of recent times, with its simple domes over cubes, belongs to the same general category. They also demonstrate that we do not have to look only among the monumental and sophisticated forms of royal architecture for purity of shape and execution, because a good many of the popular monuments reflect the same style.

Pl. 98 (312)
Pl. 99 (313)

Pl. 100 (313)

Pl. 101 (314)

If we may mention still one more cliché—the fourth in the series—we may point to the erroneous idea that overcrowded and overbuilt native quarters reflect a lack of understanding of nature. Indeed, the fact that nearly every house has a central water basin or fountain, that plants and trees are set in the courtyard, and that a well-planned, large garden outside the city is regarded as the greatest of earthly possessions indicates that this contact with nature has not been lost. Indeed, it represents an essential part of a way of life and reflects the high value and full awareness given to the surrounding world even under difficult living conditions.

Pl. 4 (20),
57 (167),
87 (291),
102 (321)

In considering still other factors which indicate an affinity or closely related attitude between the old towns and the new, one's attention is drawn to the question of patronage and how certain units are organized. In the Middle Ages, it was primarily the king and his grandees who, for their own glory and salvation and for the public weal, had major buildings erected to serve religious and secular needs. Thus, a member or members of the middle class consisting of merchants, traders, and artisans had usually nothing to do with the commission of buildings or the choice of forms used and, of course, even less so the lowly laborers. In a way this is not too different from modern conditions, where it is again not the individual or the large mass of the people who dispenses patronage or has anything to say about public buildings, but an impersonal government and its agencies. In this respect conditions are at variance with those existing in Europe from the late Middle Ages onward, when the middle classes had much greater influence on the formation of cities.

Another aspect to be considered is that since the Middle Ages, the suq or the bazaar, with its aligned buildings, always consisted of many units which were occupied by followers of the same trade; the total of these many specialized units served the business needs of the town in a compact fashion. This more or less is also the underlying principle which nowadays applies to "shopping centers," in which special care is taken that at least two if not more stores selling the same merchandise are close to each other and the needs of the whole neighborhood can

Pls. 17 (64),
18 (65), 20
(67), 23 (71),
32 (98)

98. The Prototype of the Ibn Sina Mausoleum: Gumbad-i Qabus, the mausoleum of the
Ziyarid Shams al-Ma'ali Qabus in Gurgan, A.D. 1006.

99. The Spiral Minaret "Malwiyah" of the Great Mosque of Samarra, 847-853.

100. The mosque of Ali Shah in Tabriz, the so-called Ark, 1310-20. An excellent example of thoroughly "modern" starkness and simplicity. (Photo: Donald N. Wilber.)

101.Courtyard and sanctuary of the mosque of Sultan Ahmed I in Istanbul, 1608-1614.
(Photo: Elizabeth S. Ettinghausen.)

be fully satisfied. In addition, in recent decades "professional buildings" have been developed, which also apply the principle of placing men of the same calling within one locality, only now the arrangement of units is vertically oriented rather than horizontally; in this way, greater compactness is achieved and valuable real estate more efficiently used. Thus, the modern forms of concentrated competitive shopping are not too different from the system developed in the Middle Ages. Only the secondary aspects—outer appearance and alignment—differ.

Finally, a word should be said about the general approach to modernization. There is the method used by Baron Haussmann, who cut his boulevards through Paris to provide fast arteries and streets for new major buildings. This system of new avenues imposed on the old towns has in recent years been used in the Near East, particularly in Isfahan, Aleppo, and Istanbul. Even with careful planning, such a harsh method destroys a great deal of the urban heritage. However, already in the Middle Ages a more considerate principle was developed throughout the vast region here under discussion. By building the new cities *next* to the old ones—which had reached its saturation point or was to be superseded for other reasons—opportunities were given for the old to co-exist with the new. The prime example is the capital city of Muslim Egypt. We find here seventh-century al-Fustat next to the older Heliopolis and Babylon to be replaced in turn by Tulunid al-Qata'i in the ninth century and then by Fatimid Cairo in the late tenth century, to be further increased by other aggregations in more modern times, none of which has tried to destroy its forerunner. The same system is to be found elsewhere in the Far West of the Muslim world as well as in the farther East. Thus we have Fez al-Bali, the old Fez, founded in the ninth century, to which was joined Fez al-Jadid (Fez Jdid), the new Fez created by the Merinids in the thirteenth century, and then eventually the Ville Nouvelle of the French Protectorate. The number of these cities is exceeded by Delhi, which is generally believed to be composed of seven such juxtaposed cities but actually embraces many more. The principle of peaceful co-existence has also preserved Jerusalem, as new quarters have been built beyond the old, walled town. Hence, we have here one more example of a sound principle established many centuries ago in Muslim lands; continuously practised, it does not run counter to modern concepts, and on account of its more humane and conservationist considerations it deserves to be followed.

We are fully aware that the mere preservation of an old quarter or town next to a new one does not necessarily mean a continued social and economic viability. Undoubtedly, special endeavors combined with financial efforts are needed to preserve a sound urban fabric, whichever form it may take. These are not theoretical considerations, but schemes which have proven to be successful in other settings. Thus, in his own lifetime and on two continents, this writer has witnessed the resuscitation of what were for all practical purposes the local equivalents of "madinas," which had become physically decrepit and socially rundown. In the 1920s, through spirited civic work, the *Altstadt* of his native town of Frankfurt am Main, with buildings from the Middle Ages to the early nineteenth century, was slowly and systematically renovated and thus liberated from the threats of civic death. A run-down area thus became attractive and safe again to live in, and this change was so exhilarating that it gave a new sense of pride to the people. In addition, the whole setting with its many historical buildings as well as its shops, restaurants, and places of entertainment in quaint old houses greatly appealed to the inhabitants of the newer parts of town, just as it of course became the mecca of the tourists with money to spend. (Unfortunately, the whole quarter was destroyed in the Second World War, especially during the last months in which Hitler insisted on continuing an already lost war till its bitter end.) Later in the 1930s and 1940s this writer observed a similar process which led to the revival of Georgetown, the old eighteenth-century section of Washington, D.C. It, too, had become mostly inhabited by people of the lowest income group and by the unemployed, and many of its streets were incipient slums. Again, due to a reawakened sense for the still lingering beauty of this old settlement and a new historical awareness, this part of town was restored house by house with the result that it now represents the most prestigious quarter of the nation's capital, favored by the socially and culturally prominent. These two examples show what can be done—not by outside advice but by the initiative of the people themselves.

All these considerations make it clear that old and new towns do not really represent the strict polarities that the current stereotype seems to imply. There are many aspects of the old towns which can provide connections with the new. But they have to be resuscitated or re-employed according to the concepts and technological requirements of a modern age. Once the many misconceptions about the true nature of the old have been overcome and the problem is approached with the proper empathy, there is every reason to believe in an eventual revival or a renascence based on the old traditions.

This brings us to our final point. If there is to be a true integration between the old and the new, it is necessary that the old be properly understood and appreciated. In other words, each of the nations involved should have a small body of professionals dedicated to explain the monuments and arts of their country to their countrymen and to the world. It is true that most countries have a Department of Antiquities which takes care of the physical needs of the buildings. However, this does not always imply full appreciation of the historical significance of the monuments or a keen sensitivity to their artistic beauty. This is evident from the fact that in some restorations the departments involved have proceeded too far and with little understanding. This has resulted in "rescued" buildings which, though now physically safe, resemble only vaguely their true old selves and present themselves in a distorted and unsightly fashion.

It seems essential that the proper study of the national monuments and arts be given a high priority, particularly in the curricula of the universities and art schools, so as to help shape toward them a positive attitude within the younger generation. Illustrated volumes for instruction should be published and extensive files of every preserved or otherwise known monument be kept. They would be a source of information not only for students, but also for architects who by direct assignment or in competitions are asked to submit designs for new monuments. That this is not a theoretical consideration is proven by the fact that in the past architects so approached, consulting the few general books available but lacking proper direction, selected the wrong prototype for their designs. This resulted in the construction of buildings which contain salient features characteristic of other

Muslim regions with which this particular country had no historical or geographical relations. Obviously, such a procedure cannot lead to an architecture which has a deeper significance within the national context or even one inspiring to the people, The vast sums expended were thus to a large extent wasted. With the proper knowledge, such unfortunate errors just described could be avoided, as there would be enough informed citizens to understand the issues and to criticize them in case of improper planning or procedure. Eventually, every nation and even the bigger towns would have historical societies dedicated to the preservation of ancient monuments whose work would naturally extend beyond mere physical care. Such organizations exist already in a few countries, but, as in the West, there is no limit as to the manner in which their range can be extended and their working methods refined.

As in other instances, our time is, as far as urban development is concerned, not only one of frustration and danger but also one of great promise. What seems more important than anything else is a proper understanding and respect for what has been achieved in the past so that with due measure it can serve as inspiration for the future.

BIBLIOGRAPHY

The following titles provide information about certain issues dealt with in the preceding pages:

Beaudouin, Eugène Élie. "Ispahan sous les grands Chahs (XVIIe siècle). Avant-propos par Emmanuel Pontremoli." *Urbanisme* 2 (1933).

———, and Pope, Arthur Upham. "City Plans." In *A Survey of Persian Art*. Edited by Arthur Upham Pope, vol. 2, pp. 1391-1410. London, 1938-39.

Berger, Morroe, ed. *The New Metropolis in the Arab World.* Bombay: Allied Publishers, 1963.

Berque, Jacques. "Medinas, Villeneuves et Bidonvilles." *Cahiers de Tunisie*, no. 21-22 (1958), pp. 5-42.

Brown, G. Baldwin. *The Care of Ancient Monuments: An Account of the Legislative and other Measures Adopted in European Countries for Protecting Ancient Monuments and Objects and Scenes of Natural Beauty and for Preserving the Aspect of Historical Cities.* Cambridge: The University Press, 1905.

Dettmann, K. "Islamische und westliche Elemente im heutigen Damaskus." *Geographische Rundschau* 21, no. 19 (1969): 64-68.

Faidutti, A. M. "Les Grandes Lignes du Développement Urbain de Constantine." *Bulletin de l'Association de Géographes Français*, March 1961, pp. 38-51.

Herzfeld, Ernst. "Damascus: Studies in Architecture." In *Ars Islamica* 9 (1942): 1-53; 10 (1943): 13-70; 11-12 (1946): 1-71; 13-14 (1948): 118-138.

Hourani, A. H., and Stern, S. M., eds. *The Islamic City: A Colloquium.* Oxford, 1970.

Ibn Battuta. *Travels in Asia and Africa, 1325-54.* Translated by H. A. R. Gibb. London, 1929-1958.

Lapidus, Ira M., ed. *Middle Eastern Cities: Ancient, Islamic and Contemporary.* Middle Eastern Urbanism: A Symposium (Berkeley, 1969).

Lassner, Jacob. *The Topography of Baghdad in the Early Middle Ages: Text and Studies.* Detroit, 1970.

Le Strange, Guy. *Baghdad during the Abbasid Caliphate.* London, 1924.

———. *The Lands of the Eastern Caliphate.* Cambridge, 1930.

Le Tourneau, Roger. *Les Villes Musulmanes de l'Afrique du Nord.* Alger, 1957.

———. "Implications of Rapid Urbanization." In *State and Society in Independent North Africa.* Edited by Leon Carl Brown (1966).

Marçais, Georges. "La Conception des Villes dans l'Islam." *Revue d'Alger* 2 (1945): 517-533.

———. "Les Jardins de l'Islam." *Éducation Algérienne* (1941). Republished in *Mélanges d'Histoire et d'Archéologie de l'Occident Musulman.* Vol. 1: *Articles et conférences de Georges Marçais.* Alger, 1957, pp. 233-244.

———. "L'Urbanisme Musulman." *Revue Africaine* (1939), pp. 13-34. Republished in *Mélanges d'Histoire et d'Archéologie de l'Occident Musulman.* Vol. 1: *Articles et conférences de Georges Marçais.* Alger, 1957, pp. 219-231.

Nouschi, André. "Croissance des Villes Nord-Africaines (Tunis): Vue par un Sociologue." *Annales,* no. 2, March-April 1962, pp. 362-367.

Riefstahl, Rudolf Meyer. "Trajan's Market in Rome and the Islamic Covered Market." *Parnassus* 4 (1932): 17-19.

Sarre, Friedrich, and Herzfeld, Ernst. *Archäologische Reise im Euphrat- und Tigris-Gebiet.* Berlin, 1911-1920.

Sauvaget, Jean. *Alep. Essai sur le Développement d'une Grande Ville Syrienne des Origines au Milieu du XIXe Siècle.* Paris, 1941.

———. "Esquisse d'une Histoire de la Ville de Damas." *Revue des Études Islamiques* 8 (1934): 421-480.

———. "Inventaire des Monuments Musulmans de la Ville d'Alep." *Revue des Études Islamiques* 5(1931): 59-114.

———. *Les Monuments Historiques de Damas.* Beyrouth, 1932.

Schmidt, Erich F. *Flights over Ancient Cities of Iran.* Chicago, 1940.

Shiber, Saba George. *The Kuwait Urbanization, Being an Urbanistic Case-study of a Developing Country.* Kuwait, 1964.

Sourdel, Dominique and Janine. *La Civilisation de l'Islam Classique.* Paris, 1968.

von Grunebaum, Gustave E. "Die islamische Stadt." *Saeculum* 6 (1955): 138-153.

———. "The Structure of the Muslim Town," In *Islam: Essays in the Nature and Growth of a Cultural Tradition.* Edited by G. E. von Grunebaum. American Anthropological Association, vol. 57, Memoir no. 81, 1955.

Wilber, Donald N. *Persian Gardens and Garden Pavillions.* Rutland (Vermont) and Tokyo: Charles E. Tuttle, 1962.

Wirth, E. "Strukturwandlungen und Entwicklungstendenzen der orientatlischen Stadt." *Erdkunde* 22 (1968): 101-128.

Wussow, A. von. *Die Erhaltung der Denkmäler in den Kulturstaaten der Gegenwart. . .nach amtlichen Quellen dargestellt.* 2 vols. Berlin, 1885.

11

Constancy, Transposition and Change in the Arab City
by Hassan Fathy

THE beginning of the nineteenth century marked a radical change in the hitherto continuous development of the countries of the Near East and North Africa. With the introduction of Western culture and the industrial revolution resulting from the advances of technology, the evolutionary processes of urban development were halted. These alien forces were imposed upon peoples who did not have the necessary knowledge to cope with the myriads of new problems that were created.

The task of assimilating an alien culture almost overnight is quite beyond the means of any people to achieve. As a result, a hybrid style of architecture emerged, below the level of the pure Arab or Western. Even when the European classical style adopted in Arab countries was pure, there remained the problem of "truth," which made the building look alien and false in its environment.

In recent years, when these countries changed to the so-called modern style, two factors continued to be virulently active in prohibiting design in the traditional style: 1) the municipal laws, which are based on the assumption that all buildings are extroverted, and 2) the training given to architects at the universities. Arab architecture is completely ignored in the curricula of design and theory of architecture and often considered to be "exotic" in general histories of the subject. The result is continued and widespread examples of the most inappropriate designs—witnessed in almost all cities of the Near East, such as Cairo, Kuwait, Riyadh, Baghdad, and others—while the traditional buildings are being mercilessly demolished.

In this respect, what was happening in the Arab countries was in many ways similar to what was happening in rural areas all over the world. When the moment came for the peasantry to change, they lacked the knowledge necessary to cope with the foreign influences and to develop an architectural style in keeping with their rural traditions. Instead, they took the easy way out and chose to adopt an urban style of architecture of which they knew little; but they succeeded only in creating a sub-urban style alien to the countryside, instead of a super-rural style. Arab architects likewise created a sub-European style which is now equated with "Near Eastern architecture."

Certainly, the Arab heritage in architecture is not devoid of value, and it would be unwise for the modern architect to ignore it completely as is the case today. In all cities we find architectural elements that are as valid today as they were yesterday, because the forces that underlie the process of the creation of form are constant and should therefore be preserved. Other elements may still be valid in design and concept, but the form or size may have to be altered due to changes in material or socio-economic conditions; these elements have to be transposed, and only those elements that have outlived their time and are antiquated should be eliminated.

It is the duty of the architect and planner to sort out all these elements before he gives his final verdict on their value. This implies that we must clarify the meaning of many terms that are often indiscriminately used by both architect and layman alike, such as "contemporaneity," "functionalism," and "progress." A close analysis in the light of the latest findings of science would easily show that many of the modern layouts and house designs in the Arab cities of today are far less functional and less modern than the old ones they replace in the name of functionalism and modernity.

It is the intent of this chapter to discuss ideas on subjects calling for research in areas of design, layout, and change in the planning of Arab cities rather than to give a detailed analysis of the problem of change.

THE TRADITIONAL ARAB CITY

The Layout

The major part of the Near East and North Africa is desert land, lying in the hot-arid zone between latitudes 10°-30°N. From early times, the culture of the people was nomadic. As climate was the dominant factor affecting architecture and town-planning, it is not surprising that we find a marked uniformity in the development of urbanization. From the time of the Arab invasion until the latter part of the Turkish period, all cities in this vast region bore a great similarity to one another. The typical layout was characterized by narrow winding streets with a similar arrangement of housing plots. We have only to look at aerial photographs of such traditional cities as Fez, Tunis, Cairo, or Jerusalem to see that in many ways one could be taken for the other.

By simple analysis, it becomes quite understandable how such a pattern came to be universally adopted by the Arabs. It is only natural for anybody experiencing the severe climate of the desert to seek shade by narrowing and properly orientating the streets and to avoid the hot desert winds by making these streets winding, with closed vistas.

The road system in the Arab city was a result of the patterning of buildings, not a determinant as in most modern planning. By the first attitude, such a city

Pl. 4 (20),89 (292)
Pl. 87 (291)

102. Cairo, Shoubra Palace. Reception kiosk and loggias around large basin with fountain. (From: Pascale Coste, *Architecture Arabe ou Monuments du Kaire . . . 1818 à 1826.*)

103. Alexandria, Egypt. A room in a private house, around 1800. (From: *Description de l'Egypte.*)

enabled the people to articulate space more advantageously, to experiment with ideas, and to solve problems of architecture and planning as they occurred.

House Design

In the desert, nature at ground level is hostile to man, so he shuts his house entirely to the outside, and opens it instead onto an internal courtyard, or *sahn*. The temperature in the desert drops considerably during the night; this drop amounts to approximately 20° to 40° F. during the summer. In this way, cool air deposits in the courtyard and flows into the surrounding rooms, keeping them cool to quite a late hour of the day.

In the typical Arab house of early times, the reception and living parts were composed of a courtyard to which were linked *iwans* (or evyans) preceded by loggias. This arrangement is found repeated in exactly the same way in houses of Fustat in Egypt, in the Palace of Ukhaydir in Iraq, and in the old houses of Tunis.[1]

Whereas the Arab type of town layout mentioned above is implicit, it is not the same with the house design. The variants are innumerable, and we must therefore assume that this prototype was consciously introduced from Iraq, where it would appear to have originated.

Pls. 102-103 (321)

In later years in Egypt, the whole arrangement was transposed while preserving all the elements of design; the open sahn, the semi-covered loggia, and the covered iwan, with the last element developed into a separate composite entity called the *"Qa'a."* The layout of this Qa'a was almost an exact replica of the whole reception part of the earlier houses, with a covered sahn, but, naturally, without the loggias. To provide for the semi-covered space with its special atmosphere and open quality, the loggia retained its place overlooking the sahn and served as antechamber to the Qa'a.

Assessment of the Traditional Street and House Layouts

At first sight, the plan of the Arab city, with its irregularities, might appear to have developed haphazardly. But from what was mentioned previously and from further analysis, we shall see that it has its functional and logical reasons. Indeed, it has certain distinct advantages over so many modern city plans using the gridiron system.

The narrow and winding streets with closed vistas have the same function as the courtyard in a house, namely, they act as a temperature regulator. Were the streets wide and straight, the cool night air would not be retained, and they would heat up more readily during the day.

From the aesthetic point of view, this layout creates more interest. Irregularity of the street alignment serves as a stimulus to the creativity, ingenuity, and sense of discrimination of the architect and master-builder, as shown in the accompanying example of Dardiri Street.

---

[1] On Ukhaydir, see the references in K. A. C. Creswell, *Early Muslim Architecture*, 2 vols., as well as his article "Architecture" in the *Encyclopaedia of Islam*, 2nd ed. For Fustat, see the article "Fustat" in the *Encyclopaedia of Islam*, 2nd ed., and the references cites therein. An excellent illustrated treatment of traditional residential architecture in Tunis is found in Jacques Revault, *Palais et demeures de Tunis* (Paris, 1967).

104. Dardiri Street.

105. Courtyard façade, Kritliyya
House (Cairo).

Dardiri Street

Pl. 104 (323)

The architect of the house in Dardiri Street was confronted with a bend in the shape of his plot which he wanted to correct in his first-floor plan. So he created the brackets that increase in size to take up the then triangular projection necessary to establish rectangularity in the main reception part over the irregular ground floor plan. By this solution, the architect animated the façade of the house and solved the problem in an interesting and clever way, like a musician who creates a dissonance and solves it by a sequence of chords. The more intricate the resolution, the more interesting the music.

Fig. 23. Sketch of Dardiri Street.

Kritliyya House

Pl. 105 (323)

When the same problem appeared to take place in the façade opening to the courtyard in the Kritliyya house (early Ottoman period), the architect had recourse to a more refined and intricate solution than simple brackets. He replaced them by a series of stalactites to match the more delicate character of the interior.

The configuration of streets with closed vistas has another advantage over wide, straight streets. We find almost every enclosed view in the old city wall composed, with the location of important buildings and less important ones in a certain order, increasing in importance, like a crescendo, as they approach the climax of the mosque or palace, thus giving a feeling of unity while maintaining a variety of artistic expression that could not be achieved if the buildings were of a monotonous design and layout.

Another point worthy of note in the comparison between open and closed vistas is that of a straight street with parallel sides and an open vista: the only point to attract the attention of the pedestrian at the beginning of the street is the vanishing point at which the parallel lines meet on the horizon. As these lines meet only at infinity, the pedestrian would feel psychologically tired before he had walked very far.

In the old quarters, sections of streets with closed vistas do not exceed 300 meters each, thereby making each section easy to walk. Thus, the way is subdivided into sections, each one a separate entity, almost like the movements in a sonata, with exposition, development, and recapitulation. Such subtleties are not denied the planner of today, who can be creative by recognizing the potentialities inherent in planning or design in space, and by differentiating the quality of the space— exterior and interior, public, private, or semi-private—and the grand and humble parts of house and street. In modern architecture and planning these considerations are ironed out by pure engineering.

Pls. 106-108 (326-327)

Remodelling the Old Quarters

The change taking place today, as witnessed in nearly all of the Arab cities, be it Cairo, Aleppo, or Damascus, has several detrimental effects on the historical quarters wherever they exist. As the modern house design is transformed from the introverted type, depending on the gardens and courtyards for insulation and ventilation, to the extroverted type, depending solely on the street for sun and air, it becomes necessary that narrow streets be made wider. This has led to the demolition of the façades of many of the old palaces and houses and the total destruction of the character of the space enclosed within the walls of houses bordering the streets, even though this space is no less important than the architectural details and the texture of the buildings. The character of this "perceived" space is all too often overlooked in contemporary house and city design.

The analysis of the traditional Arab house has opened a new field for research into the optimum configuration for patterning buildings, with a view toward the creation of an agreeable use of space, be it public, semi-public, or private; open, semi-covered, or covered; and surrounding man in a street, in a room, a loggia, a courtyard, or a cafe in a square. This may enrich the design, by adding to the problem tackled—a design concerned with civility and quality of life. Certainly it would contribute to the beautification of the city, bringing it up to the scale of man and not to that of the car. Most of the old quarters in Arab cities are in sad disrepair. The palaces and large family houses are falling into ruins. However, the original town plan has been preserved in many parts by the system of *waqfs*, which does not allow for property to be sold or transacted. Recently though, this system has been abolished in many areas, and the ownership of these large buildings is now divided among numerous beneficiaries. The share of each one being in most cases too small to build a courtyard house in traditional style, the heirs are now building outward-looking blocks of flats instead, disfiguring the old quarters. A successful solution to this problem is suggested by the *wikalas* and khans in which several living units are designed around a large courtyard. If these were to be designed collectively, the courtyard could then be preserved and put to good use.

Pl. 25 (72)

Problems of Change in the Arab City

In Cairo, the movement of Westernization was started by the Khedives, who adopted European classical styles of architecture. This sort of architecture by its

Examples of traditional streets laid out to lead to, and emphasize, major public buildings. 106. (opposite page) The minaret of Zitouna Mosque at the end of a major street in the old madina, Tunis. (Photo: L. Carl Brown.)

107. A scene of Cairo drawn by David Roberts showing the twin minarets of the Bab Zuwaylah in the background. (Source: David Roberts.)

108. (left) A David Roberts scene of the "Mosque el Rhamree" situated in such a way that it captures the eye of the pedestrian who uses this street, which leads to a major city gate—the Bab al-Nasr. (Source: David Roberts.)

109. Jiddah, Saudi Arabia. Modern boulevard on north side of the old city. The city walls formerly ran where the public gardens are now located. A good example of vehicular traffic "ringing" the old city. (Photo: Aramco.)

very nature, and the consequent effect on town planning, ruled out any possibility of continuing the Arab tradition in house and street design.

At the same time there was a geographical change. The Nile River was brought under control by the construction of barrages. Thus the ponds and marshland that had hitherto hindered the growth of the city westwards were reclaimed and developed. Since some of these ponds and marshes happened to lie in the middle of the old city, their reclamation produced new land for the building of whole quarters, and it became necessary to connect the new quarters with the existing main centers. Thus, planning by necessity encroached on the old city. Unfortunately, it was beyond the knowledge of the planners to tackle the problem wisely, and the new plan was simply superimposed upon the old one with no consideration for the historical buildings, which were indiscriminately destroyed.

Naturally, it is inevitable that we build wide streets in order to accommodate motor cars. However, there are better means to provide for the car than to widen the existing streets in the historical quarters and ruin their character. One proposal is to surround the old quarter with a ring road from which cul-de-sac streets could penetrate inward. This would allow easy access for ambulances and fire-engines and other emergency vehicles.

Pl. 109 (328)

As a matter of fact, modern man inherited the actual street design from a generation which was not ready for the advent of motor traffic. Nor could he anticipate the development it has reached today—like the design of the first automobile, which is now hopelessly outmoded, having taken several generations of designers to develop from a horse-cab without the horse to present styles. Cannot the same charge be levied at the unchanged street system of today, in which motor cars are mixed with pedestrians? Research is needed to develop a street system for the modern city by which traffic is segregated from the pedestrian within the city itself, as in the case of the superhighways.

If this is not easy to achieve in the existing city, at least we can make use of it in the Arab City of the future. By a system of sectoring we can divide the city into communities of a given size, from 5,000 to 10,000 inhabitants. A sector could be small enough to allow for the local daily services to be within walking distance Thus, the motor car would be kept on the periphery for external communications only, except for the points in which the use of the car is indispensable. As we shall have preserved the historical character in the old quarters through this system, we shall have likewise preserved the human scale of the community, and, by the same token, we shall have preserved the design concepts that we so highly-praised in the old city, by articulating space so as to obtain the optimum configuration with respect to the aesthetic, the climatic, and other aspects of planning for the city of the future.

Certain laudable efforts have been made in this direction, such as the Radburn[2] and the Dynapolis[3] plans. Profitable use could be made of these plans were they applied to the Arab city.

---

[2] Radburn, a town in New Jersey, was designed by Clarence Stein and Henry Wright in 1928. It is an "introverted" town in which blocks open towards a central park, almost like a huge Arab house opening onto a collective courtyard.

[3] The Dynapolis plan is a collectivity of Radburn-like towns.

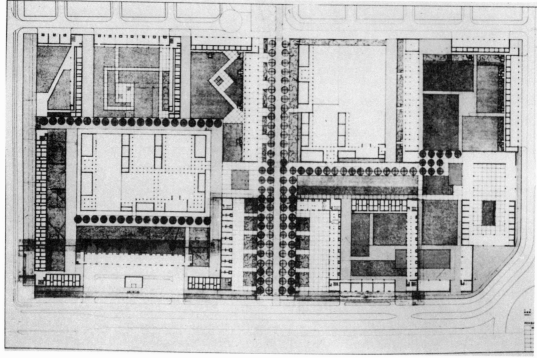

Fig. 24. (above) and 25. (below) General layout and three-dimensional view of the plans for residential quarters in New Baghdad, usefully incorporating sound scientific principles and elements of traditional Arab style. (Photo: Hassan Fathy.)

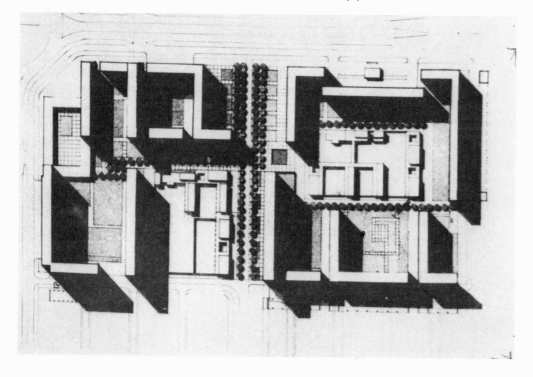

Contemporaneity for the Arab City

To achieve contemporaneity for the Arab city, the architect first has to determine the real meaning of the term and then establish a standard of reference. Contemporaneity is intimately linked with the notion of change, meaning in a sense consonance with the current stage of knowledge; as a result, the architect must determine the nature of the driving forces which motivate change. He must sense the order underlying all processes of evolution in general. He must then adjust his thought and feeling to this situation and make his knowledge guide him as he evaluates the situation at hand, and he must question recent trends in order to retain what is basic and constant and discard what is ephemeral.

While architecture deals with man and technology, planning deals with man, society, and technology. Therefore, contemporary architecture and city-design should blend the mechanical in an indissoluble relationship with the ensemble of relevant human sciences. A work of architecture not respecting any of these will be anachronistic because it does not exploit to the maximum man's present knowledge. For example, if an architect does not take into account the problem of solar radiation and designs a building with a glass wall in any of the cities of the hot-arid zone of the Near East, then he is willfully ignoring available knowledge in physics; and by the way that he fails to be contemporary, we can measure how anachronistic his building is.

We know that a glass wall lets in as much as ten times more heat than a solid wall four inches thick and that a glass wall 3 x 3 meters exposed to the direct rays of the sun lets into the interior 2,000 kilo/calories per hour, requiring two tons of refrigeration power per hour. By shading this glass, using any of the devices available, such as the *brise soleil* now mandatory in all modern buildings, we cut down this amount to one-third, which leaves us still with 300% more heat than with the four-inch wall.

So, the architect who builds such a solar furnace in Kuwait or Riyadh, for example, and then brings in a vast refrigeration plant to make it habitable is unnecessarily complicating the problem and is working below the standards of contemporary architecture. His design is anachronistic, and his anachronism is estimated quantitatively by the amount of kilo/calories in excess of the optimum for the economic ratio of building/heat.

In a similar way, if air movement through the building is unnecessarily impeded by the architectural design, because the architect has not consulted the findings of aerodynamics and physiology, then the design will be anachronistic, and the anachronism with respect to physiology can be stated as the difference between the optimum thermal comfort and the attained thermal comfort. With respect to aerodynamics, it can be stated as the difference between the optimum and the attained air movements and can be measured by the difference between the two velocities in miles per hour.

Similar anachronistic measures may develop through ignorance of economics, sociology, aesthetics, and other sciences relevant to planning and design.

This is not to say that architecture can be created by science alone, but simply that design requires a certain minimum of applied scientific knowledge. Within the fields to which science is applicable, the degree of application can be measured, thus providing a check on that aspect of contemporaneity in design.

There is for a given city at any given time a cluster of optimum configurations for the various aspects of that city, which together constitutes an ideal. A contemporary city is one in which reality coincides with the ideal. The modern Arab city is far from satisfying this condition and scientific research is urgently needed. It is odd that the most radical approach to research in architectural design for Arab countries is to be found in Europe, where there is no urgent need for it. For example, research on the courtyard-house, which should normally have been carried out in some Arab country, is being undertaken in Scotland (the Prestonpans Research Project) and in Denmark (the Elzinor Project). In America, we find that in places like Texas the house with a courtyard is gaining popularity over the stereotyped outward-looking type of house.

The High-Rise Building in the Modern Arab City: A Case for Transposition

One of the problems posed in the modern Arab city is the seemingly inevitable introduction of high-rise buildings. At first sight, there seems to be an incompatibility between the use of such buildings and the traditional city design; thus, most architects take this hasty judgment as an argument against the traditional concepts. However, closer analysis will reveal that the old concepts of city and house design are much more appropriate for these high-rise buildings than the ones currently applied.

If we transpose from the old to the new in terms of size and scale, we find that the old concept offers more freedom in applying the principal of optimum configuration with respect to the climate and aesthetic factors—such as air-movement within the built-up area, the quality of space, variegation of forms, respect of the human scale, segregation of motor traffic from pedestrians, and the like. This line of thought brings us nearer to the attitude of the old city builders in patterning their buildings in space, as described previously, and eventually may provide the opportunity to revise our actual views on town planning, which limit the city plan to the patterning of streets merely for circulation.

Figs. 24-25 (330)
An experiment in this direction has been made in the planning of the residential quarter in a project for New Baghdad. This sector is to house 19,000 inhabitants and, being adjacent to the principal center of the city, will be composed of blocks of flats.

In this experiment an attempt was made to provide seclusion by transposing the courtyard concept into enclosed private squares completely shut off from the bustle of the center of the city. For air movement, care is taken in setting the higher buildings to the lee-side of the lower buildings, and in orientating the blocks so as to embrace the prevailing wind. The large masses of the buildings are to work as wind barrages, with open parts on stilts at ground level, or at higher levels, as dictated by the principles of aerodynamics, to act as sluices for regulating the air flow and correcting the screening effect resulting from the different buildings. The open parts with stilts at ground level would provide for the same kind of contact with the open as the loggias in the traditional Arab house, at the same time that it allows for communication between the compartmented spaces of the private squares.

CONCLUSION

It is hoped that before it is too late Near Eastern architects will come to realize the intrinsic value of their architectural heritage. In so doing, they will reap the rich rewards of the accumulated experience that was left to them by their ancestors and will produce successful and enduring works of art. Let them not suppose that this tradition will hamper them. When the full power of human imagination is backed by the weight of a living tradition, the resulting work of art is much greater than any that an artist can achieve when he has no tradition to work in or when he willfully abandons his tradition.

110. Tunis, Tunisia. Newer houses built in the traditional style. The eye-pleasing diversity achieved through an apparently random cluster of domes, vaults, and squares may be contrasted with the more brutalist style of Plate 39. (Photo: William Dix, Jr.)

111. Beirut, Lebanon. Although streets are wider than in the traditional city, this scene conveys a sense of crowdedness, with its extroverted style of open balconies, larger shops and multi-use circulation system—from pedestrian to large bus. Note also the juxtaposition of public commercial and private residential. (Photo: Pan American World Airways.)

GLOSSARY

(N.B. Terms mentioned only in one context in the book, and adequately explained, are not listed here.)

ABBASID. Major Muslim dynasty of caliphs ruling from 750 to 1258. Founded Baghdad in 763.

AYYUBID. The dynasty ruling Egypt and portions of Syria from 1169 to 1252 founded by Saladin (Salah al-Din), who is celebrated for his victories against the Crusaders. Named after Ayyub (Job), Saladin's father.

BEDOUIN. Arab nomad.

BIDONVILLE (FRENCH). Shantytown.

BLED (MOROCCAN ARABIC). The countryside or hinterland.

CAÏD. (Properly, qaid) Leader. Provincial governor.

CALIPH. Literally, successor. Title of the religio-political leader of the Islamic community (umma).

CARAVANSERAI. A combination warehouse, stable and inn for transit and wholesale merchants doing business in the traditional city.

CELALI (TURKISH). Revolts against the Ottoman dynasty in early sixteenth-century Anatolia.

DAHIR. Decree or law (Morocco).

DOUAR. Bedouin camp, village and, by extension in the urban setting, a spontaneous and often illegal settlement of rural immigrants in or on the fringes of a town.

GECEKONDU (TURKISH). Shantytown.

HABOUS. Land or property held in Muslim religious trust. North African usage. The common term in the Eastern Arab world is waqf (Turkish vakıf).

HADARA (ARABIC). Civilization, conveying the idea of human concentration, sedentarization, and settlement.

HADITH. A record of the actions or sayings of the Prophet Muhammad or of his early followers. The body of hadith literature constitutes one of the major sources for the study of Islamic law and theology.

HANAFI. One of the four canonically accepted systems or "schools" of Sunni Islamic law.

HANBALI. One of the four canonically accepted systems or "schools" of Sunni Islamic law.

HARA. Quarter of a city.

HARIM. Women's quarters and their occupants (harem).

HIJRA. Emigration of the Prophet Muhammad and his early followers from Mecca to Medina (622). An event commemorated as the beginning of the Muslim calendar.

HÖYÜK (HÜYÜK). Artificial mound or hill, as over a grave.

IMAM. Prayer leader. Also, by extension, the caliph in traditional Sunni Islam.

IMARET. Kitchen for distributing food to the poor (Ottoman Empire).

JANISSARY. The Ottoman regular infantry.

KHAN. Caravanserais.

KHUTBA. The Muslim Friday Sermon given by the preacher (Khatib) at the congregational mid-day prayer.

KSOUR. In Southern Morocco, walled villages built of earth.

MADANIYA (ARABIC). Civilization, the same root as the Arabic word for city—Madina.

MADINA (ARABIC) City. In North African usage, the traditional, old city.

MADRASA (ARABIC). Religious boarding school often linked with a mosque.

MAKHZAN. Literally, a storehouse or treasury. By extension, the government (Moroccan usage).

MALIKI. One of the four canonically accepted systems or "schools" of Sunni Islamic law.

MASHRABIYA (ARABIC). Wooden latticework covering projecting window.

MIDAN. Town square.

MILLET SYSTEM. The system, brought to its fullest flowering in the Ottoman Empire, granting considerable autonomy and governmental responsibilities to religious communities.

MUFTI. An authority on Islamic law entitled to give an interpretative judgment (fatwa). A jurisconsult.

MUHTASIB. Traditional Muslim administrative official with "urbanist" duties including those of checking on weights, measures, fair prices, etc.

MUKATAA (TURKISH, FROM ARABIC). Lease of tax farm.

NESTORIAN. Eastern Christian Church important in early centuries in Persia and farther East. Especially hard hit by the Mongol invasions of the thirteenth and fourteenth centuries. The Nestorians have survived as small, scattered communities throughout the area and even in the United States where the Nestorian patriarch, Mar Shimun, resides.

QADI. Muslim judge.

QAJAR. Dynasty ruling in Iran from the late eighteenth century to 1925.

QURAYSH. Meccan tribe to which the Prophet Muhammad belonged.

SELJUQS. Name for Turkish clan that founded several different dynasties. Embraced Islam in the tenth century while steadily penetrating from Central Asia into the Near East. Responsible for defeating Byzantines and driving them out of Anatolia save for a truncated area around Constantinople.

SHAFI'I. One of the four canonically accepted systems of "schools" of Sunni Islamic Law.

SHARI'A. Islamic law.

SHAYKH (ARABIC). Elder, chief, and (in the traditional urban context) often used as head of city quarter, leader of a craft or trade organization, religious leader, etc.

SHIITE. Literally, follower (or partisan), i.e., of Ali, the son-in-law of Muhammad. The largest sectarian grouping in Islam which, in turn, is divided into a major "Twelver" sect (recognizing the authority of 12 imams [q.v.]) and several "Sevener" sects, among the best known in the West being the Ismailis under the leadership of the Agha Khan. Twelver Shiism is the majority and official religion of Iran.

SIPAHI (TURKISH, ORIGINALLY PERSIAN). Feudal cavalry.

SUFI. Islamic mystic.

SUNNI. Literally, orthodox or "of the tradition." The major body of the Muslim community comprising roughly 90% of the total world Muslim population.

SUQ (ARABIC). Market.

ULAMA. Literally "knowers." Those learned in Islamic religious sciences.

UMAYYAD. First Muslim dynasty of caliphs ruling from 661 to 750. Capital: Damascus.

WAQF. See Habous.

WIKALA. Caravanserai or khan.

INDEX

Arabic names containing the elements *Abd, abu-,* and *ibn-* are alphabetized under those elements. Those beginning with *al-* and *el-* are alphabetized under the part that follows.